Jewish Education Program

The Joseph & Faye Tanenbaum Jewish Education Program of Zeirei Agudath Israel was organized in September 1972, and since its inception has become a well-known, active force in the field of Jewish education. Its guiding principle, "Jewish power and Jewish pride through Jewish education," was formulated in response to what has become a Jewish tragedy of massive proportions, namely assimilation and its tragic by-products.

Under the guidelines of prominent Roshei Yeshivos and leaders in the field of Jewish education, and staffed entirely by B'nei Torah and Yeshiva graduates, JEP relies almost entirely on the talents and efforts voluntarily contributed by capable young Torah students.

Some of JEP's programs include: Shabbatones, in which hundreds of children from various communities in the United States and Canada experience the beauty of Shabbos in a Torah true environment; Release Hour classes for spiritually-starved public school children; programs for needy Russian immigrants; Ruach and Seminar sessions for day school students; Chavruso Big Brother Programs; High School Encounter Groups; Holiday Rallies; Yeshiva and Camp Placement; and the publication of educational material for thousands of young people. Through these and other various programs, JEP hopes to ignite the spark of Yiddishkeit deep within the hearts of these individuals, and turn it into a blazing, warmth-emanating fire. It hopes to instill within these youngsters a love of Hashem and His Torah and an understanding of Torah-true Judaism.

RABBI MOSES FEINSTEIN

455 F. D. R. DRIVE

NEW YORK, N. Y. 10002

OREGON 7-1222

משה פיינשטיין

ר"מ תפארת ירושלים

בנוא יארק

בע"ה

כבר נודע בשערים לתהלה ההצלחה שזכו הני בני הישיבה
איחוד ה"חכנית לחינוך היהודי" בשם "דשעפ" העוסקים באמונה
לקרב ילדי בני ישרא' לתורה. ועכשו אספו מדברי חז"ל
וראשונים ואחרונים חיבור מיוחד על חמשה חומשי תורה, גדוש
בחומר חיוני וחינוכי כדי להלהיב הלבבות לאהבת התורה ולקיום
המצוות.

והנה ידעתי כמה גדלה עבודתם בקירוב הרחוקים, ובראותי
הליקוט הזה שהם מוציאים לאור לחזק מטרתם, הנני בזה לעודדם
ולברכם שיצליחו להגדיל תורה ולהאדירה, וישתמשו בחיבור היקר
הנוכחי לפתוח לבותיהם של אלפי ילדים המשתוקקים באמת במעמקי
נפשם לדבר ה' לגלות להם הזוהר והיופי של יסודות אמונתנו
ולהמשיכם לחיי תורה ויראת שמים.

PREFACE

רבי ישמעאל-ל בר רבי יוסי אומר הלומד על מנת ללמד מספיקין בידו ללמוד וללמד.

R. Ishmael the son of R. Yosi said: He who learns in order to teach, is granted the opportunity to learn and to teach. (Avos 4,5)

אמר רבי יוחנן, כל הלומד תורה ואינו מלמדה דומה להדס במדבר.

R. Yochanan said: One who studies the Torah but does not teach it, is like the myrtle in the wilderness (the fragrance of which is wasted). (Rosh Hashana 23)

The purpose of this volume is to provide the English-speaking public with a Torah commentary replete with parables and examples to be used in teaching and explaining the Five Books of Moses.

The Rabbi, the Rebbi, the teacher, the speaker, the group leader, as well as the layman, will find in this sefer a wealth of material to assist them in understanding and illustrating the various lessons to be learnt from the Chumash.

The format consists of a brief summary of the Portion of the Week based on the traditional commentaries. In addition, several interesting points in each Sedra are elaborated upon, with the lessons to be gleaned from these points brought home by parables and stories of our illustrious Sages. There is no better way to teach the lessons of the Torah than by showing how our Gedolim incorporated these lessons into their own lives. The section concludes with quotes from various scriptures and Seforim.

The style is clear and concise. Everyone, including the layman, will be able to understand, appreciate, and use the thoughts contained in these pages. We have attempted to avoid being unnecessarily complex. However, we have not diluted the content.

The Rabbi, Rebbi, or group leader will find this to be an invaluable aid in teaching the weekly Torah reading, especially to young people. The layman, too, will greatly enjoy the wisdom and stories contained in this book.

ACKNOWLEDGMENTS

At this juncture, I would like to express my deepest feelings of gratitude to those who have graciously given of themselves and their time to help me in this holy endeavor:

My parents, Mr. and Mrs. Moshe Katz, and my in-laws, Mr. and Mrs. Yitzchok Berger, and all the members of my family for their encouragement and support. May Hashem grant them long life and nachas from their children for their endeavors.

Rav Yisroel Belsky and Rabbi Shlomo Frankel for their assistance and suggestions regarding the material.

I would like to thank the following chaverim who assisted in the writing and editing of this work: Larry Gewirtz, Betzalel Lerner, Dovid Zwiebel, Danny Gross, Gedalia Machlis and Matis Bloom. The finished product attests to their unitiring efforts.

I want to thank all of the people on the JEP summer staff who helped write, type and proofread the manuscripts: Malkie Kahan, Aviva Lubling, Priva Mandelbaum, Judith Sherman, Rivka Spatz, Michelle Schultz, and Mendy Eisikovic.

Special thanks to . . .

Shiya Markowitz and Nutti Goldbrenner of M & G Art Design, and his brother, Itchy Goldbrenner, for their invaluable technical assistance.

Rabbi Yosef Chaim Golding, Associate Director of JEP, Yossi Aszknazy, President of Zeirei Agudath Israel, Yehuda Spira, Barbara Silbermintz and Betty Rubin, for their assistance.

Mrs. Chavie Aranoff, Mrs. Rochel Hirsch, Mrs. Fran Shulman, Mrs. Rochel Shain, Miss Nitza Hertz, Mrs. Judy Dick, Miss Tzippy Wexler, Yaakov Rosen and Rabbi Baruch Hilsenrath for their proofreading and invaluable assistance.

My deepest gratitude and appreciation goes to my wife, Pessi, for her support, self-sacrifice, and dedication. Without her, this work would never have been completed. May her sincere and untiring efforts be rewarded in the blessing most precious to her—that our children merit to sit in the House of the Lord.

I humbly thank the Ribono Shel Olam for permitting me to accomplish this task.

Mordechai Katz

Brooklyn, N.Y.
Roch Chodesh Elul 5738

TABLE OF CONTENTS

CHUMASH BEREISHIS

Parshas Bereishis...16-19
  The Creation.. 16
  The Sun, The Moon, The Stars, And The Benefit of Modesty.......... 16
  The Sin of Odom and Chava.. 17
Parshas Noach..19-23
  Hashem Waits Patiently For Repentance 19
  Godol Hasholom—How Great is Peace! 20
  Noach and Avrohom: Silver and Gold.. 21
Parshas Lech Lecha...23-28
  How Avrohom Came To Believe In Hashem................................ 23
  Going To Eretz Yisroel 26
  Bikkur Cholim (Visiting The Sick).. 27
Parshas Veyeirah... 28-34
  Chesed (Kindness) And Hachnosas Orchim (Hospitality) 28
  Saving Lives 30
  The Akeidah 33
Parshas Chayei Sarah.. 34-37
  Sarah's Greatness 34
  Sarah's Burial... 35
  Rivkah's Chesed 36
Parshas Toldos 37-40
  The Birth Of Yaakov And Esav 37
  Kibbud Av V'aim 37
  The Blessings Of Yaakov And Esav.. 39
Parshas Vayeitzei 40-44
  Yaakov's Dream 40
  Yaakov And Lovan: Being Honest And Learning Good Even From The Wicked..... 41
  Rochel And Leah: The Importance Of Not Embarrassing Someone.................... 43
Parshas Vayishlach..45-47
  Yaakov's Humility 45
  Yaakov's Preparations... 45
  Steering Clear Of Bad Influences... 46
Parshas Vayeishev.. 48-52
  Hashgochoh Perotis (Divine Supervision)................................... 48
  Avoiding Temptation.. 50
  Judging Your Fellow Man Favorably.. 51
Parshas Mikeitz 53-56
  Faith In Hashem... 53
  Yoseph, Second To Paroh 53
  Why Yoseph Concealed His Identity: Doing Teshuvah 54
Parshas Vayigash 57-59
  Yaakov, Do Not Fear 57
  The Reunion.. 58
  Yaakov's Meeting With Paroh.. 59
Parshas Vayechi 59-62
  The Last Years 59
  Living On After Death 60
  Ephraim And Menasheh... 61

CHUMASH SHEMOS

Parshas Shemos 63-68
  Jewish Suffering In Egypt 63
  Moshe As A Leader 65
  The Burning Bush That Was Not Consumed By Fire 66
Parshas Vaeirah 68-71
  Displaying Gratitude (Hakoras Hatov) 68
  Bechira (Free Will) 70
  The Makos (Plagues) 70
Parshas Bo 72-75
  Mesiras Nefesh: Offering One's Life For Hashem 72
  The True Wealth 72
  "And You Shall Tell Your Children" 73
Parshas Beshalach 75-78
  The Miracle Of The Yam Suf (Red Sea) 75
  Massah Merivah 76
  The Mun 77
Parshas Yisro 78-81
  The Torah Is Given On Har Sinai 78
  The Acceptance Of The Torah 79
  Honor Your Father And Your Mother 80
Parshas Mishpotim 81-87
  Honesty 81
  Showing Kindness To Others 83
  Charity To Others 86
  Chukim 87
Parshas Terumah 87-89
  Hashem In Our Midst 87
  Charity 88
  Avoiding Hypocrisy 89
Parshas Tetzaveh 90-91
  Our Torah 90
  The Me'il And Loshon Ho'Rah 90
  The Bells 91
Parshas Ki Sisah 91-94
  The Eigel Ha'Zohov (The Golden Calf) 91
  Negative Influences 92
  A Half Shekel: Jews Working Together 93
Parshas Vayakhel 95-97
  Shabbos 95
  The Lineage Of Betzalel 96
  The Women's Jewelry 96
Parshas Pekudei 97-100
  Moshe Under Suspicion 97
  The Oron And The Flask Of Mun 99
  "As Hashem Commanded Moshe" 99

CHUMASH VAYIKROH

Parshas Vayikroh 101-103
   Korbonos And Prayers...101
   Donating With Your Heart..101
   Modesty...102
Parshas Tzav 103-106
   A Lesson In Consistency 103
   Not Embarrassing Others 104
   Sincere Devotion, Not Mere Habit 105
Parshas Shemini..106-109
   In Pursuit Of Peace...106
   Importance Of Respecting The Sages 107
   Kashrus..108
Parshas Tazriah-Metzorah 109-112
   Tzora'as And Loshon Ho'Rah 109
   Punishment For Loshon Ho'Rah 110
   Judging Others—And Oneself 111
Parshas Acharei Mos 112-114
   Strange Fires—Foreign Influences...112
   Yom Kippur: "Yom Hazikoron"...113
Parshas Kedoshim 115-119
   Great Expectations—Bnei Yisroel's Mission 115
   Loving Your Neighbor..116
   Prohibited Mixtures..118
Parshas Emor 119-122
   The Kohanim And Levi-im—Supporting Scholars 119
   The Shabbos For Hashem...120
   Yomim Tovim (Holidays) 121
Parshas Behar..123-125
   Shemittah And Emunas Hashem...123
   The Oral Law...124
   Taking Interest 124
Parshas Bechukosai..125-128
   Commitment To The Torah..125
   Achdus: United We Stand, Divided We Fall......................................126
   Shivisee Hashem Lenegdee Tomid 127

CHUMASH BAMIDBAR

Parshas Bamidbar 129-132
   The Holy Wilderness 129
   Your Students Are Your Children 130
   Yissachar and Zevulun 130
Parshas Nosso 132-135
   Birchas Kohanim And Material Wealth 132
   Birchas Kohanim And Praying To Hashem 133
   The Nazir 134
Parshas Beha'aloscha 135-137
   The Menorah 135
   Consistent Devotion 136
   Protecting Other Jews 136
Parshas Shalach 138-141
   Moshe And Yehoshua: Qualities of Leadership 138
   The Sin of the Meraglim: A Lack of Bitochon 139
   Achdus—Brotherhood 140
Parshas Korach 141-143
   The Rebellion Of Korach 141
   Searching For Peace By Swallowing Pride 142
   A Wife's Influence 143
Parshas Chukas 144-147
   "To Say . . ."—Influencing Others 144
   The Poroh Adumah—Law Without Any Meaning 145
   Miriam And Aharon 146
Parshas Balak 147-149
   Bilam's Duplicity And Greed 147
   Ascertaining Hashem's Protection 148
   The Jewish Family 149
Parshas Pinchas 150-152
   Pinchas' Uncompromising Attitude 150
   Pinchas' Reward 151
   The New Leader 151
Parshas Matos 153-156
   Keeping Vows 153
   Tzenius And The Yetzer Horah (Modesty And The Evil Inclination) 154
   The Request Of Reuven And Gad 155
Parshas Massei 156-158
   Cities Of Refuge 156
   Relying On Others 157
   Enumerating The Stages—Learning From Experience 158

CHUMASH DEVORIM

Parshas Devorim 159-161
  Greatness Has Many Levels 159
  Speaking The Truth 160
  The Right Association 161
Parshas Vo'eschanan 161-164
  "All The Days Of Your Life" 161
  Lifnim Mi'Shuras Ha'Din 162
  Mezuzah And Tefillin 164
Parshas Eikev 165-167
  Love Of Hashem 165
  Fear Of Hashem 166
  The Jewish Homeland 167
Parshas R'ei 168-171
  The Blessing Or The Curse 168
  Intentions 169
  Generosity At All Times 169
Parshas Shoftim 171-175
  "Justice, Justice You Shall Pursue" 171
  The Levi'im's Share 173
  A "Complete" Nation 173
Parshas Ki Seitsei 176-179
  The Right Marriage Partner 176
  Returning Lost Property 176
  The Crime Of Ammon And Moav Against Bnei Yisroel ... 178
Parshas Ki Sovo 179-182
  Doing Mitzvos Quickly And Eagerly 179
  The "Chosen Nation" 180
  Ma'Aser For The Poor 181
Parshas Netzavim 183-185
  All Stand As Equals Before Hashem 183
  Searching For The Treasure Within Yourself 183
  Returning While There's Still Time 184
Parshas Vayeilech 185-188
  A True Leader Of The People 185
  Including The Children 186
  The Hidden Face Of Hashem 187
Parshas Ha'azinu 188-190
  Forgetfulness 188
  Prosperity And Rebellion 188
  The Few Chasing The Many 189
Parshas V'Zos Ha'brochoh 190-192
  Torah Tziva Lonu Moshe, Morasha Kehillas Yaakov ... 190
  The Public Wedding 191
  The Torah Is Eternal 192

ללמוד וללמד

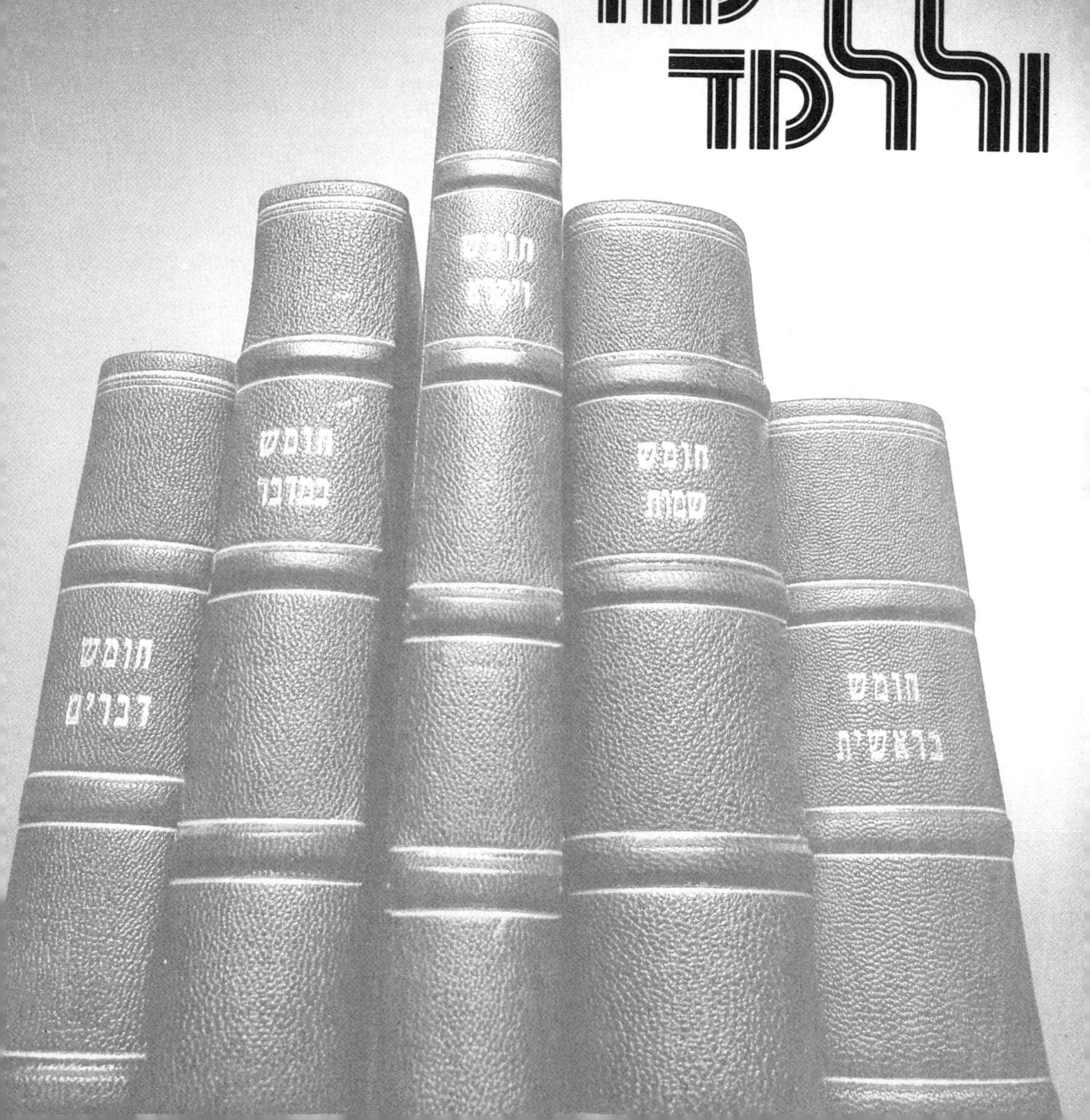

The Torah begins by stating that in the beginning Hashem created from nothingness the heaven and the earth. However, the world was yet void and without shape or order. During the first six days Hashem shaped, made and placed everything in the universe into its proper functioning position. The order of this Divine task was as follows:

First Day—Creation of light and darkness.

Second Day—Arrangement of "Rokiah" to separate between the heavenly and earthly waters.

Third Day—Accumulation of the waters allowing the

פרשת
בראשית
*Parshas
Bereishis*

THE CREATION

A heretic once asked Rabbi Akiva, "Who created the world?"

Rabbi Akiva replied, "The Holy One, G-d, Blessed be He."

"Give me a definite proof," demanded the heretic.

"What are you wearing?" asked Rabbi Akiva.

"A garment," was the reply.

"And who made it?" continued Rabbi Akiva.

"The weaver, of course," replied the startled heretic.

"I do not believe you," said Rabbi Akiva. "Prove it to me."

The heretic looked at him scornfully and responded, "Isn't it obvious that the weaver was the one who made this garment!"

"And yet you do not realize that it is just as obvious that the Holy One created the world!" retorted Rabbi Akiva.

The heretic departed, but Rabbi Akiva's pupils, who had heard this exchange, said to him, "How was your answer a clear proof?"

Rabbi Akiva replied, "My students, just as the presence of a house testifies that it was constructed by a builder, and the garment testifies to the weaver, so, too, does the presence of the world testify to the fact that Hashem, the Creator, formed it." (Meshech Chochmah, Vayikrah 19:18)

> Where is Hashem? In the heart of every questioner. (Ben Ha'Melech Veha'Nazir)
> Atheism starts as a black spot on the heart gradually growing bigger, till it corrodes the whole heart. (Mussar Ha'Philosophim)
> From my body I deduce the existence of Hashem. (Iyov 19)

A similar story is told of the Rambam. When the Rambam taught that the world

was created by Hashem, a heretic disagreed. Instead, said the heretic, the world had existed forever and no one had created it. The Rambam then asked the heretic to leave the room for several moments. When the heretic was asked to re-enter, a beautiful painting hung on the wall. The heretic admired the painting and asked who had painted it. The Rambam answered that he had spilled some paint onto a canvas and that the painting had taken shape by itself.

The heretic laughed mockingly and said, "That is impossible. Just by looking at the perfect design of the painting, anyone can tell that someone painted it carefully and purposefully."

The Rambam responded, "The same is true of the world. When examining how perfectly all its features exist and interact, anyone can tell that it was formed by an All-Knowing Creator."

THE SUN, THE MOON, THE STARS, AND THE BENEFIT OF MODESTY

The Medrash tells us that the sun and the moon were originally created to be equally large. However, the moon complained to Hashem that this was not a fair and practical arrangement, saying "Is it possible for two kings to rule one country and share one crown?"

"You are saying that you and the sun cannot be of the same size," said Hashem. "Very well, since one of you must be subservient to the other, you will be the one to be diminished in size and power. The sun will continue to burn as brightly as it did when created, and will radiate light and warmth throughout the day. On the other hand, you will provide only a small amount of illumination during the darkness of the night."

The moon was extremely sad upon hear-

dry land to be visible.

Fourth Day—Creation and placement of sun and moon in the sky.

Fifth Day—Creation of sea life and birds.

Sixth Day—Creation of reptiles, animals, and finally man.

On the Seventh Day of creation, Hashem "rested" from His work, and sanctified the seventh day as the Shabbos.

Hashem decided that it is not good for man to be alone. He brought all the animals and birds before Odom. Odom gave names to all of them, but could find no mate for himself among them. Hashem, therefore, cast a deep sleep upon Odom. He removed one of Odom's ribs and then closed the wound with flesh. He shaped, developed and completed the rib, making it into a woman, and brought her before Odom. Hashem placed them in the Garden of Eden where they could eat from anything, save the forbidden fruit of the Tree of Knowledge. However, Chava fell

ing this, and immediately regretted the fact that this development had been caused by its own rash and immodest protest.

But Hashem, with His everlasting sympathy and compassion, said comfortingly, "Because I realize that you are now sorry about your improper behavior, I will lighten the burden of my decision. I will surround you with countless luminous stars which will add to your shine with their own twinkling brilliance. You will not be alone. Yet, because you tried to claim the supremacy for yourself, your light will still be dimmed." (Chullin 60b)

How many of us, without necessarily realizing it, spend our lives pursuing Kovod (Honor). How often do we want to be on top, to be better than everyone else? Yet, what we may not realize is that this striving for selfish supremacy usually leads to bitter disappointment, as with the moon in the above story. Instead of seeking our own advancement at someone else's expense, we should be satisfied with what we have. It will result in better relations with others and fewer ulcers.

In fact, Hashem Himself guides us with the proper attitude of modesty. We find Hashem stating, "Let us make man." What is the meaning of this pronoun "us," when Hashem created everything by Himself!? Rashi replies that Hashem was speaking to the 'Malochim,' the angels, not because Hashem needed their assistance in the Creation, but to show mankind that even Hashem follows the modest practice of seeking the opinions of others. If Hashem, the All-Powerful, can Himself be so modest, certainly we can. (Bereishis Rabbah 8)

Silence and Modesty are good for everybody.

Why was man created on the Shabbos-eve and not earlier? . . . so that, should he become swell-headed, he can be reminded that the worm preceded him in the works of creation. (Sanhedrin 38) Hashem says: "With haughty eyes and proud heart I cannot be." (Tehillim 101:5) The proud in heart are an abomination to Hashem. (Midrash Ha'Godol Vayeshev)

THE SIN OF ODOM AND CHAVA

Odom and Chava were able to enjoy the countless splendors of the Garden of Eden. The Eitz Hada'as was the only tree whose fruit they were told not to eat. Yet, it was this one tree whose fruit they did eat. How did it happen that Odom and Chava were not able to observe this seemingly simple commandment?

The mistake Chava made was to reinterpret Hashem's commandment. Hashem had told her and Odom not to eat of the Eitz Hada'as's fruit. Yet, when the Yetzer Ho'rah (Evil Inclination) in the form of the serpent asked Chava, "Has Hashem forbidden you to benefit from all the trees here?," she replied, "No. It is only the Eitz Hada'as which we were told neither to touch nor to eat from." Chava added, on her own, the restriction of not touching the tree. The serpent then pushed her until she was touching the tree. Nothing happened. The serpent then said, "You see, nothing occurred when you touched the tree. Likewise, you may eat from its fruit and nothing will happen." She did, and gave some of the fruit to Odom as well, and this grave sin was committed. The error was in changing Hashem's law. This is why we are not allowed to add to, subtract

under the influence of the crafty serpent (Nochosh) and ate of the forbidden fruit and gave some to Odom as well. As a result, they received Divine punishment. They were forced to leave the Garden of Eden and begin the lives of humans, as we know it, experiencing the hardship of toiling for their sustenance and the sufferings of childbirth. The serpent was also punished by its having to crawl on the ground and to eat the dust of the earth.

Odom and Chava gave birth to two sons: Cain, who became a tiller of the land, and Hevel, who became a shepherd. Both Cain and Hevel brought offerings of their produce to Hashem. Hevel was sincere in his offering and brought before Hashem from his first-born and from the best of his flock. On the other hand, Cain was insincere and brought his worst produce. Hashem accepted Hevel's offering and a fire came down from heaven burning his offering; but not so to Cain's offering. Cain was greatly angered and highly embarrassed. While they were in the field, Cain killed Hevel, his brother.

Asked by Hashem the whereabouts of his brother, Cain replied, "Am I my brother's keeper?" Hashem punished Cain severely for his actions. Cain was cursed and as penalty was forced to be a wanderer over the face of the earth.

Odom and Chava gave birth to a third son, Sheis, as well as additional children. As each new generation reproduced, the numbers of mankind increased.

from, or reinterpret the laws of Hashem's Torah. (Avos De Rabbi Nosson 5:5)

Another instance in which a change in a basic premise led to problems is provided by the following story. Reuven visited his neighbor Shimon and asked to borrow two spoons. Shimon readily agreed. The next day Reuven returned three spoons. "But I lent you only two!" protested Shimon. "I know," replied Reuven, "but the two spoons had a baby, and I'm returning that one to you, too." Shimon thought that sounded highly unusual, but he accepted the extra spoon, thinking, "If he gives me something for free, why shouldn't I keep it?"

Soon afterwards, Reuven again borrowed some spoons, four spoons this time. Sure enough when Reuven came to repay the loan, he brought with him eight spoons. This time Shimon accepted the extra spoons with no questions whatsoever. The next time Reuven appeared, he asked for the entire silverware collection belonging to Shimon. Shimon gave this to him most eagerly, secretly anticipating the return of countless additional spoons, knives, and forks. The next time he saw Reuven, Shimon asked when the silverware would be returned. Reuven looked at him sadly and said, "I'm sorry to tell you that all the pieces of silverware became sick and died, and so I have nothing to return."

"But that's ridiculous!" protested Shimon. "Silverware can't get sick! They

aren't human!"

"But you accepted the fact that they could have children!" answered Reuven as he left.

By changing the logical law that silverware cannot have children in order to satisfy his greed, Shimon set himself up for the eventual loss of his entire silverware collection. Similarly, by changing Hashem's basic command, Chava brought about the loss of the ideal life in the Garden of Eden.

It is perhaps understandable that Chava could be fooled into sinning when she touched the Etz Hada'as and her punishment never came. Yet, why was Chava convinced that just because she did not die immediately after touching the tree that she would not be punished? Perhaps the punishment of death would come later?

Actually, the wicked strategy of the serpent (the Yetzer HoRah) was as follows: He told Chava, "You have already sinned, so you will eventually die anyway. Therefore, you might as well enjoy yourself to the fullest while you can." As a result, she proceeded to eat the forbidden fruit.

This is the same attitude assumed by many. They let themselves be convinced by the Evil Inclination, the Yetzer HoRah, that they will die in the end anyway. They have sinned a little bit, so they have nothing to lose by succumbing to more sinful acts. They lose their self-control and indulge in unlawful practices. These acts may provide momentary happiness, but they lose sight of

There were ten generations from Odom till Noach, including two Tzadikim, Chanoch and Mesushelech. However, man turned to evil and practiced immorality and violence. Hashem began reconsidering His act of populating the world with mankind. Noach, however, found favor in His eyes.

the fact that they are forsaking their permanent happiness in Olom HaBoh, the World to Come, just as Chava lost her right to everlasting contentment in the Garden of Eden for the temporary thrill of eating the forbidden fruit. One must always be on guard against losing one's self-control to the lure of the Yetzer HoRah. (Berachos 5a)

When you fear Hashem and beware of

an evil path, you will not be misled into evil. (Mussar Haphilosophim)

Avtalion said: "O Sage, be watchful of your words, lest you incur the penalty of exile and be banished to a place of evil waters." (Pesachim 102)

The fear of Hashem prolongs days but the years of the wicked shall be shortened. (Mishley 10:27)

Noach was a righteous man, even though the rest of his generation was evil. Hashem beheld the sad state of the world and decided to destroy the entire populace, with the exception of Noach and his family, by bringing a flood. He informed Noach of His decision and instructed Noach to construct a three-story ark, in which Noach and his family would dwell during the flood. Noach did as Hashem instructed, and when the ark was completed, Noach, his wife, their three sons (Shem, Chom, and Yafes) and their respective wives entered the ark. They took with them seven pairs of every

פרשת נח

Parshas Noach

HASHEM WAITS PATIENTLY FOR REPENTANCE

There was a span of ten generations between the life of Odom and that of Noach. Unfortunately, each new generation's acts represented a moral decline from those of the previous one. Mankind seemed to become morally worse and worse. Yet, Hashem refrained from punishing them. He waited, hoping that men would use their Free Will to repent from their wicked ways. Hashem hoped that they would possibly follow the example of the few righteous men and change their ways. However, these few righteous individuals alone proved unable to stem the tide, and the populace remained cruel and sinful. In fact, there was one such Tzadik (righteous person) named Chanoch about whom the Torah records "And Chanoch walked in the ways of Hashem." Yet, if we study a little further in the Chumash, we find that Hashem found it necessary to end Chanoch's life before his time. Hashem was afraid that Chanoch might somehow find himself falling under the negative influence of his wicked generation. In this way, Chanoch was able to die as

an unblemished Tzaddik and would receive his reward in the World to Come.

The evil of the era of Noach surpassed that of all previous generations and Hashem knew that the world as it existed had to undergo a drastic change. Hashem decided to destroy all sinful beings by means of a Mabul (Flood), and only the righteous Noach and his family would be spared to rebuild humanity.

Hashem, therefore, commanded Noach to construct an ark. This tedious process took one hundred twenty years (Bereishis Rabbah 30:7). Why all this unnecessary labor? There are many ways Hashem could have saved Noach without having him toil for one hundred twenty years! Actually, this was all part of Hashem's Divine plan. Hashem was providing mankind with one final chance to repent. Upon seeing Noach working so hard for so long a period of time, the people were bound to ask, "What are you doing?" Noach was then able to reply, "If you do not mend your ways, Hashem will bring a flood upon the entire face of the earth. That is why I am building an ark, to survive the flood waters. So repent, before it is too late!" By prolong-

kosher animal and bird and one pair of every other living creature. They also took into the ark all types of foods which would sustain the inhabitants during their stay in the ark. On the seventeenth day of the second month, rain began to pour onto the earth, and large quantities of water erupted from the earth's interior. This inundation continued for forty days and forty nights and almost all living beings located outside the ark drowned. The deluge was so great that almost six months elapsed before the waters subsided sufficiently for the ark to come to rest on the mountain-top of Ararat.

After almost three additional months, Noach released a raven from the ark to ascertain whether dry land had reappeared. The raven merely flew to and fro, waiting for the water on the surface of the earth to dissipate. Seven days later, Noach sent out a dove, only to have the dove quickly return to the ark for it could

ing the building, Hashem gave humanity every last possible opportunity to make the flood unnecessary. But, alas, Noach's message went unheeded.

Hashem is patient in accepting repentance (Pirkey Avos 5:1). He will go to almost any means to encourage it. The Neviim (Prophets) were sent just for this purpose. They warned the people in the name of Hashem to repent, or destruction and exile would not be far off.

One particularly noteworthy instance is in the book of Yonah. In it, we learn how Hashem sent the prophet Yonah to the city of Nineveh to try to convince the people there to abandon their sinful ways. Yonah cautioned the inhabitants of Nineveh that unless they return to Hashem, their city will be destroyed in forty days. The people of Nineveh did indeed heed Yonah's call and the entire city joined together in penitence and was saved.

> R. Levi said: "Great is repentance, for it reaches as far as the Throne of Glory." (Yoma 86)
> R. Yochanan said: "Great is penitence, for it averts the evil decree." (Rosh Hashana 17)
> A fool repeats his foolishness. (Mishley 26)

GODOL HASHOLOM—HOW GREAT IS PEACE!

In this sedra we find two generations of sinners, Dor Hamabul (the Generation of the Flood) and the Dor Haflogah (the Generation of the Division). The Dor Hamabul lost their fear of G-d. They partook in all types of immoral and destructive activity. "The earth was filled with robbery" (Bereishis 6:11). The Torah's description of the Dor Hamabul is very bad. The Dor Haflogah lost

themselves even more. They rebelled directly against Hashem's authority. They attempted to build a tower, ascend to heaven and conquer the heavens. It was defiance at its peak. (Bereishis Rabbah 38:7).

Yet, if we examine their respective punishments, we find an interesting phenomenon. The Dor Hamabul was destroyed, wiped off the face of the earth. On the other hand, the Dor Haflogah was only dispersed. Was not the Dor Haflogah deserving of a more stringent punishment? Why did Hashem punish them with such leniency?

Our Chazal (Sages of Blessed Memory) explain that there was one substantial merit that the Dor Haflogah possessed which brought lenience along with their punishment—Shalom (Peace). As wicked as they were, as rebellious and defiant towards Hashem as they were, there was peace and harmony among them. And, therefore, Hashem saw fit to be lenient in their punishment. The Dor Hamabul was filled with robbery and crimes 'Bain Odom Lachaveiro' (between man and his fellow man). The Dor Haflogah had harmony and unity on their side.

A Rav was once visiting a certain town. On Tisha B'Av (the fast of the ninth day of Av which commemorates the destruction of the Bais Hamikdosh) he was informed of a bitter feud between two groups, and was asked to mediate between them.

"We assume, however, that you will not want to hear the two sides until tomorrow, since today is a fast day," they told him.

"On the contrary," responded the Rav. "The destruction of the Bais Hamikdosh was caused by 'Sinas Chinom,' unwarranted hatred. What is more appropriate than trying to promote peace and brotherhood on this very day?"

find no resting place. After waiting another seven days, Noach again sent out the dove. This time the dove returned with an olive leaf in its beak indicating that the waters were receding. Finally, on its third assignment seven days later, the dove did not return at all, and Noach knew that the land had at last begun to dry up. Noach was then able to remove the covering of the ark. It was only then that Hashem told Noach to leave the ark. Noach left the ark after his stay of one year and eleven days, or one solar year. He offered sacrifices of gratitude to Hashem for his survival. Hashem was pleased with Noach's sacrifices and He promised Noach that He would never destroy all of mankind by means of a flood. Hashem placed a rainbow in the sky and told Noach that the rainbow will always be the symbol of this promise.

Our Chazal teach us, "Great is Sholom (peace) and hated is Machlokes (dispute)."
The master of peace desires the peace of all His creatures. (Chinuch 206)
Nothing good ever came out of a quarrel. (Shemos Rabbah 6)
R. Shimeon ben Gamliel said: "The world depends on three things: Justice, Truth, and Peace." (Avos 1)

NOACH AND AVROHOM: SILVER AND GOLD

The Torah states, "Noach was a man righteous and wholehearted in his generation "(Bereishis 6:9). Some of our Sages interpret this text as meaning that Noach was considered outstandingly righteous only when compared with the others of his generation. However, had he lived during the lifetime of Avrohom Ovinu, Avrohom's righteousness would have outshone his. Thus, Noach's character can be compared to silver coins, which look impressive when compared to brass coins, but which lose their luster when in the company of gold coins. (Sanhedrin 108a)

Noach was truly a very pious person. Unfortunately, his piety never carried itself over onto others. Besides his family, there was not one other individual who was under Noach's influence who was worthy of accompanying Noach on his journey of survival aboard the ark. We do not find one prayer uttered by Noach on behalf of the world about to be destroyed. Yes, he was pious but it was a piety that affected only himself.

Avrohom was very pious and his piety affected others. We learn in Parshas Lech Lecha about Avrohom's single-handed fight against idolatry and his helping others realize its worthlessness. We will find out

about the converts that he converted, about the Hachnosas Orchim (Hospitality) he had for everyone and how he used it to bring them closer to Hashem. Avrohom was definitely a pious person for himself but he stretched out his hand and helped others see the truth.

Avrohom understood the value of human life. When Hashem informed him (see Vayeirah) that he intended to destroy S'dome, Avrohom beseeched the Almighty to spare it. The Torah describes in great length Avrohom's prayer for the preservation of those wicked people. Avrohom was a Tzadik whose piety spread forth and shone upon others.

The Gemorrah tells us that Rav Meir also learned of the importance of trying to save others. Some robbers in his neighborhood were causing him a great deal of trouble. He, therefore, prayed to Hashem that they should die. When his wife Beruria heard this, she questioned whether this was the proper prayer. "Why don't you pray instead that these robbers should repent," she urged. "That way they will not only stop robbing, but they will also have the opportunity to do Mitzvos in the future!" Rav Meir followed his wife's advice and they did indeed repent. The prayer to save their lives was the one that Hashem responded to. (Berachos 10a)

The following tale gives another indication of the importance of saving the life of a fellow human.

A farmer and his wife once came to the Maggid of Koznitz. They were childless, and they asked the holy man to intercede on their behalf before Hashem so that they would be blessed with offspring.

The Maggid blessed them and prayed for them. The prayers were accepted and the couple was graced with the birth of a boy. Later, the child fell ill and once again the

Through the offspring of Noach's three sons, the earth became repopulated and the founders of numerous nations appeared. Yet, at this time, all of mankind spoke only one language, Loshon Hakodesh, the holy language. Unfortunately, mankind didn't learn from the experiences of the flood and returned to evil ways.

The different nations met and proposed to build a city with a tower reaching heaven. Our Chazal (Sages of Blessed Memory) explain that these wicked people were not satisfied with the earth alone for their dwelling place. Thoughts such as "Why should Hashem have the heaven all for Himself?" passed through their minds. They decided to build a colossal tower, scale the tower, and conquer the heavens. Hashem frustrated this challenge by confusing the speech of the builders, so that one could not understand the other. The city was consequently called Babel,

farmer came to the Maggid to ask for another blessing. The Maggid complied but this time the blessing did not seem to have any effect, for the child's condition did not improve. On the contrary, the boy seemed to grow weaker by the day. The child's mother kept watch at her son's bedside, never leaving it for a moment.

One night, the mother fell asleep while sitting at the bedside. When she awoke some time later, she noticed with amazement the sight of a soldier standing by the bed. In one hand he held a bottle and in the other a small spoon. When the frightened woman saw him feeding her child, she screamed and the soldier vanished into thin air. Yet, beginning at that very moment, the child began to improve and he soon was completely recovered.

Naturally, the parents were elated. However, they were deeply worried about the mysterious vision of the soldier. Perhaps it had been some demon casting a magic spell over their son. They decided to once again visit the Maggid of Koznitz and related all that happened. The Maggid assured them that they had nothing to worry about, and they left in a relieved state of mind.

As soon as the parents had left, the Maggid ordered his servant to go to the local cemetery and knock with his stick on the tombstone of a certain soldier who was buried there. The servant was told to announce that the soldier was requested to appear before the Maggid. The servant did as he was told and the soldier promptly appeared before the Maggid.

"Who appointed you a children's doctor?" the Maggid asked.

Slowly, the spirit of the soldier replied, "It happened in the following way. When I was kidnapped by the Czar's Cossacks to be a member of the Army, I was still a child of 15.

I was trained to be a soldier and I grew increasingly assimilated to the gentile ways. After a while, there was no visible difference between myself and the non-Jewish soldiers.

"One day, I was marching with my Army unit. On the road, we met a Jewish traveler who was returning from a nearby village. The soldiers soon surrounded the Jew on all sides. They searched through his pockets and found seventy-five rubles, which they immediately took from him. Because they were afraid that this robbery would be discovered, they decided to kill the Jew. They quickly hanged him on the limb of the nearest tree and left him there.

"When I watched what was happening, the Jewish soul in me was aroused and I began to pity this poor fellow Jew. I lingered behind when the other soldiers left and I quickly cut the rope from which the Jew was suspended. I was just in time, the poor man soon regained his breath, but he still looked in bad condition. I had some money with me, so I counted out seventy-five rubles and gave them to him. With this, the horror of his encounter was lessened a bit.

"As soon as the other soldiers reached the barracks, the roll call was taken and it was discovered that I was missing. A search party was organized and I was found at the tree. I had to confess to my deed and I was immediately hung on the same tree. Later, some passing travelers cut down my body and buried me in the cemetery in this area.

"When I came before the Heavenly Court for judgment, there was some question as to what my sentence should be. I was not fit for immediate paradise, for I had committed many sins during my lifetime. On the other hand, I was not sent to hell, for, after all, I had saved a soul and one who saves a soul is considered as one who has saved an entire world. It was, therefore, decided that I was to

meaning mixing, for it was there that Hashem mixed the languages of the people of the earth.

There were ten generations from Noach till Avrom. Avrom lived in Uhr Kasdim and it was there that he realized the oneness of Hashem, and it was there that he risked his life to follow Him and not to worship idols.

become a spiritual children's doctor, and that I was to give my services wherever needed. This is why I was there to help cure the couple's young son."

Thus, even a sinful man's soul can be saved if he helps save the life of another.

When we see our fellow man drowning in a river or being attacked by a wild

beast or thieves we are obliged to rescue him, for it is written: "You shall not stand idly by the blood of your neighbor." (Vayikrah 19:16)

He that sustains one Jewish life is as if he had sustained all the world. (Bava Basra 11)

The Divine call came to Avrom to leave Choran and to proceed to another land which Hashem would show him. Avrom journeyed toward the land of Canaan (Eretz Yisroel), taking with him his wife Sarai, his nephew Lot, and all their possessions. They also took with them their many followers whom Avrom and Sarai had successfully brought closer to the ways of Hashem and the Torah. Avrom reached the land of Canaan and continued on until he arrived at the city of Shechem. At Shechem, Hashem appeared to Avrom in a vision and affirmed His promise to Avrom that the

פרשת לך לך

Parshas Lech Lecha

HOW AVROHOM CAME TO BELIEVE IN HASHEM

In the time of Avrohom, most people worshipped idols. Avrohom's father Terach was also from this vast majority. In fact, he even owned a shop in which he sold idols. However, Avrohom quickly came to the realization that mere man-made, lifeless idols could not be the rulers of the earth. There had to be a superior force capable of creating the world and regulating all of nature. He gazed up at the sky and saw the glorious blaze of the sun. "This must certainly be the ruler of the earth," he said to himself, and began to worship the sun. But when night fell, the sun became eclipsed and its position was taken over by the moon and stars. "Then the moon and stars must be the real powers," he now thought, and began worshipping them, only to find that they in turn gave way again to the sun. Only then did Avrohom realize that there must be a power superior to the sun, the moon, and the stars, and that His power must control all visible bodies. This power could only be an invisible Eternal, Almighty G-d to whom Avrohom now worshipped.

One day, Avrohom's father had to leave the idol store and he left Avrohom in charge. A customer entered the store, looked around and decided to purchase a particular idol. He approached Avrohom to place his order. Avrohom listened to the order and asked, "How old are you?"

"Sixty years old," answered the startled customer.

"Woe is it to the person who is sixty years old and wants to worship an idol made yesterday" proclaimed Avrohom.

Upon hearing this the would-be customer was so embarrassed that he left the store without his purchase.

Soon a woman entered the shop carrying a large tray filled with fine flour. She gave it to Avrohom explaining that she would like this flour to be sacrificed to the idols. As the woman left, Avrohom took a heavy instrument and broke all the idols in the store except the largest idol. He then took the heavy instrument and placed it in that largest idol's hands. When his father Terach returned, he was aghast at the horrible sight of his store.

"What happened?" shouted Terach.

"A woman came into the store," explained

land of Canaan would one day be the domain of his descendants. Avrom built a Mizbeach (an Altar) to Hashem as thanksgiving for these happy tidings.

A severe hunger in Canaan compelled Avrom to temporarily sojourn in Egypt. He feared that the Egyptians would be attracted to his wife Sarai and would murder him in order to take her. Therefore, as he approached the land of Egypt, he asked Sarai to tell the Egyptians that she was Avrom's sister. When they did arrive in Egypt, Sarai's beauty was greatly admired and she was taken into Paroh's royal household. Consequently, Avrom was showered with gifts of flocks, herds, and servants. However, when Paroh and his household were smitten with mysterious illnesses, he sensed that something was wrong. He learned that Sarai was really Avrom's wife and that his taking Sarai had caused this punishment. Paroh asked Avrom to leave Egypt with his family and possessions and Avrom complied.

Avrom and his wife, with their newly acquired possessions, returned to the city of Bethel in Canaan. Because both Avrom and Lot had become very wealthy and had many flocks and herds, there was not enough pasture land for the herds of both men, and quarrels erupted between their herdsmen. To avoid conflict, Avrom suggested that he and Lot separate, and he offered his nephew the first choice of land in which to settle. Lot chose the fertile, well watered plain of Jordan, and

Avrohom, "and she brought a large tray filled with fine flour as a sacrifice for the idols. After I placed it in front of the idols, an argument broke out among them. Each one wanted to eat from the flour first. All of a sudden this big idol got up, took that heavy instrument and smashed all the other idols."

"Why are you joking with me?" screamed Terach, "You know these idols can't do that!"

"Ah-hah!" exclaimed Avrohom, "Let your ears hear what your mouth is saying! Idols are only pieces of stone and wood. They have no power to even move. How then could they control the world? There is only one great Power in the world, and that is Hashem!"

For this act, considered heretical at the time, Terach brought Avrohom to the mighty King Nimrod to be tried and sentenced.

Nimrod told Avrohom to come forward. "Before you stands the great idol of our god, worshipped by all my subjects. Behind it, there is a furnace of flames with smoke billowing furiously from its midst. The choice is now yours. The noblemen and citizens of my realm have come to see you pay penitent homage to our god—or, if you refuse to do so, to see your terrible death by fire!"

"For me there can be only one reply," said Avrohom. "I have made up my mind that I will never bow to a mere statue. Only

Hashem will receive my worship. I choose the flames of the furnace!"

Four soldiers seized Avrohom and hurled him into the furnace. The people turned away, not wanting to watch the horror of the burning. But then something unexpected happened. No screams or cries of terror could be heard. The people looked back at the furnace and saw the figure of Avrohom making its way out of the furnace. When he emerged, Avrohom had not a mark nor a burn on him. It was a miracle before their eyes. A miracle performed by Hashem in defiance of their own gods. The people there gasped in amazement.

Avrohom's brother Horon was also being tried by Nimrod and he couldn't decide what to do. Should he bow down to the idol or be thrown into the furnace. He decided he would wait and see Avrohom's outcome. If Avrohom comes out alive, he'd be ready to follow Avrohom. Otherwise, he'd bow down to the idol. Finally, when he saw Avrohom's escape, he also declared, "I will not worship the idol. Throw me into the furnace!" He was sure that what had happened to Avrohom would also happen to him.

Once again the doors of the furnace were opened, and Horon was thrown inside. But this time the people assembled there heard screams. They were Horon's, and they were his last sounds, for he was soon burned alive. He had depended on a miracle, but miracles happen only to those who have complete faith in Hashem, as Avrohom did.

pitched his tents until the city of S'dome, infamous for the wickedness of its inhabitants. Avrom settled in the Plains of Mamrei, near Chevron, and was again promised by Hashem that his descendants would one day be granted this land.

At this time, five rulers in the south of Canaan, including the kings of S'dome and Amorah, were in the midst of a revolt against Kedorlaomer, King of Elam, to whom they had paid tribute for twelve years. Kedorlaomer, in turn, sought the aid of three of his neighboring rulers. The revolt became a battle, with the four kings led by Kedorlaomer, proving victorious. The winners managed to acquire as booty all the possessions and foodstuffs of S'dome and Amorah, as well as to take into captivity much of the populace. Among those in captivity was Lot. Avrom, hearing of his nephew's plight, led his household in battle against the victors and defeated them, rescuing Lot and his possessions, as well as the rest of the inhabitants of S'dome and their possessions. The King of S'dome went out to greet Avrom upon his victory. He offered Avrom all the possessions he had freed from Kedorlaomer as a reward for having freed all the captives. Avrom, however, refused any rewards whatsoever for his efforts.

Horon's wishy-washy stand did not merit a miracle. One must be strong in his faith and ready to stand up for it wholeheartedly. Avrohom's escape demonstrated to all the existence of Hashem and the reward paid to one who fully believes in Him. (Bereishis Rabbah 38:13)

Avrohom was the first individual to come to the realization of Hashem's existence on his own. He paved the path of "Emunah" (Belief in Hashem) for all the generations to come. Even a child can perceive with his pure simple "Emunah" things that a nonbeliever may not. A gentile once asked a Jewish boy how the boy knew Hashem exists. The boy replied, "I live near the seashore. If I go there and see footsteps in the sand, I know that someone has been there. In the same way, whenever I look up and see the sun, the moon, the stars, and the wonders of nature, I know that Hashem is there. Those are some of His imprints on the universe."

When Rav Yitzchak was a child, he was brought to a Maggid, who told him, "I will give you a gold coin if you can find where Hashem is." The boy replied, "I will give you two gold coins if you can find me a place where Hashem is not."

A true test of one's faith in Hashem comes when one is forced to choose between serving Hashem and dying, as Avrohom did. Those who sacrifice their lives for Hashem and Judaism are accorded the highest honor in Jewish legacy. Among those who did so was Rav Chaninah. He was among the ten martyrs tortured by the Roman Emperor Hadrian for their continued faith in Hashem.

All ten chose to remain faithful, and died 'Al Kiddush Hashem.' Though the emperor had forbidden all forms of Torah study, Rav Chanina persisted in delving into G-d's Holy Books. He was caught with the Torah in his hands and was condemned to death by burning. To compound the torture, the Roman authorities put wool on his heart to prolong the agony of his burning, and wrapped the parchment of the Torah around him. As he died, Rav Chanina was asked what he saw. He replied, "I see parchment burning, but I see the letters on it ascending to heaven." The words of the Torah, and the soul of Rav Chanina, went on to everlasting life, but the Roman Empire eventually crumbled. (Avodah Zarah 18a)

Another person who gave his life in devotion to Hashem was not even born a Jew. His name was Potozcki, and he was the nephew of a Polish king. Although Poland was by no means a Jewish nation, it did have its share of Jews, and Potozcki found himself attracted to Judaism. He sought to learn of its laws and ideals and soon decided that it was the only true religion. As a result, he left the royal household and converted to Judaism. Potozcki was a true Ger Tzedek, a convert who practiced Judaism faithfully and learned its Torah eagerly. However, his conversion was considered an act of treason by the Polish ruler. Potozcki tried to escape the king's threatening grasp; but he was caught. Trying to reason with him, the king informed him that one day, after he, the present king would die, Potozcki would be crowned king but only if he renounced his conversion. However, Potozcki un-

Avrom, in spite of all his good fortune, was still saddened by the fact that he did not yet have a son and heir. Hashem then took Avrom outside and told him to look up at the sky and count the stars. "Surely you cannot count them" said Hashem, "so many will be your children." Hashem told Avrom that He took him out of the land of Uhr Kasdim to give him this land as a possession to be inherited by Avrom's descendants. Avrom asked Hashem, "Whereby shall I know that I will possess the land?" Hashem then made a covenant with Avrom, known as the Bris Bein HaBesorim (Covenant Between The Halves). At this covenant Hashem informed Avrom that his descendants would temporarily be enslaved in a foreign land, but that they would emerge with great wealth.

Because Sarai remained childless, she suggested that Avrom take her maid Hagar as a second wife. When Hagar realized that she was pregnant, she no longer showed respect to Sarai. This bothered Sarai very much and she complained to Avrom.

hesitatingly refused. "I am a Jew, and I will die a Jew," he announced. "So be it," said the king. Potozcki was burned as a heretic; but even to the end he retained his faith in Hashem. So great was the example set by this Ger Tzedek that the Vilna Gaon, the supreme Torah leader of his time, requested to be buried near him.

> Rabbi Akiva said: In Shema we say, "With all your Soul" implies even if it takes your life. Shimeon ben Azzai said, "With all your Soul"—with your soul's lifeblood, till your dying breath. (Nedarim 40a)
>
> The person who is willing to risk martyrdom for his principle earns the respect of his enemy, who in the end concedes his right to them, like R. Abba ben Zimma. (Yerushalmi)
>
> The righteous man lives by his faith. (Chavakkuk 2)

GOING TO ERETZ YISROEL

Avrohom was already seventy-five years old when he heard Hashem's command to leave his birthplace and sever all ties with the land he had known all his life. A lesser man might have hesitated about making this major move. Not Avrohom! Though his only instructions were to leave his native country and go to the place that Hashem would show him, Avrohom asked no questions. He readily departed, leaving his future in the hands of Hashem. His adherence to G-d was so obvious that it influenced many others, and these followers soon converted and joined Avrohom, traveling to the "mystery destination," not knowing where they were headed.

Hashem led Avrohom to the land of Canaan, which later, as Eretz Yisroel, became the homeland for the Jewish nation. Not everyone would be so ready to forsake his home to journey to the Holy Land. Many Jews later in exile in foreign countries chose to remain there rather than travel to Eretz Yisroel. Not everyone had the trust in Hashem that Avrohom displayed, to live in G-d's chosen land, though the life might not be as comfortable there as it was elsewhere.

Yet, there were those who strove to journey to Eretz Yisroel. Among them was **Rav Yehuda Halevi**, the great Jewish philosopher and poet. He was fifty years old when he decided to make the difficult and dangerous trek to the Holy Land. After much hardship, he finally arrived at the gates of Yerusholayim. He immediately tore his garments, removed his shoes, and bowed to kiss the holy soil. As he was doing so, a Turk rode over on his horse, and trampled this great Tzadik to death. Yet, Rav Yehuda Halevi had died where he had wished, on the holy earth of Eretz Yisroel.

One who was not privileged to see this dream fulfilled was Rav Chaim Krozno. He, too, decided he must travel to Eretz Yisroel. While on the ship voyage there, he was confronted with a terrible storm and his ship was forced to return. Rav Chaim and his fellow passengers escaped injury, but Rav Chaim never again had the opportunity to make the journey. As a result, for the rest of his life he remained despondent because of it. When he was about to die, he asked that only his name be inscribed on his tombstone, nothing else. He felt that he had no inscribable merits because he had not merited to travel to Eretz Yisroel.

> R. Shimeon ben Yochai said: "The Holy One, blessed be He, gave the Jews three precious gifts, and all of them were

Avrom returned Hagar to Sarai's authority, and Sarai dealt harshly with her, and Hagar fled. An angel of Hashem appeared to Hagar and told her to return, promising that the son Yishmael,that she will bear will be the founder of a large nation.

When Avrom was ninety-nine years old, Hashem renewed the covenant with him and changed his name to Avrohom, meaning "father of a multitude of nations." Hashem commanded Avrohom to circumcise himself and all the other male members of his household. Since then every male child born for all generations must be circumcised when he is eight days old. This has been the sign of the covenant between Hashem and Avrohom and his descendants. Hashem also told Avrohom that henceforth Sarai shall be known as Sarah meaning "Princess for

given through suffering. These: The Torah, the land of Israel, and the world to come." (Berachos 5)

Hashem said: "Return unto the land of your fathers and to your kindred, and I will be with you." (Bereishis 31:3)

The atmosphere of Eretz Yisroel makes one wise. (Bava Basra 157)

BIKKUR CHOLIM (VISITING THE SICK)

When Hashem visited Avrohom after his Bris Milah in order to comfort him during his recuperation, He set a standard that all of us should follow. Visiting the sick can help save a life, and is therefore, accorded a high place in the priorities of Jewish law as can be seen from the stories below.

A woman once appeared before Rav Chaim, her face moist with tears. When Reb Chaim asked what was troubling her, she replied that she needed money for her baby, who was very ill. Not only did Rav Chaim run to secure the necessary money, but he also insisted on accompanying the woman to her home. There he stayed and watched over the baby for two days, giving the mother a chance to sleep while foregoing sleep himself.

A pupil of Rabbi Akiva suddenly became sick. The scholars in the academy of Rabbi Akiva did not visit him. The sick student had not been especially outstanding in his studies, so they felt it was beneath their dignity to come to his house.

Rabbi Akiva was outraged by their insensitive behavior. He personally went to the home of the sick pupil, waited upon him, supplied him with all his needs, and took a deep interest in his treatment. After he had recovered, the student said, "My master, you have saved my life."

When his pupils assembled shortly afterwards, Rabbi Akiva began his lecture by telling them, "Be advised that not visiting the sick is equivalent to hastening their death and shedding their blood." He then nodded in the direction of the sick student, whose recovery was due largely to the moral support he had received from his Torah master.

The Gaon Rabbi Hillel, the son-in-law of Rav Chaim of Volozhen, was seen one Shabbos evening carrying a lamp through the town of Horodna. The people of the town were shocked. The Gaon was violating the Shabbos by carrying a burning lamp in the street! Soon a crowd gathered, and they followed the Gaon until he came to a house belonging to a poor family. The Gaon entered the house, and later exited without the lamp.

"Master!" the people exclaimed. "Why were you carrying a lamp on Shabbos?"

The Gaon replied, "In this house lives a person who is dangerously ill. The candle inside the house had burned up and the entire house was shrouded in darkness. As a result, those inside could not take proper care of the ill person. The family sent a messenger to me to ask what could be done. To emphasize the halacha, I took a lamp and brought it to their house on Shabbos. For it is a mitzvah to violate the laws of the Shabbos to help save the life of a dangerously ill person.

When Rabbi Akiva Eiger accepted the position as Rabbi of his town, he devoted as much time as he could to aiding his fellow Jews. Though not physically strong, Rabbi Akiva Eiger never said, "Enough," when it was a matter of coming to the assistance of someone else.

When a cholera epidemic broke out in Prussia in 1831, Rabbi Akiva often spent whole nights at the bedside of the sick. He promulgated various laws of sanitation , urged the people to boil their water, and in this way helped reduce the death toll in his and nearby communities.

all." Avrohom promptly performed the great Mitzvah of "Bris Milah," circumcision. He circumcised Yishmael and every male member of his household, and then circumcised himself. All this was done by Avrohom in the light of day without fear of what others might say or do.

This heroic work came to the attention of the Emperor, Frederick William III, who sent a special royal order of appreciation to the Rabbi. A special emissary of the Emperor came to the Rabbi's house to deliver this letter of commendation. But a royal reward is not necessary for one to help the sick. The mitzvah of Bikkur Cholim is recognized by the King of the Universe, and those practicing it will receive their rewards from Him.

Rav Eliyahu Chaim Meisels was also a Torah leader who had to cope with a plague raging in his home town. Rav Meisels made it a point to go from house to house to visit the sick and to tend to their needs. One rainy day, while making these visits, one of his galoshes got stuck in the mud and he could not remove it. Instead, he extricated his foot and made his visits that day barefooted. When people told him that he was too prestigious a person to go around like this, he replied, "Do you want to take my opportunity to visit the sick away from me? Even Hashem performed this mitzvah!"

Visiting the sick takes away one sixtieth of the illness (Yorah Deah 335)

As Avrohom sat at the entrance of his tent hoping to greet visitors and thereby perform the Mitzvah of Gemilas Chesed, three individuals appeared. Avrohom ran to welcome them and proceeded to entertain them in a most hospitable manner. These "visitors" were actually Malochim (Angels) sent by Hashem to perform special duties on this world. One of the Malochim informed Avrohom that in a year's time his wife Sarah would give birth to a son. Sarah, who was almost ninety at the time, laughed inwardly at this seemingly unbelievable news. She was rebuked by Hashem for this

פרשת וירא
Parshas Veyeirah

CHESED (KINDNESS) AND HACHNOSAS ORCHIM (HOSPITALITY)

The one virtue which permeated Avrohom's character and was actually part and parcel of his very makeup was Chesed, kindness and generosity to others. Chesed is one of the three pillars upon which the world was founded by Hashem, for without it, men could not live together in a workable society. With it, one can do wonders.

The Chesed model was provided for by Hashem. It is because of Hashem's kindness that we are supplied with food, sunshine, happiness with life itself and all the good that comes along with it. Just stop for a minute and think about it.

Avrohom recognized this abundance of kindness and succeeded in emulating Hashem's generous ways. He did not help others because of any ulterior motive, such as wealth or greatness but because he knew that this was the will of Hashem and the right thing to do.

Avrohom's Bris Milah occurred at the age of ninety-nine, and while he was recovering, Hashem strengthened the rays of the sun. The intense heat caused everyone to remain home and not come out and bother Avrohom at his tent, for if anyone had approached Avrohom's abode, he would have entertained the guests royally, pain or no pain. However, Hashem noticed that the lack of visitors and the inability to perform the mitzvah of greeting others was making Avrohom sad. Consequently, Hashem sent three Malochim disguised as men to Avrohom. When Avrohom saw them, he was so pleased at the chance to perform Chesed that he ran out to greet them. "Rest your weary feet and I will fetch some water, (Bereishis 18:4)" he told them. Yet, when he returned, it was with a complete, sumptuous meal. Avrohom was a firm believer in "Emor Mi'at V'asey Harbei"—saying little but doing a lot (Pirkey Avos 1:15). Instead of making impressive-sounding promises, he quiet-

slight indication of doubt. She should have believed wholeheartedly in Hashem's promise. Why was it so hard to believe?! Is there anything that Hashem cannot do?! Before the Malochim left Avrohom, the second Maloch performed his assignment by healing Avrohom from the pain and sickness he had incurred from his Bris Milah (Circumcision—see Parshas Lech Lecha).

The time had arrived for the third Maloch to perform his assignment, the destruction of S'dome and Amorah. Hashem decided that it would be improper not to inform Avrohom of His intention to destroy the cities. When Avrohom was informed by Hashem of His intention, Avrohom's rachmonus (mercy) was aroused. He approached Hashem with prayer on behalf of the people of S'dome and Amorah. Avrohom argued that the righteous should not be destroyed together with the wicked, and obtained Hashem's promise to pardon the entire condemned populace if at least ten righteous men could be found among them.

The two Malochim arrived in S'dome. The first one, the Maloch who had cured Avrohom, was there to finish his assignment and save Lot and his family. The second Maloch was there to destroy the city. The two Malochim, still outwardly mere human beings, were greeted by Lot and invited to stay in his house. When the word

ly went about accomplishing more than anyone expected.

The Medrash tells us that not only was Avrohom eager to fulfill the mitzvah of Hachnosas Orchim, of greeting guests, but that in doing so he also sought to impress upon his visitors the kindness of Hashem. After partaking of the meal, the visitors would thank Avrohom profusely for his hospitality. "Oh, don't thank me," Avrohom would reply. "It is Hashem whom you must thank. Hashem is the one who has given all this to you." Then he would lead his guests in offering praises to Hashem in acknowledgement of His favors. In this sense, Avrohom's positive influence on others can be compared to the effect of a locomotive on the other cars in the train. Just as a locomotive has the power to pull other cars along on its route, so too, Avrohom was able to persuade others to follow in his service to Hashem. (Bereishis Rabbah 54:6)

A story is told of how the pious Rav Yeshaya practiced Hachnosas Orchim. Once a man and his wife were traveling through a village on Erev Shabbos when they happened to notice a small house. Because they were very tired from their journey, they wanted to ask the owner for lodgings. However, they were afraid that the owner would ask too high a price for accommodating them. They were about to move on when the wheel on their carriage broke, and they had no choice but to ask the owner for a place to stay for Shabbos.

When they knocked on the door, Rav Yeshaya answered and as soon as he heard of their plight, he asked them inside. The man nervously asked Rav Yeshaya how much their accommodations would cost. Rav Yeshaya replied that it would cost five rubles, but that for this price they could eat as much food as they wanted.

The husband and wife decided that, despite the fact that this was a high price, they had to accept it for lack of any alternatives. At least they could eat as heartily as they desired.

As a result, they enjoyed the Sabbos meals very much, and they slept most peacefully. When Shabbos was over, they felt that they had received more than their money's worth, and were most willing to pay the five rubles. However, Rav Yeshaya refused their money.

"But Rabbi," the man said, "we agreed on the price. We had a wonderful Shabbos here. Why then won't you accept our money?"

Rav Yeshaya replied, "Actually, I never had any intention of taking any money from you, as the Mitzvah of Hachnosas Orchim is one that I gladly perform for nothing. However, I sensed that if I told you at the outset that I wouldn't accept money, you would feel very uncomfortable here and would not accept our hospitality. I wanted you to enjoy the Shabbos, and you did. That is payment enough."

The Medrash says that when Shlomo Hamelech was in exile, he ate at two homes. At the home of a rich man he received lavish food and accommodations, but he was constantly reminded of his unfortunate state of affairs. At the home of a poor man, though, he was made to feel most comfortable and at

spread through the wicked city of S'dome, the entire city gathered around Lot's house. The evil men of the city tried to molest these visitors and were punished by Hashem with blindness.

The Malochim then informed Lot of Hashem's intention to destroy the city. They told him to take his family and leave. Lot hesitated in leaving S'dome; he wanted to save all his money. The Malochim quickly grabbed Lot, his wife, and his two daughters, and placed them outside the city.

The Malochim warned them not to look back at the destruction of the city. They were being saved only in the Z'chus (Merit) of Avrohom and, therefore, had no right to observe the punishment of others. They also warned them not to remain in the entire plain surrounding the cities. Lot pleaded to be allowed to remain in the area in a small town later known as Tzoar. Hashem granted Lot's request. Lot and his family found refuge in Tzoar.

Hashem then caused brimstone and fire to fall upon the cities of S'dome, Amorah

ease, as a member of the household rather than as an intruder. As a result of his experiences, Shlomo said, "Better a meal of herbs that one eats at a poor man's home, where love is found, than a stall-fed ox that the rich man fed me only in order to remind me of my misfortune and hatred therewith."

The Chofetz Chaim invited guests to his house whenever possible. Occasionally, on Shabbos, he would make Kiddush as soon as he returned from shul and would commence eating immediately. Someone asked why he began eating so quickly, without first singing zemiros. The Chofetz Chaim replied, "I have guests now, and they are foremost in my mind. The Malochim can wait; they are not hungry as the guests are." (Toldos HaChofetz Chaim—Kisvei Chofetz Chaim 3)

> Acts of kindness are also one of the things the fruit of which man enjoys in this world, while the stock remains for him for the world to come. (Peah 1)
> It is worthier to shelter the stranger than to welcome Hashem. (Shabbos 127)
> Yose ben Yochanan of Jerusalem said: Keep an ever open house and let the poor feel at home with you. (Avos 1)
> In the street a stranger did not have to lodge; my doors I kept open for the wayfarer. (Iyov 31)

SAVING LIVES

S'dome is always remembered as the prototype of wickedness, especially Bein Odom Lachaveiro (Between Man And His Fellow Man). They enjoyed and practiced making the lives of others miserable and unbearable. They seemed to mirror the exact opposite image of Avrohom in their zeal to do non-chesed and wickedness to their fellow man.

The Vilna Gaon was one who devoted practically every hour of the day to studying Torah. In order not to waste his time, he notified the community leaders that he was not to be asked to communal meetings unless a new law was scheduled to be discussed.

Once he was summoned to an emergency meeting. When he arrived, he listened in shocked amazement to the proposal that poor Jews living outside the city of Vilna should not be allowed to come into the city to collect charity without special authorization.

The Gaon arose and asked, "Is it for this proposal that you have taken me away from my Torah studies? I was under the impression that this meeting was called to discuss a new law."

"But that is exactly the case," explained the head of the community. "We are trying to draw up a new law against the outside poor."

"Do you call that a new law?" asked the Vilna Gaon scornfully. "Why, that law was introduced thousands of years ago in S'dome and Amorah!"

Though S'dome and Amorah were destroyed, Avrohom's nephew, Lot, was able to escape this fate. One of the reasons for this is that he was helped by the z'chus of his uncle Avrohom. This is made clear by the response to a question that is raised about the destruction of S'dome and Amorah. Three Malochim were sent to Avrohom, each one assigned a different task, for Malochim can perform only one task at a time. One Malach informed Avrohom that he would soon be blessed with a son; another informed Avrohom of the impend-

and the entire surrounding plain. The area was overturned and destroyed. Lot's wife disobeyed the Malochim's warning; she turned back and gazed at the destruction. She was punished and was turned into a "pillar of salt."

Lot feared living in Tzoar due to its promixity to the destroyed city of S'dome. He, thus, moved to a cave in a nearby mountainous area. It was there that the founders of the nations of Ammon and Moab were born to his daughters.

After this dreadful catastrophe, Avrohom traveled to the Negev (the south of Eretz Yisroel) to Gerar. He once again took the precaution he had earlier taken in Egypt, and declared that Sarah was his sister. She was taken into the palace of Avimelech, the king of Gerar, and Avimelech's entire household was smitten by Hashem with an illness. Hashem came to Avimelech in a dream and told him that he had committed a grave sin by taking Sarah into his palace. Hashem warned Avimelech that he would die if he did not return Sarah to her husband. The next

ing destruction of S'dome and Amorah; and a third Malach came to heal Avrohom and to save Lot. Yet, if a Malach is limited to one task, how could the third Malach have performed the twin tasks of healing Avrohom and saving Lot? The answer is that the fates of Avrohom and Lot were intertwined as really one task. For it was through Avrohom's z'chus that Lot was saved, and if Avrohom had not recovered from the Milah, his nephew would have also perished.

Our Chazal (Sages of Blessed Memory) explain that Lot was also saved for a Chesed he had done. When Lot had traveled with Avrohom to Egypt, he heard Avrohom tell Paroh that Sarah was his sister. Lot knew that Sarah was actually Avrohom's wife but remained quiet. For this seemingly small act of kindness he was saved from the horrible fate of S'dome. (Bereishis Rabbah 49:6)

One never knows which good deed might come in handy in a time of need. "Tzdakoh Tatzil Mimoves-Charity saves from death." (Mishley 10)

The Gemorrah relates that according to Divine Judgment, the daughter of Rabbi Akiva was to die on the day of her wedding. However, that morning, a beggar came to the house asking for aid. Rabbi Akiva's daughter was the only one home at the time and she generously gave him more than enough for his needs. Later, while she was at the wedding ceremony standing under the chuppah to be married, a hairpin started slipping from her hairpiece. Not having the time to fix it, she removed it from her hair and stuck it into the wall behind her. After the wedding, it was discovered that a poisonous snake had been located behind the wall, ready to strike at Rabbi Akiva's daughter, but that the placement of the hair-

pin had pierced and killed it. Had the daughter not been so charitable that day, her wedding might have ended tragically. Her act of Chesed had saved her life.

A similar tale is told of Shmuel, who was observing a workman carrying boxes. Suddenly, the top box fell down, and out of it fell a snake—a dead one. Had the snake been alive, the man would certainly have been bitten and would have died.

Shmuel asked the man what he had done to deserve being saved. The man did not reply. Later, Shmuel discovered that it was the practice in the town for the men to take turns distributing food. One day, the food supply was short and someone was left without any food. Instead of seeing this person go hungry, the workman had willingly given up his own portion of food. Now Shmuel knew what merit had saved him. (Shabbos 156b)

The Talmud relates that Binyomin the Virtuous was in charge of the public charity chest. One year, when a drought plagued the town, a woman came to him and begged for help. Although Binyomin felt sorry for the woman, there was no money left. The woman, in desperation, cried, "If you do not help me, a woman and her seven children will surely die!" Not wanting to bear the thought of this happening, Benyomin, poor as he was himself, gave her money from his own pocket.

Sometime later, Binyomin was seriously ill and the doctors had given up hope for his recovery. The ministering angels appeared before the Almighty and exclaimed, "Lord of the Universe! You have said that whoever saves one Jewish life is regarded as if he had saved the entire world. Should then Binyomin the Virtuous, who saved the lives

morning Avimelech returned Sarah to Avrohom together with many valuable gifts. Avrohom prayed for Avimelech, and Hashem cured the king and the members of his household of the illness they had contracted.

It was now a year later and Hashem remembered Sarah as He had promised. Sarah gave birth to a son whom Avrohom called Yitzchak. Avrohom circumcised Yitzchak when he was eight days old as Hashem had commanded him (see Parshas Lech Lecha). As her son grew up, Sarah felt that Yishmael might prove to be a negative influence on Yitzchak, and she urged Avrohom to send Hagar and Yishmael away. Avrohom was unhappy with the request, but Hashem appeared to Avrohom and told him that he should follow Sarah's advice. Hashem also promised him that Yishmael will also develop into a large nation. Avrohom took bread and water and gave it to Hagar and sent her and Yishmael away from his house. Hagar

of a woman and her seven children, die in the prime of his life?'' Immediately, the sentence of death was annulled, and, instead, 22 years were added to Binyomin's life. (Bava Basra 11a)

Once it occurred that many people were spared great hardships due to their performance of the mitzvah of Hachnosas Orchim.

This came about after Rabbi Mendele of Riminov issued an order that all those who lived in small villages must leave their dwellings and move into the larger cities. His reasoning was that because the small villages were isolated, they often lacked Rabbinical supervision, and were not functioning as true Jewish communities. They had no Minyonim, Mikvaos, or Yeshivos, and those living there were in danger of going astray from Yiddishkeit.

When this decision became known, it caused quite an uproar. Though its intent was clear, it would cause great hardships to all those who would now have to leave their homes and jobs to begin life anew. Yet, the word of the Rabbi was law. What could they do? The people of the small towns decided to turn to the Ropshitzer Tzaddik for advice, for they knew that Rav Mendele often listened to the Ropshitzer's suggestions.

The Ropshitzer was moved by the plight of the people. Though he understood Rav Mendele's reasoning, he also felt that the resulting burden of Rav Mendele's new law on the people would be more than they could bear. He knew that he must convince Rav Mendele to reverse his decision.

The Ropshitzer ordered his coachman to prepare his horse and wagon for a trip to Rimonov. This was during the winter and the trip in bitter cold weather was a hard one. When the Ropshitzer arrived in Rimonov, he went straight to the house of

Rav Mendele. It was obvious to everyone that the trip had left the Ropshitzer ill and exhausted. Rav Mendele made provisions for the Ropshitzer to be put to bed, and then came in to inquire how his friend was feeling.

"It was a most difficult journey," the Ropshitzer told him. "Previously, when I made this trip, I used to stop at a few homes along the way. There the people in the small villages were most hospitable and they provided for my every need. That way, I was able to escape the full fury of the winter weather. Now, however, as all the villagers are preparing to leave their homes, there is no place left for me to stop on the way. As a result, the trip has become a real Sakonos Nefoshos, a threat to one's health."

"Is that so?" said Rav Mendele in amazement. "What you are saying is that if my order is followed, no one will be left to greet and care for the visitors during their long journey. That means that from now on all travelers on this route are in danger of losing their lives!" Rav Mendele thought for a moment, and then exclaimed. "I will not allow it! I did not realize the side effects of my decision. I will rescind my decision immediately!"

And so, because the villagers had shown kindness to visitors in the past, the kindness was now returned to them and they were allowed to remain in their homes.

What shall a man do to deserve children? Rabbi Eliezer advised: "Let him distribute money among the poor. Rabbi Nechemia's disciples asked him: "What have you done to prolong your life?" He answered: "I have been generous with my money." (Megillah 28)

If you are a generous giver, you will

and her son wandered about in the wilderness for days. When it appeared that they might die from thirst, a Maloch of Hashem appeared and miraculously showed her water and assured Hagar of her son's future. Yishmael grew up to be a bowman, and lived in the wilderness of Paran where he married an Egyptian woman.

Avrohom was a true servant of Hashem. In the course of Avrohom's lifetime, Hashem had placed him through nine very difficult tests to ascertain his loyalty. Avrohom had always passed these tests with flying colors; his sincere loyalty and devotion to Hashem had always carried him across any pitfalls in the way. Yet, the last test, the tenth one, was the most difficult of all. Hashem commanded Avrohom to take his only son, the one he loved, the son of his old age, Yitzchak, and to offer him as a sacrifice on one of the mountains in Moreeyah.

Avrohom did not hesitate for a moment. He arose early the next morning, made the necessary preparations, took his son Yitzchak and journeyed to the place which would be revealed to him by Hashem. On the third day he arrived at the appointed mountain. Avrohom built the Mizbeach (Altar), arranged the wood and bound Yitzchak's hands and feet together. He placed Yitzchak on the Mizbeach upon the wood. Avrohom lifted his hand and took the knife, ready to slaughter his son. All

never come to harm. (Derech Eretz Zutta 2,4)

THE AKEIDAH

The Akeidah represented the final and most difficult of the ten tests designed by Hashem to determine Avrohom's worthiness of being the founder of the Chosen People.

The difficulty included in this task was that Hashem was asking Avrohom not to give up property or money, but rather to sacrifice a dream. For if Avrohom were to kill Yitzchak, his visions of serving Hashem as the ancestor of the Children of G-d would vanish into thin air. After all, he had been promised a son, had had to wait until he was 100 years old and almost past hope to receive one. Now he was being asked not only to lose this son, but to kill him with his own two hands! This act was contrary to the very nature of all the Chesed Avrohom had always performed. It was almost like the acts that Avrohom had fought against all his life for he had constantly disputed those around him who had worshipped their gods by sacrificing their sons to them. And now Avrohom was being asked to perform this very same murderous task by his own G-d!

Yet, Avrohom did not dispute the command for a moment. He immediately set out to comply with Hashem's request. To show his loyalty, he saddled his donkey himself rather than ordering his servant to do so, in order to save time. This way he could perform the command as quickly as possible.

The journey to the designated mountain

was not an easy one. The way was riddled with obstacles set by Satan to prevent Avrohom's compliance with Hashem's order. At first, Satan appeared to Avrohom in the guise of an old man and asked, "Where are you going?" When Avrohom replied that he was going to pray to G-d, the Satan demanded, "Then why are you carrying all those knives and pieces of wood?"

"We may stay a day or two," Avrohom told him, "and with these utensils we will be able to prepare our own food."

The Satan then said, "Don't try to fool me. You are the fool. It took you one hundred years to have a son, and now you want to sacrifice him! This you were not commanded to do by Hashem, for He would surely never give such a command. It must be your imagination. Don't do it."

But Avrohom realized that this was in reality an obstacle placed in his way to prevent his carrying out Hashem's wishes, so he moved on.

However, the Satan persisted. This time he caused a large flowing river to appear at a spot which Avrohom and his retinue had to pass over. When Avrohom came to the river, he remembered that he had never seen a body of water at this spot before, and that this too must be the work of the Satan. He took Yitzchak with him, and the two began to cross the river. They finally came to a point where the water had reached their backs, and if they had gone any further they would certainly have drowned. At this moment, Avrohom lifted his eyes towards heaven and

of a sudden, a Maloch's heavenly voice was heard calling, "Avrohom, Avrohom!" The Maloch instructed Avrohom not to touch Yitzchak nor to cause him any harm. It was now evident that Avrohom was truly G-d fearing and there was no need for the actual sacrifice of Yitzchak. Avrohom found a ram caught by his horns in the trees and sacrificed the ram instead of Yitzchak. Hashem promised Avrohom that in the Z'chus (Merit) of this great deed he had performed, Hashem will bless him. These children will be many and his descendants will inherit their enemies' cities

prayed that he be allowed to continue and fulfill Hashem's request. Immediately, the water disappeared and they traveled on. (Bereishis Rabbah 56:4)

Finally, they reached Mount Moriah. Avrohom took Yitzchak (who was already thirty-seven years old and who complied with all this most willingly) and bound him to the altar he had built. He took the knife and was about to bring it down on Yitzchak when he heard a Heavenly voice call out, "Stop, Avrohom! I do not want you to kill your son. I wanted to see if you were willing to follow My words wholeheartedly, and you have certainly done so. I am now certain of your belief and trust. Return home, and from your son Yitzchak will emerge a nation —My nation."

R. Abbahu said: The reason why we blow a Shofar on Rosh Hashanah is because Hashem said: "Sound me a Shofar so that I may remember on your behalf the sacrifice of Yitzchak, the son of Avrohom, and I shall account it to you as if you had offered yourselves to Me." (Rosh Hashanah 16)

S arah died in Hebron at the age of one hundred twenty-seven. Avrohom, upon hearing the sad news, came quickly from Be'er Sheva to mourn and eulogize her. Avrohom bought the nearby field and cave of Machpelah from Ephron the Hittite as a permanent burial place for Sarah. Avrohom then buried Sarah in this cave of Machpelah.

Avrohom, now at an advanced age, grew anxious to marry off his son Yitzchak. He called his loyal servant Eliezer and entrusted him with the crucial task of finding the proper mate for Yitzchak. Avrohom insisted

פרשת
חיי שרה
*Parshas
Chayei
Sarah*

SARAH'S GREATNESS

The Torah lists Sarah's age at her death as being "One hundred years, and twenty years, and seven years" (Bereishis 23:1). Why was it necessary for the Torah to divide the years of her life into three separate segments? Our Sages reply that in this fashion the Torah indicated to us the following about Sarah: When she was one hundred, she was as lacking in sins as she was at the age of 20; and when she was twenty, she had the same beauty as she did at the age of seven. This immediately raises the question of how is it possible that a girl aged seven can be more beautiful than one aged twenty? However, the Torah is telling us that just as Sarah did not use her innocent beauty at age seven for anything immoral, so, too, she did not use her more mature beauty at age twen-

ty for anything immoral. (Bereishis 23:1, Rashi). And Avrohom came 'Lispod L'Sarah V'Livkosah (Bereishis 23:2) "to eulogize Sarah and to weep over her." In regard to the writing of the word V'Livkosah in the Torah we find something very interesting. The letter "kaf" is smaller in size than all the other normal letters of the Torah! Why this variation in graphics?

When Sarah died, Avrohom did not mourn excessively. He realized that her death, sorrowful as it was, was not a tragedy for Sarah had lived a full and rewarding life. She had accomplished much during her stay on earth and her good deeds were innumerable. She had aided Avrohom with his devotion to Chesed by opening her house to as many guests as possible and by taking care of all their needs. Because of her out-

that Eliezer swear that he will not take a mate for Yitzchak from the daughters of the Canaanites. Rather, he should return to Avrohom's native land and from there bring back a suitable wife for Yitzchak.

Eliezer took ten camels laden with his master's best possessions and embarked upon his journey to Avrohom's kindred in Aram Naharayim. He arrived towards evening and stopped at the well outside the city. He prayed to Hashem that he meet the proper girl for Yitzchak. He went on in his prayer to ask Hashem to make him successful in the following manner. He will ask a girl at the well for a drink of water. The girl who will reply, "Drink and I will draw water for your camels as well" is the girl chosen by Hashem for Yitzchak.

Before Eliezer finished his prayer, Rivka arrived at the well and filled her pitcher. Eliezer ran toward her and asked for a sip of water from her pitcher. Rivka gave Eliezer water to drink, then quickly drew water for all Eliezer's camels. Upon seeing

standing righteousness, Hashem bestowed upon her special personal qualities. In fact, we are told that in terms of prophecy she was even greater than her husband Avrohom.

Therefore, the small "kaf." Avrohom definitely mourned and wept over Sarah but not in an excessive fashion. The loss was great but the comforting realization of her fulfilled life made it much easier to accept.

Those who, like Sarah, spend their lives assisting others benefit in both this world and the World to Come. Their memories are cherished fondly and their good deeds and accomplishments are cherished and commemorated forever. On the other hand, those who become negatively influenced during their stay on this earth are both vilified by later generations and suffer in the World to Come.

In a case in point, Reb Chaim Elazar met an assimilated Jew by the name of Shemer. During their conversation, Reb Chaim Elazar learned that Shemer, who considered himself 'enlightened,' had written several books. "In fact," said Shemer, "I have just published a new one named 'Apostate for Spite.'" "Then I certainly do not envy you," said Reb Chaim Elazar. When the irreligious Jew looked at him questioningly, Reb Chaim Elazar explained: "You see, authors are usually named after their works. I, for example, am known as the 'Nefesh Chaya,' for that is a sefer I have written. That name will therefore probably appear on my tombstone. But think of what will be written on your tombstone, "Here Lies 'Apostate for Spite!'" Not very inspiring, is it? Yet, it is certainly true that what we accomplish during our lifetime will be accredited to us forever."

No monuments are to be raised to the pious, their deeds are their monuments. (Yerushalmi Shekalim 2)
The memory of the righteous is blessed. (Mishley 10)
The righteous are greater in death than in life. (Chullin 7)

SARAH'S BURIAL

Immediately after Sarah's death, Avrohom went to find a proper burial place for her to pay her departed soul full respect. Man was created from the dust of the earth and he must be returned to that dust when he dies.

Once when Rabbi Yisroel Slanter was in the middle of Tefilas Shachris, he heard a loud argument between the heads of two Chevra Kadishas (Burial Societies). A poor woman had died and each society claimed that it was the other's obligation to bury her.

In the middle of his prayers, Rav Yisroel removed his Talis and Tefilin, gathered together a few of his 'talmidim' and told them to join him in the burial of the woman. Since neither society wanted to perform the burial, it was a "Mais Mitzvah" (when no one else is available to perform the burial) and everyone must drop whatever he is doing to do this final 'Chesed' with the deceased.

There was a time after the destruction of the Second Temple that Jews who were killed by the Romans were, on orders of the authorities, made to lie without burial. However, a great miracle occurred. The dead bodies neither rotted nor emitted a foul odor, as usually occurs. Because of this miracle, we recite the Berochoh of "HaTov V'HaMetiv" in the Birchas HaMozon. (Berachas 48a)

To bury Sarah, Avrohom purchased a

this, Eliezer, hoping silently that his prayers had been answered, presented Rivka with a gold nose ring and two gold bracelets. Eliezer was overjoyed to discover that Rivka was actually the granddaughter of Nochor, brother of Avrohom. He bowed and blessed Hashem for having bestowed this great kindness upon his master Avrohom.

Rivka took Eliezer to her home and he told her family the entire story of his journey. They agreed to the match and to allow Rivka to go to the land of Canaan to marry Yitzchak. Eliezer showered Rivka with more gifts and gave presents to her family. Eliezer brought Rivka back to Canaan, where she met and married Yitzchak.

Avrohom took another wife, Keturah, and had additional children with her. He gave them beautiful gifts as a legacy, but he left everything he owned to his favorite

cave called the Machpelah for the large sum of four hundred shekels weight of pure silver. The Machpelah was a unique place because Odom and Chava had been buried there; later Avrohom, Yitzchak and Rivka, and Yaakov and Leah joined Sarah in this eternal resting place. Today, the M'oras HaMachpelah in Chevron remains a most holy site and Jews flock to it to offer prayers which we hope will, through the merits of our Forefathers, be answered speedily.

The righteous are greater at death than in life. (Chullin 7)

The road to a grave should have no limits, so that countless people can come to honor the dead. (Bava Basra 100)

RIVKAH'S CHESED

After Sarah's death, Avrohom wanted to ensure the continuation of his lineage by seeing that Yitzchak was properly married. Avrohom told his servant Eliezer to find a bride for Yitzchak exclusively from the members of his own family, not from the Canaanites. Why this distinction? Weren't the members of Avrohom's family in Aram Naharayim just as devoted idol-worshippers as were the Canaanites?

Avrohom in his deep wisdom, understood that there are certain characteristics which are inherited by children from their parents. Mercy and compassion towards others can be taught only to a certain degree; it must be a part of the person, inherited from his parents. On the other hand, idol worshipping is dependent upon a person's intellect, his mind. An individual can select or reject idol worshipping. (Ran)

Avrohom was searching for someone to become one of the future mothers of B'nei Yisroel. The nation for whom the identifying symbols are, "merciful, bashful and

doers of Chesed," surely needed a mother exemplifying all these traits. Avrohom knew that in Canaan these traits were not to be found. In his home town, in his family, he knew these traits were to be found and to be inherited. True, they were idol worshippers, but that is something a person such as Rivka could reject. But her inherited traits of goodness and kindness would serve as a good basis for her role as one of the founding mothers of the nation of Israel.

Eliezer asked Hashem to aid him in his search for the proper bride. When Eliezer and his attendants came to the well, they asked Rivka for a drink of water. Not only did she offer to provide both him and his camels with water, but she made sure that his needs would be taken care of first, so that he would not have to drink with the animals. In addition, she made sure to draw enough water so that the animals would be completely satisfied. Can you imagine how much water must have been needed to satisfy the thirst of all those camels? Yet, Rivka provided all this, for she was a genuine person of Chesed.

It was this quality that Avrohom was searching for in a daughter-in-law. This was one of the qualities that made Rivka a most worthy member of Klal Yisroel's founding family.

The quality of Chesed and concern for others is something we should also search for in our own families. A wealthy Jew once visited the Leipniker Rav, and proposed a match between his son and the Rav's daughter. The rich man then noticed that the Rav looked upset. "A child in this town is dangerously ill, and I am worried about him," explained the Rav.

"But why are you so worried about a strange child?" asked the visitor.

son, Yitzchak. Avrohom died at the age of one hundred seventy-five, and was buried by his sons Yitzchak and Yishmael in the cave he had bought, the cave of Machpelah.

Upon hearing this, the Rav decided that his daughter should not marry into this man's family. Anyone coming from a family that shows so little concern for others could not be a desirable match for his family.

"Like father, like son" (Eruvin 70)
"A man always looks out for the good of his son."(Bava Basra 142)
"A woman is beautiful when she is virtuous." (Shabbos 25)

פרשת תולדות

Parshas Toldos

For the first twenty years of their marriage, Yitzchak and Rivka were childless. They prayed to Hashem. Hashem heard their prayers and they were blessed with twin sons. Esav, the elder, was a man of the field, a hunter; Yaakov, the younger, was a scholar who sat and studied Torah. Each parent had a favorite son. Yitzchak showered his affections upon Esav, while Rivka preferred Yaakov.

Esav came home one day from the field and was very tired. He noticed that Yaakov was cooking some red lentils. Our Sages explain that Yaakov was cooking len-

THE BIRTH OF YAAKOV AND ESAV

When, after twenty years of childlessness, Yitzchak and Rivka learned that Hashem had answered their prayers and that they were to be parents, they were overjoyed. Yet, Rivka's happiness was soon diminished. For while pregnant, she was experiencing some strange sensations. Every time Rivka would pass a place of learning or prayer, she would feel her unborn baby kicking. Yet, the same thing would happen every time she would pass by a temple of idol worship. Rivka did not understand these seemingly contradictory signals, and so she sought advice from Shem and Eiver, the Torah leaders of her generation. She was told that she would give birth to twins and that one twin would follow the ways of Torah, while the other would be attracted to idol worship. (Bereishis Rabbah 63:6)

In due time, the twins were born. The elder was named Esav, for when born he was covered with red hair. The younger was called Yaakov, for when born he was holding on to the heel ("eikev") of Esav, as if he was striving to be the first-born.

As had been predicted, the brothers began gravitating to different lifestyles. Esav became a hunter, enjoying the chase and the kill; Yaakov became a scholar, prizing peacefulness. Yaakov realized the importance of the birthright while Esav considered

it a worthless distinction.

Esav returned from a long session of hunting one day, clamoring for food. He saw Yaakov preparing some lentil soup and agreed to exchange his birthright for the soup. After all, what good was the birthright when he could trade it for some immediate pleasure? However, Yaakov had enough foresight to realize that as the B'chor, the first born, he would have the opportunity to inherit the right to continue Avrohom's heritage. This would bring him all the closer to Hashem, a prospect that meant little to Esav. To Esav, his lineage wasn't worth as much as a bowl of soup!

Righteous—one is so of himself; wicked —one becomes so through others. (Yoma 35)

A man gets the soul he deserves—if he raises it, it will be exalted; if he lowers it, it will become low and disintegrate. (Pninei Ha'Melitzot)

People are like grass on a field: some sprout and some rot. (Eruvin 54)

KIBBUD AV V'AIM

Though Rivka recognized Yaakov's superiority to Esav, Yitzchak lacked this insight. He was misled by Esav's practice of Kibbud Av, honoring his father, and as a result he did not appreciate Esav's true character. He thought that Esav was just as

tils for his father, Yitzchak, because it was the day of Avrohom's funeral. Said Esav to Yaakov, "Give me quickly some of that red stuff to eat for I am very tired."

Yaakov answered, "Sell me, in turn, your privileges as first-born." Yaakov knew that until Hashem chose Aharon and his descendants to serve as the priestly family, it was the first-born who would serve as priests to Hashem. Esav was not worthy of this sanctified work.

"Of what use are the rights of the first-born to me?" reasoned Esav.

"Swear to me," said the wary Yaakov. And so it was. Yaakov gave Esav some bread and lentils in return for the rights of the first-born for which he had shown very little regard.

To escape the grip of a famine, Yitzchak moved temporarily to Gerar. Hashem appeared to Yitzchak and promised to uphold the promise He had made to his father, Avrohom. Hashem promised Yitzchak to make his children as numerous as the stars of heaven and that Yitzchak's descendants would inherit the land of Canaan.

Taking the same precautions that his father, Avrohom, had taken (see parshas Lech Lecha), Yitzchok told the people of Gerar that his wife, Rivka, was his sister. Avimelech, king of Gerar, discovered the truth and ordered that anyone who would harm Yitzchak or his wife would be put to death. With Hashem's help, Yitzchak soon became very prosperous. This aroused the envy of the local populace, and Avimelech asked Yitzchak to leave the area. While staying in the valley of Gerar, Yitzchak dug his father's old water wells. Yitzchak eventually moved to Be'er Sheva. Before long, he was visited by Avimelech who now recognized that Yitzchak was a holy person, favored by Hashem, and they agreed to a peace treaty. Meanwhile, Esav brought grief to his parents by marrying two Hittite women.

Yitzchak had grown old and blind and felt that the time had come to bless his eldest son. He, therefore, requested that Esav go to the field to hunt and prepare the game he captured as a tasty dish, so that Yitzchak could partake of it and then bless him. Rivka, overhearing the conversation, dressed Yaakov in Esav's clothing, covered his hands and neck with goat-skin to make them feel as hairy as Esav's, and sent him to Yitzchak bearing a tasty dish of young goat's meat and bread which she

scrupulous in observing all mitzvos as he was in showing respect to his parents. This shows the power of Kibbud Av, for it could make Yitzchok believe that even one as degenerate as Esav was an honorable person.

If Esav, for all his wickedness, still was careful to honor his parents, then how can we claim to be good Jews if we fail to do the same? **To appreciate the lengths** that we should go to in order to practice Kibbud Av V'Aim, we should remember the story of Damah, a gentile boy. Damah's father had a precious diamond which he kept under his pillow for its protection. One day, while his father was asleep, some businessmen came to Damah's house and asked to buy the diamond. Damah replied that he could not obtain the diamond for to do so he would have to wake his father and he did not want to do this. The men offered greater and greater sums of money, but Damah still refused to

bother his father. Finally, in desperation, the men left and Damah lost his chance to make a fortune. Yet, for his devotion to his father, Damah received a just reward. Within his herd was born a Poroh Adumah, a totally red cow, needed by Jews for purity purposes, which he was able to sell at a very high price.

Damah also had a mother who had emotional problems, and who yelled and spit at him for no apparent reason. Though he was greatly embarrassed by her actions, he did not speak to her harshly. She was, after all, his mother, and for all the hardships she caused him, he treated her royally. (Kiddushin 31a)

If Esav and Damah could show such concern for their parents, so certainly should we.

Many stories are related of how our Sages honored their parents.

One day Rabbi Avuhu asked his son,

made. Yaakov's voice aroused Yitzchak's suspicions, but they were allayed when he felt Yaakov's hairy hands which Yitzchak was sure belonged to Esav.

Yitzchak, now ready to bestow upon his son the blessings, called him forward. Yaakov came forward and kissed his father. Yitzchak blessed Yaakov saying, "May Hashem give you from the dew of the sky and the fat of the land, and plenty of grain and wine. Nations shall serve you and kingdoms shall bow down to you. Those who curse you shall be cursed and those who bless you shall be blessed."

No sooner had Yaakov left, did Esav return and the truth was discovered. However, Yitzchak did not revoke his blessing to Yaakov. Instead, he agreed to bless Esav as well and foretold that Esav's future descendants would live by the sword and would serve Yaakov's descendants so long as the latter behaved properly. However, when the descendants of Yaakov stray from the path of the Torah, Esav's descendants will be free of this servitude.

Esav was quite upset at Yaakov's ruse and plotted to kill his brother as soon as their father died. To prevent this, Rivka instructed Yaakov to leave home and stay with her brother, Lovan, in Charan. Yitzchak gave him similar counsel and expressed the wish that Yaakov choose a wife from among his uncle's family. Yitzchak then blessed Yaakov again that the blessings of Avrohom be fulfilled through him and his descendants, to inherit the land of Canaan. After Yaakov had

Rabbi Avimi, for some water to drink. Rabbi Avimi brought the water, but his father had fallen asleep. He stood next to his father with the water in his hand the entire time, until he awoke. (Kidushin 31b)

A man once came to Rabbi Chayim Soloveitchik of Brisk with the following question: His father had become ill in a distant city and he felt obligated to take a trip to visit him. However, since the law of "Kibud Av V'Aim" does not require a person to spend his own money to honor his father, and the train trip would cost him money, was he still obligated to go?

Rav Chaim's sharp reply was, "True, you aren't obligated to spend your own money on a train. Walk!"

When Rabbi Leib of Kelm was a young man he once came home very late at night from the Bais Hamedrash. His parents were already sleeping and he didn't have a key with him. In order not to awaken them, he remained in the street all night despite the extreme cold.

One child gives his father roast pheasants to eat but with such harshness that he will be punished therefore, while another child puts his father to work turning a mill-wheel but with such kindness that he will be blessed therefore. (Kiddushin 31) Rabbi Shimeon ben Gamliel said that although he honored his father, he did not even honor him to the extent of

even one hundreth part of how Esav honored his father. (Bereishis Rabbah 65)

THE BLESSINGS OF YAAKOV AND ESAV

Yitchak granted Yaakov the blessing that all nations would come to serve the people who would emerge from his descendants. However, Yitzchak indicated that this blessing would come true only if the Bnei Yisroel adhered to the Torah of Hashem. Once the Jews abandoned the ways of the Torah their enemies would gain superiority over them.

History has borne out this prediction. While the Jews acted properly, they enjoyed the graces of Hashem and were granted the presence of His Beis Hamikdosh. However, when they refused to heed His warnings to repent, they suffered the loss of the Holy Temple and were reduced to living under gentile oppression in exile. Later, Jews tried to assimilate and become like the citizens of foreign countries such as Greece, Rome, Russia, and Germany. What they forgot was that the gentiles, the sons of Esav, have always been their enemies. As a result, all attempts of the Jews to assimilate have been met by oppression, pogroms, and wars. It was only when Jews remembered that they are Jews and tried to comply with the laws of the Torah, that they emerged supreme, self-confident, and happy.

Hashem says: You have treated Me

left Be'er Sheva, Esav tried to please his parents by marrying a daughter of Yishmael.

uniquely by saying Shema, so I shall do the same by saying: "Who is like Your people Israel a unique nation on earth?" (Berachos 6)

In his journey from Be'er Sheva to Choran, Yaakov reached the mountain of Moriah and slept there overnight. In a dreamlike vision, he saw angels ascending and descending a ladder standing on the earth with its top reaching the heavens. Hashem then appeared to Yaakov and promised him that the land he was now resting on would be given to him and his descendants, and that he would return home under Hashem's protection. Upon awaking, Yaakov anointed and consecrated the stone he had placed under his head as an altar to Hashem. He vowed that when he

פרשת ויצא
Parshas Vayeitzei

YAAKOV'S DREAM

On his way to Lovan, Yaakov left Be'er Sheva and stopped to pray at Mount Moriah. The sun suddenly set and Yaakov decided to spend the night there. He took some stones and arranged them around his body like a fence to protect himself against wild animals. The stones began to quarrel, each demanding the right to have the righteous Yaakov rest his head on it. To settle the quarrel, Hashem joined the stones together and they became one large stone upon which Yaakov fell asleep.

During this sleep, Yaakov saw the vision of a ladder thousands of miles long. The ladder rested on the ground but it extended up to the heavens. Three angels resembling humans began to ascend the ladder. They represented steps, and then descended. The one representing Modai rose fifty-two steps, and then came down. The one representing Greece climbed one hundred eighty steps, and then climbed down. Finally, the one representing Edom ascended countless steps, and seemed to keep climbing higher and higher. "Does this one not descend?" Yaakov asked with fear.

"Fear not," Hashem replied. "Though this nation appears to be reaching great heights, it too will descend." (Bereishis Rabbah 68)

In this manner, Yaakov forsaw the rise and fall of nations and their cultures. Why did this dream come to Yaakov at this particular time, when he was in flight from his brother and on his way to choose a wife?

Yaakov, later named Yisroel, is the final founder of the Bnei Yisroel, the Jewish people. He represents the Jews in exile and wandering; like him, the Jews have known the uncertain passage from one nation to another. And, like Yaakov during his dream, they have observed the rise of various heathen nations, only to see their eventual fall. Sometimes, though, Jews wonder if the reign of a particular nation will ever come to an end; certain nations seem to be too powerful to ever decline. They ask, as Yaakov did, "Does this one not descend?" However, Hashem's reply still holds true. All nations will eventually descend and only the Jewish nation will reign supreme in the end.

Do not worry for the morrow, for you know not what the morrow may bring. (Ben Sira)

Hashem can cause even the mightiest person's immediate downfall, if He so chooses. The evil General Titus had just destroyed the Bais Hamikdosh. He took all the vessels of the Bais Hamikdosh, wrapped them in the Paroches (the curtain-partition separating the holiest of holies in the Bais Hamikdosh), and was on his way home to show off his might and glory. On the boat going home, large waves erupted and the boat began to sway dangerously. Recognizing Hashem's influence, he still remained defiant. "You see, the Jews' G-d can attack me only when I am on the water. If he is really so mighty let him come on the dry land and fight me!"

A heavenly voice cried out, "Wicked person the descendant of Esav the wicked! I

returned safely to his father's home, he would offer to Hashem one-tenth of all the possessions Hashem would give him. He would return to worship and pray to Hashem at the altar he had just consecrated.

Yaakov arrived at a well of water in a field in the outskirts of Choran. He noticed that three flocks of sheep and their shepherds had gathered around the well and were just sitting idly. Yaakov approached them and asked, "From where are you?" "We are from Choran," was the reply.

"Do you know Lovan the son of Nochor?" continued Yaakov.

"We know him. And there is Rochel, his daughter, coming with the sheep," pointed out the shepherds.

"The day is yet long, it is not the time of gathering the sheep, why don't you give the sheep their water and take them out to pasture?" wondered Yaakov.

"We cannot, until all the flocks gather and all the shepherds together roll the stone off the well and then we can give the sheep their water," explained the shepherds.

As they were conversing, Rochel drew nearer with her father's sheep. When Yaakov saw this he went over to the well and rolled the heavy stone off the well

have a small insect in my world. Go to the dry land and fight with her!"

The boat reached the shore. However, as Titus stepped on to the land, a tiny insect entered Titus' head through his nose. Titus tried to shake the insect away, but the insect did not emerge. Soon thereafter, Titus began to experience painful headaches. All the royal Roman doctors tried to treat him but the headaches grew worse and more intense. Finally, they drove him almost literally out of his mind and he died a tortured death. When the Roman doctors conducted an autopsy, they found the little insect had grown enormous and had penetrated his brain and had been devouring his brain matter. Thus, even the self-proclaimed mightiest of men can be quickly humbled by the All-Powerful Hashem. (Gittin 56b)

> Hashem steers the sinner to go to meet his own punishment. (Meleches Machsheves)
> The evil will slay the evil-doer. (Tehillim 34)
> The wicked do not repent even at the threshold of Gehenam. (Eruvin 19)

YAAKOV AND LOVAN: BEING HONEST AND LEARNING GOOD EVEN FROM THE WICKED

Our forefather Yaakov made a special point of practicing honesty throughout his life, even in the potentially corrupting environment of Lovan's home. When taking care of Lovan's sheep, he cared for each and every one of them and made absolutely sure that no harm came to any of them, though they were not his own possessions. He even stayed up during the cold nights to protect the sheep, for he had promised Lovan he would care for the sheep and he wanted to fulfill that guarantee. Naturally he did not take any of the sheep for himself without permission, though Lovan would probably not have noticed the loss of a few sheep. Yaakov was a firm believer in the statement, "Truth is the tree of life whose fruits you shall eat all your days."

Our Rabbonim learned from and copied Yaakov's admirable traits. They recognized that one must be honest at all times. For even if one feels that no one is noticing his deception, Hashem is always watching.

Rav Saffra owned a store. One day, while he was reciting Krias Shema, a man entered the store and asked to buy a certain item. Not noticing that Rav Saffra was reciting Krias Shema, he offered a certain price for the book. However, Rav Saffra did not reply as he was in the midst of Krias Shema. The man thought that Rav Saffra's silence meant that his offer was too low, so he raised his offer. Again Rav Saffra was silent, so again he raised the amount of his offer. Finally, Rav Saffra finished the prayer and turned to the man. Though he could easily have gotten the higher price, he said, "Sir, I will accept your original offer. For originally I had decided in my mind to sell it to you for that price. The only reason I did not respond to it earlier was that I was praying, and if I accepted more money than you were originally willing to offer, I would be dishonest." (Makos 24a)

singlehandedly, and gave Lovan's sheep water to drink.

He then acquainted Rochel with their familial relationship and she quickly ran to inform her father of the arrival of their visitor. Lovan welcomed Yaakov who agreed to work as Lovan's shepherd for seven years in order to marry Rochel, whom he had come to love. Lovan consented, but after the seven years had elapsed, he tricked Yaakov by substituting his elder daughter Leah in place of Rochel under the wedding canopy. His excuse for this deceitful breach of promise was that Leah was older and therefore should be married first. Yaakov had no choice but to accept the situation. He soon after married Rochel as well, on the condition that he would work another seven years for Lovan.

Hashem saw that Leah was not as well liked as Rochel, and He consequently caused Leah to have children while Rochel remained barren. Leah gave birth to Yaakov's first four sons: Reuven, Shimon, Levi and Yehudah. Rochel saw that she was not having children, so she followed Yaakov's grandmother Sarah's example and offered her handmaiden, Bilhoh, to Yaakov as a wife. Bilhoh bore Yaakov his next two sons, Dan and Naftali.

Rabbi Pinchas ben Yair lived in a city in the south of Eretz Yisroel. Two poor men who came to seek a livelihood in that region stopped at his house and left a small amount of barley seeds in his care. They left, and failed to reclaim the seeds. In their absence, Rabbi Pinchas planted, sowed and reaped the barley year after year and stored all the proceeds in the barn.

Seven years later, the two men happened to pass by Rabbi Pinchas's home and they suddenly remembered the seeds. "Please return the seeds to us, if you still happen to have them," they told Rabbi Pinchas.

Instead of giving them a few seeds, though, Rabbi Pinchas led them to the barn and opened the doors. Noting their surprise, he told them, "It is all yours. Now go and bring donkeys and camels and take away your treasure." (Bava Mezia 28b)

Rabbi Pinchas ben Yair could easily have given the men a few seeds and kept the barley all for himself. However, Rabbi Pinchas wanted to be absolutely honest in his dealings

In a bathhouse, the Chofetz Chaim once saw a person using an article that belonged to someone else. The Chofetz Chaim went over to him and whispered, "A person who washes himself with something that does not belong to him ends up dirtier than when he started."

The Chofetz Chaim once arrived a few minutes late at the train station. He had wanted to send some books on the train that was about to depart but it was past the time when parcels could be processed for that train. The clerk in charge greatly respected the Chofetz Chaim, and smilingly told him that he would place the parcels in the freight train for free. The Chofetz Chaim, however, refused.

"Only the owner of the train company has a right to forego payment," he said. "Since a clerk is merely an employee, it would be considered robbing not to pay the proper amount."

It sometimes seems such a simple, inoffensive matter to gain a few dollars or a few points by telling a little white lie, or by doing a little unnoticeable cheating. What could be wrong with this? But it *is* wrong, and overcoming the desire to do so is one of the greatest tests we face. Yaakov Ovinu's acts are proof that the test can be passed.

Truth is a heavy burden, therefore its bearers are so few. (Mishley 3)
Truth proves itself. (Adnei Kesef 1)
Accept the truth from whomever it is. (Rambam, Shemona Perekim 4)

Another admirable trait exhibited by Yaakov was his ability to learn how to improve himself from even the most despicable of persons. Yaakov stayed in Lovan's home for 20 years. Not only didn't he adopt this idol worshipper's ways, but he learned how to enhance his own Avodas Hashem. For he noticed that whenever Lovan was practicing deceit, Lovan did so with great enthusiasm. "If only I could show the same enthusiasm when serving Hashem!" thought Yaakov, and so he began worshipping Hashem with added zeal.

Rabbi Levi Yitzchok of Berditchev was another who derived a positive lesson from the wickedness of someone else. Rabbi Levi

Leah saw that she had stopped giving birth and she also gave her handmaiden Zilpoh to Yaakov as a wife. Zilpoh bore to Yaakov his next two sons, Gad and Usher. Leah herself then gave birth to two sons, Yissocher and Zevulun. She also gave birth to a daughter named Dinah. Then Hashem remembered Rochel and listened to her prayers and she gave birth to a son whom she called Yoseph.

With Hashem's help, Yaakov became very wealthy. However, he noticed the jealousy of Lovan's sons and the cool attitude of Lovan himself, and he decided it was time for him to leave. Consequently, he took his wives, children, and flocks with him while Lovan was away, and began the journey homewards. Before they left, Rochel, without Yaakov's knowledge, stole her father's idols. She reasoned that in this manner she would be able to prevent her father from worshipping them. Three days later, Lovan was told of Yaakov's departure, and Lovan pursued him, overtaking him at the mountains of Gilad. Hashem appeared to Lovan at night in a

Yitzchok was on a mission to raise funds for *pidyon Shivuyim,* to free Jewish prisoners. After much pounding on doors, Rabbi Levi Yitzchok found that he was not collecting much. Frustration set in, and he wondered, "Perhaps I am wasting my time trying to collect money when I could be back home learning Torah instead."

Rabbi Levi Yitzchok was just then asked to visit a certain prisoner who had been caught stealing and had been placed in jail. He agreed. When he arrived in the prison he told the culprit, "Look what troubles you have caused yourself, my son, by stealing. I hope this will be a lesson to you, so that when you are released from jail you will not return to your evil ways. For, you see, not only didn't you get to keep the money you stole, but you were also placed in jail."

"That's all right," said the robber. "If I didn't succeed in the crime this time, I will succeed next time."

When Rabbi Levi Yitzchok heard this, he said to himself, "If, after all his suffering, this thief doesn't become discouraged and is willing to try to steal again, then what right do I have to become discouraged in raising money? Forget about returning home! If I did not succeed in raising funds today, then I will succeed tomorrow."

The same lesson for *Zerizus,* enthusiasm, can be learned from the lowly ant. The ant is small, but it is far from lazy. It goes about gathering one piece of food after another for its tribe, though it eats only a small portion of that food. If we could be only half as zealous in our performance of Mitzvos as the ant is in his work, we would be in a much better position. (Mishley 6)

Rav Yisroel Salanter was once watching a tightrope walker very carefully. When he was asked why he was so immersed in observing the man walk across a wire, he replied, "Imagine the concentration that goes into every step the tightrope walker takes. His life hangs on every move. One false step, and he may plunge to his death. We should remember to say our prayers with the very same concentration and devotion. You never know, our lives may be hanging on every word we say."

He who has chosen good will flee from evil.

The wicked are ruled by their hearts, the righteous rule their heart. (Bereishis Rabbah 34)

ROCHEL AND LEAH: THE IMPORTANCE OF NOT EMBARRASSING SOMEONE

Although Lovan solemnly agreed to marry off his daughter Rochel to Yaakov in exchange for Yaakov's labor, Lovan had nothing of the sort in mind. Yaakov was aware that Lovan might try to trick him, and so he gave Rochel some secret codes so that he would know it was Rochel under the bridal canopy. However, when Rochel learned that her father was planning to marry off Leah instead, she revealed these codes to Leah. She felt that she could not let her sister, who was older than she, be embarrassed under the bridal canopy. So Rochel, who had waited seven long years to marry Yaakov, delayed her chance for happiness simply because she did not want to see her sister embarrassed. This act of selflessness is a lesson to us all. (Megillah 13)

Mar Ukvah was similarly intent in avoiding causing someone else embarrassment. Once when he was raking coals in his furnace, he had his back turned and another

dream and warned him not to try in any way to influence Yaakov to return to Choran. Lovan upbraided his son-in-law for having left so hurriedly, and accused him of the theft of his idols. Yaakov denied the theft, and unwittingly declared that anyone who had taken the idols would die. Lovan began a methodical search through all of Yaakov's possessions for the idols. Rochel hid them and Lovan's search proved fruitless. Yaakov and Lovan then parted after completing a peace treaty, and Yaakov and his household headed homewards. Yaakov met angels of Hashem during his travels. The place where Yaakov saw these angels he named Machanoyim (Groups).

In this Parsha, the birth of the shevatim (12 tribes) is mentioned. They are: Reuven, Shimon, Levi, Yehudah, Yissochar, Zevulun, Dan, Naftali, Gad, Usher, and Yoseph. The birth of Binyomin is mentioned in Parshas Vayishlach.

person entered the room. The other person thought this great Rabbi was the lowly servant and he playfully kicked him and ordered him about. Though his feet were beginning to get scorched from the heat of the coals, Mar Ukva did not turn around. He knew that if he did so, the other man would be utterly embarrassed at his crass act, and Mar Ukva wanted to avoid this. (Bava Metzia 59a)

> R. Nechunya ben Hakonah was asked by his disciples as to what he attributed his longevity. He answered them: "I have never gained honor from a colleague's disgrace." (Berachos 43)

A Rabbi once delivered a sermon about the "Lechem Haponim" which were offered in the Beis Hamikdosh every Shabbos, and how unfortunate we are in no longer being able to have this mitzvah. The sermon left a deep impression on a poor man. This man decided that he would use the purest and finest flour he could find to bake two challahs and leave them on the Aron Hakodesh on Erev Shabbos.

The Shammos of the shul came there Erev Shabbos, smelled the two delicious-looking loaves and took them home for Shabbos. When the poor man came later and noticed the loaves missing, he assumed that Hashem had accepted them, and he was overjoyed.

The Rabbi heard about what was happening, and learned that the poor man was leaving challahs in the shul every Friday night. He scolded the poor man, telling him he was naive in thinking that Hashem would eat his challahs. The poor man was ashamed and walked away crestfallen.

Soon afterwards, a message came for the Rabbi from Rabbi Yitzchok Luria, telling the Rabbi to make out a will because the Rabbi was destined to die within the next few days. The Rabbi rushed to Rabbi Yitzchok Luria to find out what he had done wrong to deserve this sudden fate. Rabbi Yitzchok Luria replied that nothing since the days of the destruction of the Beis Hamikdosh had caused Hashem more pleasure than the challahs baked with such sincerity by the poor man. By shaming the poor man and causing him to think he was in the wrong, the Rabbi had sealed his own fate.

Embarrassing others is a most grievous fault and we are told never to gain personal honor through another person's disgrace. For if we kill someone, he dies only once, but if we embarrass him, he dies many times over.

> R. Eleazar of Modayin said: "He who insults his fellowman in public . . . forfeits his portion in the Hereafter, although he has Torah and good deeds to his credit." (Avos 3:15)
> You can only kill a man once; but when you shame him—you kill him many times over. (Midrash Eliyahu 42)

In his journey home, fearful for his family's safety, Yaakov sent messengers to his brother with a conciliatory message. However, they returned with the news that Esav was approaching with four hundred armed men. Yaakov was now very frightened that Esav would try to carry out his previous intention of killing him (see Parshas Toldos). Preparing for the worst, Yaakov divided the people with him and his possessions into two camps. In this way, if one camp was attacked, the other would have a chance to escape. Yaakov chose this fearful moment to pray to Hashem

פרשת וישלח
Parshas Vayishlach

YAAKOV'S HUMILITY

The Torah tells us that when Yaakov heard that Esav was heading towards him, he grew afraid. At first glance, this seems hard to understand. Hadn't Hashem promised Yaakov protection wherever he went?! Was Yaakov now doubting Hashem's guarantee?!

No, surely Yaakov had no doubts that Hashem would keep His word. A true tzadik, Yaakov doubted only himself. He understood that Hashem's promise would be fulfilled, but only on the condition that he remained meritorious to deserve this promise. If Yaakov had sinned in the meantime, Hashem might remove His protection. Yaakov's fear was, therefore, not that Hashem would prove unreliable but that he himself had not met Hashem's standards. (Berachos 4a)

This is the manner of a Tzadik. He knows that Hashem will always be true to His word. However, he constantly checks his own deeds to make sure that he is worthy of Hashem's aid. This is the way all of us should act. We must not take Hashem's kindness for granted. We must, rather, always be concerned that perhaps we do not deserve it.

Rav Moshe Eiber, a talmid of the Vilna Gaon, was one who viewed himself in this way. He constantly avoided honors. "If I accept the honor, then perhaps I will start believing that I really deserve it," he said. Instead, he devoted his life to helping the poor, a task without many honors, and always strove to improve himself. He considered himself a man with few z'chusim (merits) and, therefore, when he did experience Hashem's kindness he was overcome with gratitude. It is an attitude that can help us better appreciate life.

The righteous say little and do much.

(Bava Metzia 87)
Danger threatens the complacent, not the watchful.
One who prays should cast his eyes downwards, and direct his heart upwards. (Eichah 3:41)

YAAKOV'S PREPARATIONS

When Yaakov learned that Esav was approaching, he prepared to meet him in three ways. He prepared a gift to appease Esav, he prepared a prayer for Hashem to assist him, and he prepared for war. Yaakov knew that, when faced with danger, man should make his own fight for survival rather than give up all hope or rely on miracles.

When problems arise, we should first try to solve them peacefully. To this end, Yaakov sent gifts to Esav. Perhaps Esav's brotherly affections would be aroused by the sight of Yaakov's presents and bloodshed would be avoided. Peace and brotherhood are goals we should always pursue.

At the same time, prayer is an indispensable aid during times of crisis. Those who can pray never feel lost.

It was prayer that saved the Jews of Yerusholayim at the time of Napoleon. Reb Mordechai was praying at the Kosel HaMa'aravi, the Western Wall, when suddenly five brilliantly white letters "aleph"! appeared. He stared at them for a while, and then they seemed to vanish. Reb Mordechai was frightened, not knowing what they portended.

The next day, his fears seemed to be confirmed. He learned that the Pasha (the Turkish ruler of Yerusholayim) had decided that all Jews living within ten blocks of the Kosel had to vacate their homes immediately. Not waiting for the Jews to comply, the Pasha's soldiers began looting the Jews' homes. Now Reb Mordechai knew what the

that he be saved from the hands of his brother Esav. He also sent a succession of valuable gifts to his brother, thereby hoping to pacify him.

Yaakov took his wives and children and helped them cross the ford of Yabok. Yaakov then supervised the conveyance of all his possessions across the ford. He, too, was ready to cross when an individual appeared. He began fighting with Yaakov and the two wrestled until dawn. The individual, who our Chazal explain was actually the angel who represents Esav and his descendants in Heaven, was unable to overcome Yaakov. However, he managed to injure Yaakov's thigh. Yaakov managed to restrain him and refused to release his opponent from his grasp until he received a blessing from him. His wish was granted, and the angel blessed him and assured him that he will thereafter be known as Yisroel.

Yisroel was limping as he left the spot upon which the battle had occurred. It is for this reason that we do not, until this very day, eat the "Gid Hanosheh" (Sinew of the Thigh) of any animal.

When Yaakov saw Esav and his followers approaching, Yaakov placed each of his children near his respective mother. First came Bilhoh, Zilpoh and their children. Next, Leah and her children, and finally Rochel and Yoseph. Yaakov himself, approached Esav in front of his family, bowing seven times on the way. It was then that a miracle occurred. Esav, witnessing this entire scene and seeing Yaakov bowing low before him, was greatly touched. He ran to Yaakov, embraced

five "alephs" represented: the words "Omar Oyeiv Erdof Asig Achalek Sholol—the Enemy said, 'I Will Pursue, I Will Overtake, I Will Divide the Spoils."

All seemed lost. Many despaired but not Reb Mordechai. He prayed to heaven and his prayers gave him added incentive to persevere. He urged his fellow Jews not to give up hope.

That very day the unexpected happened. Reb Mordechai received instructions to present himself immediately to the Pasha. When he arrived, the Pasha said, "I have just received word that the army of Napoleon is approaching. I am desperate. If Napoleon comes, all is lost. My only hope rests with you. You must pray to your G-d not to let Napoleon take over the city."

Reb Mordechai looked at the Pasha angrily and replied, "How can you expect the Jews to pray for you if you ordered us to stay away from the holy Kosel?"

Upon hearing this, the Pasha immediately reversed his evil decree. The Jews, once again allowed to live and pray at the Kosel, prayed for the safety of Yerusholayim. The city was saved as the result of prayer.

However, if all else seems to fail, Jews must be prepared to defend themselves by physical means. Yaakov knew this and armed his camp for war. Rav Meir Yecheal Halevi was noted for his devout praying and fasting, yet he did not hesitate to order that

every Jew over the age of 13 should stand ready to fight the enemy during the Blood Libels. When the enemy did approach, they took one look at all the Jews prepared to fight and they turned back. And the Sage Rabbi Menachem Zemba did all he could to encourage the Jews' courageous fight against the Nazis in the Warsaw Ghetto. Once we take the necessary steps to help ourselves Hashem will step in and save us, if we but deserve this.

Yaakov Ovinu, then, outlined the different steps that Jews should follow in times of danger. They must search for peace, pray to Hashem, and prepare for battle. It is hoped that, if they do this, Hashem will find them worthy of His salvation.

Prayer is also a refuge from disappointment and despair. As both R. Yochanan and R. Eleazar said: Even when a sharp sword rests on a man's neck, he should not desist from prayer. (Berachos 10)
"Out of the depths have I called you O Hashem." (Tehillim 130:1)

STEERING CLEAR OF BAD INFLUENCES

We have much to learn from our forefathers' acts that can be applied to our own lives. As a result, it is most useful to study the deeds of our Ovos, Avrohom, Yitzchok, and Yaakov, for they provide us with clues as to how we should behave to-

him and kissed him. The two brothers cried. Hashem's promise of safety on the journey home had been fulfilled.

Yaakov parted from his brother and eventually reached Shechem. There he purchased some land, pitched his tent, and gratefully built an altar to Hashem.

The prince of Shechem kidnapped Dina and forced her to live with him. No one in Shechem's city protested this inhuman behavior. Shimon and Levi went to the city and rescued their sister. They punished the perpetrator and all those who either aided Shechem or could have helped Dina but didn't.

At Hashem's bidding, Yaakov returned to Bais-El, where Yaakov again built an altar in gratitude to Hashem. Hashem appeared to him and renewed His promise to give the land to Yaakov and his descendants. Yaakov then poured wine and oil upon the altar he had erected on his way to Lovan's house. (See Parshas Vayeitzei)

As the family left Bais-El and was just a short distance away from Bais Lechem, Rochel died while giving birth to Binyomin. She was buried there and Yaakov erected a monument over her gravesite. Finally, Yaakov reached Chevron, where he was reunited with his father. Yitzchok died at the age of one hundred eighty and was buried by his sons, Esav and Yaakov.

Esav had become very wealthy and there was not enough land in Canaan for both him and Yaakov to tend their flocks. Esav, therefore, resettled with his family in Mount Sair, in the land of Edom, a land that his descendants inhabited for many years to come.

day.

One such example is Yaakov's relationship with Esav after their reunion. Esav urged Yaakov to stay and accompany him. However, Yaakov politely declined this offer. He knew that it would be best to avoid his brother's possibly harmful influence. For, as we Jews have learned throughout history, gentiles often court the Jews' favor for a while, only to turn on them in the end. Jews who tried too eagerly to become part of gentile society, like those in Germany and Russia, soon learned of the goy's intolerance. And even if Jews are accepted in non-Jewish society for a while, they are likely to be corrupted and lose their Jewish identity and their belief in Hashem. So it is best to keep a distance from possible harm, as indicated by the following story:

A certain man had been a failure at everything he had attempted. He seemed at a dead end in life when he decided to try something new. He would become a wagon driver. He therefore went to the guild and submitted his application for the position. The members of the guild were doubtful whether he was suited for the job in light of his previous failures. However, they decided to give him a chance by trying him in a test

of wits.

"What would you do if your wagon got stuck in the mud?" they asked him.

"I would get a lever and pry it out," the man answered proudly.

"And what if that didn't work?" they went on.

"I would get a rock to raise it even higher."

"And if the mud was too deep for even that?"

"I would get a few horses to try to pull the wagon out."

"And what if that didn't work either?"

The man had no answer to this. "What would *you* do?" he asked them instead.

The members of the guild grinned and replied, "We would have made sure to avoid the mud, and that way we wouldn't have let the wagon fall into it in the first place."

We Jews, too, must avoid, the pitfalls of corrupting influences, and the best way to do so is to stay as far away from them as possible, as Yaakov Ovinu did.

Woe to the wicked and woe to his neighbor. (Succah 56)

The rotten date-tree seeks out the society of the barren tree. (Bava Kama 92)

Yaakov's favorite son was Yoseph, his "Ben Z'kunim," son of old age. Yaakov made for Yoseph a multi-colored silk coat as a sign of distinction and lordship. This aroused the jealousy of Yoseph's brothers until they actually hated Yoseph and could not even talk to him congenially.

Yoseph dreamt two dreams with the same obvious message. His brothers' hate intensified as they heard Yoseph's dreams. In the first dream, the sheaves of his brothers bowed down to his own sheaf, which was standing upright in their midst. In the second, the sun,

פרשת וישב
Parshas Vayeishev

HASHGOCHOH PEROTIS (DIVINE SUPERVISION)

Whatever happens in this world is planned and controlled by G-d. Some may occasionally question this statement. "If G-d controls everything," they ask, "how come certain unfortunate things happen? What is the reason for this?" Often we may not be able to perceive the reason behind certain events. However, this does not mean that there is no explanation. What we lack is the ability to see events in total perspective from the vantage point of hindsight. What might seem tragic today might prove to be wonderful tomorrow. Life is like a puzzle with all the pieces scattered about, and we seem unable to fit them together into a logical form. However, Hashem designed the puzzle and it is He who will eventually link together all the pieces into a perfectly comprehensible whole. The truth of this can be seen from the story of Yoseph.

The events of Yoseph's early life probably seemed very tragic at the time they occurred. He was his father's favorite son, and yet he was thrown into a pit by his jealous brothers, seemingly doomed to die. The brothers then moved away from the pit so as not to hear Yoseph's cries for mercy. Then, in apparent coincidence, they noticed a caravan of travelers which "just happened" to be passing by. The traveling merchants removed Yoseph from the pit and "just happened" to take him to Egypt. There, instead of becoming a menial slave toiling in the fields, he "just happened" to be sold to an important member of Egyptian society. Then again Yoseph's fate seemed to take a downward turn when he was unjustly thrown into jail. At this point, an observer might have thought that Yoseph was being punished for no obvious reason. However, it was in jail that Yoseph "just happened" to meet and in-

terpret the dreams of the butler and the baker. This eventually led to his becoming second in command to Paroh, which in turn led to the immigration of all of B'nei Yisroel to Egypt. It was in Egypt that Yoseph was able to support his family and keep B'nei Yisroel alive even during the terrible hunger. So what seemed to be a series of unreasonable hardships for Yoseph finally resulted in the sustainment of the Jewish nation. Hashem's Divine Hand had been in command of the situation throughout, and His Divine plan finally became clear in retrospect. (Bereishis Rabbah 85:1)

Reb Yitzchak was another individual who learned that every event that takes place has a reason behind it, however vague at the moment. Reb Yitzchak was once strolling on a cliff near the city of Kasria. He noticed something rolling towards him. As he drew closer, he observed that it was a bone. "This is dangerous," he thought to himself. "Someone might not notice the bone lying there and might trip over it and fall off the cliff." Consequently, he took the bone and buried it in the nearby earth.

However, the bone would not stay put. The earth seemed to open and the bone once again began rolling towards him. Once again, Reb Yitzchak took the bone and placed it in the earth.

Then the same thing happened for a third time. Reb Yitzchak began reconsidering. "If this bone keeps rolling back, there must be some Divine reason for it. I had better leave it as it is, instead of trying to fight fate."

A few days later, Reb Yitzchak learned that a government courier had come to the same spot he had traveled on, had tripped over the bone, and had fallen over the cliff to his death. Some Jews who found the courier's body found that he had been carrying documents urging punishments for the

moon, and eleven stars, (representing the rest of Yoseph's family) bowed down to him. The implication of these dreams was that all the members of Yoseph's family would become subservient to him. Yaakov rebuked Yoseph for arousing his brothers' enmity, though he personally noted and waited for fulfillment of the dreams.

When Yoseph's brothers were away tending their father's flock in Shechem, Yaakov sent Yoseph to see how they were faring. Yoseph was on his way to his brothers when they noticed him from a distance. The brothers decided that this was their chance to conspire to kill him, throw his body into a pit, and then conceal their act by saying he had been eaten by a wild beast.

Reuven knew that this was wrong. He wanted to save Yoseph but saw that the other brothers would not heed his word. However, he was able to convince them not to kill Yoseph but rather to cast him alive into a nearby pit. "Let it not be your hands that directly injure Yoseph," argued Reuven. Reuven reasoned silently that later he would return, after the brothers had left, and save Yoseph. When Yoseph finally arrived, the brothers stripped him of his silk coat and, as Reuven had suggested, threw him alive into the pit.

Jews. The documents disappeared and the punishments were not carried out. Reb Yitzchak smiled to himself. "I have now seen the hand of G-d at work." (Midrash Rabbah)

Because Hashem controls all earthly occurrences, it is, therefore, a good idea for men to realize that all that occurs is G-d's will. Even the occurrences which may seem bitter and detrimental are actually beneficial in the long run. For otherwise why would Hashem cause them to transpire? One who made a special practice of doing so was Nachum Ish Gamzo. "Gamzo" means 'this too,' and Nachum was thus named because of his tendency to say, after every setback, "Gamzo L'tovah"—"this too is for the good."

One time, the Jewish community decided to send a gift to the Caesar. But who should represent the Jewish people with this tribute to the Caesar? Nachum Ish Gamzo was the right person, it was decided, for miracles were constantly occurring around him.

So, Nachum set out on his journey carrying a large chest filled with precious stones to be offered to the Caesar. On the way, he stopped at an inn to spend the night. In the middle of the night, the greedy innkeepers arose, emptied the chest of its precious contents and filled it with sand.

Not realizing what had happened, Nachum woke up the next morning and made his way to the Caesar. He presented the chest in the name of the entire Jewish community. The Caesar was appreciative of the precious gift and approached the chest to

open it. But when he opened it, lo and behold, it contained sand.

The Caesar was furious. He started making plans to wipe out all the Jews in his kingdom. But, Nachum was not overwhelmed. His Bitachon (Trust) in Hashem was firm and he pronounced fervently those familiar and meaningful words, "Gamzo L'tovah."

Eliyahu Hanovi, the prophet, was sent to help Nachum and the Jews. He appeared as one of the king's soldiers and told the king, "Maybe this is from the sand of the Jews' ancestor Avrohom. When Avrohom threw sand at his enemies the sand turned into swords!"

There was one province which the Caesar could not conquer. He decided to test out this sand on this province. He tested it and it worked! He conquered that province thanks to the miraculous sand.

The Caesar took the same chest and filled it with gold and precious stones as a present to the Jews. He sent off Nachum with much honor and fanfare. Nachum returned to the same inn. When the innkeepers saw the great honors bestowed upon Nachum by the Caesar, they were bewildered. They approached Nachum and asked, "What exactly did you bring to the Caesar that you received such honors?"

"Whatever I took from this inn I brought to the Caesar," replied Nachum.

Upon hearing this, the innkeepers quickly gathered together sand from their inn and brought it to the Caesar. The Caesar tested their sand also but to no avail. It was just

A caravan of Yishmaelites bearing spices to Egypt approached, and the idea occurred to Yehudah to sell Yoseph as a slave rather than to directly cause his death. The brothers accepted this new plan and sold Yoseph to the traveling Yishmaelites for twenty pieces of silver. Reuven, away while this was happening, returned to find no trace of Yoseph, much to his grief. The brothers then dipped the silk coat in the blood of a goat (whose blood is similar to that of a human being) and brought it to Yaakov, who concluded that Yoseph had been devoured by a wild beast. Yaakov mourned Yoseph's loss for many days.

Meanwhile, Yoseph was being sold and resold many times. The Yishmaelites sold him to Midianite merchants, and the merchants sold him in Egypt, to Potiphar, an officer of Paroh.

Yehudah had married the daughter of Shooa, a merchant, who bore him three sons. The first son later married a woman named Tamar, but died soon after the marriage. The second son then married her, as it was the custom that the husband's surviving brother marry the childless widow (Yibum). However, this second hus-

---

plain sand. The Caesar had the innkeepers put to death. (Taanis 21a)

Nachum's faith in Hashem had eventually proved correct, Gamzo L'tovah.

Nothing happens to man in life without it being decreed by the Holy One blessed be He. (Sefer Chassidim)

The physician's error is the Creator's design.

AVOIDING TEMPTATION

The wicked are summoned before the Court of Hashem after their deaths and are asked why they did not comply with the laws of the Torah. If they respond that they were too readily exposed to temptations and therefore succumbed to wickedness, they are told, "Were you really more tempted than Yoseph?" Yoseph was extremely handsome, and the wife of Potiphar made every attempt to seduce him. She urged him daily to consent to her wishes and her words could not be taken lightly, for she was the master's wife. However, Yoseph steadfastly refused. When she threatened to lock him up in jail, he replied, "Hashem opens all locks." When she threatened to scratch out his eyes, he replied, "Hashem gives sight to the blind." When she threatened to torture him, he replied, "Hashem strengthens the faithful." One time when he seemed to weaken, the vision of Yaakov, his father, came to him and this inspired him to resist all temptations.

Like Yoseph, we must resist all evil influences and impulses. When we sense we are losing our self-control, we should bear in mind the story of Yoseph. Just as Yoseph was rescued from temptation by retaining the image of Yaakov, so, too, should we keep the image of someone important in mind during trying moments. In this way, our defenses against immorality will remain high. (Yoma 35b)

The power of such an image acting as a "protecting angel" can be seen from the story of two brothers during the days of the Spanish Inquisition. The one named Rapahael was firm in his dedication to Judaism, whereas the other named Sancho was an opportunist who became a Marrano when he saw the government opposing Judaism. As a result, they went their separate ways. Rapahael, the loyal Jew, became involved in many anti-government plots, thereby hoping to save his brethren. Even when he had been caught and partly blinded, he continued in his revolutionary ways. Sancho, on the other hand, sought to ingratiate himself with the government by turning traitor against the Jews whenever possible.

One day, a meeting was held in which Rapahael explained his plan to save some Jews held prisoners by the Spaniards. Because of its importance, the plotters tried to keep the plan as secret as possible. However, Sancho soon learned of it through his usual informants and prepared to reveal the plan to the government in exchange for his personal gain.

On the night before his planned meeting with the Spanish leaders, Sancho fell into a deep sleep and had a strange dream. In it, he saw the figure of his father come towards him, looking most upset. "What is it, Father?" he heard himself asking.

"It is you," his father replied, sternly. "You are upsetting me, Sancho. I raised you

band also soon died. Yehudah feared that his third son would die if he married Tamar, so he asked Tamar to wait in her father's house until his youngest son grew up and was ready to marry her. Yehudah was only putting her off; he had no real intention of ever having the marriage take place. Realizing through a prophecy that the Kings of Yisroel will descend from Yehudah, Tamar disguised herself and deceived Yehudah so that she should bear his child. When her pregnancy was discovered, Yehudah, not realizing that it was his own child that Tamar was carrying, condemned her to be burned. However, Tamar was able to prove that it was Yehudah himself who was the father of her unborn child. As Tamar was taken to be burnt, she sent to Yehudah his staff and other personal possessions, saying, "By the man who owns these objects I am pregnant." Yehudah thereupon realized and acknowledged that it was his child. He admitted that she was right for he had not allowed Tamar to marry his remaining son, and she was saved from death.

to be a true and loyal Jew. Now what did I see you doing? Nothing less than betraying your fellow Jews, all for money and glory. Well, you can keep your money and glory, but you are no longer a son of mine!" And the image of his father disappeared.

Sancho woke up quickly, both frightened and chastened. Had he really been such a disgrace to the memory of his father? Was he really such a menace to his own people? The true impact of his actions had only just hit him. Then he must do something to compensate for his perfidy. He must start immediately!

The next morning, the Spanish officials waited impatiently for their informer, but Sancho never appeared. Impatient, they came to find him themselves. But Sancho refused to talk. "We know you have some information," they told him menacingly, but he remained silent. No threats or punishments could pry any information from his lips. He was severely beaten, but his father's memory kept him from divulging Rapahael's plans. Thanks to Sancho's silence, those plans were carried out successfully, and the Jews were freed. The image of his father had saved the day.

He who has chosen good will flee from evil.

He who rears his children in the proper way will have peace in his home.

(Derech Eretz 2)

JUDGING YOUR FELLOW MAN FAVORABLY

Yoseph was treated harshly by his brothers. Did he deserve this treatment? In a certain way, he did. For he was not as careful in judging his brothers as he could have been. Much of what he said, however in-

nocently, had the effect of arousing their jealousy, such as his reporting his dreams of superiority. And he made the additional error of mistakenly accusing his brothers of a crime. When Yoseph saw his brothers eat the meat of an animal that seemed to be moving, he ran to Yaakov and accused them of eating meat of a new born animal. What he did not know was that they were eating the meat of a baby animal taken out of its mother's womb, which is permissible if the mother was slaughtered according to halacha. In his readiness to condemn his brothers he disregarded a major Jewish principle, to judge every person in a favorable light. For this mistake, he deserved his brothers' enmity.

One who did all he could to find the good in others was Rav Levi Yitzchak of Berditchev. One Shabbos, he was surprised to find a Jewish neighbor of his smoking a cigarette. Rav Levi Yitzchak came over to him and said, "You probably began smoking because you didn't realize that it was Shabbos."

"Oh, I know that today is Shabbos," replied the man.

"Then you probably didn't know that one is not allowed to smoke on Shabbos," Rav Levi Yitzchak went on.

"Oh, I know that too," said the man.

"Then I suppose you are smoking because it is necessary for your health."

"No, not at all,"

At this point, Rav Levi Yitzchak lifted his eyes up to the heavens and, speaking directly to Hashem, said, "See how honest your people are? Even when they commit a sin, they do not make it worse by lying about it!"

Another such example of trying to judge another person without suspicion is related

Hashem was with Yoseph and he was very successful in all his endeavors. Potiphar, realizing this, appointed him to the position of overseer of his household. Potiphar's wife tried to seduce Yoseph but Yoseph rejected her daily advances. Potiphar's wife finally became insulted and reacted viciously by accusing him of molesting her, and Yoseph was sent to prison.

Even in prison Hashem was with Yoseph, and he found favor in the eyes of the prison warden. The warden placed Yoseph in charge of all the prisoners and everything that took place in the prison was controlled by Yoseph. While there, Yoseph came in contact with two royal officials, Paroh's chief butler and baker. They had offended Paroh and were in prison awaiting word of their fate. One night, each had a dream which they revealed to Yoseph. Yoseph interpreted the dreams to mean that the butler would be pardoned by Paroh, but the baker would be executed. The events occurred exactly as Yoseph had foretold. Yoseph asked the butler to intercede with Paroh on his behalf, but the butler forgot this request as soon as he was released from prison.

in the Gemorah in the following manner. There was once a worker who worked for an individual for three years. At the end of this period, on the day before Yom Kippur, he approached his employer. The worker explained that he felt it was time to return to his family and he would like his wages for the years of devoted labor he had served his employer.

The employer replied, "I am sorry, but I have no money at the moment."

"So pay me in produce," said the worker.

"I have no produce," was the employer's reply.

"Then I'll accept my wages in land or in livestock or in housewares," decided the worker.

The employer shook his head solemnly, "Sorry, I possess none of those either."

The dejected worker set out on his way home with empty pockets without a word. Right after the Yomim Tovim (Holidays), the employer took the worker's wages and three donkeys laden with food, drink and delicacies, and went to the worker's home. After he paid him his wages and they had partaken of the delicacies the employer had brought, the employer asked the worker, "What did you think when I told you I had no money to pay you?"

"I thought maybe you had just been offered some goods at a bargain price and had spent all your money purchasing these wares."

"And when I told you I had no livestock or land, what did you think?"

"I thought maybe you had rented them to people," answered the worker.

"And how did you understand that I had no produce or housewares?" was the next question.

"Well, I figured you couldn't give me produce because you hadn't yet given Ma'aser (Tithes) from them, and about housewares I guessed you must have donated all your property to the Bais Hamikdosh," explained the worker.

"Yes, yes, you're right! That's exactly what happened," exclaimed the employer. "You have judged me favorably, may Hashem always judge you favorably!" (Shabbos 127b)

True greatness lies in the ability to see the good points of others. This was especially illustrated by Rav Levi Yitzchok of Berditchev who was renowned for always judging people favorably and seeing their positive side.

It is told that he once saw a wagon driver fixing a wheel on his wagon while reciting the morning prayers and wearing his Talis and Tefillin. Rav Levi Yitzchak explained, "Ribono Shel Olam, look how Your servants think only of You even when they are engaged in the pursuit of earning their livelihood."

Joshua ben Perahiah stated: ". . . Judge every man charitably." (Avos 1:6)

Hillel: ". . . judge not your fellowman until you have put yourself in his place." (Avos 2:5)

"May Hashem judge you charitably for having so charitably judged me." (Shabbos 127)

Two years after the chief butler was freed from prison, Paroh dreamt two unusual dreams. In one, he saw seven lean cows devouring seven well-fed cows and nevertheless, remaining lean; in the other, he saw seven thin ears of grain swallowing seven full ears of grain and still remaining thin. Paroh was disturbed by these dreams and was not put at ease by any of the explanations offered by his advisors. It was then that the chief butler, recalling Yoseph's ability to interpret dreams, told Paroh of Yoseph's talent.

Yoseph was immediately summoned before Paroh.

פרשת מקץ
Parshas Mikeitz

FAITH IN HASHEM

After Yoseph had correctly interpreted the chief butler's dream, he depended on the butler's help in getting out of prison. However, he languished there for another two years. Our Sages say that this extended imprisonment was a punishment for relying on the butler, rather than Hashem, for freedom.

However, it seems difficult to understand why Yoseph was punished for this. We know that Hashem sends his help to us through natural means, so what was so wrong in Yoseph's depending on help from the butler? The answer is that a person as great as Yoseph, who had so clearly seen the role of Hashem in all that had happened to him, should not have placed his full reliance on his fellow man alone. Furthermore, if he did place some faith in others, he should have chosen a righteous person to rely on, not the disreputable butler. (Midrash Rabbah, Parshas Mikeitz)

Having total faith in Hashem is not an easy task, but it is a necessary one. We must remember to retain this Bitochon, faith, at all times.

A man once came to a Rav to complain that he did not have enough funds to live comfortably. The Rav replied, "Have complete faith in Hashem. If you do, then He will provide you with one thousand dollars." The man left, reassured.

However, a month later, he was back. "I've been waiting quite a while for the money, and I haven't received anything yet," he protested.

"Have you retained full faith in Hashem, that He will give you the thousand dollars?" asked the Rav. The man nodded. "Well," continued the Rav, "I have five hundred dollars here, would you take that instead of the thousand dollars?"

The man replied eagerly that he would.

The Rav shook his head. "This shows that you do not have complete faith in what I told you, for if you truly did, then you would not be willing to accept the five hundred dollars instead of the thousand you were promised."

Having Bitochon can help calm our fears and can prevent us from leading nerve-wracking lives. We know that we will not always have to worry about the future if we lead Torah-true lives today.

Once, Rav Levi Yitzchak of Berditchev saw a man running. "Where are you racing to?" he asked.

"To my Parnassah (Livelihood)," replied the man.

Rav Levi replied, "How do you know your Parnassah is in front of you and not in back of you? Have a little faith in your eventual success, and don't run around so furiously. Stop a little sometimes and learn Torah. Appreciate what you are working so hard for. Have faith in Hashem, and you won't have to run so hard!"

I chose the path of faith, your judgements I set before me. (Tehillim 119:30)

For the faith Jews had in Hashem, the Holy Spirit came to rest on them, as it is stated: "and the children of Israel had faith in Hashem and Moses His servant." (Shemos 14:31)

YOSEPH, SECOND TO PAROH

Yoseph had satisfactorily interpreted Paroh's dreams and had suggested that Paroh appoint a food manager. Paroh immediately appointed Yoseph himself to the post. Why did Paroh choose Yoseph so quickly? How did he know that Yoseph could be trusted with such an important job?

There is a parable that helps explain Paroh's quick decisions. A merchant once

Paroh told him that he had dreamt a dream which no one could satisfactorily interpret and that he had heard that Yoseph is capable of interpreting dreams. After proclaiming that it is not his own wisdom with which he interprets dreams but rather it is Hashem who will interpret the dream for Paroh through him, Yoseph proceeded to listen to Paroh's recounting of his dreams and to interpret them. He explained that Paroh's two dreams were actually conveying the same message from Hashem as to what He was about to do. The seven well-fed cows and the seven full ears of grain represent seven years of economic prosperity for Egypt. The seven lean cows and the seven thin ears of grain are symbolic of seven years of severe economic depression resulting in a severe famine which will follow the prosperous years. The seven years of famine will be so devastating that the seven good years will be forgotten. Furthermore, the duplication of this message through two dreams meant that the beginning of the seven years was imminent.

Yoseph advised Paroh to appoint a wise person to administer the Land of Egypt. Food must be stored and preserved under the auspices of Paroh during the seven good years for sustenance during the years of famine. Yoseph's interpretation and counsel were completely accepted by Paroh and all his servants. Paroh, therefore, immediately chose Yoseph, himself, for the aforementioned position, and, at the age of thirty, Yoseph became Egypt's royal viceroy.

Paroh officially installed Yoseph. He placed on Yoseph's finger his own royal signet ring, dressed Yoseph in garments of fine linen, laid a gold necklace on his neck, and placed him on the viceroy's chariot. Paroh gave Osnas bas Potipherah to Yoseph as a wife. She later bore him two sons, Menashe and Ephrayim. Yoseph began storing food in the cities during the years of plenty and amassed so much food that records of amounts were meaningless and no longer kept.

The bountiful years were over; now came the years of famine as predicted by

owned a large store in a certain city. The store was extremely well stocked with all varieties of expensive merchandise. Soon after the store opened for business, the city government began taxing the owner greatly, assuming that the owner of such a store had to be a very wealthy man.

The merchant came to the tax collector and protested vigorously. "How can you tax me so highly? How do you know all this merchandise is mine? Perhaps I bought it all on credit, and do not own anything?"

The tax collector replied, "It may be true that you bought much of the merchandise on credit. However, this only confirms my guess that you are a wealthy man. No one would extend so much credit to a pauper! The fact that you were given so much on credit indicates that you must have a lot of financial backing, and your credit rating must have been carefully checked before you were loaned so much."

Paroh took the same attitude. He told Yoseph that he understood Yoseph to be wealthy in wisdom and understanding. Yoseph replied, "Whatever wisdom I have comes from Hashem."

"It may be true that your abilities come from your G-d," answered Paroh. "However, since your G-d saw fit to give you all these abilities, you must be a most worthwhile individual and must be the right man for the job. If your G-d can trust you, so can I."

This very attitude is one we should assume towards our Torah leaders. If Hashem entrusted them with so much wisdom, then we must accept them as our guides and mentors. Instead of feeling that we are our own best guides, we should follow those in whom Hashem has placed His wisdom.

Blessed is the man who trusts in Hashem and whose hope is Hashem. (Jeremiah 17:7)

Cast your burden upon Hashem and He shall sustain you. (Mishley 3:4)

Trust in Hashem and do good so you shall dwell in the land and verily shall you be fed. (Tehillim 37:3)

WHY YOSEPH CONCEALED HIS IDENTITY: DOING TESHUVAH

Yoseph's conduct towards his brothers

Yoseph. Yoseph opened all his storehouses and sold the provisions stored within to the Egyptians. The neighboring lands also suffered from the famine, and their inhabitants came to Yoseph to purchase food.

The severe famine in Canaan compelled Yaakov to send his sons to Egypt to buy food, but he made the youngest, Binyomin, remain at home lest he suffer harm during the trip. When Yaakov's sons arrived, Yoseph recognized them instantly. However, his appearance had changed and they did not recognize him. Yoseph acted to them as a stranger and did not reveal his identity to them. He spoke harshly to them and accused them of being spies. They strongly denied this and said that they were all brothers who had come just to buy food. They explained to Yoseph that they came from a family of twelve brothers, that one brother had disappeared and the youngest brother was still at home with their father. "No, I am right," said Yoseph. "You are spies. This shall be your test. Send one brother from amongst you and let him bring back your youngest brother. Then I will know that you are telling the truth."

Yoseph placed all the brothers in prison for three days. After three days, Yoseph released them. However, he informed them that one brother, Shimon, would remain behind until the rest would return with their youngest brother. The brothers now remembered with regret their treatment of Yoseph. They attributed this terrible anguish to divine punishment for the sin they had committed. The brothers did not know that Yoseph understood their language, Hebrew, for when they had conversed with him their words had been translated into Egyptian for Yoseph to understand. When Yoseph saw this display of regret from the brothers, he walked away from them and wept.

had long puzzled our commentators. For what purpose did Yoseph falsely denounce them? How could he ignore their plight and their hunger, and how could he cause his father such worry through the threats to Shimon and Binyomin?

However, one thing is clear. Yoseph cannot be accused of being driven by a desire for revenge. Though Yoseph's brothers suspected that he would hate them and requite the evil which they did to him, Yoseph avoided all acts of vengeance. Had he wanted to, he could easily have ordered all his brothers killed. That he did not do so indicates that he was after a different goal.

What then was Yoseph's motivation? The Torah states that when Yoseph saw his brothers, he remembered his dreams and noted that they had not yet been properly fulfilled. His dreams had indicated that all eleven of his brothers as well as his parents would some day bow down to him. Because the first dream stipulated that his eleven brothers would be the first to bow to him, he made sure that Binyomin would come to Egypt, without Yaakov. Had he revealed his true identity immediately, Yaakov would certainly have arrived at once. But it was only in the second dream that Yoseph saw

his parents bowing to him! Therefore, he hid his true identity for the time being and demanded Binyomin's appearance. After Binyomin arrived and the first dream's prophecy had been fulfilled, Yoseph removed his mask and revealed his identity. Eventually, Yaakov arrived and the second prophecy was also substantiated.

The Rambam provides another explanation for Yoseph's actions. Yoseph's brothers, the other B'nei Yisroel, were guilty of a grievous injustice towards Yoseph. The spiritual honor of the House of Yaakov could be restored only if this wrong were righted. How could this injustice be atoned for?

The answer was that the brothers must do Teshuva, penitence. How is Teshuva accomplished? In its true form, it occurs when one is confronted with the same temptation to which he had previously succumbed. If one stands the test and resists this time, he has fully repented.

How, then, could the brothers of Yoseph do Teshuva? If they discovered Yoseph's identity and showed him their regret, this would not be true Teshuva, for they might be penitent only out of fear for their lives. No, the only way they could achieve true

Yoseph returned to them and took Shimon and jailed him before their eyes. Yoseph then secretly commanded his servants to fill his brothers' vessels with grain and to replace their money inside their sacks of grain.

As the brothers were returning home, one of them opened his sack of food and found inside the money he had paid for the food. Not knowing that Yoseph had ordered their money secretly returned to them, the brothers were very afraid that they would be accused of theft. Upon returning home, they recounted to Yaakov all that had happened. As they were emptying their sacks they each found their money among the grain. However, Yaakov still refused to let Binyomin accompany them to Egypt for fear that misfortune would befall him on the trip.

The famine in Canaan was very severe. Soon the food that they had brought from Egypt was gone. Yehudah sought to ease his father's fears by offering to take responsibility for Binyomin's safety. Yaakov regretfully agreed to allow Binyomin to accompany them to Egypt.

The brothers arrived in Egypt and were escorted to Yoseph's house. There they met Shimon and dined with Yoseph. Yoseph ordered his steward to supply the brothers with food, and to once again restore each brother's money. He also ordered that his silver goblet be placed in Binyomin's sack. The brothers set out on the journey home, but were soon overtaken by Yoseph's steward (sent by Yoseph), who accused them of ingratitude by stealing his master's goblet. They protested their innocence and readily agreed to be searched. When the goblet was found in Binyomin's sack, they tore their clothes in grief and returned to the city. Yehudah offered to have himself and his brothers taken as bondsmen, but Yoseph refused to detain anyone but the offender. Binyomin, he said, would be detained, and the rest were free to return to their father.

Teshuva would be for them to face the same situation they had previously failed. They had to show that they would not allow their father's favorite son to lose his life this time.

To accomplish this, Yoseph brought Binyomin to Egypt and accused him, and only him, of stealing his goblet. Now the brothers had a valid excuse for leaving their youngest brother to his fate. They could easily claim that they had no choice but to surrender Binyomin, for how could they fight off the entire Egyptian army?! However, they steadfastly refused to abandon Binyomin. If he were taken prisoner, they declared, they would all go with him. Once the brothers said this, Yoseph knew that they were truly sorry for what they had done to him, and that they would never allow something like it to happen again. It was then that they achieved true Teshuva, and it was then that he felt free to reveal his true identity. (Yoma 86b)

He that comes to cleanse himself from sin will be assisted by Hashem. (Yoma 39)

The standing that the penitents have before Hashem, even the most righteous have not. (Berachos 34)

After Binyomin was accused of stealing Yoseph's goblet, Yehudah approached Yoseph and presented an eloquent appeal. He pointed out to Yoseph the special love and affection that their father Yaakov had for Binyomin, his only remaining son from his wife Rochel. The love was so intense that Binyomin's soul was as dear to Yaakov as his very own. In fact, Yehudah continued, when Yaakov will see that Binyomin has not returned with them, it will surely cause his death. Yehudah also explained that it was he, himself, who had personally guaranteed the safe return of Binyomin, and failure would result in Yehudah's excommunication in this world and the world to come. Therefore Yehudah implored that he be allowed to remain in Egypt as a slave in lieu of Binyomin, and Binyomin allowed to return to his father with his brothers.

פרשת ויגש
Parshas Vayigash

Yoseph could no longer restrain his strong emotions and he ordered the departure of all persons from the room except for his brothers. Yoseph, then alone in the room with his brothers, raised his voice in weeping. He exclaimed, "I am Yoseph!" and quickly inquired, "Is my father really still alive?" His brothers could not answer him for they were ashamed of the wrong they had committed. Yoseph realized this and called them to come closer to him which they did. He comforted them and told them not to be sad that they had sold him, for Hashem had actually sent him here to keep them alive during the years of famine. He urged them to quickly return to Canaan and tell his father to come down to Egypt with all his children and grandchildren and all his possessions. They would live in the land of Goshen (the finest pasture land in Egypt) and Yoseph would supply them with sufficient food for the remaining years of the famine.

The news of the arrival of Yoseph's brothers reached Paroh. Paroh told Yoseph to tell his brothers to bring back Yaakov and their households to Egypt. Paroh further commanded Yoseph to tell them to take wagons from Egypt to convey their wives and children. Yoseph presented each of his brothers with sets of different clothing as gifts and he gave Binyomin five such sets and three hundred silver s'loim (amount of currency). He also gave them provisions for the journey. To his father he sent ten donkeys laden with the best of the land of Egypt and ten asses laden with all types of food for the journey.

YAAKOV, DO NOT FEAR

When Yaakov was journeying to Egypt, Hashem found it necessary to calm his fears and to reassure him that all would turn out well. Why was Yaakov afraid? Wasn't he on his way to see his long-lost son, and shouldn't this have, therefore, been an occasion for rejoicing? What was the cause for Yaakov's trepidation?

Actually, Yaakov's uneasiness stemmed from the fact that Hashem had already told Yaakov that his children would be taken into bondage. Now, when Yaakov heard that Yoseph was in Egypt and that he and his family must follow, he was worried that the moment of bondage had arrived.

Yaakov did not fear for his own safety, but for the welfare of his descendants. He knew that they would have to remain in the foreign land of Egypt for quite a while, and he was not sure whether they could withstand the challenge of an alien society. Yaakov was afraid that his children would lose their identity as Israelites and would turn into Egyptians at heart, never to return to their homeland. What then would become of Hashem's promise to create a Jewish nation of Israel for the descendants of Avrohom? It was to these fears that Hashem responded. The Almighty reassured Yaakov that, though they would spend many years in Egypt, his descendants would indeed

The brothers left Egypt and came to Canaan, to their father Yaakov. They informed their father that Yoseph was still alive, and that he ruled over the entire land of Egypt. Yaakov's heart skipped a beat; he did not believe them. The brothers then told Yaakov everything Yoseph had told them. Yaakov heard all this and saw the wagons Yoseph had sent for him and then he realized that Yoseph had indeed become a king in Egypt. Yaakov then exclaimed, "There is still much joy in my life for Yoseph is still alive. I will go and see him before I die." Yaakov set forth on his journey and reached Be'ersheva where he offered sacrifices to Hashem. Hashem appeared there to Yaakov in a vision and told him not to be afraid of going to Egypt for it is there that Hashem will make him into a large nation. Hashem promised Yaakov that He will accompany him down to Egypt and will later bring Yaakov back to Eretz Yisrael (meaning that Yaakov will be buried in Eretz Yisrael). Yaakov went down to Egypt with all his children and grandchildren. There were seventy persons of the house of Yaakov that came into Egypt.

Yoseph personally harnessed his chariot and went to meet his father. In an emotion-filled scene, Yoseph finally meets his father. Yoseph falls upon his father's neck and cries continuously. Yaakov proclaims, "If I would die immediately after having seen you now, I would be consoled, for you are still alive."

Yoseph told his brothers and their households that he was going to inform Paroh of their arrival. He advised his brothers that when Paroh calls them and asks them their occupation, they should reply that they are herdsmen. This will assure them that they will live in Goshen, a good pasture land, away from the Egyptians, because every shepherd is an abomination to the Egyptians. (Since the Egyptians

return to Canaan stronger and more numerous than when they went down.

Trust in Hashem with all your heart and lean not unto your own understanding. (Mishley 3:4)

There is not a man who does not suffer. (Midrash)

A worry in your heart—suppress it. (Mishley 12)

THE REUNION

Before Yoseph was finally reunited with Yaakov, our sages tell us that Yoseph sent his father a gift of old wine. Why this particular present? It was meant as not only an expression of endearment, but also a reassurance to Yaakov. Yoseph was trying to convey to his father the fact that he himself had remained faithful to his father's principles throughout the years of separation. For just as old wine remains the same even when in new bottles, so, too, did Yoseph remain intrinsically pure despite his new outward appearance. And just as wine improves with age, so too, did Yoseph improve in his personal traits throughout the years.

When Yaakov and Yoseph did, at long last, come face to face with each other, they embraced and the Torah says, "He cried." The obvious question is why the Torah did

not say that they cried, referring to both Yoseph and Yaakov. The Sages respond that only Yoseph cried, for Yaakov was occupied with a different matter. He was saying Shema, praying to Hashem. (Rashi, 46:29)

Now, why was Yaakov reciting the Shema at this particular moment? He had waited for this meeting with his son for twenty-two long years. Now that it had finally arrived, why was he praying to G-d instead of crying along with Yoseph?

Certainly, Yaakov was intensely affected by his reunion with Yoseph. It aroused in him the ultimate feeling of joy. But Yaakov was on too high a spiritual level to expend all his emotions on his son. He knew that he could not forget the Almighty at this supreme moment, for it was He who had brought it about. Therefore, while Yoseph was expressing his love for his father, Yaakov was expressing his love for Hashem by reciting the Shema. In this manner, Yaakov included thoughts of G-d in this pinnacle of his life.

"With all your soul"—with every part of your soul, man has to praise Hashem with every breath he draws. (Tehillim 105:6)

The root of prayer—the joy of the heart is the love of Hashem. (Sefer

worshipped sheep as a god). Yoseph presented five of his brothers to Paroh, and the brothers followed Yoseph's advice in their conversation with Paroh. Paroh then told Yoseph to have his father and brothers settle in the land of Goshen. Yoseph brought his father before Paroh and Yaakov bestowed his blessing upon Paroh.

The famine had reached a critical stage, and Yoseph collected all the money in the lands of Egypt and Canaan through the sale of food. Yoseph brought all this money to Paroh's house. To obtain food, Yoseph required as payment from the Egyptians first their cattle and later their land. The Israelites lived in the land of Goshen, where they acquired more property and they increased in population.

Chassidim)
He who worships out of love, all his worship is love. The essence of worship is love. (Mitzva B'lev)

YAAKOV'S MEETING WITH PAROH

When Paroh greeted the father of his most trusted assistant for the first time, he asked Yaakov, "How many are the days of the years of your life?" (Bereishis 47:8) This seems like a most awkwardly-phrased question. Instead of asking simply, "How old are you?" why did Paroh stress the number of Yaakov's days?

In reality, Paroh's question was most aptly expressed. Though Paroh was head of one of the mightiest nations in the world, he was impressed with Yaakov's saintly bearing. He recognized that Yaakov was one who fully

appreciated life and its possibilities for doing good. Yaakov was, therefore, one of the few who understood that one should make the most of every single day that he is granted on earth. Consequently, Paroh asked Yaakov how many were the days of the years of his life, for to Yaakov every day was a new and meaningful experience.

Does the worth of a thing depend on its age?—Nay, it is on its quality that it depends. (Bava Basra 143)
Wisdom is with the aged. (Iyov 12)
All things—the older the better, except dates, beer, and little fishes. (Bava Basra 91)
Wisdom without experience and zest is not worth anything. (Tzemech Tzedek)

Yaakov had reached the age of one hundred forty-seven, and the end of his days was approaching. He sent for Yoseph and made him promise that he would bury Yaakov in Canaan, the resting place of his fathers, rather than in Egypt. Sometime later Yoseph was informed that Yaakov was ill, and Yoseph visited him with his two sons Ephrayim and Menasheh. Yaakov told Yoseph that Ephrayim and Menasheh would be counted among Yaakov's own sons. They would each be the head of a Shevet (Tribe) as Yaakov's own sons. Yoseph brought these sons closer to Yaakov and Yaakov kissed and hugged them.

פרשת ויחי
Parshas Vayechi

THE LAST YEARS

In contrast to his early years of wanderings and tragedy, Yaakov's final years were ones of peacefulness and contentment. He lived to be reunited with his son and to see him become the second most powerful leader in Egypt. This was Hashem's reward to him for not having complained during the many years of hardship.

We often find Tzaddikim enjoying the final years of their existence on this earth,

after they had earlier gone through much uncertainty and suffering. This was certainly true of Sarah, whose final thirty-seven years on this world were her happiest, for it was then that she experienced the joy of raising Yitzchok. The closing years are ones of peaceful reward for the righteous. However, for the wicked, the process is reversed. Often their early years are spent hoarding temporary pleasures, while their final years are spent in abject misery as punishment for

Yaakov stretched out his right hand and placed it on Ephrayim's (the younger son) head and his left hand on Menasheh's (the elder son) head. Yaakov then blessed his two grandchildren. Yoseph saw that his father's right hand was placed on Ephrayim's head and thought this was wrong. Yoseph lifted his father's hand and explained to his father that Menasheh was the oldest and, therefore, his right hand should be on him. Yaakov refused to change the position of his hand, predicting that though Menasheh will become a nation and will be great, Shevet Ephrayim will be even greater.

Yaakov now called all his sons to his bedside. He spoke to each of his sons and blessed them.These famous blessings are known as "Birchos Yaakov" the blessings of Yaakov, full of prophecy about the future of each Shevet (Tribe) and the description of each tribe's special attributes and characteristics.

their recklessness.

Yaakov was in such a high state of satisfied bliss towards his death that he gathered all his sons together and decided to reveal to them the date of the coming of the Messiah. However, this power of prophecy was removed from him just as he was about to use it. Why did Hashem prevent Yaakov from disclosing the date of the Messiah's arrival? Would it not make life more confident for his descendants if they knew exactly when the Messiah would appear? However, Hashem did not want to, thereby, cause the Jews to lose their Bechirah, their free choice to do good or evil. If Yaakov had been allowed to reveal that the Messiah would come in a specific year, then the Jews might behave improperly until then, knowing that even if they did so, the Messiah would come anyway. In order to give every generation the chance to hasten the Messiah's arrival through their good deeds, Hashem left the date of his coming a secret.

Nevertheless, the Malbim, among other Gedolim who lived over three thousand years after Yaakov, did make predictions as to when the Messiah would come. (Malbim on Daniel) When asked why he did so when Yaakov was not allowed to, he replied by way of a parable:

A father and his son began their journey to a fair located quite a distance from their home. They had hardly begun the trip when the son asked, "When will we get there?"

The father quieted him down and gave him no response. They continued on their travels. Days passed, and the son again asked, "When will we get there?" This time the father responded by telling him exactly when they would arrive.

"Why didn't you give me that information the first time I asked you?" the son wondered.

"Because the first time you asked we had hardly left home and our destination was very far away," answered the father. "However, now that we are so close to it, your question has become pertinent and deserves a response."

When Yaakov sought to predict the coming of the Messiah, explained the Malbim, the date for his arrival was far off, so no revelation was forthcoming. However, now that we have gone through so much and are approaching our destination of the Messianic age, the question of when the Messiah will come is a pertinent one, and deserves an answer!

The ingathering of the exiles is as great as the day on which the heavens and earth were created. (Pesachim 88)
Whoever partakes of the three statutory Shabbos meals will be saved from the pangs of Messiah. (Shabbos 108)
The Son of David will not appear until redemption has been despaired of, when there seems to be no supporter and helper for Israel. (Sanhedrin 97)

LIVING ON AFTER DEATH

If one examines the Torah, he will find that nowhere does the text use the expression, "And Yaakov died." Why was the word "death" not used in connection with Yaakov?

Actually, there are two deaths that can be associated with a person. One is his physical death, the cessation of his bodily functions, and this death occurs to everyone sooner or later. The other possible death is the end of one's influence and impact on the world. In the case of many, both deaths occur at the same time. They have accomplished little of lasting value on this earth, so when they

Yaakov commanded all of his sons to bury him in the M'oras Hamachpelah which Avrohom purchased from Ephron (see Parshas Chayei-Sorah). Yaakov finished commanding his sons, gathered his feet into the bed and "returned to his people."

Yoseph fell on the face of his father and wept over him and kissed him. Yoseph commanded the physicians to embalm Yaakov which they did. The Egyptians mourned Yaakov for seventy days. Yoseph received Paroh's permission and he, his brothers, and their households, together with the elders of Egypt were able to go to Canaan to bury Yaakov. Yoseph and his brothers had done as they were commanded; they had buried Yaakov in the M'oras Hamachpelah.

On their return to Egypt, Yoseph's brothers, now afraid that Yoseph would seek

pass away neither their memory nor their life's work lingers on. This was not the case with Yaakov, though. True, he no longer functioned physically after the age of one hundred forty-seven. However, he had achieved so much during his years of existence that his influence and his example are felt even today, as if he were still alive. He helped found the still thriving nation of Israel, and his noble traits and his devotion to Hashem are guides for us all. Therefore, Yaakov can be considered more a part of this world than many who are actually alive today. (Taanis 56)

Rav Yehuda ben Bava was also one who realized that one's life work can survive his death. Rav Yehuda ben Bava lived during the days of Roman oppression, when the government decreed that the granting of semicha, Rabbinical ordination, was forbidden under penalty of death. Nevertheless, Rav Yehuda ben Bava assembled five of his disciples and, when hidden from view, secretly ordained them. However, just as he had finished doing so, his disciples heard the footsteps of the Roman's soldiers coming to kill them.

They began to make their escape, and shouted to their mentor, "Come, flee from the pursuit of the enemy! If you do not run, you will be killed!"

But Rav Yehuda ben Bava refused. "I am an old man. You run and save yourselves, but I will stay. I have completed my life's work, and even if the Romans do kill me, they cannot kill my accomplishments. The world of Hashem's Torah will live on!"

Soon afterwards, the enemy soldiers did indeed catch up with Rav Yehuda ben Bava. They so riddled him with spears that his punctured body resembled a sieve. However, his disciples escaped to transmit Torah to others, and in this way, Rav Yehuda has

continued to live with us today. (Sanhedrin 13b)

It should, therefore, be our goal in life to survive in this world even after death. For, though we must all die physically, if we accomplish something worthwhile during our lives, the achievements of our existence will live on.

Hashem will give to each and every righteous person three hundred and ten worlds. (Sanhedrin 100)

Hashem kills and brings to life, He brings down to the grave and brings up. (I Shmuel 2:6)

Your dead men shall live, together with my dead body shall they rise. Awake and sing you that dwell in the dust; for your dew is as the dew of light and the earth shall cast out the dead. (Isaiah 26:19)

R. Shimen ben Abba said: From the fact that you renew our lives every morning we knew that your faithfulness is great to resurrect our dead. (Bereishis Rabbah 76)

EPHRAIM AND MENASHEH

Parents who bless their sons say, "May you be like Ephraim and Menasheh." Why are sons specifically compared to the two sons of Yoseph? Because, of Yaakov's family, they were the only two who were born in Golus (Exile), and despite the corrupting temptations that Golus can offer, they remained as true to G-d's principles as Yaakov himself.

Another who retained her Jewish identity even in foreign surroundings was Queen Esther. Though she was forced to live in the King's palace, away from her countrymen, and to hide the fact that she was Jewish, she remained faithful to the laws and the spirit of the Torah throughout. It was partly

vengeance against them, sought his pardon for their past misdeeds. However, Yoseph reassured them that he had no vengeance in mind. Yoseph calmed them and told them that he would support them and their children. Before Yoseph's death, he made the children of Israel take an oath to take along his remains with them when Hashem would return them to the Promised Land. Yoseph died at the age of one hundred ten and he was embalmed and placed in a coffin in Egypt.

because of this merit that the Jews of Shushan were saved from the wicked plot of Haman.

Therefore, in praying that their sons should become like Menasheh and Ephraim, parents ask Hashem to protect their offspring from the pitfalls of Golus and to help them remain loyal and steadfast Jews.

Another admirable trait shared by Ephraim and Menasheh was their mutual lack of envy towards one another. Though Menasheh was older than Ephraim, and though Ephraim received a blessing greater than that granted Menasheh, they found no cause to rival each other. They knew that jealousy and hatred would only split their nation, and so they avoided it.

The Ari Hakodesh commented that when the two "yud"s signifying the name of Hashem are written together, then the letters cannot be erased. However, if one "yud" is higher than the other, then it is not the name of Hashem and can be erased. The reason for this is that the two "yud"s must not be rivals and must consider themselves equal, and only then do they symbolize Hashem. Similarly, two Yiddin (Jews) can evoke Hashem's spirit only when they work together harmoniously, and not when one considers himself above the other. Egotism, on the other hand, leads to destruction.

Rivalry and hatred can only cause the downfall of the B'nei Yisroel. It is when the Jews are united and accept each other as equals that the B'nei Yisroel will thrive and flourish, and bring credit to Hashem and His Torah.

The memory of the righteous is blessed. (Mishley 10)

Israel is the light of the world. (Shir Ha'Shirim)

The descendants of Yaakov were now all in Egypt where they flourished in numbers. The new Paroh, fearful that the Israelites might join with enemy forces to overthrow him, initiated a policy of oppression by reducing the Israelites to slaves. Supervised by cruel taskmasters, the Israelites were forced to build the fortresses and storage cities of Pithom and Rameses on Egypt's frontier. However, Paroh's attempts to reduce the Jewish population numerically proved ineffective, as their birth rate increased steadily. Taking a drastic approach, Paroh ordered the Hebrew midwives to kill

פרשת שמות

Parshas Shemos

JEWISH SUFFERING IN EGYPT

One who studies Jewish history may come to the conclusion that the Chosen People seem to have been chosen to suffer more than their due throughout the years. The Jews have undergone more banishment, pain, and humiliation than any other people. Their very beginnings in Egypt were marked by the anguish and torture of exile and slavery! What was the cause for this experience of misery in Egypt, and why has it been followed by so many similar examples in the years since?

There are a number of explanations for the suffering in Egypt. One concentrates on the basic error committed by the Israelites living in Egypt, an error committed by many following generations of Jews. Their mistake was their desire to assimilate into the alien society.

When the children of Yaakov first came to Egypt, they indicated that they intended to make their stay there a temporary one. However, they soon changed their attitude; instead of remaining sojourners, they became settlers. After all, Egypt was a flourishing nation full of riches. So they left their secluded community in Goshen and were soon to be found in all sections of Egypt. In this way, they made it easier for themselves to become as Egyptian as the Egyptians. They put themselves in danger of losing their separate Jewish identities and of forsaking the G-d of their fathers. It was because of this attempt to assimilate that they received their punishment. (Meshech Chochmoh, Vayikrah 26:44). Instead of accepting them as equals, the Egyptians turned on them and treated them like slaves. They could no longer make the mistake of forgetting that they were Jews, for the Egyptians would not let them.

Despite the lessons of Egypt, Jews have continued their attempts to assimilate, and they have continued to be punished for it. The Jews in the days of Esther were faced with annihilation at the hands of Haman. Why? Because they had attended King Achashveirosh's banquet to mingle with the local gentiles, showing a desire for non-Jewish influences and pleasures. It was only through their repentance that Hashem decided to save them. Similarly, the Jews at the time of the second Beis Hamikdosh were often influenced by Greek concepts and pastimes (the evils of Hellenism), and were in danger of forsaking their Jewish ways. They received the punishment of foreign domination, and it was only when the Maccabees reminded them of their separate national consciousness that they were able to regain independence.

During the past century, Jews have placed increasing emphasis on gaining entrance into the goyish society. Jews have adopted the gentile dress, the gentile methods of having fun, and the gentile goals for success. They have changed their names and their appearances to be able to mingle freely in the gentile world. But have the gentiles always accepted them as equals? Hardly. The drive towards assimilation first gathered steam in Russia and Germany. It was in these two countries that anti-Semitism was unleashed in its fullest fury, as we now tragically know.

Those who think that they can blend easily into gentile society are deluding themselves. The results can often be disastrous, as the Jews of Egypt learned.

Our Sages state: You shall be set apart. "For I, Hashem, your G-d, am Holy." Just as I am set apart so should you strive to be. "I have separated you from the peoples to be mine."—if you are separated from the peoples then you

the male infants at birth. However, fearing Hashem, the midwives disobeyed Paroh. Thereupon, he decreed that every newborn male should be drowned in the Nile.

Amram and Yocheved, members of the tribe of Levi, were parents of two children, Miriam and Aharon. Soon after Paroh's death edict, Yocheved gave birth to a second son. After Yocheved could no longer keep the news of this son's birth a secret, she placed him in an ark which she left among the reeds on the bank of the Nile (under Miriam's supervision). Paroh's daughter came to bathe in the Nile, saw the ark, and sent one of her maidens to fetch it. She realized that it was a Hebrew child and, touched with pity, decided to adopt it. Miriam came forward and, receiving the princess' permission to find a nurse, returned with Yocheved under whose care the boy was later taught the traditions of his ancestors. The boy was taken to the royal palace and was called Moshe (Moses), meaning "drawn out of the water."

After he had matured, Moshe went to be among his fellow Israelites and he

belong to me; otherwise, you belong to Nebuchadnezzar King of Babylon and his associates. (Sifrey, Kedoshim).

Another explanation for the suffering in Egypt is that the Israelites' travails were not so much a punishment as the refining and purification of the new Jewish nation. (Sefer Yalkut Meam Loaiz, Parshas Shemos). In this view, Egypt was the "iron furnace" (Devarim 20:6), which helped mold the Jews into a holy and cohesive people. Their impurities were removed and the experience gave them a common bond making them ready for Matan Torah. In this way, they were like iron, which must go through fire before it loses its dross and becomes hardened.

Fortitude strengthens industry and its fruit—Success. (Mussar Ha'philosophim)

"I have refined thee (Israel) in the crucible of affliction." (Isaiah 48).

A third approach to the misery in Egypt is that it helped the Jews to better appreciate Hashem's bountiful gifts. For the harder it is to achieve something, the more welcome it is when it is attained. After the suffering in Egypt, the Jews were in a position to fully value their freedom as a nation under Hashem's guidance. They were like a man who is allowed to eat after being starved the whole day, and they eagerly accepted the spiritual nourishment of the Torah.

Whatever the Holy One blessed be He gives man in this world, whether peace or suffering, is kindness on His part. (Kad HaKemah)

A certain young man once considered leaving Yeshiva. It was suggested to him that he consult the Chofetz Chaim, ZT'L, before making his final decision. The young man

agreed and traveled to Radin to the home of the Chofetz Chaim. When he entered the house, he saw the Chofetz Chaim pacing the floor, tearfully reciting T'hilim (Psalms). This did not seem in keeping with the peaceful atmosphere of the rest of the household. Inquiring about the source of the Chofetz Chaim's distress, he was told, "A stranger whose relative was ill came to ask the Chofetz Chaim to pray for the recovery of his relative."

Overwhelmed by this display of love for a fellow Jew who was a complete stranger, the young man realized that only the study of Torah could cultivate such powerful compassion, and he became a disciple of the Chofetz Chaim.

Even as a young boy, the Chofetz Chaim showed the kind of compassion for which he was renowned in later years. A group of mischievous children in his neighborhood would fill up the water-carrier's pails with water and leave them outside overnight to freeze. When the unfortunate man awoke in the morning, he had the difficult task of removing the frozen ice from the pails.

When young Yisroel Meir discovered the prank, he would go late at night to the well to empty the pails, thus saving the water-carrier much distress. (Der Chofetz Chaim, pg. 15)

When Rabbi Eliyahu Dushnitzer would walk up or down the steps of his Yeshiva at night near the rooms where the students slept, he would take off his shoes. He would say, "I might awaken one of the students with the noise of my steps, and that would be stealing sleep." (Nachalas Eliyahu, pg. 23)

The Holy one Blessed be He, said: "Since you treat the flock of mere flesh

observed their sufferings. He noticed an Egyptian overseer savagely beating one of the Hebrews. Seeing no one else around, Moshe killed the cruel Egyptian and buried his body in the sand. The next day, Moshe intervened in a quarrel between two Israelites. One of the two tauntingly asked Moshe what right he had to judge others and did he intend to kill them as he had already killed the Egyptian? It became instantly clear to Moshe that his deed was now known and that his life was in danger. Therefore, before Paroh could seize him, Moshe fled to Midian in the southeastern region of the Sinai Peninsula. He came to a well where he protected the seven daughters of Yisro (the spiritual leader of Midian) from unfriendly shepherds. He was welcomed by Yisro and tended his sheep. Moshe soon married his daughter Zipporah, who bore him two sons, Gershom and Eliezer.

During Moshe's stay in Midian, Paroh died. His successor continued the oppression of the Jews with an even greater severity, and the Israelites cried out to Hashem

and blood with such tenderness—By your life! You shall shepherd my flock, Israel!" (Shemos 3:1)
Abba Shaul commented: "Emulate His attributes. Just as He is compassionate, so must you be." (Shabbos 133)

MOSHE AS A LEADER

Why was it that Moshe was chosen by Hashem to be the leader of the Israelites at their time of crisis? What personal attributes did he have that made him most suitable for this task?

One hint of Moshe's leadership capabilities is given by the Torah statement that, as a young man, Moshe went out to his brethren and looked on their burden. This was no mere once-over glance. Rashi explains that Moshe directed his heart and mind to share the experiences of his fellow Jews. Although he himself enjoyed the privileges of a palace upbringing, he empathized with the plight of those Jews who were treated like slaves. This quality of concern for the commitment to others helped make Moshe an outstanding leader.

These same attributes were visible as well when Moshe became Yisro's shepherd. Not content to simply let the sheep wander off, Moshe ran after every stray sheep and treated it as he would his own. He exhibited this personal concern for both man and animals. (Shemos Rabbah 2:3). It is interesting that a number of Jewish leaders were originally shepherds. Another example was Dovid HaMelech. As a shepherd, Dovid made it a point to always bring the smaller sheep to pasture first so that they would be able to graze on the tender grass. Hashem decided that one who exhibited such care for His smaller creatures was fit to lead His chosen people.

Many other Jewish leaders likewise displayed this characteristic of personal concern. This was certainly true of Rav Yisroel Salanter, who arrived in shul one Yom Kippur eve unusually late. Later, Rav Salanter explained that on his way to shul he had heard a baby crying. He investigated and found that the infant was all alone inside a nearby house, with no one to care for it. The parents had apparently gone to shul themselves. Rav Salanter decided that he could not allow the baby to remain in misery. Therefore, he stayed and tried to comfort the infant until it was peacefully asleep, and only then had he come to shul. Though Rav Yisroel Salanter was a widely revered Torah leader, he hardly thought it beneath his dignity to care for a baby.

Another of Moshe's outstanding qualities was his *Anivus*, his modesty. Anyone else might have leaped at the chance to become the powerful leader of Bnei Yisroel, but Moshe declined the honor several times before he finally agreed to accept. He actually believed that he was not worthy of this great honor and that others could fill the post much better than he. However, it was for this very reason, his humility and lack of arrogance, that Hashem considered Moshe fit to be a leader of Israel.

Modesty has been a leading characteristic of many great Rabbonim, including Rabbi Akiva Eiger and Rav Yaakov of Lisa. These renowned Torah giants were once traveling together to town by coach. As they approached the town, they noticed a large group of Jews, apparently waiting to honor the visitors. Rabbi Akiva Eiger, noting the crowd, immediately assumed that the people had come to pay tribute to Rabbi Yaakov. Therefore, he slipped out of the coach and

for aid. While tending Yisro's sheep at Chorev, Moshe saw an extraordinary sight; a bush that was afire but was, nevertheless, not consumed. As Moshe turned to gaze at this wonder, Hashem addressed him for the first time and commanded him to remove his shoes, for he was standing on holy ground. Hashem then informed Moshe that he was to be Hashem's messenger to bring the Israelites out of Egypt and into the Promised Land. Moshe responded that he was unworthy of this awesome task, but he was assured of Divine assistance. Moshe then inquired as to what reply he should give when asked by the Israelites for G-d's name. Hashem replied that He could be revealed by the declaration, "Eyeh Asher Eyeh," "I will be what I will be." Moshe was then told to inform the Elders of Israel of Hashem's appearance, and that they were to demand that Paroh allow the Israelites to offer sacrifices to Hashem in the wilderness. Paroh would refuse, but after he had been smitten by Hashem's plagues he would be forced to relent, and the Israelites would leave Egypt laden with riches.

Moshe protested that he would not be believed by the people, whereupon he was

began helping to push the coach to its destination. At the very same time, Rabbi Yaakov came to the conclusion that the crowds had gathered to honor Rabbi Akiva Eiger, so he, too, slipped out of the coach and joined in pushing it. When the coach reached the crowd, the people were amazed to find the coach empty and the two Torah giants walking alongside it and pushing it! Then the people learned that each man had considered only the other worthy of honor, while feeling that he himself could not be the cause of any tributes. Naturally, this display of modesty by both Rabbonim only made the populace respect them all the more.

"With the Humble is wisdom."
(Yerushalmi Berachos)
He who runs after Honor, Honor shuns him. (Eruvim 136)
The wise man forfeits his wisdom through pride, the prophet, his gift of prophecy. (Pesachim 66)

THE BURNING BUSH THAT WAS NOT CONSUMED BY FIRE

How are we to understand the sight of a bush burning, yet not being consumed? Was this revelation through fire designed merely to attract Moshe's attention, to make him look up and stare? Was it intended to shock and prepare him for what was to come? In any event, the fact that this was a bush and that it did not burn up does not seem to have any special significance.

However, our Sages have given several interpretations for this unusual occurrence. Each one offers a different explanation why Hashem appeared specifically in a thornbush and why the bush did not burn up.

(Shemos Rabbah 2:5) They include the following:

1) The thornbush is a seemingly insignificant creation, small and apt to cause prickles of pain. Yet, it was from a thornbush that Hashem chose to appear to Moshe, rather than from the lofty peaks of a mountain. Hashem wanted to point out that even the lowliest of creations can miraculously become inflamed if filled with Divine sparks, a lesson that even the humblest of men can make history if filled with Hashem's holy spirit. In addition, Hashem demonstrated that He empathized with the children of Israel, who were at that time suffering as lowly slaves. So He appeared in a lowly thornbush, to emphasize His appreciation of their plight.

Rabbi Chanina ben Ida said: "Why are the words of the Torah compared to water? This is to teach you, just as water flows from a higher level to a lower, so too the words of the Torah endure only with him who is lowly. (Taanis 17)

2) If someone thrusts his hands into a thornbush, he suffers no pain for the thorns are bent downwards. However, if he tries to remove his hand, the thorns become imbedded in it. In this sense, the thornbush symbolized the Jews' experience in Egypt, which had at first welcomed them but which then refused to let them go.

The evil impulse has a sweet beginning and a bitter end. (Yerushalmi Shabbos 14:3)
Rav Assi stated: "The evil impulse is at the beginning like the thread of the spider but at the end like a rope." (Succah 52)

given the power to perform three miracles. His rod, when thrown on the ground, turned into a snake. Upon being seized by the tail, it returned to its original form. Then Moshe was told to place his hand on his chest. When he removed it, the hand was white with leprosy; yet, when he repeated this process, the hand emerged once again healthy. Finally, if the Israelites still remained unconvinced, Moshe was to pour water from the Nile onto dry land and the waters of the Nile were to change into blood. Moshe continued to hesitate, protesting that he lacked the necessary speaking ability. Hashem consequently informed him that his brother Aharon would serve as his spokesman.

Moshe was met by Aharon at Mount Chorev and Moshe told his brother all that had occurred. Upon reaching Egypt, they assembled the Elders of Israel and revealed to them the words of Hashem. After Moshe had performed the miracles, the Israelites voiced their belief that Hashem was responding to their cries for help and all bowed down to worship Him.

Moshe and Aharon appeared before Paroh and asked that he let the Jews go and deliver offerings to Hashem in the wilderness. Not only did Paroh reject this re-

3) The burning thornbush that was not consumed by fire was a way of assuring Moshe that the Jews of Egypt would not be destroyed. Just as the thornbush survived the power of the flames, so, too, would Bnei Yisroel emerge from the oppression in Egypt intact with the aid of Hashem.

> Just as the world cannot be without winds, so cannot the world be without Jews. (Avodah Zarah 10)
> Generations come and go, cruel edicts come and go, but Israel lives forever. (Sippurei Ha'Shalom)
> Israel had been promised: "No warring nation that is formed against you shall prosper." (Isaiah 44:17)

Not only did Egypt lack the means of destroying the Jews, but neither does any nation have the ability to completely annihilate Hashem's Chosen People. This is one of the reasons Jews are spread throughout the earth. (Pesachim 87b). If one nation persecutes its Jews, the Jews of another nation will still survive. Certainly many countries have done their best to rid the earth of Jews, but none have succeeded and none ever will. For the Jews have a special "weapon" on their side, as was pointed out by Rav Yehoshua. **The Roman Emperor Hadrian** once praised the resiliency of the Jews by remarking, "How great is the lamb who stands against seventy wolves!" But Rav Yehoshua replied, "How great is the Shepherd that guides and watches this lamb!" (Midrash Tanchuma, Parshas Toldos 5).

The Jews have witnessed many miraculous salvations throughout the ages and they will hopefully witness many more, if they deserve it. In this connection, it is written that if someone reads the Megillah backwards, he has not fulfilled the Mitzvah of Megillah. (Megillah 17a). What is the meaning of reading a Megillah backwards? One explanation is that if someone says that the events of the Megillah happened in the past but can no longer occur, then he is looking at the Megillah in a backwards manner and he has not fulfilled his obligation of believing in Hashem's eternal assistance. Hashem is always aware of plots against Jews, during any era, and He will continue to defend the Jews if they are worthy of His help.

One can never know how Hashem will send aid, and, therefore, one must always practice good deeds for they may someday prove directly beneficial. This is what occurred to the famed Nodeh B'Yehudah, Rav Yecheskel Landau. He once noticed a gentile boy shivering and crying in the winter cold. Rav Landau tried to calm the boy and asked what was the matter. The boy replied that he had been sent by his parents to sell some wares, but some local ruffians had stolen all the money he had made. He was now afraid to face his parents without a penny. Taking pity on the young boy, Rav Landau gave the boy some of his own money which the boy accepted most gratefully.

Many years later, on Erev Pesach, Rav Landau was preparing for the Seder when he heard a knock at the door. He opened the door to find a tall gentile youth there, a most uncommon sight. Rav Landau was afraid that the youth was there to rob him and was

quest, but he imposed even harsher decrees against the Jews. They would be expected to deliver the same number of bricks daily, but they would no longer be supplied with the straw that facilitated the brick building. The Hebrew foremen were flogged because their charges could not perform such an impossible task. Their appeal to Paroh for mercy was turned down and they accused Moshe and Aharon of worsening the situation. However, in response to Moshe's expressions of frustration, Hashem assured him that Paroh would eventually be compelled by the Divine might to let the people go.

about to shut the door when the young man said, "Don't you remember me, Rabbi? I am the boy you once comforted by giving money to in the street. And now I have come to return the favor which I have never forgotten. I overheard the non-Jewish bakers talking about how Jews always buy bread from them right after Pesach when they have none of their own. I heard the bakers say that this year they were planning to poison the bread and in this way kill all the Jews, and I thought you should know of this." Rav Landau thanked the youth and told his fellow Jews that because of a mistake in the calendar they should refrain from eating bread an additional day. When the bakers complained to the king that the Jews were not buying from them as they always did, Rav ‿andau said he would buy the bread, provided the bakers took a bite from it first. When the bakers showed a reluctance to do so, their evil plot was discovered. The Jews of the town were saved, thanks to Hashem's aid and Rav Yecheskel Landau's kindness to the gentile boy.

Hashem revealed Himself to Moshe as the One whose promises to the Patriarchs would now be fulfilled, for the Israelites would be redeemed from bondage and taken to the Promised Land. The Jews, crushed in spirit, refused to listen to Moshe when he delivered Hashem's message. This in turn frightened Moshe, for he wondered how the great Paroh would listen to him if his own brethren did not do so, especially when Moshe's speech was impaired. Again he was told that Aharon would be his spokesman and that Paroh would refuse to let the Jews go until Hashem had inflicted severe punishments upon the Egyptians.

פרשת
וארא
Parshas Vaeirah

DISPLAYING GRATITUDE (HAKORAS HATOV)

The Torah records that Moshe called upon Aharon to initiate the first three plagues upon the Egyptians; Blood (Dam), Frogs (Tzifardeia), and Lice (Kinim). Why did Moshe rely upon his brother for these acts? Wasn't Moshe the leader chosen by Hashem to confront Paroh?! Why did he not initiate these three plagues himself?

The answer lies in Moshe's desire to exhibit appreciation for past favors. All three of the above-mentioned plagues involved some slight hurting of the forces that had aided him in the past. For instance, the plague of Blood caused the waters to become unusable. These same waters of the Nile had once saved Moshe's life, for it was on their shores that Moshe's mother hid him from Paroh. Similarly, the plague of Lice was produced from the ground. Yet, this same dust of the earth had once protected Moshe by hiding from view the Egyptian that Moshe had killed. Therefore, because the waters and the earth had proved beneficial to him, Moshe reciprocated by showing his gratitude to them and he refrained from starting plagues involving them. He let Aharon bring about these plagues, instead, for he believed in being thankful to forces that had helped him in the past. (Shemos 13:18, Rashi).

Gratitude is one of the pillars that sustains human society. Without it, we would be cold, insensitive individuals; with it, we can establish satisfying relationships with

Moshe was eighty years old and Aharon eight-three years old when they set forth to carry out their mission. Knowing that Paroh would be impressed by a wondrous manifestation, Aharon cast down his rod before the Egyptian leader and it turned into a serpent. However, the Egyptian magicians were able to duplicate this feat. Even though Aharon's rod swallowed the magicians' rods, Paroh remained unimpressed.

The first plague was now brought upon Egypt. After warning Paroh of what was to happen, Aharon followed Moshe's instructions and waved his rod over the Nile and its waters, canals, and reservoirs. All of them became rivers of blood. The fish died, and this created an unbearably foul odor. The Egyptians, faced with a lack of water, were forced to beseech the Jews for some, for the plague had no effect upon the water of the Jews. The plague continued for seven days. Since the miracle was again duplicated by the Egyptian magicians, Paroh retained his stubborn attitude.

Consequently, Paroh ignored the threat of a plague of frogs. Once again, Aharon stretched his hand over the Nile and frogs swarmed over the land. Paroh pleaded

others. By being grateful, one rewards those who had aided him. He shows that he recognizes their efforts rather than taking them for granted. How many individuals simply expect assistance from their parents, their teachers and their friends? How many demand something from others as a matter of course and then don't bother to thank them when assistance is given? If they would stop and think of all the favors they are receiving, the care and sustenance provided by their parents, the wisdom imparted by their teachers, the kindness showed by their friends, their uncaring attitudes might be different. What would they do if these helpers were not around?

Rabbi Levi of Berditchev was one who made his feelings of gratitude very clear. When he arrived at a small town one evening, he found himself without lodgings. He was forced to trudge from house to house seeking shelter. However, because no one knew who this stranger was, he was turned away from each home. There remained only one rather run-down residence and Rabbi Levi was not too optimistic about his being accepted there. Nevertheless, he knocked at the door and when it was opened, he repeated his request for a night's lodging.

"Well, I am only a poor man with few furnishings," was the reply. "But if you wouldn't mind staying in a poor man's home, it would be an honor for me to welcome you."

Rabbi Levi gladly accepted the invitation and thanked the man profusely when he left the next day.

Some years later, when Rabbi Levi had become known far and wide as a saintly Sage, he again paid a visit to the town. The townsfolk, who were now aware of the identity and fame of their visitor, gathered before him and competed for the honor of having this Torah leader lodge with them. But Rabbi Levi shook his head.

"I will stay with the poor man at the edge of town, if he will admit me," he announced. "It was he who took me in the last time and it is to him that I must express my everlasting gratitude. Once someone performs a favor for you, you must never forget it."

Sometimes, one gets an opportunity to show his gratitude many years after the favor. A certain yeshiva student, new to the school, moved into the yeshiva's dormitory. Unfortunately, his behavior was not of the best and his antics caused many disturbances in the dormitory. It was decided that, while the student could continue his studies in the yeshiva, he would have to live elsewhere. But where would he find lodging? The school authorities were stumped until they received a surprise offer. The Rosh Yeshiva himself suggested that the student live in his own house and dine with his own family!

The offer created quite a stir. Why would the Rosh Yeshiva take such a special interest in a student who had proved so disruptive? Soon, though, the reason became known. When the Rosh Yeshiva had himself been a young man, he had studied in a yeshiva that had been founded by the rebellious student's great-grandfather. Though the Rosh Yeshiva had never known the founder of the yeshiva, he nevertheless felt a sense of gratitude towards him. Now, at last, he had found the means to express it, by welcoming

with Moshe to stop the plague's effects and promised to reciprocate by allowing the people to leave and sacrifice to Hashem. As soon as Moshe prayed to Hashem, the plague ceased. However, Paroh steadfastly refused to fulfill his promise.

Aharon then struck the dust with his rod and the dust turned into lice which swarmed over man and beast. This time, the Egyptian magicians were unable to do likewise and they were forced to admit the superiority of Hashem's power. Nevertheless, Paroh's heart remained hardened towards the Jews.

Moshe warned Paroh that swarms of wild animals would invade the homes of the Egyptians, but that the land of Goshen, where the Jews lived, would be unaffected. Paroh remained obstinate. However, the devastation caused by this fourth plague forced him to agree to let the Israelites sacrifice to Hashem in the land of Egypt. Moshe, though, demanded that the Jews be allowed to journey for three days into the wilderness to offer sacrifices, to escape any harrassment by the Egyptians. Paroh yielded, but as soon as the plague was halted, he again refused to let the Jews leave.

Moshe then warned that Murrain (A Cattle Plague) would devastate Egypt (again

---

the unruly student into his own home. And this favor, given in return for a previous favor, had a very gratifying effect, for the student who had caused so much trouble eventually became a highly-respected Rabbi in his own right.

Naturally, we should express our ultimate gratitude to the One who created us and supplied us with all our needs and happiness, Hashem Yisborach. We can never take for granted the benefits that Hashem provides. It is for this reason that we daven to Him daily, and utter blessings over the food that we eat. In this way, we will never forget His unceasing kindness. (Rambam, Hilchos Berachos, Perek 1 Halachah 3).

> *The whole world is fed by the benevolence of Hashem. (Berachos 17)*
> *You are truly a true G-d, though I have not seen you; but I have at all times experienced the abundance of Your Grace.*

BECHIRA (FREE WILL)

Though Hashem oversees all earthly events, He has graced each human with the gift of Free Will. Men are not robots. They have the ability to make a choice between right and wrong, between good and evil. Because of this, we are responsible for the decisions and actions we take, and we are rewarded and punished accordingly. (Rambam, Hilchos Tshuvah, Pereks 5, 6).

However, the principle of Free Will seems to be contradicted by the case of Paroh. Every time a plague ceased, Paroh became stronger in his opposition to the Jews' departure. It would seem that Hashem removed Paroh's ability to decide to let the Jews go.

Did Paroh lack the power of Free Will?

Not really. Actually, anyone who saw the ten plagues in Egypt no longer had the free will to deny Hashem's existence. Who else but Hashem could have the power to perform these miracles? To counteract this influence, Hashem restored the power of Free Will to Paroh. He was given the ability to make his decision on whether to let the Jews go regardless of Hashem's obvious presence. It was under these conditions that Paroh, entirely on his own and with full power of decision, decided not to let the Jews of Egypt go.

> *When there is no free will there are no good and evil impulses. (Karo, Toldos Yitzchok)*
> *Proof of man's intelligence is his freedom of choice.*
> *The wicked are ruled by their heart, the righteous rule their heart. (Bereishis Rabbah 34)*
> *The wicked do not repent even at the threshold of Gehenam. (Eruvin 19)*

THE MAKOS (PLAGUES)

Hashem devastated Egypt with many different plagues (Makos). Why was it necessary to bring so many plagues upon the Egyptians? Wouldn't one powerful plague have been sufficient?

The answer lies in the fact that the 'Makos' had a two-fold purpose: to punish the Egyptians and to impress the Jews. Through the plagues, Hashem made it crystal clear to the Jews that it was not a one-shot accident of nature that caused their freedom from Egypt, but a well-planned,

sparing Goshen) if Paroh would not capitulate. Paroh refused to budge and the murrain hit with full fury, causing the Egyptians' cattle to die while the cattle of the Jews were not harmed. Still, Paroh remained unmoved.

Next, Moshe sprinkled ashes towards the heavens, in Paroh's presence. The ashes turned into dust and this caused an epidemic of painful boils to erupt among man and beast alike. Paroh's magicians were likewise affected but Paroh did not change his mind.

Paroh was then told that if he did not relent, Egypt would be hit by a torrent of hail which would cause calamity for the crops and the remaining cattle. He was advised to shelter both people and animals to save them from death. Some of the Egyptians heeded the warning and shielded themselves and their cattle. Then Moshe stretched his rod towards the heaven and a terrible storm of thunder, lightning and hail raged over Egypt (except for Goshen), killing man and beast and destroying crops. (The hail was of an unusual nature. It was composed of fire on the interior and ice on the exterior, and was as huge as a boulder). This time Paroh openly acknowledged his error, but when the storm ceased, his heart once more turned to stone.

Heavenly-caused series of events. Hashem wanted to demonstrate for all time that He is prepared to come to the aid of the Jews whenever they deserve His assistance, and for this we must be eternally grateful.

Another demonstration of His Divine intervention to save us, somewhat camouflaged in the guise of nature, occurred during the time of King Chizkiyahu, during the time of the first Beis Hamikdosh. Sancheirev, the leader of the Assyrian army, appeared at the gates of Jerusalem, ready to conquer the Jewish nation. The Assyrians had no doubt whatsoever that they would easily be victorious against the weak Israelite army. However, they did not reckon with Hashem's opposition. That night, while they slept, the soldiers of the Assyrian army were suddenly struck down by a plague. The army was so devastated that Sancheirev was forced to flee and his well-laid plans of conquest turned into a rout. Once again, as in Egypt, the Jews had escaped an apparently overpowering enemy, through Hashem's help.

Sometimes Hashem's assistance is given directly to individuals. One such case happened during the dark days of World War I. A conquering colonel decided to show off his power by ordering a Rav to bathe with women. The Rav, well aware of the halochos against this, refused, and the colonel vowed to kill him. When the townsfolk heard this, they pleaded with the Rav to flee for his life. However, the Rav replied that he had full faith in Hashem who had saved the Jews of Egypt at their time of need, and who, he prayed, would save him as well. Just as the Rav was engaged in fervent prayer, the colonel rode through the town and, furiously noting the Rav's presence, came charging towards him. Just as he was about to make a lunge at the Rav with his sword, the colonel's horse stumbled to the ground. The colonel was thrown high into the air and landed on his sword, dying instantly. The Rav knew that this miracle had been engineered by none other than Hashem, and his thanks to the Almighty never ceased until the end of his life.

It is G-d who ultimately contrives that the sinner go forward to meet his own punishment. (Meleches Machsheves) The physician's error is the Creator's design.

After Moshe warned Paroh that on the following day a plague of locusts would destroy Egypt's crops, Paroh's courtiers urged him to let the Israelite men depart. However, Moshe and Aharon insisted that the women, children, and flocks of the Israelites also be allowed to leave. As a result, they were driven from Paroh's presence. The next day Moshe extended his rod, and an east wind carried into Egypt a swarm of locusts which devoured the country's vegetation. After witnessing this disaster, Paroh admitted his error and begged Moshe and Aharon to pray for the removal of

פרשת
בא
Parshas
Bo

MESIRAS NEFESH: OFFERING ONE'S LIFE FOR HASHEM

Hashem was willing to save the Jews from their Egyptian captivity. But were the Jews ready to accept Hashem as their G-d? How would Hashem know, for man has Free Will with respect to fear of G-d. How could Hashem be sure of the Jews' loyalty?

There was really only one way to be sure. If the Jews would offer to sacrifice their own lives for the sake of Hashem's word, they would be worthy of His assistance. It was for this reason that Hashem asked them to prepare the Korban Pesach, the Pascal sacrifice, publicly. First they were to procure the lamb, then lead it through the streets, and then slaughter it and sprinkle its blood on their doorposts. The reason for this very noticeable process was that the lamb was considered a god by the Egyptians. Only one who was willing to put himself in jeopardy and face possible Egyptian hostility by sacrificing the Egyptian god could show complete adherence to Hashem's commands. By bringing the Korban Pesach, the Jews indicated that they deserved the deliverance from Egypt.

The bringing of the Korban Pesach had the beneficial effect of reminding Hashem of another Jew who had put his progeny and his happiness on the line, Avrohom Ovinu. It was Avrohom who had willingly agreed to sacrifice his son Yitzchak, and Yitzchak himself complied with the preparations for his own death. By proving that they, too, were willing to die for Hashem, the Israelites showed that they were on the holy level of Avrohom and Yitzchak.

Kiddush Hashem—martyrdom—ranks even higher than the most profound mastery of the Torah. Rav Papa asked Abaye why miracles were not in his generation just the same as it was to the previous ones. He answered: "My son, the former ones gave their lives for the holiness of His name; We do not give our lives for the holiness of His name." (Berachos 20)

In addition, the blood of the Korban Pesach, placed by the Jews on their doorposts, demonstrated that within the house lived a Jewish family, who were not to be harmed by the Makas Bechoros (Death of the Firstborn). Because they had performed the Mitzvah of the Korban Pesach, the Jews were spared a great tragedy.

A similar tale of one saved by the performance of a Mitzvah is told of the wife of Rav Hershele who had gone to the Meoras Ha Machpela to say Tehillim. While fervently immersed in her prayers, she forgot to keep track of the time, and found, to her dismay, that she had been locked in the cave with no way out. She was frightened, and in terror tried to grope for an exit.

Suddenly the cave shone with a brilliant illumination. She turned to its source and saw an old man standing before her, wearing a crown and carrying a small Sefer Torah and a lamp. The man said that he was Dovid HaMelech and that because she had recited his Tehillim so sincerely he had come to assist her.

Leading her step by step, he guided her through the labyrinth to the exit from which she was able to make her way home in safety. Once again, the performance of a Mitzvah had proved to be its own reward.

THE TRUE WEALTH

After Hashem told Avrohom Ovinu that his descendants would suffer greatly as slaves in Egypt, He promised that they would "go forth with great abundance of wealth" as free men.

Our Sages tell us that this "great abun-

the plague. They complied and a strong west wind drove the locusts into the Red Sea. However, once again Paroh reverted to his stubbornly negative attitude.

Moshe then brought the next plague upon the Egyptians, a total darkness, which descended upon the Egyptians for 6 days, 3 of which they were unable to move about. Only the Israelites were granted light within their dwellings. The resulting nightmarish chaos proved too much for Paroh to cope with, and he now offered to allow all Israelites—men, women, and children—to leave, provided the flocks and herds were left behind as surety that the Israelites would return. Moshe rejected this stipulation and Paroh forbade him to appear again in the royal presence. Moshe replied that there would be one final, devastating plague; one that would cost all Egyptian firstborn their lives. Moshe and Aharon then departed for the last time.

Hashem informed Moshe that the redemption was near and that henceforth the year would begin with the month of their deliverance (Nissan). On the tenth of this month, each head of a household was to set aside an unblemished male lamb to be kept until the evening of the fourteenth day, when it was to be sacrificed. Some of its blood was then to be smeared on the lintel and doorposts of the house as a sign that the inhabitants were Israelites. That night the meat of the sacrifice was to be eaten when roasted with unleavened bread and bitter herbs. Any of it remaining in the morning was to be burnt. Furthermore, it was to be consumed in haste and the

dance" refers to the Torah they received at Har Sinai. But if this were so, why were Bnei Yisroel commanded to ask the Egyptians for money and jewels before leaving Egypt?

The Maggid of Dubno answers this apparent problem with the following Moshol:

A young man had hired himself out to a wealthy merchant for six years. At the end of his service, he would receive a bag of silver coins. When the six years had elapsed, it occurred to the master that a bag of silver was too small a reward for the splendid services the servant had rendered him. He, therefore, put the silver aside and instead wrote out a check in an amount many times that of the total value of the silver coins. However, when he saw the check, the servant looked very despondent and he glumly stuffed the check into his pockets. He had been promised silver coins and he now felt cheated.

The next day, the young man's father called at the merchant's house and said, "You have been most generous to my son and I want to thank you. But my son is still young and he doesn't understand the value of a check. He expected to receive a bag with shiny new coins and got a plain sheet of paper instead. I would be most grateful, therefore, if you would let him have at least part of his wages in silver."

In the same manner, Avrohom approached Hashem and said, "You have in-

deed been generous in promising the Torah to my descendants. But the Israelite nation will be too young and inexperienced to understand the value of the Torah, and if they emerge from slavery empty-handed, they will say, 'It is true that Hashem fulfilled one part of His promise; we did become slaves. But what about the great abundance He promised us at the hour of our deliverance?' "

It was for this reason that Bnei Yisroel were commanded to take gold and silver from the Egyptians. This way, they would be leaving with tangible wealth, something they could appreciate at that time, more than the Torah. It was only as Israel grew in wisdom that she came to understand that true wealth lay not in the coins and trinkets gathered in Egypt, but in Hashem's gift of the Torah which has ensured our survival and moral richness to this very day.

R. Chanania ben Akashia said: "The Holy one blessed be He, desired to give Israel an opportunity for achieving merit; He, therefore, heaped on them Torah and Mitzvos." (Makos 23)

The reward of a 'mitzvoh' is not in this life. (Kiddushin 39)

"AND YOU SHALL TELL YOUR CHILDREN"

Part of the observance of Pesach, in fact, the basis for reciting the Hagodoh, is recoun-

participants were to be prepared to start on a journey. That night would be the one when Hashem would smite all the Egyptian firstborn but would spare those in houses sprinkled with the lamb's blood. In the future, this festival was to be observed annually as Pesach, a permanent reminder of the deliverance from Egypt. Only unleavened bread was to be eaten for seven days, and the first and seventh days of the festival were to be observed as days of holy assembly when all work would be forbidden. The sacrifice of the Pesach offering was to be observed in Canaan after the conquest, and its significance was to be explained to the future generations.

At midnight exactly, Hashem smote all Egyptian firstborn, both man and animal. Paroh and his fellow Egyptians rose in the middle of the night to bitterly lament their loss. They then asked that the Israelites leave, as Hashem had predicted, speaking not from a position of power, but from one of subjugation.

The Israelites left in such haste that their leavened dough had no time to rise. (As a result, Jews have been eating unleavened bread, or Matzoh, on Pesach ever since.) There were six hundred thousand men who began the journey and they brought with them their wives and children. They also carried a large supply of gold and silver, which the Egyptians had given them. The Jews were ordered to bring a Kor-

ting the story of Pesach to children. The unusual foods and customs at the Seder are meant to prompt questions from the children, and we must respond to these questions, regardless of the source.

The bright, righteous child is eager to learn and tries to comprehend the commandments of Pesach. He wants to know the reasons for all of the Mitzvos. We reply to him that the Mitzvos and the observances we keep are in recognition of and in appreciation for the wonders that Hashem performed on our behalf in Egypt. (Hagodoh Shel Pesach). Jews must be especially careful in satisfying the curiosity of their children, and in serving the Torah. They are essential links in the chain that keeps Torah tradition strong and growing. Parents who raise a child properly are considered the real heroes of Jewish survival and their work can never be sufficiently praised.

Reb Chiya was one who recognized this. His wife did not have a very agreeable personality and it was difficult for anyone to get along easily with her. Nevertheless, whenever Rav Chiya saw an item that he thought she would like, he would purchase it and bring it to her as a gift.

Noticing this, Rav asked him, "She is always annoying you. Why do you bring her so many presents?"

"I know she is a difficult woman," replied Rav Chiya. "Yet she has raised our children, and for that alone she is worthy of all the treasures in the world." (Yevamos 63).

Sometimes when raising a child, it is necessary to discipline and admonish him. This is indicated in the story of the wicked son, who asks, "What is all this labor to you?" This question shows that he considers himself separate from the Jewish nation and considers the observation of Pesach as a mere task. In reply, he is told, "If you had been in Egypt at the time of the redemption, you and those like you would not have been saved. You would have remained in Egypt and died there." In fact, this is what happened to the wicked Israelites in Egypt. They enjoyed Egyptian life and did not want to leave, so they perished along with the Egyptians during the plague of darkness. (Shemos 13:18, Rashi). Because it was so dark, the Egyptians did not know that the Israelites were also dying.

Rav Yitzchok Elchonon Spector knew how to admonish a Jew who was unfaithful to his religion. A free-thinker once met Rav Spector on the train and confessed that he was surprised to find that the Rav was so Orthodox, for he had always thought he was a modern Jew, not an old-fashioned one.

"On the contrary," replied Rav Spector, "I am of the modern generation. It is you who are the old-fashioned one!"

"In what way?" asked the free-thinker.

"Very simply," said Rav Spector. "On Pesach we read in the Hagodoh: In the beginning our ancestors were idol worshippers!"

Parents certainly have a powerful and im-

bon Pesach every year on the fourteenth day of Nissan. The Jews were commanded to redeem their firstborn male child in all future generations, and to wear Tefillin "for a sign on your hand and for a memorial between your eyes" to remind them of the salvation from Egypt.

portant influence on the upbringing and eventual character of their children. The Seder on Pesach is a reminder for them to always raise their children in a manner loyal to Hashem and His Torah.

> He that brings up the child is called "father", not the one who begets the child. (Shemos Rabbah 46)
> The world is preserved only by the innocence of the school children. (Shabbos 119)

> Instruct the child in that to which he is inclined: even in his old age will he not part from it. (Mishley 22)
> The one who teaches his neighbor's child the Torah, it is as if he had himself begotten him. (Sanhedrin 99)
> Rabbi Neharia said: "I put aside all the crafts in the world and I teach my son only Torah." (Kiddushin 82)

W hen the Israelites left Egypt, Hashem did not lead them to Canaan by the direct route, through the land of the Phillistines, lest they encounter hostile armies there and come to regret their departure. Instead, the people journeyed in the opposite direction led by a pillar of cloud by day and a pillar of fire by night. Moshe did not forget to take the remains of Yoseph with him, as Yoseph had been promised. The Israelites had reached Etham on the edge of the wilderness when they were commanded to turn back and camp by the Red Sea. There, Paroh would pursue them, thinking they were

פרשת בשלח

Parshas Beshalach

THE MIRACLE OF THE YAM SUF (RED SEA)

There are always those who will deny the existence of miracles. They claim that the works of Hashem are simply natural phenomena. This was the attitude that many non-believers assumed in regard to the splitting of the Red Sea. It was caused by an earthquake, they might claim; it was just a freak accident of nature.

To forestall any such beliefs, Hashem magnified the miracle of the Yam Suf. He split not only the Red Sea, but also all the waters in the world. (Shemos 14:21, Rashi). Even water that was in a cup gravitated to two separate sides! Because of this, no one could deny that the splitting of the Yam Suf was a true miracle, a true Act of G-d, just as were all the plagues in Egypt.

As Bnei Yisroel were standing at the shores of the Yam Suf, watching their enemy draw closer by the minute, they seemed petrified. What could they do? Then one of the greatest among them, Nachshon ben Aminodov, stepped forward and jumped into the waters of the Yam Suf, fully

confident that Hashem would save him. At the very moment that he touched the waters, they parted, and the Israelites walked through them. (Sotah 37a). It was Nachshon's unwavering faith in Hashem that led directly to the miracle that saved the Jews.

This is but one of the many examples of Jews standing at the edge of disaster, watching the enemy approaching and yet, because of their faith in Hashem, surviving intact.

Another such example was provided by Rabbi Shimon ben Gamliel. When his son was born, there existed harsh decrees against the Jews, one of which prohibited the Bris Milah. Those who performed a Bris on their children were threatened with death. Nevertheless, Rabbi Shimon ben Gamliel went ahead with the ceremony.

The emperor soon heard rumors that Rabbi Shimon had disobeyed the law, and summoned him for a trial. On their way to the trial, Rabbi Shimon and his wife stopped at an inn and befriended a noble aristocratic family who were lodging there. The wife of

trapped in the wilderness, but Hashem would again provide their salvation.

As soon as the Jewish people had left, Paroh regretted letting them go. He assembled his whole army, which consisted of many soldiers and chariots, and pursued the Israelites. The Egyptians were soon at the heels of the Israelites who panicked and complained bitterly to Moshe. "It would have been much better for us to serve in Egypt than to die in the wilderness," they cried. However, Moshe assured them that Hashem would once again fight for them. The guiding pillar of cloud moved to their rear, creating a veil of darkness that hindered the Egyptian advance. Moshe, at Hashem's bidding, stretched out his hand over the Red Sea and a strong east wind blew and divided the water. This enabled the Israelites to cross the sea on dry land. The Egyptians followed them into the seabed but were thrown into confusion by Hashem. Their chariot wheels became stuck in the wet sand. Then Moshe stretched out his hand over the sea again, and the waters began to flow over the Egyptian army drowning the Egyptians and their animals.

A song of triumph was sung by Moshe and the children of Israel in which they praised Hashem's infinite power in destroying the enemy. He would guide Israel safely into Canaan whose inhabitants were terror-stricken upon hearing of the Egyptian destruction.

The Jewish march continued southwards through the wilderness of Shur to a place called Marah (Bitterness), so named because of its bitter waters. The people, their mouths parched with thirst, murmured against Moshe. He in turn was shown a tree which when thrown into the waters, made them sweet. The Israelites refreshed themselves and then moved on to the oasis of Elim.

the aristocrat had also just given birth to a child, and when she heard of Rabbi Shimon's plight, she offered to temporarily exchange her son for his.

Therefore, when ordered to present his baby, Rabbi Shimon displayed an obviously uncircumcized son. The charges against him were dismissed, and his child grew up to become the great Sage, Rabbi Yehuda Hanassi (Tosfos, Avodah Zarah 10b).

> *Everyone has to regard the miracles done to the nation in the past as of direct relevance. The Talmud states: "Anyone who reads the Megillah backwards, has not fulfilled his duty." On this, Baruch of Meziboz used to say: Just as everyone must look upon himself as if he himself had been delivered from Egypt, so, too, everyone must feel as if he had been through the miracle of Mordechai and Haman. (Sippurei Hassidim)*

MASSAH MERIVAH

Bnei Yisroel had left Egypt. They were now in the wilderness, and would journey there for the next forty years. Soon, they began complaining to Moshe that they would have been better off if they had died in Egypt rather than in the desert. One of

their complaints was the lack of water to drink. Hashem responded by telling Moshe to hit a rock, which caused water to flow from it.

We can well imagine that Hashem responded angrily to this incident. Hashem had performed miracle after miracle for the Israelites, and the only way they saw fit to thank Him for His efforts was to complain! In fact, they said they would rather have died in Egypt! Consequently, Hashem caused Amalek to attack them, as punishment for their not having had full faith in Him.

This is similar to a father who put his son onto his shoulders to protect the boy from the dangers of the road. The two traveled for a way, and then a man passed by. "Have you seen my father?" the boy asked this third individual.

Upon hearing this, the father became angry and said, "I have been carrying you single-handed all this way, and you didn't even appreciate it, or realize I was there!" As a result, the father ordered the son to dismount, and the boy began walking by himself. A moment later, a dog came and bit him (Shemos 17:8, Rashi).

In the case of Bnei Yisroel, the dog was the tribe of Amalek, who attacked the un-

Proceeding inland, they entered the wilderness of Sinai one month after their departure from Egypt. Soon the lack of food made them wish that they died amid the luxuries of Egypt. Hashem made it known that He would cause bread to rain from the heavens for them and would test whether they would obey His law. In the evening, migratory birds called quails came to the camp, and in this way the people were provided with meat. In the morning, the ground was covered with Mun (manna), which had the taste of whatever its consumer desired. The Israelites were commanded to gather no more than an Omer (a measurement of just under four pints) of Mun per person every day. However, on the sixth day a double portion was to be gathered to provide food for the Sabbath as well, when no work was permitted. An omer of Mun was placed in an earthenware pot kept before the Ark in the Mishkon, a testimonial to Hashem's kindness.

At Rephidim, which lay further south, the people again quarreled with Moshe complaining of a lack of water. At Hashem's bidding, Moshe struck the rock on nearby Mt. Horeb with the staff he had used in Egypt, and streams of water gushed forth allowing the people to drink to their hearts' content. The place where this miracle occurred was called Massah-Meriva.

The tribe of Amalek attacked the Israelites at Rephidim. The Israelites, led by Yehoshua, fought back. While the war raged, Moshe ascended to the top of the hill holding his staff. He was accompanied by Aharon and Chur. They supported his hands when he became tired, for Israel prevailed only when Moshe held up his hands praying to Hashem. The battle lasted until sunset, and Amalek was decisively defeated. Moshe was told to record this incident and impress its occurrence upon Yehoshua, who would lead the Israelites into Canaan. Because of their treachery in

grateful son (Bnei Yisroel) of the unappreciated father (Hashem).

The Jews certainly have much for which to be eternally grateful to Hashem. It would be extremely disastrous for us to deny appreciation, and to instead complain to Hashem about what we do not have. If we take this attitude, the dogs of punishment will swiftly be upon us.

The archer is shot with his own arrow and is repayed with his own action. (Pesachim 28)

G-d steers the sinner to meet his own punishment. (Maleches Machsheves)

THE MUN

Every morning, the Mun, manna, dropped down from the heavens at the command of Hashem. Every Jew was ordered to collect only a set amount of Mun per person; no amount was to be left over and no extra amounts were to be taken. Whatever Mun was left over began to rot and serve as a breeding place for worms. The reason for this was that those who took more than they were told to were exhibiting a lack of faith in Hashem. Hashem had said that this certain amount of Mun would be sufficient and that the Mun would appear daily. Those who

took more indicated that they did not trust His word. They did not believe that the Mun would reappear the next day, as they were told. However, they were wrong. Whoever believes today that Hashem will not come to the aid of the Jews is just as wrong.

In fact, Hashem is always performing miracles for His people. The fact that the Jews are still in existence after hundreds of years of exile and persecution is in itself a miracle. (Chovos Halvovos, Shar HaBchena). So are many of the daily events of life. Take the rain cycle. Without rain, crops cannot grow and man would starve. But this does not usually occur. The waters of the seas constantly evaporate, causing the creation of clouds in the atmosphere, which in turn leads to the falling of the rain. The rain drops water into the seas, which again leads to evaporation, and the cycle continues indefinitely.

The problem is that, like the Jews of the desert, we often take these daily miracles for granted. They happen all the time, so we do not bother to think about them. It is important to really take the time to appreciate all the marvels of Hashem's nature and to perceive that miracles are actually happening at all times.

attacking Israel, the tribe of Amalek was to be totally destroyed and its memory eradicated.

> *Hashem told Iyov: "I have created countless raindrops in the clouds; for each one, I have its own source. Were drops to issue from a single source, they would dissolve the soil and it would not produce fruit. I have never failed to distinguish between one raindrop and another." (Iyov 25)*

פרשת
יתרו
Parshas
Yisro

While Moshe had carried out his mission in Egypt, his family had returned to Midian. Now that the Bnei Yisroel were in the Midbar, Moshe's father-in-law, Yisro (Jethro), brought his daughter, Zipporah, and Moshe's sons to Rephidim. Moshe welcomed Yisro affectionately and related all that Hashem had done for the Jews. His father-in-law fully acknowledged Hashem's power and offered sacrifices to Him. Observing that Moshe was overburdened with judicial duties, Yisro advised his son-in-law to appoint judges to assist him, while concentrating only on the difficult

THE TORAH IS GIVEN ON HAR SINAI

The Medrash states that when Hashem decided to give the Torah to Bnei Yisroel, all the mountains of the desert vied with each other for the honor of being the site for this great event. Each thought itself the most fitting setting for the giving of the Torah. Only one mountain, Mt. Sinai, did not make any such claim. It felt itself unworthy of being selected for such greatness. Yet, when Hashem made His decision, He chose Mt. Sinai, a lowly site for the transmission of the Torah. In this manner, Hashem demonstrated to all of mankind the importance of modesty and humility, in contrast to overbearing self-confidence and pride. This, certainly, is the path preached in the Torah.

In addition, Hashem wanted all of mankind to note that the Torah was presented in the most barren of areas, a desert. Through this, man was to observe that the Torah can provide its own glories and does not require the trappings of a shiny exterior to appear great. Similarly, a person is judged on the basis of his inner qualities rather than on the gaudy exterior he presents. He should, therefore, seek the road to internal righteousness and avoid searching for materialistic goals. The Torah, rather than money and luxuries, can provide all the satisfaction he needs.

R. Yose ben Kisma said: *"If you should give me all the silver and gold, precious stones and pearls that are in the world, I would not dwell anywhere except in a place of Torah; for in the hour of departure of a man from the world there accompanies him neither gold nor silver, nor precious stones nor pearls, but Torah and good deeds alone. (Avos 6) If, for the sake of study, one abases himself as the desert that everyone treads upon, his learning will endure. (Eruvin 54)*

The daughter of an emperor once approached a Torah Sage who had a rather homely appearance and asked, "Why did G-d insert so much wisdom into such an ugly vessel?"

The Torah Sage replied by asking, "Where do you keep your wine?"

"In earthen vessels," was the response.

"But why not keep the wine in precious gold containers which would be more fitting for the delicious wine?"

The princess thought this over and decided it was a proper suggestion. She immediately went home and transferred all the wine in the royal household from earthen to gold containers. Two weeks later, she held a party and she ordered that the butlers carry in the wine in their new, glistening containers. However, at their very first taste, all the guests came to the same conclusion; the wine had turned sour. The golden vessels had looked magnificent but they had provided poor protection for the wine.

The princess went directly to the Sage the

cases. Moshe acted on this sage advice and Yisro returned to Midian.

On the first day of the third month (Sivan) after they had departed from Egypt, the Bnei Yisroel arrived in the wilderness of Sinai and camped in front of the mountain. Moshe approached the mountain and heard the voice of Hashem instructing him to remind the people of how He had delivered them from Egypt. If they obeyed Him, they would be transformed into a "kingdom of priests and a holy nation." Moshe descended from the mountain and repeated Hashem's words to the Elders and to the people. A united nation responded, "All that the L-rd has spoken we will do!" Moshe reported these words to Hashem and was told that Hashem would appear in a thick cloud and speak to him before the entire assembly of Jews. That way, His Divine mission would never again be doubted. The people were to prepare themselves for three days in anticipation of the great event of the acceptance of the Torah. They were not to touch the boundaries around the mountain under penalty of death.

After these three days had elapsed, and the sixth of Sivan had arrived, thunder and lightning erupted and a dense cloud descended on the mountain. The call of the trumpet was heard and Moshe brought the people to the foot of the mountain. Mount Sinai was enveloped in smoke and Hashem summoned Moshe to its summit. Hashem bade him to warn the Bnei Yisroel not to gaze upon the Divine Manifestation. Moshe did as ordered.

Then followed the supreme moment in the history of the world. The voice of

next day and asked what had happened. "What you have just witnessed," replied the Sage, "is how unimportant outward appearances are. The earthen containers may have appeared drab, but they kept the wine tasting sweet, something that the shiny gold vessels could not do, for all their splendor. The same is true of the appearance of humans. Some individuals might look fair of form and face. Yet, this does not mean that their inner spirit is just as beautiful. In fact, their interest in their own appearance may cause them to become vain and selfish. On the other hand, one who is ugly may appear repulsive, but he might also be kind and wise, and inwardly beautiful. Appearances can be deceiving. Therefore, do not always assume that if something looks impressive, it must be superior. Sometimes it is the humble-looking item or individual that is the greater treasure (Nedarim 50b).

This, then, is the lesson of Har Sinai. Despite its humble-looking appearance, Har Sinai was selected as the site for the world's most outstanding event.

THE ACCEPTANCE OF THE TORAH

The world and the Torah were developed in conjunction with one another, with the Torah intended as the eternal guidebook for a good life. In order to give all of mankind the option of living according to the Torah's precepts, Hashem offered the Torah to each nation in the world.

Hashem first approached the nation of Amalek and asked, "Will you accept the Torah as the basis of your lifestyle?"

"What does the Torah contain?" asked the Amalekites.

"One commandment is, 'You shall not kill.' "

"No killing?" was the response. "But our entire existence is based on the permissibility of killing. We kill to live, and live to kill! If the Torah forbids killing, we cannot accept it."

Hashem then asked the nation of Yishmoel if it would be willing to receive the Torah. "What does the Torah contain?" asked Yishmoel.

"The Torah states, 'You shall not steal.' "

"If that is so," replied Yishmael, "then we cannot possibly accept the Torah. If we cannot steal, then we will starve. Take the Torah and give it to some other nation."

And so it went, down the line. Nation after nation refused to accept the Torah, for they could not agree to live according to its laws. Finally, Hashem approached the nation of Israel: "Will you accept My Torah?"

The reply of the Israelites was brief and to the point: "Na'aseh V'nishma"—"We will observe and then we will hear what the Torah contains." In other words, not only

Hashem Himself was heard by every man, woman, and child as He declared the foundations of religious and moral conduct for all time:

1—I am the L-rd your G-d who delivered you from the land of Egypt . . .
2—You shall have no other gods before Me . . .
3—You shall not take the name of the L-rd your G-d in vain . . .
4—Remember the Sabbath day to keep it holy . . .
5—Honor your father and your mother . . .
6—You shall not murder.
7—You shall not commit adultery.
8—You shall not steal.
9—You shall not bear false witness against your neighbor.
10—You shall not covet your neighbor's house. . .

The people were so awed by all they had witnessed that they withdrew from the

was Israel willing to receive the Torah, but was willing to do so before even knowing what it contained. This, then, was the nation that truly deserved the gift of a Torah treasury (Avodah Zarah 2b; Sifrey, Vezos HaBrocho).

The above suggests that the Jews accepted the Torah of their own free accord. However, this seems to be contradicted by a statement in the Gemorrah that Hashem threatened Yisroel by suspending a mountain over their heads until they agreed to receive the Torah. (Avodah Zarah 2b, Shabbos 88a). Did Bnei Yisroel then accept the Torah willingly or not?

The answer is that their acceptance was immediate and enthusiastic. No threats were needed to make the Jews become the People of G-d. When the Medrash refers to force, it pertains to the later generations of Jews. We, who live now, no longer have the right to reject the Torah that was given to our ancestors. The transmission of the Torah to the Jews was meant for eternity and we must continue the Jewish adherence to its laws. Our ancestors were wise enough to perceive the great prize that Hashem offered and we cannot undo their good work by forsaking that gift.

In fact, the Torah was presented by Hashem Himself, and not through any intermediaries, even one as great as Moshe, to impress upon the Jews that the Torah is a timeless, Divine present. It cannot be changed by future generations, for it applies to all ages. If one were to alter any of the basic Torah laws, he would be challenging the wisdom of Hashem Himself.

Hashem said to the Earth: If Israel accepts the Torah, you will remain intact; otherwise I shall turn you back to chaos. (Shabbos 84)

He who exerts himself in the Torah stands, as it were, all day on Mount Sinai and receives the Torah. (Zohar)

Israel is the light of the world. (Shir Hashirim)

The Holy One Blessed be He, the Torah and Israel are all one. (Zohar)

HONOR YOUR FATHER AND YOUR MOTHER

The Asseres Hadibros (Ten Commandments) are separated into two general categories. The first five commandments comprise laws of relationships between man and G-d, while the last five apply to laws of relationships between man and his fellow man. This dichotomy is clear-cut in all respects but one; the law to honor one's father and one's mother is included in the first grouping. Why should this law be considered one dealing with a man-G-d relationship rather than a man-man relationship?

The Talmud provides the following explanation. Whoever honors his parents honors Hashem, and, therefore, honoring one's parents becomes a law pertaining to one's relationship with Hashem. Why is this so? Because those who honor their parents indicate a willingness to accept authority and to carry on the Jewish tradition. On the other hand, those who reject their parents' authority will tend to deny Hashem's authority and will not continue the chain of tradition. They will turn their backs on the ties that have upheld the Jewish nation from the time of Mattan Torah.

This is also why the Torah states that those who honor their parents will thereby prolong their days. This refers to both their

mountain and pleaded with Moshe to speak to them in place of Hashem lest they die.

Moshe then drew near to the thick darkness and received a series of laws. The first four precepts dealt with important aspects of Divine worship: the prohibition of idolatry, the creation of an altar made of earth for sacrifice offerings but only where Hashem commands that an altar of stone must be built of unhewn rock and not fashioned by iron instruments, and, to establish propriety, the law that the priest should ascend to the altar not via steps but on a slope.

own individual lives and also the endurance of the Jewish people. Whoever exhibits respect towards those who brought him into the world will receive the same respect from his own children, and his life will consequently be a more serene one. Conversely, whoever abuses his parents will set a poor example for his own children, who will eventually treat him in the same manner.

For instance, the story is told of a small boy who observed his mother drop a dish. "You clumsy idiot!" the boy yelled. "Can't you do anything right?"

The boy's father happened to hear this outburst, and rushed over to reprimand him. "What's wrong with you?" he shouted back. "Is that any way to talk to your mother?"

The boy looked at the father sheepishly and replied, "Well, that's the way she yells at Grandma when her hands shake and she

drops something."

Disrespect for one's parents had obviously been handed down from one generation to another.

And, of course, whoever learns the basis of Jewish tradition from his parents and then puts his knowledge into practice becomes a full-fledged member of the Jewish nation, and thereby perpetuates the never-ending linkage of Jewish generations. In this way, Judaism will never perish.

The Sages taught that whenever a man honors his parents it is as if he had brought down the Divine Presence to dwell with them and honored G-d Himself. (Kiddushin 30-31)

If you do not respect your parents, your children will not respect you. (Guide for the Perplexed).

Parshas Mishpotim lists many laws basic for the preservation of a civilized existence among the Bnei Yisroel. The first group of laws promote the humane treatment of slaves. A Jew who was sold as a servant to make restitution for a theft must be set free after a maximum of six years of service. If he was married when entering slavery, then the master must support his Jewish wife and children during his servitude, and must release them upon its completion. However, if his master provides him with a woman slave (Shifcha Canaanes), then the wife and any children she bears, re-

פרשת משפטים
Parshas Mishpotim

HONESTY

There might be those who think that Jewish law consists essentially of the Ten Commandments. However, this is a fallacy. Whereas the Ten Commandments provide the foundation of all laws, they are also the basis for many other laws, all of which are designed to strengthen Jewish society. Among the different categories of laws are the Mishpotim.

The Mishpotim are those civil laws that protect the moral fiber of society. They help

regulate relationships between men, encouraging truthfulness, sincerity, and kindness, while condemning immorality and deceit. They emphasize the Mitzvos Bein Odom L'Chaveiroh (Mitzvos Between Man and His Fellow Man). Those who make sure to learn Torah daily, to pray devoutly, and to eat only Kosher food, and who then conduct dishonest business deals or who fail to treat others with respect are certainly lacking in their Judaism.

Rabbi Shimon ben Shetach set the proper

main with the master when the Jewish slave is freed. If the slave becomes so attached to his master and family that he insists upon remaining with them after the years of servitude have expired, he makes a declaration to this effect before the judges, and the master pierces his ear against the door of the house with an awl. Then the slave remains in servitude until the year of the Yovel (Jubilee—the fiftieth year).

A man may sell his daughter to be a maidservant until she is twelve years old. If she displeases her master, she cannot be consigned to slavery in a foreign country. Rather, her relatives are allowed to redeem her from the master. If the son of the master marries her, she is to be treated as a free-born Jewess. She cannot be denied her marital rights if either the man or his son marries another woman, in which case she goes free.

If a man strikes his non-Jewish slave, and the slave dies, the master is punished according to the determination of the judges. If, however, the slave dies after a day or two, the master is not punished for it is assumed that he did not intend to kill the slave. If, though, the master maims the slave, the slave is immediately freed.

The death penalty is imposed for the following crimes: willful murder (though when one causes a death accidentally, he can escape the vengeful survivors of the victim by fleeing to a city of refuge), cursing a parent with the name of Hashem, kidnapping, practicing witchcraft, practicing bestiality, and sacrificing to idols.

The following are included among the laws of torts: If one injures another during a fight, he is held responsible for the victim's loss of earnings and for his medical fees, as well as compensating him for pain, embarrassment, and physical injury. If, while battling with another man, someone accidentally strikes a woman and causes her to miscarry, he is responsible to pay for the damages caused. If the owner of a dangerous animal fails to take proper precautions and the animal causes the death of a human, the animal is to be put to death and the owner is to be punished; if an animal kills a non-Jewish slave, the slave's owner is given thirty shekels of silver as compensation.

example for one who seeks to be a sincere Jew in his relations with men and G-d. Needing a donkey for his travels, he bought one from an Arab. At the time, neither he nor the Arab noticed that the donkey bore a small package in his saddle. Some time later, one of Rabbi Shimon ben Shetach's students found the package and opened it. He was amazed by what he found.

"It is a diamond, Rebbe!" he exclaimed. "A perfect diamond! It must be worth an enormous amount. Sell it, and you will never want for money. Imagine all the Mitzvos you will be able to do with the new-found money!"

Rabbi Shimon ben Shetach shook his head. "I may be able to perform many Mitzvos with the money, it is true. But they will never be able to cancel the demerit that will be mine if I keep property that is not mine. No, I will return the diamond to its rightful owner, the Arab."

"But Rebbe," protested the student, "why not keep the diamond? The Arab will never

know of his loss!"

"Possibly. But Hashem will know what I have done. I did not earn the diamond, and so it is not mine. If one claims to be a good Jew, he must be truthful at all times."

Rabbi Shimon ben Shetach was true to his word, and returned the diamond to the astonished Arab.

"I don't believe that anyone could be that honest," said the Arab. "The Jews must truly have wonderful laws. Blessed Be the G-d of Rabbi Shimon ben Shetach!" (Yerushalmi Bava Metziah, Perek 2; Choshen Mishpat 266).

Rabbi Shimon ben Shetach's strict adherence to the Mishpotim created a tremendous Kiddush Hashem, and should remind all that one should fulfill all of Hashem's Mitzvos with equal zeal.

He who does not keep his word is likened to one that would worship an idol. (Sanhedrin 92)

"He that engages in deceit shall not dwell within My house; He that utters

Compensation must also be paid for damage to property. If an animal dies after having fallen into an uncovered pit, the one responsible for the negligence must repay the value of the animal to its owner and deduct the price of the carcass. If someone's ox kills another man's ox, the surviving ox is sold, and the owners divide the proceeds from both oxen.

If one steals and then slaughters or sells an ox, he must pay five times the value to the owner, whereas he must pay only fourfold if he stole a sheep. If the thief is caught with the animal in his possession, he pays double. A homeowner can plead justifiable homicide if he kills a burglar breaking into his home during the night; however, he is charged with murder if he kills a burglar during the day. A thief who is too poor to offer repayment is sold into slavery.

When a man knowingly allows his animal to wander into another man's field or vineyard and causes damage, the best parts of his fields are evaluated as a basis for assessing the restitution. A similar penalty is imposed upon a man who lights a fire and allows the sparks to set fire to his neighbor's property.

If money or property entrusted to the care of a non-paid individual is stolen, then the owner may be paid double the value of the missing object. This fine is paid by the thief if he is caught, or by the trustee if he is caught, or by the trustee if he is found guilty of embezzlement, or by witnesses who falsely accuse the trustee of having the object in his possession. The trustee can absolve himself from liability if he takes an oath that he is in no way responsible for the object's loss.

falsehood shall not be established before My eyes." (Tehillim 101:7)

SHOWING KINDNESS TO OTHERS

Selfishness is an unfortunately common trait among men and women. If there is a question whose interests should take precedence, one usually decides in favor of one's own. After all, isn't it true that I am really more important than everyone else, and that others (especially strangers) should naturally honor me?

The Mishpotim show us that this isn't necessarily so. In fact, it is the welfare of others that should take precedence in one's mind. Certainly, the Torah stresses the importance of treating others, especially strangers, as equals rather than inferiors. After all, the Jews were themselves strangers in Egypt and are strangers in Golus today as well. The Jews ask others to treat them with respect; how then can they abuse the rights of strangers in their midst?

Rather, Jews are told to show patience and kindness towards others. If they do so, they will be exhibiting to all others the beneficial effects of adhering to Hashem's Torah, in which the spirit of brotherhood is given a very high status.

Rabbi Yisroel Salanter was certainly one who practiced the Mishpotim of Gemilus Chassodim (Kindness) and patience towards others. It is said that he was in the habit of washing his hands with the exact minimum amount of water needed. When asked why he was being so stingy with the water, he replied, "I, of course, consider the Mitzvah of Netilas Yodayim (Washing of One's Hands) a most important one. However, I noticed that whenever I use up the contents of the barrel of water, my maid has a terrible struggle bringing in a new barrel. Therefore, the more water I use, the more barrels she will have to lug, and the more hardships she will experience. To spare her this, I use as little water as possible."

Likewise, Rabbi Yisroel refrained from rising too early in the morning to attend shul. He knew that whenever he awoke, his maid would have to rise as well to tend to his needs and he did not want to curtail her sleep. When he was asked what aspect of baking Matzos provided the biggest Mitzvoh, he replied, "Making sure that the widows who work in the Matzoh factories are not yelled at."

Rabbi Yisroel also knew how best to deal with strangers, even seemingly rude ones. He once found himself sharing a train compartment with a young man who appeared unusually disrespectful. Although they were sitting in the "No Smoking" area, the young man insisted on taking out a cigarette, lighting it, and practically blowing the

When an animal entrusted to a paid watchman for safekeeping dies or is injured or is carried off by robbers, the trustee can also take an oath that he was in no way responsible. However, if the animal is stolen, he is liable. If the animal is mauled by wild beasts, the trustee is not liable if he can produce the carcass. A borrower is responsible for the borrowed animal's death or injury, unless the owner is present at the time of the accident.

The Torah warns that a foreigner is not to be wronged or insulted in any way, for the Jews were strangers themselves in the land of Egypt. Similar consideration must be shown to the widow and the orphan, for Hashem Himself will wreak vengeance on anyone who takes advantage of them in their vulnerable situation.

Loans are to be made interest-free. If one takes a garment which is used as a blanket at night for a pledge, he must return the garment to its owner before sunset.

The perversion of justice can be the greatest danger to the survival of a civilized society. It can be caused by any of the following: A witness who gives false evidence on behalf of a guilty individual; the witness who does not remain firm in upholding righteousness but who, instead, follows the majority in the wrong; the judge who administers justice on a partial basis; and the judge who accepts a bribe to influence his decisions.

One must extend a helping hand to his fellow man even if there is a rivalry

smoke in Rabbi Yisroel's face.

Rabbi Yisroel said not a word. He merely opened the window slightly to let the smoke out and some fresh air in. A few moments later, the young man began complaining violently.

"Don't you see how cold I'm getting? In a minute I'll be freezing to death. Can't you close that window and show some consideration for others?"

Rabbi Yisroel silently closed the window.

A few minutes later, though, the young man was at it again. "Look, I'm practically choking here," he gasped between coughs. "You'd think this place was a furnace. Come on, open the window. Hurry!"

Rabbi Yisroel opened the window without a word of protest. He remained quiet for the rest of the journey, despite the frequent mutterings of the young man.

When the train arrived at its destination, the young man glanced out the window, and was amazed to see a crowd gathered at the station. "Who in the world could they be waiting for?" he wondered aloud. "Is there someone famous aboard the train?"

Rabbi Yisroel shrugged. "Everyone is important and famous in his own way," he said.

The young man disembarked at the same time as Rabbi Yisroel, and was astonished to see the crowd surge forward towards his traveling companion. "Who are these people honoring?" he asked a nearby observer.

"Why, Rabbi Yisroel Salanter, the great leader of Klal Yisroel!" was the response. "Were you on the same train as Rabbi Yisroel? What an honor!"

"Do you mean . . . I was riding with the famous Rabbi Yisroel?" The young man sighed deeply, and then drove himself through the surging crowd until he came to the great Godol. "Rabbi Yisroel, can you ever forgive me for the terrible way I treated you during the train trip? In all honesty, I didn't know who you were. Can you find it in your heart to forgive me?"

Rabbi Yisroel motioned the man to draw close. "My son, I am very pleased to see you again, and even more so to hear your words. Can you pay me a visit tomorrow, when we can get to know each other better without the discomforts of the train interfering?"

The young man called on Rabbi Yisroel the next day, continuing his profuse apologies. Rabbi Yisroel found out that the young man had come to the town to learn more about Judaism, and he secured for him not only a teacher but also room and board. Within a short time, the young man was progressing very satisfactorily in his studies.

A companion who had heard the story of the young man asked Rabbi Yisroel why he had aided one who had been so impertinent to him. "When he asked me for forgiveness," Rabbi Yisroel replied, "I did so immediately. After all, if Hashem forgives us for our sins when we do Teshuva, it is certainly our job to forgive our fellow men. Then, to make sure that I bore the man no

between the two. If one happens upon the lost animal of his rival he should return it to its original owner. Similarly, if one finds an animal lying helplessly under its burden, one should assist it and ease its pain.

The first fruits and produce of land and vineyards are to be offered to Hashem, who has provided man with these gifts. Similarly, the firstborn of men and animals are to be dedicated to Him.

Other laws include the prohibition against eating Treifeh (the meat of an animal torn by beasts in the field). The seventh year of the Shemitta cycle is to be a Sabbatical year, during which the land must be neither sown nor reaped, but must lie fallow. The Sabbath is to be commemorated by means of a complete abstention from work on the part of every member of the household, including the servants and even the cattle. Three times a year (on Pesach, Shevuos, and Succos), every adult Israelite is to make a pilgrimage to the Sanctuary, bringing offerings as an ex-

personal malice, I went out of my way to help him. In the long run, I have found that kindness and patience are more successful in winning others closer to Yiddishkeit than are anger and exasperation."

That Rabbi Yisroel's conclusion was a sensible one can be seen from the detrimental effects of hostility towards others. In one such instance, hostility resulted in the destruction of the Beis Hamikdosh.

The Romans held sway over Yerusholayim, but the Beis Hamikdosh still stood, and with it remained the dream of Jewish independence. In Yerusholayim, there lived a wealthy man who decided to celebrate a simcha with a party. His invitations were coveted by many, and he sent a messenger to deliver an invitation to his good friend Kamtzoh. The messenger was one who did not know the wealthy man well, and he mistakenly delivered the invitation to an individual named Bar Kamtzoh instead. This might not have proved calamitous but for the fact that Bar Kamtzoh and the wealthy man were bitter enemies. Bar Kamtzoh was surprised to receive the invitation, but assumed that the wealthy man wanted to end their rivalry, and he decided to attend.

The moment he made his entrance at the party, though, Bar Kamtzoh realized that his coming had been an error. The wealthy man took one look at him, walked over, and snarled angrily.

"What are you doing in my house? What nerve you have to come here! Pick yourself up and leave immediately!"

The host's outburst had captured the attention of the guests. Bar Kamtzoh looked around to see everyone staring at him. He turned to the wealthy man and said to him in a low, pleading voice,

"It must have been a mistake for me to think you invited me. But please don't shout at me; everyone is watching."

"Let them watch," the host replied. "Let them see that I do not allow persons like you in my house."

"Not so loud, please," begged Bar Kamtzoh. "Don't worry, I'll leave and never set foot here again. But please, just this once, let me stay—just to avoid a scene. I ask your help; I'll even pay for half the feast. Only save me the embarrassment of having to make an exit this way."

"I make no deals with you, you cur," said the host. "Words won't help you. You'll leave now, and that's final!"

By now, everyone was watching closely. Bar Kamtzoh had no choice but to make his departure, under the contemptuous gaze of the assembled persons. "They may shame me now," he muttered as he was leaving. "But the day will come when they will suffer."

Bar Kamtzoh was as good as his word. Still stung by this display of intolerance, he concocted a plan to punish those who had embarrassed him. He came before the Roman Emperor and accused his fellow Jews of conspiring against the Romans. As proof of his claims, he cited the fact that the Jews would not allow a sacrifice selected by the Emperor to be offered in the Beis Hamikdosh. The Emperor decided to investigate this charge. He appeared at the Beis Hamikdosh with a sacrifice, but Bar Kamtzoh had made sure to render the offering unfit beforehand, and the Kohein was forced to refuse the Emperor's demands. The Emperor was outraged, and he set in motion the intensified oppression that eventually resulted in the destruction of the Beis

pression of gratitude to Hashem. One is forbidden to seethe a kid in its mother's milk.

In a concluding message, the Israelites are promised that if they obey the Divine laws, Hashem Himself will support them in their gradual conquest of Canaan, and their victory will be assured.

Moshe returned from the heights of Mount Sinai and, after writing down all the precepts conveyed to him by Hashem, offered sacrifices and read the Book of the Covenant to the people. They instantly responded by stating, "All that Hashem has spoken we will do and we will hear." At Hashem's bidding, Moshe, Aharon, Nadav, and Avihu, together with the seventy Elders, ascended the mountain, where they witnessed a mystical vision of the Divine Glory. After their descent, Moshe was summoned alone to receive the two tablets of stone on which Hashem had inscribed the Ten Commandments so that they could be taught fully to the people, while Aharon and Chur were left to govern in his absence. Followed by Yehoshua

Hamikdosh, a tragedy that came about because of one Jew's hostility towards another (Gitten 55b).

> The Torah begins and ends with acts of kindness. (Sotah 14)
>
> Acts of kindness are so important, that without them man would not have been created. (Bereishis Rabbah 8)
>
> The world couldn't exist even one hour —without acts of kindness!
>
> The world stands on three things: on the Torah, on worship and on kindness. (Avos 1)
>
> The Medrash tells us that Hashem prefers acts of kindness above all the sacrifices offered to His name. (Yallus Hosea 247, 522)

CHARITY TO OTHERS

The Mishpotim that cement our interpersonal relationships ask us to help others not only with our kindness but also with our possessions and money. Some persons are more than willing to offer their time and efforts for the sake of others, but are a little more reluctant to part with their hard-earned money. However, as the following story illustrates, a little charity can result in a manifold repayment.

The leader of the Jewish community of Pressburg came to Rabbi Moshe Sofer for advice. He had invested his life savings in a business which had failed. He had also invested the savings of widows and orphans in this venture, and all was now lost. He now had an opportunity to recoup these losses at the Leipzig fair, but he did not have any money to take advantage of the chance. Would Rabbi Sofer have any suggestions?

Without uttering a word, Rabbi Sofer

went to his safe, emptied it of all its money, and handed everything over to the visitor. "I am lending you this money," he said. "Go to the Leipzig fair. Invest this money safely, and may Hashem help you in recouping not only your own money, but also that of the orphans and widows."

At the fair, the merchant invested in a cargo of coffee. The purchase proved to be a very successful one, and he was able to sell the coffee for a large profit. The man earned enough money to repay all those whose funds he had previously lost.

Soon afterwards, the man returned to Rabbi Sofer. "Here is the money you lent me," he announced, "and here is a diamond ring I bought especially for you to repay you for your kindness."

But Rabbi Sofer shook his head. "No, I cannot accept your kind gift," he said. "My reward in this matter is the knowledge that I was able to carry out the Mitzvah of Charity. Give the ring to your wife instead."

Reluctantly, the man took back the ring. However, he did not give the ring to his wife, as Rabbi Sofer had suggested. Instead, inspired by the Rabbi's example, he donated the ring to charity.

> Each day G-d lauds the rich man who distributes charity in private. (Pesachim 112)
>
> What shall a man do to deserve children?—Rabbi Eliezer advises: "Let him distribute money among the poor." (Challah 2)
>
> Rabbi Nechemiah's disciples asked him: "What have you done to prolong your life?" He answered: "I have been generous with my money."(Megillah 28)

(who remained on the lower part of the mountain), Moshe mounted Har Sinai, which was surrounded by a cloud. Then he passed into the mists of the cloud and remained on the mountain for forty days and forty nights.

CHUKIM

Among the categories of laws contained in the Torah are the Chukim. These are commandments whose rationales are somewhat unclear to us, such as Sha'atnez. Because the reasons for these Mitzvos are not specifically stated, there have been some Jews throughout the ages who have considered these laws irrelevant and have refused to perform them. However, they forgot that these laws come directly from Hashem, as do all other laws, and He, of course, knows the full reason for all His commandments. Therefore, our ignorance of His purpose should not lead us to believe that these Mitzvos are unimportant. It is only our lack of perspective that keeps us in the dark about them.

This is similar to a man observing a painting in a museum. He notices crowds gathering in front of the painting and admiring its beauty and design. However, to the man, the painting appears to be just a series of dark and ugly blotches, and he cannot understand the painting's popularity. He complains aloud that the painting makes no sense at all, but then someone notices that he is looking at the painting through smeared up darkened glasses, and that this is altering his view of it.

Likewise, when we do not always see the beauty of the Torah's logic, it does not mean that the beauty does not exist, only that our ability to see it has been clouded.

The law of truth G-d gave to His prophet, who was faithful in his house. (Siddur, Yigdal)
G-d will not alter, nor change His law forever for another. (Siddur, Yigdal).

Hashem commanded Moshe to build a Mishkon (Sanctuary), symbolizing His presence among the people and constructed according to Divine pattern. For its erection, Bnei Yisroel were asked to voluntarily supply offerings of precious metals, fabrics, skins, wool, oil, spices, in. ense, and precious stones. The Sanctuary consisted of the Chotzeir (Outer Court) containing the altar for burnt offerings and the laver used by the Kohanim (Priests) and the Tabernacle which was divided by a curtain into two chambers. The outer chamber was called the Kodesh (Holy Place), to which

פרשת תרומה
Parshas Terumah

HASHEM IN OUR MIDST

After the Jews had been freed from their Egyptian bondage and been forged into the Nation of Israel, Moshe was commanded to build the Mishkon, a temporary, portable Temple, which would accompany the Bnei Yisroel during their desert wanderings. Why was this necessary? Doesn't Hashem's Divine Presence permeate every single particle of space in the universe? Why then did He issue the command to build a special and limited dwelling place?

Furthermore, the language employed by the Torah in this instance seems unusual. "V'osu Le Mikdosh V'Shochanti B'Sochum," says the Torah (Shemos 25:8): "And let them make Me a Sanctuary, and I will dwell in them." Basic grammatical consistency would dictate that the verse should read, "And I will dwell in it" rather than "in them". What, then, is the cause for the plural usage?

The response to the first question may be that whereas the human being may learn that Hashem's presence exists everywhere, the human intellect cannot readily conceive of this possibility. The human senses are too limited to fully comprehend Hashem's omnipresence. Therefore, in a gesture to man, Hashem provided for a specific, concrete site for His Presence, one which men could readily see and accept. This site was the Sanctuary, later called the Beis Hamikdosh.

Unfortunately, we have not been privileged with the presence of the Beis Hamikdosh for the past nineteen centuries.

only priests who performed sacred duties had access, and which contained the Shulchan (Table of Showbread), the Menorah (Candelabra) and the Mizbeiach HaKatoress (Altar of Incense). The inner chamber was called the Kodesh HaKodoshim (Holy of Holies), which only the Kohein Godol (High Priest) entered and only on Yom Kippur. It contained the Oron (Ark), the most sacred of the ar-

However, this does not mean that we can no longer experience the presence of the Holy Shechina. The Shechina is not reserved for the Beis Hamikdosh alone. Every home, every synagogue and every house of Jewish assembly that exhibits a Jewish manifestation, through prayer, learning, or Mitzvos, is itself a haven of holiness. Every home, synagogue, and Jewish assembly place must be made worthy of this holiness. It is for this reason that the Torah uses the plural in stating "V'shochanti B'Sochum"; to remind us that Hashem will dwell in the midst of all of us, if we are deserving of this privilege. (Midrash in the Shloh).

> *Wherever you go Hashem accompanies you. To this the following refers:*
> *"What nation . . . has Hashem so near to them as Hashem our G-d whenever we call on Him?" (Devarim 4:7)*
> *"Do I not fill the heavens and earth?" says Hashem. (Jeremiah 23:24)*
> *Where is Hashem? In the heart of every questioner.*

CHARITY

To aid in the construction of the Mishkon, the Bnei Yisroel were asked to make two types of contributions. One type consisted of any amount the individual desired to give, while the other was a set amount that each individual, rich or poor, had to give on an equal basis.

These two categories of charity should guide us in our own approach to charity. The free-will donation, of whatever the individual could afford, is one that all those blessed with riches should make. Naturally, the millionaire is in a better position to contribute large sums to the poor than is the average working man. However, the equal contribution given by all Jews for the Mishkon underlines the need for all of us, rich and poor alike, to give Tzedokoh. Even those whose worldly possessions are relatively few, should recognize that whatever they do have comes from Hashem, and that they should use part of their possessions to assist those more needy than they.

Rabbi Yechezkel Landau, the Rabbi of Prague, clearly understood the importance of all Jews sharing in the Mitzvah of Tzedokoh. He was approached by two community leaders to aid in ransoming Jewish captives. Without hesitation, Rabbi Landau asked them how much was needed.

"Three hundred dinarim," they replied.

Immediately Rabbi Landau went into his private office and returned with a bowl of gold dinarim. "Here," he announced. "You will find in this bowl 290 gold coins. Gather the other ten dinarim from others in the town."

The two visitors were surprised. "With all due respect, please explain to us your generous but puzzling offer. On the one hand, you were extremely charitable in offering an immense amount of money, and Hashem will surely bless you for this. Yet, on the other hand, you refused to contribute the remaining ten dinarim, which you could no doubt have done. Why?"

"It is very simple," responded Rabbi Landau. "Our Sages say that he who wants to give charity but who desires that others not give is considered to have an evil eye towards his fellow man (Pirkey Avos 5:13). In other words, why should I try to get credit for the entire Mitzvah without giving others an opportunity of sharing in the deed?"

In essence, Charity includes giving away to the poor even your dearest possessions.

Before every Succos, Rabbi Mordechai had the practice of purchasing wood and boards, and then distributing them to the poor so that they could build succos. One Erev Succos, a poor, lame person approached Rabbi Mordechai for some of the wood, but Rabbi Mordechai was forced to reply sadly that he had none left. A few moments later, Rabbi Mordechai saw the cripple groveling in the nearby mud, searching for stray pieces of wood with which to build a succah. Immediately, Rabbi Mordechai ordered one of his assistants to go to his home.

"Go there and dismantle my succah, so that you can bring the boards I used to this man. Then we will both help him build his

ticles in the Sanctuary. The Oron held the two tablets of stone inscribed with the Ten Commandments. It was from the Oron that Hashem, through Moshe, revealed His commandments to the Bnei Yisroel. The instructions to construct all the utensils and the actual building needed in the Mishkon are mentioned in minute detail.

succah with them."

That year Rabbi Mordechai spent the entire holiday of Succos as a guest in the succah of the lame man.

Even the poor man who is himself maintained by charity should give charity. (Gitten 6)

Give much or give little, only give with your heart for the Sake of Hashem. (Shavuos 14)

If you are a generous giver, you will never come to harm. (Derech Eretz Zutta 2, 4)

AVOIDING HYPOCRISY

The central feature of the Mishkon was the Oron, the Holy Ark. Hashem commanded that there be three such arks, each one larger than the other, with two made of gold and one of wood. When they were assembled, the wooden one was placed between the two gold ones, thus being completely surrounded, both inside and out, by gold.

This arrangement provides a lesson for every individual. Just as the Ark was golden from both within and without, so, too, should every person be righteous both inwardly and outwardly. Instead of behaving one way in the glare of public life and another way in private, one should remain virtuous at all times. He should at all times practice what he preaches (Yoma 72b). If he means wholeheartedly whatever he says, then others will take him and his thoughts seriously. On the other hand, if one puts on a display of greatness in public only, and then acts immorally behind closed doors, he is branded as an untrustworthy hypocrite. One who deceives others deceives himself.

It was said that when Socrates, the famous Greek philosopher, was caught in a disreputable, inappropriate act, he said, "Now I am not Socrates the philosopher, just Socrates the man." This implies that he had a double standard for himself. Contrast this

with the attitude of the Jewish Sages, who believed in remaining just and righteous at all times. That way they were able to impress others towards following their righteous ways.

The Chofetz Chaim was known for never assuming a facade of goodness. Whoever saw the Chofetz Chaim knew that they were seeing his true self. His character was perfect, and he had no faults to hide.

One day the Chofetz Chaim visited a town he had never before entered. He lodged at an inn and had a lengthy conversation with the innkeeper. After over an hour of talk, the innkeeper finally asked, "Could you tell me your identity?"

The Chofetz Chaim was reluctant to reveal this, for he did not want the innkeeper to go to extra bother to serve him. He hesitated, but before he could come up with any reply, the innkeeper said, "Wait—you must be the Chofetz Chaim. I have never before seen you, but from what I have heard, it must be, for we have talked for a very long time and you have not yet said even a hint of a bad word about anyone."

This, then, characterizes a Torah Sage. One who can be easily identified by his great deeds and character. It was the Chofetz Chaim who drove home the concept of brotherhood by closing his store early so that other businessmen in the area could also prosper. If someone overpaid him, he would search to the ends of the world to be able to repay that person.

These are the characteristics of our leaders, and it is hoped that we will be wise enough to learn from their examples.

Do not judge the jug by its exterior but by what is in it. (Avos 4)

A Scholar who is not what he appears to be is no scholar. (Yoma 73)

He who poses as a scholar, and is not a scholar, will not be admitted into the presence of Hashem. (Bava Basra 98)

Aharon and his sons, Nadav, Avihu, Elazar, and Isamar, were chosen by Hashem to serve as Kohanim (Priests). One of their tasks was to keep the lamps of the Menorah burning continuously in the Sanctuary. The oil for the lamps was provided by the members of the general community. While officiating in the Sanctuary, the Kohanim were to wear special garments. Aharon, as the Kohein Godol (High Priest), was to be robed in especially distinctive vestments made by skilled craftsmen.

The investiture of Aharon and his sons was con-

פרשת תצוה

Parshas Tetzaveh

OUR TORAH

The term "Torah Ohr," the Torah is like a light or a fire, is a common one in Jewish parlance. Like a flame, the Torah illuminates the proper path for Jews. Without it, our lives remain darkened.

However, it is not sufficient for us to bask in the flames of the Torah only in our own homes. Rather, we must take the approach of Avrohom Ovinu, who spread the light of Torah to all the surrounding areas. In this sense, he acted like a candle, which can kindle other candles while continuing to burn brightly on its own. Similarly, the light of the Torah never diminishes, no matter how many individuals benefit from its fire.

"The Jews had light . . . ." (Esther 8:16)
—Light is Torah. (Megillah 15)
It has been taught in the name of R. Meir: Just as light is superior to darkness, so is Torah superior to things of vanity. (Koheles Rabbah 2)

In addition to being a source of light, the Torah is also a source of life.

A woman once appeared before the TaZ, crying bitterly that her only son was at death's door. Doctors had abandoned all hope for his survival. As a final desperate gesture, she had come to the TaZ for help.

The TaZ suggested that the woman pray to Hashem for her son's recovery. "But I have prayed already, and will continue to do so," she responded. "Can't you offer your own prayers on my son's behalf?"

Overcome with compassion, The TaZ became lost in deep thought. Suddenly, he lifted his face and said, "For two agonizing weeks I have been racking my brains to discover the answer to a complex Torah question. I pray to Hashem that the merit of my torment should serve as a blessing for your sick son."

The prayer was fulfilled, and the son recovered, due to the benefit of the Torah.

Just as fire descended from heaven, so, too, the law was given from heaven. Just as fire supports life in the world, so, too, the words of Torah. (Sifrey)

THE ME'IL AND LOSHON HO'RAH

Among the garments worn by the Kohein Godol was the Me'il, the coat. The Me'il was worn as a Kaporoh, an atonement for sins involving Loshon Horah, derogatory speech about others (Erechin 16a). This is indicated by the fact that the color of the coat was blue, as is the sky, an indication that our words rise to the sky, and that we should therefore be wary of what we say. Furthermore, we are told that the neckline of the Me'il was tight, yet it never ripped. This is a reminder to us to tighten our mouths when the desire to speak Loshon Horah is felt. The Me'il also had bells hanging from the bottom. These bells were of two varieties, gold and cloth. The golden bells tinkled, while the cloth bells were silent. This indicates there are times that an individual should speak, while there are other times when he should not. The opportunity to perform a Mitzvah should encourage one to speak out, while one should remain as silent as a cloth bell when the opportunity to attack others arises.

"Death and life are in the power of the tongue, and they that indulge in it shall eat the fruit thereof."
Four classes of men will not be received by Hashem: the scoffers, the liars, the flatterers, and the slanderers. (Sanhedrin 103)
He who slanders, he who listens to slander, and he who bears false witness against his neighbor—deserve to be cast to the dogs. (Pesachim 111)
Gossip brings hatred into the heart, and he who talks to you about a third person

firmed by a number of symbolic acts. Aharon was presented with his robes by Moshe and was anointed with oil. This was followed by the investiture of the other Kohanim. Various sacrifices were brought to the Sanctuary, placed on the hands of the Kohanim, waved before the altar, and finally burnt, to symbolize the right of the Kohanim to offer sacrifices. These rites were repeated daily for seven days.

Among other obligations, the Kohanim were charged with the duty of bringing a daily burnt-offering of a yearling lamb, both in the morning and the evening, on behalf of the whole Jewish community.

will be the first to curse you and the first to speak ill about you to others. (Mussar Ha'Philosophim)

THE BELLS

As mentioned above, the coat of the Kohein was adorned by bells hanging down from its edge. What was the purpose of these bells?

Our Sages comment that the bells were there to remind the Kohein Godol of the need for humility in his actions. The clanging of the bells as he entered was a method of asking permission before entering the House of Hashem.

This emphasis on humility seems to contradict the image of the Kohein Godol's clothing displaying a sense of impressive royalty. However, there is no contradiction. What provides the Jews with a royal status? Simply their sense of humility and awe in the presence of the Holy One. It was, in fact, because of this humility that Hashem chose

the Jews from among all the other nations of the world to fulfill the royal position of the Chosen People. Whereas other nations constantly proclaim their greatness, we acknowledge our unworthiness of Hashem's favors. It is for this very reason that the Jews are exalted above all other nations in the eyes of Hashem.

Beware of the front seat, since it is the leading one.

Pride is like a mountain; He who climbs it will fall.

Great is humility in that it levels both great and small. (Taharas Hakodesh)

The Chofetz Chaim, ZT'L, once told someone who was speaking Loshon Hora, "Some people are preparing a telegram in the next room. Notice how carefully they scrutinize and consider each word. That's how careful you must be with your speech."

"Think before you speak." This piece of advice was written by the Ramban to his son in his famous "Igeres HaRamban."

When the census was taken of male Israelites over the age of twenty (who thereupon became liable for military service), each man was to make a token payment of half a shekel of silver. This silver was used for the construction of the Sanctuary. A brass laver was to be made for use by Aharon and his sons as a washing basin. The laver stood in the Court between the altar of burnt-offering and the entrance to the Sanctuary. Oil made from four prescribed aromatic herbs mixed with olive oil was to be used for anointing the priests and vessels, and incense made from selected sweet spices was to be prepared for sacred use.

פרשת כי תשא

Parshas Ki Sisah

THE EIGEL HA'ZOHOV (THE GOLDEN CALF)

Many who read the passages involving the creation of the Eigel HaZohov wonder how this episode was possible. After all that Hashem had showered upon them in the way of miracles and benefits, how could the

Bnei Yisroel suddenly turn to the worship of a golden calf, especially right after they had just accepted the Holy Torah? How could they be so hypocritical?

However, the story of the Eigel HaZohov is not as simple a matter of wrong-doing as it might seem. True, the Bnei Yisroel erred

Betzalel of the tribe of Yehuda, and Oholiav of the tribe of Dan were Divinely chosen to apply their skill in craftsmanship by supervising the work of the construction of the Sanctuary. Although the building of the Mishkon was of the greatest importance, it could not supersede the observance of the Shabbos, and the people were commanded to cease all work on that day.

Moshe had been on Mt. Sinai for forty days and forty nights, and the people, fearing that he would never return, clamored for a visible object which they could worship. They persuaded Aharon to fashion a molten image of a golden calf out of their golden jewelry. They brought burnt and peace offerings to this idol, around which they sang and danced. Hashem's anger was aroused at this display of heresy, and He sent Moshe down from the mountain, informing him of Israel's sin and declaring that he would destroy this treacherous nation. Moshe entreated Hashem to be merciful and not give the Egyptians the opportunity to gloat over the Israelites' misfortune, but instead to recall his eternal covenant with the Patriarchs. On hearing this plea, Hashem granted the people a new lease on life.

Descending from the mountain on the seventeenth of Tamuz with the two tablets of the law engraved by Hashem on stone, Moshe heard the cries of revelry, witnessed the disgraceful behavior of the people, and threw the tablets to the ground. He then destroyed the golden calf by throwing it into the fire, after which he ground it into powder and threw it into a stream. He made the people drink from

grievously in creating the golden calf; but, their motives were not entirely heretical. What prompted their unfortunate act was a mistake in calculation on their part. Moshe had told them that he would be on Mt. Sinai for forty days and forty nights, and that after forty full days he would return. However, when Moshe departed in the middle of the day the Bnei Yisroel mistakenly considered this a complete day in itself. They, therefore, expected Moshe to be back in their midst thirty-nine days later, and when he did not appear, they panicked. Their fears ran rampant and influenced by the Yetzer HoRah and the Eirev Rav (those gentiles who had joined the Jews when they left Egypt), they came to believe that Moshe had died. Consequently, they clamored for a new, visible leader, one in whom they could place their full trust. This led to their asking for the creation of the Eigel, which they intended as an intermediary between themselves and Hashem.

Their sin consisted, then, not of seeking another god, which they definitely did not do, but of choosing another leader without first consulting Hashem. They sought to decide for themselves what was good for them. However, they forgot that their status of being the Chosen People meant that they survived at the Will of Hashem, and that only He in His infinite wisdom can know what is proper and desirable for the well-

being of the Jews.

When you fear Hashem and beware of an evil path, you will not be misled into evil. (Mussar Ha'Philosophim)

NEGATIVE INFLUENCES

The primary instigators of the construction of the Eigel HaZohov were the Eirev Rav. They were those non-Jews who, impressed with the might and riches of the Jews at the time of Yetzias Mitzrayim, decided to cast their lot with them. They, too, became Jews, not necessarily because of any basic belief in Hashem, but because they believed the Jews were the great power of the moment. Consequently, when Moshe did not return on schedule from Mt. Sinai, they were among the first to abandon faith in Moshe's words. The Jews now seemed leaderless and lost, and it was they who moved to adopt a new man-made guide. Their plan had a devastating effect, for they influenced many Jews to subscribe to their ideas. Like a rotten apple, they infested the righteous among them with their poisonous influence.

This instance is one of many in Jewish history which remind us to beware of alien influences. Unfortunately, when Hurkinus and Aristobulus were vying for control of the kingdom during the First Commonwealth, they forgot this lesson of the Eirev Rav and brought disaster upon

this. He reproached Aharon who replied that he had been forced to carry out the people's demands. Moshe called upon all his supporters to rally around him, and the tribe of Levi responded immediately. At his command, the members of Levi went through the camp, slaying about three thousand leaders of the revolt. Moshe's love and compassion for his people led him to implore Hashem to forgive them, for if they were destroyed he had no desire to live. The reply he received was that only those who had willfully sinned would be punished, but, in view of Moshe's interceding on their behalf, the people would be led to the Promised Land by Hashem's messenger, though not by Hashem Himself. On learning of Hashem's disapproval of their actions, the Israelites mourned and removed their ornaments as a sign of grief.

Moshe pitched his tent outside the camp which had been defiled by the golden calf. In intimate communication with Hashem, he asked for a revelation of the Divine attributes to assist him in leading the people. Hashem reassured him that He would be merciful and lead the people into Eretz Yisroel, for Moshe had personally found favor in His eyes. In reply to a further request that he be able to behold the Divine Glory, Moshe was told that no mortal could see Hashem and still live.

themselves. During their power struggle, they called for the support of Rome, and Rome, ever eager for an easy way to establish control, not only intervened but eventually established their own crushing authority over the kingdom (Sotah 49a, Bava Kama 82a). The Jewish leaders had relied upon the help of strangers, only to find those very strangers turning against them. When the Jews became too susceptible to the influence and control of others as they also did with the Greeks, the Spanish, and the Germans, tragedy resulted. Judaism is a supreme guide to life, and there is no need to dilute it with additives from other lifestyles.

The same warning to avoid corrupting influences applies to individuals as well as to groups. Every individual must choose his companions with care; a single bad influence can cancel out the moral teachings of teachers, parents and Rabbis. The Yetzer HoRah is a very powerful force, and it can easily run rampant when given a boost by one's new-found "friend". It is usually much simpler to learn from another's bad habits than from his good habits. This is why our Sages have said, "Woe to the wicked person—and woe to his neighbor" (Negaim Perek 12 Mishnah 6, Toras Kohanim, Vayikrah 14:40).

> *Think before you act. (Peninei Ha'Melitzos Katzar)*
>
> *He who associates with the unclean becomes unclean himself. (Bava Kama 92)*
>
> *The rotten date tree seeks out the society of the barren tree. (Bava Kama 92)*

A HALF SHEKEL: JEWS WORKING TOGETHER

When a census of the Israelite men was taken, each man was required to contribute the coin of one-half shekel. The coins were then counted, and the total indicated how many men had been numbered.

This process raises several questions. Why weren't the men counted by heads? Why was each one required to donate a coin instead? Our Sages have replied that the method of counting by means of coins signifies the fact that every single person numbered has his own individual worth. However, this leads to a different question. If so, why did each man have to donate only half a shekel, rather than a whole one? Why not have each individual show that he is whole and complete?

In fact, this is just the point, to emphasize the fact that no individual is complete when alone. No man, and certainly no Jew, is an island. He can reach the ultimate heights of Jewish spirituality and brotherhood only when he associates and cooperates with other Jews. If he goes out of his way to help others, to learn from others, and to join others in positive group efforts, then he is a true member of the Jewish nation. On the other hand, if he remains aloof from others, then he stands alone and is truly lacking in character (Rambam, Perek 4 Hilchos Teshuvah Halacha 1).

The importance of working together with others is shown in the tale of a man who lost his way while in a huge, dense forest and kept on walking around in circles. Eventual-

Nevertheless, Moshe was allowed a glimpse of the Divine Radiance from behind a cleft in the mountain rock.

Once again, Moshe ascended the mountain alone, carrying with him the two new tablets of stone he had been commanded to prepare. Hashem descended in a cloud. He revealed Himself as the L-rd of Mercy, Kindness, and Truth, and renewed His covenant with Israel by repeating the chief commandments given previously. These included the prohibition against the idolatry, the command to observe the festivals, and the command to sanctify the Sabbath.

Hashem Himself inscribed the Ten Commandments on the two tablets of stone, while Moshe recorded the contents of the renewed covenant. After spending an additional forty days and forty nights on the mountain, during which he abstained from all food and drink, Moshe descended the mountain and returned to the camp. His face shone with a Divine glow and communicated the words of Hashem which he had heard on Mt. Sinai to Aharon, the Elders, and the whole assembly in turn. After he had finished speaking, he covered his radiant face with a veil. Thereafter, he removed it only when he entered Hashem's Divine presence or when he delivered his message to the people.

ly, he came upon a second person, also thrashing his way through the forest. "Can you show me the way out of the woods?" he asked.

"No, not yet," said the second man. "However, through my travels I have already found out which roads not to take. Maybe together we can find the right way."

And so it was. Each one offered his own knowledge of the forest's roads, and with their pooled information they soon found the right way. Had each remained alone, each would have wandered for much longer.

This reasoning is the basis for our praying with a Minyan, an assembly of at least ten Jewish males. The union of prayer has a force and power all its own.

This is explained by means of a parable. A king was once asked to decide which of two towns deserved a certain royal privilege. Both towns sent gifts to the king to win his favor. The members of the first town sent their gifts individually, at different times. As each gift arrived, the king examined it and usually managed to find fault with each one. The second town, however, sent their gifts in one shipment. When this bundle of gifts arrived the king was at once impressed by the enormous number of gifts, and did not feel inclined to look at each gift individually. As would be expected, the second town won his favor.

In a similar vein, if each of us would pray separately, Hashem would examine each of us on an individual basis and would no doubt find us deficient. On the other hand, if we pray in a group, as part of a Minyan, then our combined prayers are conveyed to Hashem, and hopefully the merits of the entire group will outweigh the deficiencies of each individual in the group.

Two are better than one. (Koheles 4)
Knowledge of the Torah cannot be thoroughly acquired unless studied in a group. (Berachos 63)
What is the acceptable time to pray? When the congregation prays. (Berachos 69)

Moshe transmitted to the Bnei Yisroel the details of Hashem's commands relating to the Sanctuary and its contents, but first emphasized the holiness of the Sabbath, on which no work was allowed. When asked to contribute towards the construction fund for the Sanctuary, the Bnei Yisroel responded most generously, each individual donating what he could. Women with the requisite skills spun the linen material. The princes of each tribe offered precious stones for the breastplate, as well as oil and spices for the incense. Some women even donated their mirrors of burnished copper for the

פרשת ויקהל

Parshas Vayakhel

SHABBOS

Shabbos is one of the mainstays of the Jewish religion. It provides an aura of holiness for our mundane lives, and supplies a peak for the activities of the week.

Yet, throughout history, there have been those who have either scorned or mocked the laws of Shabbos. They have claimed that the laws of Shabbos are too restrictive or irrelevant. After all, they ask, if Shabbos is a day of rest, why is watching television or taking a pleasure cruise prohibited? Why should carrying a heavy book inside the house be permissible while carrying a mere handkerchief outside the house be forbidden? Above all, why do we need a Shabbos day to begin with?

Of course, the basis for the observance of Shabbos is the verse in the Torah stating, "And He (G-d) rested on the seventh day from all His work which He had made" (Bereishis 2:2). An immediate question is why G-d found it necessary to rest? Isn't G-d all-Powerful and Omnipotent; therefore, can He possibly become fatigued!

Obviously, then, Hashem was not required to rest in any physical sense. What the Torah means is that Hashem paused from the basic work of Creation on the seventh day, for the world had already been completed. The seventh day was one which Hashem set aside for admiring His creations and to consider the earth as a totality. In this way, Hashem set the standard for humans to sanctify the Shabbos as a day on which to turn away from everyday, earthly concerns, and instead, to view life in its totality. What is life for, and how can we elevate ourselves spiritually?

It is for this reason that creative work, such as the type of work performed in the Mishkon, is banned on Shabbos. Similarly, all activities that are of a weekday nature,

such as watching television, which do not elevate one spiritually are frowned upon. The Shabbos is a day to acknowledge Hashem's creation of and mastery over the world. It is, therefore, a day one should devote to prayer and family togetherness rather than to humdrum matters. We have six days of the week during which we can worry about business affairs and school work. We can set aside one day to reflect on the purpose of all our efforts. This one day, then, is Hashem's day, during which His Holiness should permeate our actions and thoughts.

Those who observe Shabbos strictly show all the world that they accept Hashem's authority. Shabbos is like the sign on a shoemaker's shop. As long as the sign remains over the shoemaker's door, the people of the town know that he is still in business, but when the sign disappears they know that he has retired. Similarly, the observance of Shabbos is an indication to all others that the Jew is still in business as a G-d fearing Jew. Once the Jew no longer keeps Shabbos, he shows others that he has "retired" from his belief in G-d.

Yet, there are those who insist that one cannot survive financially if he must refrain from working on the Shabbos. True G-d fearing Jews, though, do not believe this and adopt the attitude displayed in the following parable:

A man was riding his horse down a long, winding road one day when he passed a man trudging along. The man was old, and he grunted under the load of an obviously heavy package.

"Would you like a lift?" asked the rider.

The old man readily agreed, and mounted the horse. He took a seat, yet he did not remove the heavy package from his back.

After observing the old man for a while,

creation of the laver and its vase.

Moshe made special mention of the fact that Hashem had singled out Betzalel of the tribe of Yehudah, a man of wisdom, understanding, and experience, to supervise the details of the construction. He was aided by Oholiav of the tribe of Dan,

the rider's curiosity got the better of him. He turned to the old man and asked, "Why don't you remove the package from your back and place it on the horse's?"

The old man shook his head. "You were nice enough to give me a lift. How can I have the nerve to impede your trip by placing such a heavy burden on your horse?"

"Don't worry," responded the rider. "The horse will be bearing the weight of the burden whether you place it on your back or the horse's. You may as well make matters easier for yourself and place it directly on the horse."

Likewise, we should have enough faith in the Power of Hashem to trust His ability to bear the burden of our troubles during the Shabbos. After all, it is He who carries us through every other day of the week. Therefore, there is no need to fret that if one observes the Shabbos he will suffer great losses. In the long run, the Shomer Shabbos has only to gain from his Emunas Hashem.

R. Yochanan said in the name of R. Eleazar ben R. Shimeon: The Holy One, blessed be He, said unto Israel: My children, borrow on my account to celebrate the holiness of the Shabbos day and trust Me, and I will pay (Baya 15).

Keeping the Shabbos is tantamount to keeping the whole Torah. (Pesikta)

He who delights in the Shabbos is granted his heart's desires. (Tehillim 37:3)

THE LINEAGE OF BETZALEL

Moshe selected only those Jews who had an all-encompassing wisdom, both mechanical wizardry and wisdom of the heart, to assist in the construction of the Mishkon. Names are usually listed in the Torah without any elaboration. However, this norm changed dramatically with the mention of the name of Betzalel. Here the Torah lists not only Betzalel's name, but also those of his father Uri and his grandfather Chur. Why the sudden need to list Betzalel's entire family tree?

The reason becomes clear when we learn that Chur was one of the few individuals

who emerged from the episode of the Eigel HaZohov with distinction. When the Bnei Yisroel began insisting upon the construction of a golden calf, it was Chur who tried to bring them to their senses. He lectured them severely, warning that their act was sacrilegious and that they would later be sorry. But this opposition only aroused the Jews' fury, and they compounded their sin by killing Chur (Sanhedrin 7a).

Chur, then, made very noticeable his loyalty to Hashem. By way of reward, he was blessed with a grandson who, helped by Chur's merit, became the chief craftsman of the Mishkon.

R. Shimeon b. Elazar said: For whatever commandment Israel was willing to accept martyrdom rather than perform violation in his time, will be strictly and stoutly adhered to even thousands of years later in our time.

THE WOMEN'S JEWELRY

As was mentioned earlier, the golden calf was fashioned from the ornaments solicited from Jewish women. However, the Torah indicates that the collection of the jewelry was not a simple matter. On the one hand, we find Aharon suggesting that the women donate their jewelry for the Eigel; on the other hand, we see the men handing this jewelry over to Aharon. This implies that the women did not contribute their jewelry willingly, and that the men had to take it by force. Obviously, the women were most reluctant to contribute anything for the service of idol-worship.

As a reward for this, the women were given the right to contribute first to the construction of the holy Sanctuary. They did so most eagerly, donating their very best jewelry with impressive zeal, in obvious contrast to their unwilling assistance in the construction of the Eigel. This time they knew they were aiding a most worthy cause, and they were enthusiastic about offering their riches for Hashem's desired goal.

The daughters of Israel are beautiful. (Nedarim 66)

Honor your wife that you may prosper. (Bava Metzia 59)

who was a talented engraver and weaver.

The gifts for the building of the Sanctuary became so plentiful that the workmen were able to report that they had more material than they needed. Soon, section by section, the Sanctuary and its contents began taking shape. The people were then asked to refrain from donating additional items.

A woman is beautiful when she is virtuous. (Shabbos 25)

Among the other loyal Jews who refused to contribute their possessions for an unworthy cause was Rabbi Yitzchok, the father of the great Torah commentator, Rashi.

Rabbi Yitzchok was the owner of a uniquely beautiful gem. His jewel won widespread fame, and even the Sultan learned of its existence. He promptly sent his emissaries to Rabbi Yitzchok and instructed them to purchase the gem for an enormous sum of money.

When these messengers made their offer, Rabbi Yitzchok was overwhelmed. He saw himself using his new-found wealth for the performance of countless Mitzvos, and he felt extremely grateful to Hashem. Suddenly, though, a look of apprehension replaced his smile.

"What does the Sultan want to do with this gem?" he asked.

"He wants to use it as the eye of his idol," was the reply.

Rabbi Yitzchok was aghast. "Never will I give you the gem for that purpose!" he exclaimed, and he asked the messengers to leave.

The Sultan's agents then hit upon a new scheme. A message was sent to Rabbi Yitzchok informing him that there was a Jewish family being held captive on a boat in a nearby harbor. They would be released,

but only if Rabbi Yitzchok appeared and redeemed them with his gem.

Rabbi Yitzchok did not hesitate for a moment. He grabbed the gem and rushed to the boat, whose whereabouts had been pinpointed in the message. The moment he boarded, though, he was met by the Sultan's agents.

"There is no Jewish family here," they told him. "This was all just a trick to bring you aboard with your gem. Now we intend to hold you captive here until you sell us the gem. Will you make matters easy for yourself and agree?"

Rabbi Yitzchok stared at the agents for only a moment. Then, with speed that astonished them, he raced to the side of the ship and dropped the precious gem overboard.

"I would rather lose all my riches than see them used for the wrong purposes," he declared.

The Sultan's agents were so amazed and impressed by Rabbi Yitzchok's attitude that they released him immediately. At that moment, a heavenly voice declared, "Rabbi Yitzchok, you threw away your fortune for the sake of Hashem. Know that you will be repaid with a son whose knowledge will be more valuable than all the jewels in the world."

At Moshe's command, the total cost of the Sanctuary construction was computed. The work was inspected and approved by Moshe, who blessed the people for their assistance in this magnificent achievement.

On the first day of the month of Nissan, almost a year after the Jews' departure from Egypt, the Mishkon was erected under Moshe's personal supervision and the contents were arranged in the prescribed order. A cloud covered the Mishkon, which was suffused with Hashem's glory. Whenever the cloud lifted, it signalled Hashem's desire that the Israelites continue their journey.

פרשת
פקודי

*Parshas
Pekudei*

MOSHE UNDER SUSPICION

What was the primary reason for Moshe's detailed accounting of the costs of the Sanctuary? Our Sages comment that there were apparently some who suspected that Moshe might have kept some of their Sanctuary contributions for his own use. As a result, Moshe was prompted to show one and all that every single coin and article contributed was indeed used for the Sanctuary (Shemos Rabbah, Parshas Pekudei).

The importance of not judging another hastily is depicted in a story about Rabbi Bunim of Parshischo. Two valid witnesses appeared before the rabbinical court to testify that they had personally seen Rabbi Bunim eating cake and coffee on Yom Kippur after Kol Nidre.

The Rabbis investigated the matter and found out exactly what had actually happened. Rav Bunim's daughter-in-law gave birth right before Yom Kippur. About an hour into Yom Kippur, Rav Bunim asked if she had eaten anything, since one is required to eat despite the fast in such circumstances. When he was told that she refused to eat because it was Yom Kippur, he insisted that she take some refreshments. She refused to eat unless her father-in-law personally gave her the food. Since this was a matter of saving a life, Rav Bunim took cake and a drink in his hands and brought them to her. Just at that moment, the two witnesses passed by the window and saw Rav Bunim holding the food. They mistakenly assumed that he was going to eat the food himself. (Eser Zchuyos, pg.102)

The renowned Tzaddik, Rabbi Aryeh Levine, was well-known for his care in judging everyone favorably. He once related to someone how he acquired this attribute: "It happened when I attended the funeral of Rabbi Eliezer Rivlin, a prominent treasurer of charity funds in Yerushalayim. The deceased had an intimate friend named Rabbi Shmuel Kook with whom he had worked together for 30 years. When the funeral procession began, I noticed that Rabbi Shmuel Kook entered a flower shop and purchased a flower pot.

"I was shocked and went over to Rabbi Kook to rebuke him. 'Is this the way to act at the funeral of a lifelong friend?' I censured him. 'Couldn't you find a more appropriate time to buy a flower pot?'

"He then explained his behavior. He had befriended someone who was hospitalized with a highly contagious disease. The day before, that person had died. The doctors, who weren't Jewish, understandably ordered

that all of that person's belongings be burned. When Rav Shmuel found out about the orders, he pleaded with the doctors not to burn the deceased's Tefillin, but to allow him to bury them instead. They finally agreed that if he would obtain an earthenware flower pot, they would permit the Tefillin to be buried in it. But they warned him that he had only until twelve o'clock to bring the flower pot. Therefore, he had to leave the funeral procession of his best friend in order to meet the deadline.

"At that moment, I made a resolution to always judge people favorably." (Ish Tzaddik Haya, pg.102)

The suspicious attitude of some of the people in this instance contrasted notably with their tolerant attitude towards their contributions for the Eigel HaZohov. We find that the Israelites donated a great deal of their gold and silver for the construction of this surrogate leader, and all that emerged was a small golden calf. Yet, no one suspected that someone had appropriated their riches. They were too enthused over what was occurring to complain. On the other hand, when their money was being used for a noble and holy cause, the construction of the Sanctuary of Hashem, they wanted to make absolutely sure that they did not donate an unnecessary cent.

How many of us assume the very same suspicious attitude? We are extremely generous and indulgent when spending money for our own benefit. We spend money recklessly when purchasing a car or paying for a pleasure cruise. But contributing money to Tzedokoh? This becomes another matter entirely. Here we become as cost-conscious as possible, watching over our pursestrings like hawks, making sure that we do not give more than absolutely necessary. Perhaps it is time that we also make a detailed accounting of our priorities.

The beginning of evil is suspicion. Suspicion will never overtake the humble. (Taanis 21)

It is the duty of every man to preserve his good name and keep himself above suspicion. R. Shmuel ben Nachmon stated: "The Torah demands that we have to satisfy human standards of behavior just as we have to satisfy divine ones." (Yalkut Shimoni)

THE ORON AND THE FLASK OF MUN

We find that both the Oron (Holy Ark) and a container of Mun (manna, food from the heavens) were hidden. Why were these two specific items hidden? Perhaps we can comprehend that the Oron, containing the holy Torah written on Mt. Sinai, was too sanctified to be open to full public view. However, the Mun was gathered by the people regularly. Why, then, was the Mun paired with the Oron in this regard?

The matter becomes clearer when we realize that both the Oron and the Mun are also symbolic of two aspects of life. The former represents the spiritual qualities, while the latter, being food necessary for the body, represents materialism. Both are necesssary if life is to flourish. Our Sages have commented: "If there is no flour, there is no Torah. If there is no Torah, there is no flour" (Pirkey Avos 3:17). In other words, we cannot exist physically and learn Torah if we do not at the same time tend to our bodily needs; conversely, if we disregard the Torah, then our physical existence becomes meaningless. It is for this reason that the Oron and the Mun were associated. The aspects of life that they symbolize must be unified by man.

Unfortunately, there are many who concentrate solely on satisfying their materialistic needs while neglecting their spiritualistic requirements. They do not realize the treasure they are overlooking. They are like the farmer who worked extremely hard to make ends meet, and who applied all his energies to the functioning of the farm. He worked so persistently, in fact, that he had no time to read the few letters he received in the mail and continued working. Unfortunately, the effort took its toll, and the farmer, suffering from exhaustion, took to his bed. His family was summoned and one of the relatives tending to him noticed the unopened mail lying neglected on a desk. She opened the letters and came upon one containing a check for an enormous sum of money. It was an inheritance that had been sent to him many years earlier. When she showed it to the farmer, though, he merely sighed.

"For years I'd been driving myself to the grave trying to make the farm profitable," he said. "If only I'd known about this letter earlier! Imagine all the suffering I would have avoided! But now it's too late."

Those who toil an entire lifetime to procure luxuries, only to find that they are too exhausted to enjoy them, have neglected an opportunity to avoid miseries. Had they noticed the lifestyle of the Torah, they would have learned that their valiant efforts were really misguided, and that the spirituality of the Torah could have provided the very same contentment with much less exhaustion.

Some ignore the eternal life for a momentary one. (Shabbos 9)
One cannot exist on bread alone. (Shabbos 51)
The slave is free when he is content with his lot and the free is a slave when he seeks more than his daily bread.
The fruit of contentedness is tranquility.

"AS HASHEM COMMANDED MOSHE"

Parshas Pekudei contains one specific phrase a total of eighteen times. This is "Ka'asher Tziva Hashem Es Moshe—As Hashem Commanded Moshe." Every time the Torah mentions an action performed in the Sanctuary, it adds that it was performed "as Hashem commanded Moshe." The Torah usually weighs every single word very carefully. Why, then, this constant repetition?

The answer stems from Moshe's championship of the Israelites during the crisis of the Eigel HaZohov. When Hashem had threatened to eradicate the Bnei Yisroel at that time, Moshe had responded, "If You will not forgive their sin, then wipe me out, too!" Moshe was willing to forego the establishment of a nation derived entirely from his descendants, in order to obtain a pardon for his fellow Jews.

As a result, it was Moshe who was largely responsible for the supreme moment of the dedication of the Sanctuary in the midst of the Jewish nation. To emphasize his role in this event, and to reassure him that his name would be enshrined, rather than blotted out, the Torah stresses that Hashem had commanded Moshe to oversee the Sanctuary.

The number eighteen, notable here as the number of times the above-mentioned statement is listed, has additional significance. It is, of course, equivalent to the word "Chai," meaning "Life." And it represents the number of original blessings in the Shemoneh Esrei prayer recited three times daily. It is as if we deserve life and are able to pray to Hashem through the merit of the service rendered by our great leader Moshe. The nineteenth blessing in the Shemoneh Esrei (added later as an indictment of heretics), corresponds to the Torah statement "As Hashem had commanded so they (the people—not the heretics) did." It should also be noted that these eighteen Torah phrases consist of one hundred thirteen words, equivalent to the number of words in the closing benedictions of the Shemoneh Esrei blessings, and both equal the number of times the word "Lev" (Heart) appears in the Torah. This emphasizes the need to devote one's entire heart and soul to the service of Hashem.

One should pray with the devotion of the woman whose son was wasting away from disease. Though told that her child was doomed to die, she placed her last fragment of hope into a prayer emitted from the depths of her being: "Hashem, spare my child! Transfer his illness to me, instead!" Immediately thereafter, the child began a slow road to recovery—and the woman, laid low for a while with the same disease that had struck him, soon joined him in full recuperation.

He who prays for his friend, while being himself in the same need, will be answered first. (Bava Kama 92)

The Holy One, blessed be He, longs for the prayer of the righteous. (Yevamos 64)

Prayer is also a refuge from disappointment and despair. As both Yochanan and R. Eleazar said: Even if a sharp sword rests on a man's neck, he should not despair from prayer. (Berachos 10)

The five principal Korbonos (Sacrifices) which could be offered by an individual are:

1) The Olah: Consumed offering. Consumed entirely by fire on the Mizbeiach (Altar).

2) The Mincha: Allegiance—Gift. Unlike the other Korbonos which consisted of animals, this was an offering of flour usually brought by a man of modest means.

3) The Sh'lomim: Peace Offering. A means of expressing thanks to Hashem on joyous occasions. Also included is the Korbon Todah (discussed in Parshas Tzav).

פרשת ויקרא

Parshas Vayikroh

KORBONOS AND PRAYERS

What are Korbonos? What is their purpose? A clue to the answer comes from an examination of the word Korbonos, which contains the word "Korov," meaning "near." A Korbon then, is a means of approaching Hashem, supplicating for Divine forgiveness or demonstrating appreciation for Divine assistance, and thereby bringing one closer to the Holy Shechina.

Today, because we are tragically without a Beis Hamikdosh, we are unfortunately unable to offer Korbonos. However, we have been granted an alternate method to express our contribution and/or gratitude, and that is through prayer.

Our prayers now serve the same two basic purposes as did the Korbonos. They testify to the fact that we acknowledge Hashem's mastery of the world, and they allow us to ask for Hashem's assistance.

When we pray to Hashem, we do so with the knowledge that Hashem is everywhere and that He will hear our prayers no matter where we may be. Our prayers provide us with a direct spiritual link to our Creator; the Tefillos we say provide us with our own "hot line" to the Almighty. This was the outlook displayed by a Sage, who was told a century ago, about a new invention called the telephone, with which one can speak to someone else a great distance away without even seeing him.

"What is so new about that?" commented the Sage. "I have been communicating with Hashem like that for years and years through my prayers."

By always remembering through our prayers that Hashem is everywhere, we can spare ourselves the pitfalls of many a sin, for we will never make the mistake of trying to sin behind closed doors. To Hashem, there are no closed doors.

This point was driven home to a certain carriage driver who was transporting a Torah sage through a town. The sky was darkening, when the driver suddenly halted the journey. The sage glanced out the window and noticed that the driver had left the carriage and was approaching a nearby field. Catching the sage's gaze, the driver said, "Please let me know if you see someone else watching." He then tiptoed toward the field and to the sage's astonishment, began selecting fruits that belonged to the field's owner. The driver had just begun amassing the fruits when he heard the sage calling frantically, "Get back, quick! Hurry! Someone's watching!"

The driver, alarmed, dropped the fruits and dashed back to the carriage. He sped away from the scene as quickly as he could. After a few breathless minutes he turned to the sage and smiled. "Thank you for warning me. If the owner of the field had caught me, I would have been finished."

"Oh, the owner of the field wasn't watching, but someone else was," explained the sage with his finger directed heavenward, "And if you had kept the fruits, you certainly would have been in big trouble."

DONATING WITH YOUR HEART

"Nefesh Ki Sakriv" says the Torah when referring to someone who offers a Korbon Mincha, the Korbon consisting of flour. This phraseology is somewhat unusual. It translates "and the Soul who will offer a Korbon." Would not the term "V'odom Ki Yakriv" "and a person who will offer a Korbon" be more appropriate? Is it not the entire person offering this Korbon, not just the soul alone?

4) The Chatos: Sin offering. An atonement for certain sins committed unintentionally by an individual, including the Kohain Godol (High Priest), the King, or the Sanhedrin (Supreme Court) as a whole. These include prohibitions punishable by Koros when done intentionally. Some examples include eating Chometz on Pesach or doing a Malacha on Shabbos.

4A) Korbon Oleh V'Yored: A special type of sin offering which varies with the wealth of the sinner. These are required for the following transgressions:

a) Swearing falsely that one had not seen or heard evidence needed for testimony.

b) Entering the Bais Hamikdosh (Sanctuary), or eating Kodshim while Tumah (Unclean).

c) Failing to fulfill a vow.

Yet, our Chazal (Sages of Blessed Memory) who enlighted our very beings with their keen insight, interpret that the Torah wishes to imbue us with a profound lesson. Let us remember that the Korbon Mincha is ordinarily offered by a poverty striken individual. It is not simple for such an individual to offer this Korbon. Yet, this poor person sacrificed his personal needs, scrimped and saved, in order to have the Z'chus (Merit) of bringing this Korbon to Hashem. Such a sacrifice is "Nefesh Ki Sakriv"—in the Al-mighty's eyes it is as if the Nefesh, the very soul of this person was sacrificed. This is the essence of giving Tzedokoh or offering Korbonos; to make sacrifices on behalf of Hashem and on behalf of the poor, of offering, in a way, our own soul, that which is very dear to us.

Those who wonder how this can be accomplished can ponder the story of a certain Rabbi of a small town. He was visited one day by a widow who, soon after she arrived, began sobbing bitterly. "My daughter wishes to get married," she explained, "and a very fine young Torah scholar has asked for her hand. But I have no money to offer as a dowry, no money to pay for a wedding. What shall I do?"

"If only I were wealthy, I would gladly give you the money," replied the Rabbi. "But wait a minute, let me think. . . ."

After a moment, the Rabbi rose and walked to a cupboard in the next room. He returned with two extremely impressive silver candlesticks. "Someone gave these to me as a present," he explained, "and they must be very valuable. Here, take them, and may your daughter be blessed with a wonderful marriage."

The widow thanked him again and again, and left with a radiant smile on her face. The Rabbi then went into the kitchen where his wife was preparing dinner. "Do you have two potatoes we could use?" he asked her.

"Certainly. What for?"

"They will serve as our new candleholders," he explained. "I gave our silver ones to a poor widow."

"But you always admired those candlesticks so!" said his wife.

"I know," said the Rabbi happily. "And now I realize what true Tzedokoh means."

MODESTY

Another noticeable point in this Sedrah is that the word "Vayikroh" contains an Alef that is much smaller in size than the other letters of the Torah. Again, this is done deliberately, to provide a lesson for us. The word "Vayikroh" means "called," and the verse "Vayikroh el Moshe" indicates that Hashem called Moshe. However, Moshe, in his modesty, felt that it was not proper to state that one so holy as Hashem called on a mere mortal like himself. Therefore, when transcribing the Torah, Moshe purposely made the Alef in the word very small, so that it would appear to be "Vayekar," meaning "met," indicating that Hashem met Moshe by accident. This would then downplay Moshe's importance.

Why did one so elevated as Moshe, the only human ever to speak to Hashem "Ponim el Ponim," feel the need to be so modest? Could he not flaunt his greatness just a little bit?

It seems, though, that Moshe's personal philosophy was the antithesis of the above. The greater he became, the higher the level of holiness he attained, the more modest he became. In Moshe's view, one who had been granted so deep an understanding of Hashem's teachings as he had should be a far greater person than he actually was. The more learned and pious a person is, the

Conscience stricken, the wrongdoer confessed his misdeed and was obliged to bring this sacrifice.

5) The Oshom: Guilt Offering. Offered as part of the penitence required for certain improper acts; such as,

    a) unintentionally using property set aside for Hashem (Kodshim),

    b) retaining another's property by swearing falsely.

In each case, the wrongdoer, after confessing his guilt, must first restore the property, plus an additional one fifth of its value to the rightful owner, before he could offer the sacrifice and receive Divine forgiveness for his sin.

better an example he must set for others. The higher he attained, the more every tiny failing and minute blemish became noticeable. This realization made Moshe modest and humble, despite his greatness.

Certainly, if Moshe Rabbeinu felt the need to be modest, how much more so should we downplay any little greatness we might think we have. If Moshe Rabbeinu refused to boast, how can we do so?

One who emulated Moshe Rabbeinu in this respect was the renowned Torah scholar Rabbi Akiva Eiger. Because he had a widowed daughter, he wrote to the equally noted Sage, the Chasam Sofer, asking for suggestions for a second husband for her. The Chasam Sofer showed the letter to his trusted colleague, Rabbi David Prosnitz. It was Rabbi Prosnitz who replied to Rabbi Akiva Eiger, proposing as a mate none other than the Chasam Sofer himself, whose wife had also died some time before.

Soon afterwards, Rabbi Prosnitz received a new letter from Rabbi Akiva Eiger. This one stated that he would be most delighted to have such a Torah giant as the Chasam Sofer for a son-in-law, and that he felt that a woman as upright as his daughter was worthy of such a husband. However, he was afraid that the Chasam Sofer would want to marry the daughter of a Talmid Chochom, and that, therefore, the Chasam Sofer would not accept him as a father-in-law. Rabbi Akiva Eiger felt that he was too insignificant a Rabbi to merit the approval of other Torah scholars.

Before Rabbi Prosnitz could inform the Chasam Sofer of this reply, the Chasam Sofer offered his own opinion on the matter to him.

"I would be greatly honored to marry the daughter of such a great Godol B'Yisroel. But how could he ever accept me as a son-in-law?"

Rabbi David Prosnitz smiled. "The fears of both of you are now dissolved," he said— the marriage was indeed performed. It was fitting that two Sages of such great modesty should be members of the same family.

פרשת צו

Parshas Tzav

The Kohanim were given the mitzvah of "T'rumas Hadeshen"—lifting the ashes of the daily "Olos" (Consumed Offerings). They were also told to keep the fire on the altar burning continuously. Aharon, the Kohein Godol, was instructed to bring a meal-offering each morning and evening.

Additional laws were given specifying the duties of the Kohanim and the portions of the offerings they were to receive as their due. They could eat of the meal, sin, and trespass offerings only if they were ceremonially clean, and only within the Court of the Sanctuary.

A LESSON IN CONSISTENCY

Two separate flames were evident in the Mishkon, the Ner Tomid, and the Eish Tomid. The former was a flickering light which burned continuously on the Menorah, while the latter was a fire of powerful warmth that blazed without a stop on the Mizbeiach (Altar).

The fact that both flames burned continuously is significant. We, too, have a heavenly spark within our souls, but it can warm us only if we keep it continuously kindled. This can be accomplished if we learn and live Torah, with the warmth and

In an impressive ceremony conducted in the Court of the Sanctuary, Aharon and his sons were installed in their offices by Moshe, with the assembly watching. After the Kohanim had bathed, Moshe dressed Aharon in his distinctive garments, and anointed the Tabernacle and its contents (the Ark, Table of Showbread,

enthusiasm indicated by the fire on the Mizbeiach. We must exhibit the "Hislahavus" of the Jewish spirit, the exuberance in serving Hashem in all that we do. Yet, to prevent us from becoming arrogant and "hot-headed," we have before us the example of the flickering Ner Tomid. The Ner Tomid was not a powerful fire which is so impressive, but rather a modest flickering light. We must bear in mind that modesty is also essential, for if we act too proudly the fragile flame we bring into this world will be snuffed out.

What we must remember above all is the fact that the fires burned continuously. This tells us that we, too, must continuously act in accordance with Hashem's wishes, and that we must remain consistent in our Yiddishkeit, showing both enthusiasm and modesty in our constant pursuit of Torah. This means that we cannot put on an impressive display of religion one day and be only minimally religious the next day. For instance, we cannot go to Shul and be pious only on Yom Kippur, but must do so every day of the year. When we give Tzedokoh, we should not do so only when we are in the proper mood, but under all conditions. We cannot make religion a matter of convenience. No! Our religious observance must exist at all times, as did the flames in the Mishkon.

The need for consistency in Yiddishkeit was underscored by the Dubno Maggid in one of his famous parables. The Maggid noted with alarm that many Jews attended his shul during the Yomim Noroim (High Holidays) only, failing to appear during the other days of the year. To counteract this, he related the following story:

A storekeeper arrived for work one day to find all his warehouses going up in flames. After the fire had been put out, he found to his dismay that all his possessions had been ruined. He was penniless, and worse, he now had a large debt, for all his merchandise had been bought on credit. What could he do?

Near despair, he went to the manufacturer and told him his tale of woe. The manufacturer's pity was aroused, and he agreed to not only wipe the debt off the books, but to

also give the storekeeper some more goods on credit. That way, the storekeeper would be able to go back into business and repay the loan.

Word spread about the manufacturer's generosity. Soon, another man arrived at the manufacturer's door and began pleading for money. "How dare you?" said the manufacturer. "You don't deserve a penny, so leave!"

"But you gave the storekeeper all that credit," replied the man. "Why did you help him but not me?"

"How can you possibly compare yourself to the storekeeper?" said the manufacturer. "I've done thousands of dollars of business with him for years! I know him and I can trust him; he's always paid me back before. Therefore, when something tragic happened to him, I gave him the gift of some credit and the benefit of the doubt. But in your case, I don't know you at all. If I lend you some money, how do I know that you'll ever pay me back?"

"This," said the Dubno Maggid, "is the plight of a Jew who is not consistent in his observance of Judaism, as opposed to one who is constantly faithful. The person who has a good credit rating with Hashem, through his regular attendance at shul and his constant observance of Mitzvos will be given the benefit of the doubt during times of need. But the person who, because he does not perform Mitzvos regularly, is a stranger to Hashem, doesn't deserve to receive Hashem's favor when he requires it."

Shammai said: "Make your study of Torah a permanent fixture." (Avos 1:15)

NOT EMBARRASSING OTHERS

There was no particular place specifically designated for bringing the sacrifice of the Korbon Chatos, the sin offering, in the Miskhan (Sotah 32b, Yerushalmi Yevamos Perek 8 Halacho 3). This is significant. The Korbon Chatos was offered by one who had sinned and now wished to repent. If there was a specified physical location for these sacrifices, the identity of the sinners would become readily known, and this might in

Candelabra, and Altar of Incense), as well as the Altar of Burnt Offering, and the laver and its base (all of which stood in the Court of the Sanctuary). He then poured the anointing oil upon Aharon's head, thus sanctifying him. Finally, the regular Kohanim were invested with their garments. A sin-offering and burnt-offering

itself discourage repentance. Because the Korbon Chatos was offered in the same place as was the Korbon Olah, no one could be certain that the bearer of the Korbon had actually sinned. In this way, the matter would remain a private one between man and G-d, and the sinner would be spared public embarrassment.

If Hashem's Torah laws deliberately avoid the shaming of others, then we should certainly be careful not to embarrass our fellow man. Our Sages say that whoever insults his fellow man in public forfeits his place in the world to come. (Bava Metziah 59a). The reason is a simple one. One can kill a man only once with a knife, but he can slay him many times over with a shameful word.

Rabbi Akiva Eiger once invited a poor man to his home on Friday night. At the meal, a beautiful white tablecloth covered the Shabbos table. When the poor man lifted his glass of wine, it slipped out of his hand, and the red liquid spilled over the pure white cloth, leaving an ugly blotch.

Seeing the poor man squirm in embarrassment, Rabbi Akiva immediately lifted his own glass of wine, and also "accidentally" spilled it over the tablecloth. As the poor man looked on in great relief, Rabbi Akiva Eiger remarked, "It seems as if the table or the floor is shaking, doesn't it?"

He had been willing to make himself look careless (and to soil a nice tablecloth) just to spare the shame of another.

On one occasion when Rabbi Noson Finkel was leading the congregation in prayer, he kept stumbling on the pronunciation of the words. Those present were amazed, since he always pronounced each word precisely. The congregants soon understood the reason for the Rabbi's uncharacteristic difficulty.

There was a mourner in the Shul who had difficulty reading Hebrew, and when he read from the Siddur, people laughed or smiled. In order to lessen the mourner's embarrassment, Rabbi Finkel acted as if he could not read any better. (Chayei Hamussar, vol. 2, pg.204)

Rabbi Moshe Feinstein, Shlita, left his lecture room for a few minutes. One of his students carelessly pushed over an inkwell and the blue ink spilled onto a beautiful volume that lay on Rabbi Feinstein's desk. Some students strongly censured their colleague for being so clumsy, since they knew how much Rabbi Feinstein cherished this set of Talmud. When Rav Moshe returned, he perceived the distress of the student who spilled the ink, and said, "Oh, it looks wonderful with the blue color." (Bastion of Faith, pg.12)

Whenever a maid would drop and break something in his home, Rabbi Yitzchak Elchonon Specter would tell the members of his household that he broke it. By this means he would save the maid from being verbally abused.

> *"You can only kill a man once; but when you shame him you can kill him many times over." (Midrash Eliyahu 42)*
>
> *"Let a man throw himself into a burning furnace rather than disgrace another in public." (Kesubos 68)*

SINCERE DEVOTION, NOT MERE HABIT

The word "Tzav" (Vayikra 6:2), which begins this Parsha, means "Command." It is deliberately expressed in a form that can refer to both the past and the future. In other words, the commandments of Hashem are as applicable today as they were when first promulgated. The Torah is not "old-fashioned." The rules governing man's behavior and man's devotion to G-d are timeless.

Consequently, our observance of the Torah should not be marked by tired, listless efforts. When we pray, we should not stumble and mumble through the Tefillos out of habit. Rather, we should remember Whom we are addressing, and say each word carefully. The same applies to our observance of Shabbos and our Torah learning. They should not be routine, but rather, should be moments of inspiration.

The following story, told by the Chofetz Chaim, illustrates the fallacy of reciting our prayers mechanically and by rote. When we pray, we should really mean every word we

were then brought by Moshe. These rites were repeated for seven days, during which Aharon and his sons remained within the Court.

say.

"All employees report to the manager's office."

The call went out over the factory's public address system and soon all the workers were assembled before the manager. This procedure had been going on each day for several weeks, ever since the company owner had left the country on an important business trip. He had always directed the factory's operations but now he had appointed a manager to oversee the work of his employees and to assure that everything functioned smoothly during his absence.

Now all of these employees listened, bored, as this manager read aloud the instructions left behind by the boss. He carefully pronounced each word just as the owner had ordered and did a masterful job of delivering the instructions.

When the boss returned he was shocked to see the condition of his factory. Machines needed repairs and workers stood around idle. He angrily called in the manager and asked him for an explanation.

"Did you follow the instructions I left behind with you?"

"Why, of course," the manager defended himself. "I read them to all of the workers every day while you were gone."

"Now I know why there is such a mess!" cried the boss. "You only read these instructions but didn't bother to see that they were carried out. The lazy workers took advantage of your foolishness and almost ruined my entire business. Do you think that I left behind these instructions only for reading? I gave them to you so that you would know how to run the factory in my absence. Reading them has not achieved this goal."

The behavior of the poor manager is similar to that exhibited by people who study Torah and pray daily only out of force of habit. They recite the words, but they consider them as reading material, not as a plan of action. The Torah and the Tefillos are like the list left by the master, a set of instructions on how to act practically. If we do not realize this, and we do not actually practice what we say, then our words have no meaning or purpose at all.

"The heart of the matter is what matters." (Berachos 15)

Rabbi Shimon said: "Be careful with the reading of Shema and with prayer, and when you pray make not your prayer a habit, but an appeal for mercy." (Avos 2:18)

The Kohanim assumed their duties after the seven days of initiation. At this time, the whole congregation stood reverently before the Altar while Aharon offered sacrifices for himself and for the entire nation. After he had blessed the assembly, Aharon joined Moshe inside the Mishkon, and upon their return, portions of the sacrifice still on the altar were consumed by Divine fire. The people, seeing this, fell in worship before the L-rd.

Nadav and Avihu, Aharon's oldest sons, offered incense on unconsecrated fire not taken from the altar. Such an offense by Kohanim, who were to set an exam-

פרשת שמיני
Parshas Shemini

IN PURSUIT OF PEACE

The name of Aharon has been accorded a special place of affection in the history of the Jews. When he was alive, he was exceedingly popular, and when he passed from the earth, he was deeply mourned. Why was Aharon so well loved? Because Aharon was renowned as an "Ohev Sholom V'Rodeph Sholom," one who loved and pursued peace

(Avos De Rabbi Nosson Perek 12, Nedarim 10b). He deeply desired the well-being of his fellow humans, and tried to improve their ways, not through harshness, but through friendship.

When Aharon became aware that two people were quarreling, he felt personally bereaved. Settling the argument became his first priority. He would go to one of the par-

ple for the rest of the assembly, was unpardonable. The two of them were therefore punished by being consumed "by fire which came from before the L-rd," and they died instantly. Aharon was overwhelmed with grief at this tragedy, but Moshe explained to him that the Kohanim had a special responsibility to maintain the high standard of sanctity demanded of them by Hashem. To prevent the remaining Kohanim from becoming defiled by touching the dead bodies, Aharon's cousins, Mishael and Elzaphon (who were not priests) were told to bury the bodies. Aharon and his two remaining sons, Elazar and Isamar, were instructed not to exhibit any mourning, thereby demonstrating their submission to Hashem's will. The Kohanim were also warned not to drink any strong liquor (as Nadav and Avihu had) before discharging their duties in the Mishkon or instructing the people.

ties and say, "Your rival told me that he feels sorry about the fight you both had. In fact, he would like to apologize to you, but he feels too embarrassed to do so. Maybe you could help matters by going over and forgiving him." Then he would tell the other party the exact same thing. As a result, when the two individuals would encounter each other, they would express their sorrow over the argument, and peace would be achieved. Peace is a very fragile treasure, but Aharon knew how to secure it. In fact, he would go to the extent of suffering personal abuse to encourage tranquility.

The following story may help illustrate this important point. Reb Meir, who strove to emulate Aharon's trait of seeking peace, had demonstrated this characteristic by the way he settled a dispute between a husband and wife. The wife was a devoted follower of Reb Meir and was a frequent attendee at his Torah discussions. The husband's jealousy was aroused, and he began asserting that her interest was in Reb Meir himself rather than in his words. When the woman protested, her husband replied, "I will believe you, but only if you go to him and spit in his eye several times. That way I will know that you are not personally involved with him."

The next time Reb Meir saw the woman, he noticed that she was unusually downcast. When he asked why, the woman explained the situation, and told him what her husband had demanded. Reb Meir nodded and said that he understood.

At the next assembly, Reb Meir approached the woman. "There is something wrong with my eye," he said. "If you spit into it several times, perhaps it will get better."

The woman was shocked at this suggestion, but eventually complied, in full view of others. Word of the occurrence eventually

reached the husband, and he was now satisfied that his wife was doing nothing wrong. Their quarrel had been settled, and Reb Meir was most pleased. His dignity may have suffered, but he had achieved his goal.

If both Aharon and Reb Meir were willing to go to such great lengths to bring about peace, we, too, must struggle to achieve the same results!

In the same vein, a certain Rav once used his wisdom to secure true peace. Two Jews came before him and requested that he resolve their dispute. It seemed that they had both purchased burial plots in the same area, and each one wanted the better-looking spot.

After listening to the claims of each, and pondering for a moment, the Rav announced his decision: "Both of you have valid claims. Therefore, I say that the nicer spot will go to the one who dies first."

There was a long silence and from that moment on, there was no more argument about the burial plot!

One must use all of his or her resources to bring about peace. "The Master of Peace desires the peace of all his creations."

> *"Even if peace eludes you—go after it and you will catch up with it." (Midrash Shmuel 4:20)*
> *Rabbi Levi says: "Beloved is peace, for all blessings end with it; the blessing of the priests too, ends with the words: 'And give you peace.' " (Bamidbar 6:26)*
> *"The learned increase the peace and happiness in the world." (Berachos 84)*

IMPORTANCE OF RESPECTING THE SAGES

Despite the greatness of Aharon, he suffered the loss of two of his sons, Nodov and Avihu, through unnatural means. A spark of Hashem consumed them, and they died (Medrash Tanchuma, Shemini). But why?

Aharon and his sons neglected to eat their share of the sin-offering brought on behalf of the people, and the sacrifice became completely burned. This was contrary to the command that a certain portion of the offering was to be eaten by them within the Mishkon. In reply to Moshe's rebuke, Aharon explained that since the Korbon became unclean and there was not a specific commandment by Hashem regarding how to deal with this, it was forbidden to be eaten.

Purity and holiness were to be the principles underlying everyday life among the Jews. Although man was permitted to eat the meat of animals, he was restricted in his choice of food by being told to abstain from impure, non-Kosher items. Only those quadrupeds which had completely split hooves and which chewed their cud

What had they done to deserve such an untimely fate?

There have been several explanations offered for their deaths. One centers around the idea that Nodov and Avihu had expounded the law in the presence of their teacher Moshe (Eruvin 63a, Yoma 23a). This may seem harmless, but in reality, it is quite a severe matter. By doing so, they had shown a lack of respect for their teacher's authority, and this in effect, challenged Hashem's authority as well. One who challenges the Torah Sages, those imbued with Hashem's wisdom, denies the whole basis of the Torah. Because the Rabbonim are the earthly representatives of the Almighty, both they and their laws must be accorded the highest respect. Therefore, when one had a doubt about a law, or about how he should conduct himself, he should take the matter to a Rav instead of deciding it on his own.

"He who passes upon a question on law in the presence of his teacher does not deserve to live." (Berachos 31)

Though Rabbi Akiva was one of the greatest of our sages, he refused to disobey the words of the Rabbonim. Because of his adherence to the Torah, Rabbi Akiva was imprisoned by the Romans. While he was in jail, Rabbi Yehoshua would bring him a jug of water daily. One day, Rabbi Yehoshua was stopped by a sadistic prison keeper, who cruelly spilled out half the water in the jug. Rabbi Yehoshua hurried to deliver the remaining water to Rabbi Akiva, and explained what had happened.

"There is not enough water here for you to both drink and wash your hands," noted Rabbi Yehoshua. "Why not use all the water for drinking?"

Rabbi Akiva shook his head. "My fellow Rabbis decreed that one must wash his hands before every meal. How could I go against this dictum of theirs? No, I will use

this water for washing; if any water is left, then I will drink." "I would rather die than transgress a Rabbinical opinion." (Eruvin 21b).

"The ordinances of the Rabbis are as authoritative as the Torah." (Avodah Zarah 32)

KASHRUS

Parshas Shemini lists the varieties of foods which Jews may and may not eat. This subject is referred to as Kashrus. Throughout the years, there have been many rationales offered for the laws of Kashrus. Some have asserted that the laws of Kashrus were only a temporary health measure. For instance, pork was prohibited so that Jews would not be stricken with the disease of trichinosis, and the laws of salting meat were a way of preserving the meat before refrigeration was discovered. Thus, they claim, the laws of Kashrus are no longer applicable in our more sanitary age.

However, this approach is wrong. While it is certainly true that the Torah is concerned for people's health and sanitation, this is not the only rationale for Kashrus. The Torah is also concerned with our spiritual well-being, and with our inner purity. Therefore, when the Torah tells us to avoid certain foods, it thereby provides for our spiritual cleanliness. Foods which are inherently unclean and disgusting, such as the meat of animals that died of disease, or the products of insects and the unsanitary pig, are not Kosher, and those who eat them have little regard for their own purity. Similarly, foods of naturally vicious animals, birds of prey and beasts of the forest, are prohibited, while products of domesticated animals like the chicken and the cow, are allowed. We are, in a way, influenced by what we eat. Therefore, we must base our characters on the peaceful ways of the animals that are permitted.

could be eaten. (This meant that species like the camel, hare, and pig were prohibited.) Only fish with fins and scales were permitted as food. (This excluded shell fish, seals, and other such species.) And as for birds, all birds of prey were declared prohibited. Some insects and creeping creatures were classified as unclean.

Thus, a distinction was made "between the unclean and the clean, and between the living things that could be eaten and the living things that could not be eaten."

Because there is a spiritual basis for the laws of Kashrus, in addition to the health basis, the laws of Kashrus are not limited to any specific era. They are timeless.

Because of this, we must be very careful of the food that we allow to enter our bodies. We must make sure that the ingredients in the foodstuffs we buy do not contain any non-Kosher items. We should ascertain that the meat we buy was prepared under the supervision of an acknowledged Rabbinical authority. We cannot take anything for granted in this respect, and we should not rely solely upon our own judgment. We should be as careful of eating non-Kosher foods as we are of eating poison.

A "Godol" was once in a distant land where people didn't recognize him. A simple Jew upon seeing the distinguished looking Rabbi thought he might be a "Shoichet" and asked him to slaughter a chicken for him. He declined because he wasn't a Shoichet.

"Could you lend me $1,000?" the Rabbi asked the simple Jew.

"I don't know you, I'm not sure you'll pay me back," was the reply.

"Since you don't know me, how could you rely upon me to slaughter the chicken according to Halacha (Jewish law)?" the Rabbi asked.

"Rabbi Eliezer ben Azariah stated: A man should not say, I cannot eat pork or I cannot indulge in forbidden sex relations, but rather I can, but what can I do when my Father in heaven has forbidden them from me? From the text: "I have separated you from the peoples to be Mine." He deliberately separates himself from transgression and accepts the yoke of heaven upon him." (Sifrey, Kedoshim)

"Religion is built on cleanliness inwards and outwards."

After giving birth to a son, a mother was not permitted to enter the Sanctuary for 40 days; if she had borne a daughter, the period was 80 days. At the termination of this period, the mother brought burnt and sin offerings to the Sanctuary and was then considered ritually clean once again.

Anyone who contracted the disease of Tzora'as (similar to leprosy) was not allowed to enter the Sanctuary. Consequently, when one's skin color indicated that he might have the disease, he was examined by the priest. If the Kohein, after scrutinizing the spots or scabs on the person's skin was unable to give a definitive verdict regarding the Tzora'as, the person was put in isolation for seven days, and then re-examined. If the appearance of the skin remained un-

פרשת
תזריע
מצורע
Parshas Tazriah Metzorah

TZORA'AS AND LOSHON HO'RAH

Our Sages say that tzora'as was the punishment meted out to those who had spoken spitefully of their fellow man (Erechen 16a). For instance, it was with tzora'as that Miriam was stricken after she spoke ill of Moshe (Vayikrah Rabbah, Metzorah).

Loshon HoRah then, is considered a most heinous crime. One who speaks Loshon HoRah about another person is, say our Sages, burdened with the other person's sins. This may seem to be an unfair punishment for an apparently minor misdeed. After all, making a nasty comment about someone seems much less damaging than physically

changed, the person was confined for an additional seven days. Then a final examination was conducted. If the mark had still not spread, the person was declared ritually clean. On the other hand, if the blemish had spread, the person was declared a metzorah, a person afflicted with Tzora'as. He was then sent to live outside the camp of the assembly, with his clothes torn and his hair unkempt. He was told to call out "Unclean, unclean!", as a warning for others not to touch him.

When the Tzora'as subsided, the person was again examined by a Kohein outside the camp, to ascertain whether or not the recovery was complete. The elaborate cleansing ceremonies which followed took place over an eight day period, on the first and last on which special rites were observed. Sacrifices were offered by the priest, and both cedar wood and hyssop were used in the process of purification.

assaulting him. Yet, this is not necessarily true. Granted, one who has just been hurt feels a very definite pain, but often, the pain subsides in a short while. A disparaging remark, on the other hand, can linger on to haunt the victim for years. Someone who makes the stray comment that a prospective job applicant looks "untrustworthy" may cost him not only this particular job, but many other job offers as well. Word spreads very easily, especially if it's a bit of juicy gossip. Loshon HoRah can be compared to one opening a bag of feathers. Even if one wanted to regather them one cannot, for they have been spread all over by the wind.

A marriage was once proposed to the son of a certain Rabbi. The Rabbi approved of the match, and he traveled a lengthy distance to the house of his son's prospective in-laws to meet them. On the way, he paused for the night at an inn. There he met several acquaintances of the family he was to meet. Within a few hours, he had begun hearing evil, not only of the bride, but of all her relatives as well.

The Rabbi interrupted their comments by saying, "Now I know why Hashem caused a miracle and enabled Eliezer, Avrohom's servant, to complete his journey to find Rivka so quickly. If Eliezer had stopped at an inn, he would have heard false gossip that would have harmed the shidduch."

Loshon HoRah can demolish in a minute a reputation that took a lifetime to establish. It is for this reason that we are advised to be extremely careful of whatever we say. Even displaying a negative facial expression towards others or just listening to unkind comments about others, can be considered Loshon HoRah. This is why we must carefully consider what we want to say before we say it.

"One should not even relate the good qualities of his friend, for speaking of his good qualities will bring up his bad qualities." (Bava Basra 165)

The Chofetz Chaim's caution in avoiding Loshon HoRah was legendary. He wrote several *seforim* devoted to the subject, and his essays on it have been compiled in English under the title of Guard Your Tongue. They are required reading for every Jew interested in self-improvement.

The Chofetz Chaim once paid a visit to a prospective supporter of his yeshiva. When he arrived, the man, a wealthy businessman, was in the midst of preparing a telegram to his business partner. He rose to greet the Chofetz Chaim and engaged him in conversation. Soon it became apparent to the Chofetz Chaim that the discussion was leading to talk about a certain individual, and that Loshon HoRah might ensue.

The Chofetz Chaim suddenly arose and glanced at the telegram on the man's desk. "It looks as if you had carefully thought out every single word here," he commented, "for you've rewritten this several times."

"I certainly have" said the man. "Every unnecessary word here will cost me extra money."

The Chofetz Chaim marveled at this. "If only everyone was as careful as this when choosing what to say!" he noted. "Don't they know that every unnecessary word they speak will cost them dearly in the World to Come?"

"Keep your mouth from evil talk and live a life of peace." (Derech Eretz Zuta)

PUNISHMENT FOR LOSHON HO'RAH

Why do people speak Loshon HoRah? Some do so in the belief that, by belittling others, they gain status themselves. They often don't realize the suffering they are causing others. Perhaps if they, too, ex-

The former Metzorah was then pronounced a full-fledged member of the community once again.

The laws of Tzora'as applied equally to a garment and to a house. If a garment showed signs of Tzora'as, depending on the situation, it might be burnt. If a house suddenly became marked by green or red streaks, it was boarded up for seven days. If the streaks then spread, the affected stones of the house were removed and replaced with new ones. The house was replastered, and the old stones and dust were thrown in a specially designated unclean area outside of the camp. If signs of Tzora'as still lingered in the walls, the whole building was demolished, and its building materials were discarded in the unclean area outside the camp.

Certain physical impurities rendered a man or woman ritually unclean, thus

perienced belittlement, if they knew what it was like to become isolated from others, they would be more considerate of others.

This is perhaps why the punishment for Loshon HoRah is Tzora'as. The Metzorah, the one afflicted with Tzora'as, becomes, literally, an outcast. He must leave the three camps of Israel and maintain an isolated existence. He is looked down upon and avoided by others. He is considered impure. This is exactly the condition he caused the libeled person to experience. Now that he knows what it is like himself, he will be more careful in the future. When he avoids later opportunities to speak Loshon HoRah, he has learned his lesson.

Hopefully, such severe punishment is not necessary before the average person realizes that Loshon HoRah is detrimental. Everyone should reach the conclusion that one way to a more peaceful life is to avoid Loshon HoRah.

Rabbi Yannai once observed a peddler striding through town and chanting, "Who wants to buy the elixir of life?" Rabbi Yannai approached the peddler and asked him to reveal his secret potion to a lengthy existence. The peddler refused, and Rabbi Yannai persisted. Finally, the peddler responded, "You do not need any special potions. The key to a long, happy life is contained in your holy books, which state, 'Who is the man who desires long life . . . Guard your tongue from evil. . . .' "

Rabbi Yannai turned to his companions and said, "I did not fully understand the feeling of this verse until the peddler clarified it. He brought it to my attention that avoiding Loshon HoRah is in itself a remedy for the torments of life. If one keeps away from speaking ill of others, and if one keeps away from animosity and arguments, then he has a better chance of living a calmer, more peaceful, and, therefore, longer

life. That, indeed, is the elixir of life." (Medrash Rabbah, Metzorah; Avodah Zarah 19b).

> *"Four classes of men will not be received by G-d: The scoffers, the liars, the flatterers, and the slanderers."* (Sanhedrin 103)
> *"He who slanders, he who listens to slander, and he who bears false witness against his neighbor, deserves to be cast to the dogs." (Pesachim 111)*
> *"Said the wise man: Whoever lends an ear to gossip will soon be abandoned by all his friends, even though he was formerly well-known and loved." (Mivchar Pninim)*

JUDGING OTHERS—AND ONESELF

When someone sees white spots on his skin, what should he do? Examine them himself? No, says the Torah. He must go to the Kohein, who will look at them and determine if they constitute tzora'as," as a person does not see his own faults" (Negaim Perek 2, Mishnah 2).

Note that it is the expert, the Kohein, who must do the examination. Why can't the person himself determine his condition? The answer is clear. The person is not the best objective judge of his own character. He might look in the mirror and see only perfection, carefully avoiding any blemishes obvious to others. Therefore, he might consider the few white spots to be insignificant while the Kohein can see clearly that they are signs of tzora'as. Before someone can properly judge himself, he should solicit an unbiased opinion from others.

Why should one go to the Kohein for a tzora'as examination? Because the Kohein is well-versed in what constitutes tzora'as and what does not. The Kohein does not decide this matter entirely on his own; the Torah gives him the necessary criteria for his

preventing them from entering the Sanctuary or touching or partaking of sacred articles. This state of uncleanliness was ended after the prescribed time by special purifying ceremonies.

judgement. He must base his opinion on the objective laws of the Torah, and then his diagnosis will be correct.

This is a lesson that all judges should heed carefully. When deciding a court case, the judge must base his opinion on the law, not on his personal desires. He should render a fair decision, and should not let himself be swayed by the identities of the opponents. If the plaintiff is rich and the defendant is poor, or vice versa, the judge should not allow this to influence his verdict. Justice should be his only guide, and then justice will prevail.

פרשת אחרי מות

Parshas Acharei Mos

After his sons Nadav and Avihu had died as punishment for their improper service, Aharon was told to enter the Kodesh Kodoshim (Holy of Holies) once a year only, on Yom Kippur. On this day, atonement was made for the sins of the community, including those of the priesthood, and the Sanctuary was cleansed because it might have been entered by those ritually unclean.

On this day, the Kohein Godol himself, attired for most of the time in white garments rather than golden ones, offered all the sacrifices. These consisted of his personal sin and burnt offerings, which he paid for

STRANGE FIRES—FOREIGN INFLUENCES

Aharon was given explicit instructions as to how to approach the Sanctuary, to enable him and future Kohanim to avoid the fate of Nadav and Avihu. These sons of Aharon had been killed because they had offered a "strange fire" on the altar. One explanation of this term is that they had added their own man-made fire to that already provided by Hashem. Because they had done so against instructions using their own ideas as to what was needed rather than relying upon Hashem's decisions, they were Divinely smitten.

Since the days of Nadav and Avihu, there have been many Jews who have been snared by this same error. They have felt that the laws of the Torah were not sufficient, or not relevant to their own times. Consequently, they have felt it necessary to add their own ingredients to the Torah. They have undertaken to add and subtract from the Torah laws, to reform the Torah to make it more palatable to them. They may have felt that this new form of Judaism was more convenient and more appealing than the original one. Yet, they did not learn the lesson of Nadav and Avihu. The additional fire, however well-meant, is still a "strange fire,"

a desecration of the original flame supplied by Hashem. Therefore, if one decides that it is permissible to drive a car to shul on Shabbos, or to remove all shul Mechitzos (Dividers), and thereby thinks that he is strengthening Judaism, he is sadly mistaken. His fate in the World to Come will be that of Nadav and Avihu in this world, Divine retribution.

Moses Mendelssohn thought he was aiding Judaism by ushering in the Reform movement. What he did not foresee was that this "strange fire" would result in his descendants and followers converting to Christianity within a very short time.

Some people fail to understand the seriousness of assimilation and its detrimental effect on the future of Judaism. It is like a stab at the heart of the Jewish people.

One Rabbi related the method he used to dissuade young men who were considering intermarriage:

"I usually meet the young man late in the evening at the synagogue and ask him to come into the main Sanctuary. The atmosphere is quiet, with over five hundred empty seats; the only lights are in the back and a few near the Ark. Then I say to the young man, 'Open the Holy Ark.' He may ask, 'Rabbi, now?' and I answer, 'Yes, now.'

himself, and similar communal offerings brought on behalf of the populace. As part of the ritual, Aharon gathered a handful of incense, and entered the Kodesh Kodoshim. He then cast the incense upon coal taken from the altar, and the cover of the Ark was enveloped in a cloud of smoke.

Two male goats were provided by the people for their offering, and the Kohein Godol cast lots to determine which of the two was to be sacrificed. He laid his hand upon the head of the other animal, called "Azazel", over which he confessed the sins of the people. This goat was thrown off a cliff, symbolizing the removal of sin from the populace. The commandment was given for Jews to permanently observe this day as a most solemn Sabbath, on which every member of the house of Israel is to afflict himself by means of a fast, and to repent from his misdeeds.

The people were again cautioned that sacrifices could be offered only on the altar in the Sanctuary. Offering sacrifices in one's own chosen spot was considered an act of idolatry. In addition, if anyone desired to slaughter an animal for eating during the wilderness period, it was to be brought as a peace offering.

After he opens the Ark, I ask him to take out the Torah scroll. Again he may ask, 'Right now?' and I answer, 'Yes, now.' Then I tell him emphatically, 'Throw the Torah on the floor! Stamp on it and spit on it!!' Invariably, the young man says, 'Rabbi, you must be kidding.' Than I take the Torah from him and return it to the Ark. Immediately, I say strongly to him, 'By marrying out of your religion you are throwing down, stamping and spitting on the holy Torah,' " (How to Stop an Intermarriage, p. 72)

The Chofetz Chaim said: "The Torah says, "Whoever touches the mountain Sinai shall die." If touching the mountain means death, how much more so if one dares to change the Torah itself!"

YOM KIPPUR: "YOM HAZIKORON"

If Shabbos is the most significant day of the week, so Yom Kippur is the most significant day of the year, the "Shabbos Shabbosone" (Vayikra 16:31). It is on Yom Kippur that one's deeds during the previous year receive Divine examination. It is also on this day, therefore, that one must personally review his own actions of the previous year, to learn from his mistakes, to atone for them, and to decide how to avoid them during the coming year. It is for both these reasons that Yom Kippur is referred to as the Yom HaZikoron, the Day of Remembrance.

We say the words "Forgive Us" at the conclusion of Yom Kippur. This may seem to be a misplaced prayer, for hasn't one just spent the entire day asking for forgiveness? Why renew the plea so late in the day?

This situation can be compared to one in which a king was passing through a field incognito. As he was doing so, one of the workers in the field came over to him, yelled that he had no business being in the field, and kicked him.

The men who were accompanying the king wanted to slay the man on the spot, but the king restrained them. "Let him be, for he did not know who I am," said the king. "If he knew me, he would not have done that. Instead, take him to the palace and teach him the meaning of respect and good manners. Then, we will see if he will change his ways."

The king's men did so, and, after a while of palace training, the man came to understand the importance of respect. In a state of shame, he approached the king, and pleaded, "Forgive me! When I kicked you, I was but a simple, ignorant person. It is only now that I understand how great my sin was!"

If we have experienced Yom Kippur properly, then we have used it as an opportunity to grow in understanding. We might have begun the day ignorant of the effects of our sins. Yet, by the time Yom Kippur reaches its conclusion, we should have searched our souls sufficiently to realize the magnitude of our errors. We should have come to understand the importance of proper behavior, and therefore we should have felt our shame more directly. Therefore, it is only appropriate to ask Hashem for forgiveness at the *end* of Yom Kippur, when the realization of what we have done is more clear.

R. Levi said: "Great is repentance, for it reaches as far as the Throne of Glory." (Yoma 86)

The laws forbidding the eating of meat from an animal which had died without having been ritually slaughtered, and forbidding the intake of any blood, were promulgated.

The people were reminded that a high level of moral conduct was expected if they were to remain a people of G-d. Consequently, adultery and illicit marriages were outlawed. Other nations were destroyed because their members had exhibited immoral behavior, and the same fate would befall Bnei Yisroel if they acted likewise.

It would be a mistake to think of Yom Kippur as a complete expiation of all our sins. If we pound our chests and acknowledge our sins on this one day, that does not mean that all will be well. Yom Kippur should be just the beginning of a process that leads to true Teshuva, a complete improvement in our behavior.

The Dubno Maggid expressed this concept by referring to a man who lives in a small town. The town's fire-fighting equipment was very limited, and if a fire broke out, disaster usually followed.

One day the man journeyed to a distant, large city. When he was there, he noticed the smell of smoke in the air and saw a far-off commotion. Then he heard the dramatic clanging of bells and thumping of drums. "What does that mean?" he asked one of the city dwellers.

"That means that there is a fire in the area, but that it will soon be out," was the reply.

The villager decided to investigate; when he reached the scene of the fire, he saw that, sure enough, the blaze had been extinguished. The man was extremely impressed.

When he returned to his small town, he called upon the town elders and told them. "I just saw something wonderful in the big city that might help us. It seems that whenever they have a fire there, they clang bells and bang on drums, and, sure enough, the fire goes out. Why don't we try that here?"

The elders assumed that the ways of the city were superior to their own, and so they accepted the man's suggestion. They readied the bells and the drums, and the next time a fire was reported, they rang the bells and banged the drums with great exuberance.

Then they proceeded to the site of the fire, and discovered, much to their shock, that the fire had burned down half the town and was still raging! They quickly reverted to their own method of drowning the fire with water. When the fire was finally out, they ran the poor man out of town.

Stunned and puzzled, the man returned to the city he had just visited. "I don't understand," he told someone. "When you rang the bells and banged the drums, the fire went out; but when we tried it in our town, nothing happened."

"Are you serious?" was the reply. "Don't you know that the bells and the drums were only a signal for the fire engines to arrive and put out the fire? The action of the firemen is what put out the fire, not the noises."

The same is true of our Yom Kippur observance. True, the wailings and the chest-poundings we exhibit on Yom Kippur are most important, for they signal the fact that we recognize our errors. But they are not, in themselves, sufficient. They must be followed by positive actions, by noticeable improvement in the way we act, by renewed concern for others and stricter adherence to Torah laws, if our pleas for forgiveness are to be answered. It is only after we take these positive steps to extinguish the fires of our errors that we will accomplish true and full Teshuva.

R. Yochanan said: "Great is penitence, for it averts the evil decree." (Rosh Hashanah 17)

Resh Lakish said: "Great is repentance, for as a result of it premeditated sins are counted as inadvertent ones." (Rosh Hashanah 17)

Bnei Yisroel are told to be "Kedoshim," of an elevated, holy nature. This high spiritual level can be achieved if one respects his parents, observes the Shabbos, and rejects idol worship. The repulsive heathen customs of sacrificing one's children to Molech, the god of the Ammorites, and of practicing witchcraft are punishable by death, for they contravene this holiness. Also forbidden are the heathen mourning rites of mutilating or tattooing parts of the body. Causing the creation of irregular mixtures, such as through the interbreeding of animals or the interweaving of wool and

פרשת
קדושים
Parshas
Kedoshim

GREAT EXPECTATIONS—BNEI YISROEL'S MISSION

In this Parsha, Bnei Yisroel are told to strictly avoid specific sexual relationships. They are not to imitate the practices of the nations around them. If they do not observe these restrictions, then the "land will vomit you out" (Vayikra 18:25). In other words, they will be expelled from Eretz Yisroel, as previous nations had been. But there will be a further punishment, too: "For whosoever shall do any of these abominations, even the souls that do them shall be cut off from among their people . . . I am the L-rd your G-d" (Vayikra 18:29). The final words indicate that, if Bnei Yisroel refuse to honor these commitments, Hashem will inflict the most severe punishment.

This seems quite unfair. If Jews indulge in perverse acts, why should they receive a punishment for this far beyond that given to the other nations? This seems like a sign of Hashem's intolerance towards the Jews. But is it really? Or is it a sign of His greater affection for us?

Perhaps the matter can be clarified by means of a story. The tale is told of a rich man who possessed great wealth, but who had only one son. In order to provide his son with some companionship, and to prepare him for competition in life, the man took into his home an orphan boy. The boy would be given every privilege in exchange for serving as a companion to his son.

Unfortunately, the arrangement proved to be disappointing. One day, the man checked on the two boys to see how their studies were progressing. He found to his dismay, the two boys counting the money they had stolen from a neighbor's house.

The man immediately ordered the orphan boy to leave his house. Then the man turned to his son, and vented the full force of his

fury on him for the next hour. After the heated lecture was over, the son looked at his father and asked, "Why are you yelling only at me? My friend was just as guilty as I. Yet you let him leave with hardly a word, and you've saved all your anger for me. Is that fair?"

"You are foolish," the father replied. "Think before you speak! The orphan boy meant little to me. I was glad to have him here as long as he behaved himself, but when he showed he couldn't be trusted, I just told him to leave. But your situation is different. You are my son, someone brought up in my house who watched my ways. I expected better from you. Therefore, if I find you acting improperly, I am really disappointed. Yet, I can't send you away from home, for then I'd have no sons. Instead, by yelling at you, I'm trying to bring you to your senses. Maybe after the proper punishment you will change back to your old ways. You are too important for me to lose."

Such is the relationship between Bnei Yisroel and Hashem. Because the Jews have been given the Torah, and have been raised according to Hashem's laws, more is expected from them. If they sin, the disappointment is all the greater. To shock them back to their senses, Hashem must often inflict upon them a punishment more severe than that given to other nations. Yet this is a sign of Hashem's continued concern, not abandonment. Hashem wants the Jews to remain His people, and to rise above the moral level of the other nations. It is our duty to fulfill these great expectations, and to see Hashem's punishments as a portion of His undying love for us.

"Whether you be good or bad, you are the children of G-d." (Kiddushin 36)
"G-d does not wound the Jews unless he first provides a remedy for them."

linen ("Sha'atnes") is prohibited, for it offends the Divine laws of Nature. One may not eat the fruits of a tree for the first three years after its planting.

The Jew must distinguish himself by being a compassionate individual. He should show special consideration to the poor person and the stranger, for our ancestors were strangers in the land of Egypt. Consequently, he should leave the corner sections of his field, as well as the stray gleanings, for the poor. He must deal

(Megillah 14)
"G-d has done a kindness to the Jews by dispersing them among all the nations. (For when they are killed off in one country there are survivors in another country)." (Pesachim 48)

LOVING YOUR NEIGHBOR

"V'ohavtoh L'reiachoh Komocho" (Vayikra 19:18), says the Torah. "And you shall love your neighbor as yourself." A very noble idea. Certainly, one who loves his neighbor as he does himself will definitely treat others with great respect.

But is this practical advice? Can it, in fact, be carried out? Or is it just too much to expect for one to show others the same concern he lavishes on himself? Can one really be so selfless?"

Obviously, reaching this high level is difficult. It can be done though, even if a slow, step-by-step approach might sometimes be necessary. Thus, when a gentile asked Hillel to explain to him the whole of the Torah while he was standing on one foot, Hillel replied, "Do not do anything to others that you would not like them to do to you" (Shabbos 31a). Note the different approach here. Hillel was cognizant of the fact that loving others unreservedly is difficult. Therefore, he suggested that men avoid detrimental acts against other. They must refrain from acts of revenge, from verbal attacks and from harboring baseless hatred. From the avoidance of negative acts, which is mostly a matter of self-control, one can achieve positive acts of love. Perhaps the following is an indication of how supreme the love of one's fellow man can become.

Moshe and Meir had long been the best of friends. But man can often find no better way of settling their differences than through war, and Moshe and Meir one day found themselves living in two opposing warring towns.

Moshe was captured by the enemy, and was condemned to death by the king. Before the execution could be carried out, Moshe asked for and received permission to speak

to the king. "I realize that, according to the rules of war, I deserve to be killed. Yet, if you will kill me now, my children will be left in poverty forever. Please, let me return to my home, collect all the debts due me, arrange for my family's security, and I promise you I will return to you by the end of the next month."

"Do you think I am a fool?" said the king. "If I set you free now, how do I know you will actually return?"

Moshe thought for a moment, and then answered, "I have a friend in this town named Meir, and I think he will be willing to take my place here until I return."

Meir was contacted, and agreed not only to take Moshe's place in prison, but to also receive the sentence of execution if Moshe did not return. The month passed, but Moshe failed to appear. The King merely shrugged, and ordered that Meir be readied for beheading. The hour for the execution drew nearer, but still no Moshe. The executioner raised his knife, Meir cringed . . . and then, at the very last moment, in rushed Moshe. He pushed Meir out of the way, and indicated to the executioner to chop his own head off instead. But Meir was having none of this, he would rather lose his own life than to see his friend die. Soon the two were struggling for the right to die for the other, and neither would relent.

The king watched this with amazement. Finally, he spoke. "I have never seen two men more willing to save each other. Certainly there have never been two men more deserving of life. Free them both!"

Not everyone is willing to die for his fellow man's sake. Yet, Jews especially, must realize that their neighbors are their allies in life. Anti-Semitism will set gentile against Jew, and Jews will survive only if they recall that "Kol Yisroel Areivim Zeh LoZeh"—All Jews are Responsible to Each Other (Sanhedrin 27b; Vayikroh 26:37, Rashi). It is this sense of love and unity that must exist if peace, harmony, and progress are to emerge triumphant.

A short while after Rabbi Yitzchok Zev

with his fellow man on a totally honest basis. Therefore, such acts as stealing, lying and slandering must be strictly avoided. The employer must pay his workmen promptly. The shopkeeper must maintain complete honesty by ensuring that his scales and weights are absolutely correct. The judge should show no bias to either the poor person or to the influential one. One who defames a person, or who misleads a blind or naive person is denounced. A Jew must do everything possible to save the life of a Jew who is in danger. He must also admonish his erring fellow man. On the other hand, he should not hate anyone else, but should rather love his

Soloveitchik became the Rabbi of Brisk, a group of soldiers came to him with the news that a Jewish soldier was sentenced to be shot that day. His crime was having fallen asleep while on guard duty. The prisoner requested the opportunity to speak to a Rabbi before he died. The anti-semitic officers added that if the Rabbi would not come, they might punish the people of the town. Nevertheless, Rabbi Soloveitchik refused to go with them.

The people of the town were puzzled by their Rabbi's refusal to speak to the prisoner. Moreover, his refusal was endangering the lives of others. A second group of officers came to the Brisker Rav and repeated the same request as before. Again Rabbi Soloveitchik refused to go with them. The people were astounded by the conduct of their newly appointed Rabbi. Even when they begged him to change his mind, the Brisker Rav refused to go.

Finally, when a third group of officers came to the Brisker Rav, the inhabitants of Brisk were sure that now they would be punished for what seemed to be their Rabbi's foolhardy stubborness. To the surprise and relief of everyone, the officers announced that the Brisker Rav was no longer needed. The prisoner's family had meanwhile appealed to a higher court, and the execution was stayed. Everyone was amazed at what appeared to be a miracle, and they asked the Brisker Rav for his comment.

"I merely followed the directives of the Rambam in 'Hilchos Yesodai Hatorah' that if a fellow Jew does not deserve capital punishment, we are forbidden to hand him over to be killed even if our lives will be put in danger. This unfortunate person didn't deserve to be killed; he wasn't starting a revolution. Had I gone to him, it would have caused his death, for immediately afterwards they would have shot him. I, therefore, had no right to go. Because I followed the halacha, I saved this person's life." (Rabbi

Moshe Mordechai Shulzinger in "Rabbosainu, pp. 193-5)

"Jews are responsible for one another." (Shavous 39)

"When one Jew is being beaten all Jews feel it." (Midrash, Song of Songs 6)

"Do not do unto others what you would not have others do unto you." (Shabbos 31)

Telling others that they are wrong might seem to be an act diametrically opposed to the command to love them. Yet, they are, in fact, two approaches to the same goal. When someone has great affection for another person, he will do all he can to help his friend. If he knows the person is in danger, he will certainly attempt to save him. Admonishing others, can lead to the same result. If a Jew sees his fellow Jew behaving improperly either by neglecting the Mitzvohs or his responsibility to others, one must correct him. If he does not, the person might easily meet a fate more calamitous than any imaginable on this earth. Admonishing others can save them from punishment in both this world and the next. By giving them "Mussar," one shows his concern for their welfare (Shulchan Oruch, Orach Chaim 608). A person should realize that when another admonishes him, he means it for his own good.

Even in his youth, Rabbi Aryeh Leib Alter, author of "Sfas Emes," studied Torah diligently. One evening he was so engrossed in his studies that he studied the entire night. During the day he took a short rest to refresh himself. Unaware that Rav Aryeh Leib had studied the entire night, his grandfather rebuked him for sleeping excessively. Someone who knew the truth asked Rav Aryeh Leib why he did not tell his grandfather the reason for his short nap in the middle of the day.

"To hear admonition from my grandfather was an opportunity that I didn't want to miss," said Rav Aryeh Leib, who later became known as the Gerrer Rebbe.

fellow man as he would himself.

Finally, he should refrain from the abhorrent sins of adultery, incest, and bestiality. The heathen nations were destroyed because they practiced such abominable acts, and Israel will suffer the same fate unless its members observe all

In effect, when one admonishes his fellow Jew, he is also benefitting himself. The sinful Jew is like a raging fire in the midst of Klal Yisroel. His sins are causing great harm to his own soul, and may play a part in the corruption of others too. If this fire is not extinguished, it will very likely rage out of control and cause the destruction of others as well. Therefore, it is the Jew's obligation to try to eradicate this fire, this sinful attitude, before it can damage himself as well.

"Rabbi Jose bar Hanina said (Bereishis Rabba 54): "Reproof leads to love, as it was said: (Prov. 9:8) 'Reprove a wise man and he will love you.' That is why according to Rabbi Jose, any love which is not accompanied by reproof is not true love, and according to another Tanna, Reish Lakish, any peace unaccompanied by reproof is not true peace."

"Whom G-d loves he admonishes." *(Proverbs 3)*

Another approach to this situation is to see the sinful Jew as sitting in a rowboat in the sea along with his fellow Jews, and then drilling a hole under his seat. If the other Jews do not repair the hole, all of them will drown; if the other Jews do not try to curtail his sinning, they will also be held responsible for it.

This is why the Chofetz Chaim used to say, "If I knew that by falling down before a sinner's feet and kissing his dirty shoes I would help him to repent, I would gladly do so. For how can the cleanliness of my mouth compare to the importance of a Jew observing the Mitzvos?"

But while giving "Mussar" is essential, it is also important for one to know how to do so effectively. Criticizing others out of anger or spite can be counterproductive. "Mussar" is best avoided when there is no hope that it will produce a change for the better. Sometimes a patient, friendly approach is the most effective way of getting one to reevaluate his actions.

The Chofetz Chaim was well aware of this. He once arrived at an inn where he noticed a Jew seated at a table without a yarmulkah, gulping down his food without first making any Brochos. The Chofetz Chaim in-

quired as to his identity, and was told that this was a Jew who had been forcibly taken into the Czar's army as a teenager and who had now been in the army's employ for over twenty years.

The Chofetz Chaim was warned not to approach the man, for he might turn violent. Nevertheless, the Chofetz Chaim walked over and said, "Is it true that you have been in the Czar's army for over 20 years?"

The man looked at him suspiciously and nodded.

"In that case," continued the Chofetz Chaim, "I give you my highest respect. You are on a much higher level than the rest of us Jews, for you have faced much greater challenges and yet you have remembered that you are still a Jew."

The man listened to these words in amazement. Here was the great Jewish leader, coming not to condemn him for his ways but to actually praise him! Yes, this indeed made him feel a part of the Jewish people, and made him want to rediscover his Jewish identity. For as the Chofetz Chaim went on, "Imagine how much greater you could yet become if you also kept all the Mitzvos." Because of these gentle, friendly words, the man became a Ba'al Teshuva (Introduction, Sefer Machneh Yisroel).

Nowadays, many Jews are finding anew the value of Torah-true Judaism. It is the task of all Jews to welcome and guide these Ba'alei Teshuva, and to accept them fully.

"The virtuous man is a mirror to his fellowmen, for he shows them their good and bad points." (Pninei Melizot 48)

Rabbi Ilai stated in the name of Rabbi Eliezar ben Rabbi Shimon: "Just as one ought to utter reproof, so one ought to refrain from an ineffective one." Rabbi Abba added: "It is a must as it is said: "Do not reprove a scorner, or he will hate you." (Prov. 9:8) (Yevamot 65)

"Don't rebuke your fellow for the fault which is your own." (Bava Metzia 59)

PROHIBITED MIXTURES

Chukim are Torah laws for which there is no explicit explanation. Among the Chukim

of Hashem's laws faithfully. Bnei Yisroel are expected to maintain a superior life style and to remain morally pure.

in Parshas Kedoshim are those forbidding the wearing of wool and linen interwoven in a garment, and the interbreeding of different animals. Though the Torah gives no specific reason for these prohibitions, it seems clear that it is cautioning against the mixing of inherently different items.

These laws should give our thinking some clear framework. While it is true that all men have some basic similarities, it is also true that certain inherent differences exist, some due to heredity, others to environment. So while Jews share with all others a basic humanity, they also have their unique qualities, as do all other groups. Therefore, while Jews can join gentiles to further mankind's progress, they should remember that they are also different. They cannot intermingle with gentiles if this will cause the loss of their special identity. They cannot intermarry, for this will cause not only personal problems but also the depletion of the Jewish race. Assimilation is therefore a crime against the Jewish nation, for it means that the special nature of Judaism is being denied.

You might indeed think that Chukim (laws without reasons) are idle ceremonies. Therefore Scripture says: "I am the L-rd," (Lev. 18:4, 5:15-16), that is to say that: I, the L-rd, have decreed them, and you have no right to criticize them! Thus, Maimonides warns not to commit the sin of depreciating those laws whose reason we cannot discern. (Mishna Torah, Meila)

"I have separated you from the peoples to be mine"—if you are separated from the peoples then you belong to me; otherwise, you belong to Nebuchadnezzar, King of Babylon and his associates. (Sifrey, Kedoshim)

Because of his privileged status, the Kohein had to maintain an especially high standard of purity and perfection. He was forbidden to attend the funeral of anyone but his nearest relatives, for contact with the dead defiled him and prevented him from performing his holy duties. In addition, he could not marry an unchaste or divorced woman. Even more rigid rules applied to the Kohein Godol, who was not to attend the funeral of even his closest kin, and who could marry only a virgin. Any physical defect disqualified the Kohein from officiating in the Mishkon, although he

פרשת אמור

Parshas Emor

THE KOHANIM AND LEVI'IM— SUPPORTING SCHOLARS

Over the years, there have been those who have looked down upon the Kohanim and Levi'im. They have been considered to be parasites of society, avoiding the hard labor of others and living off other people's incomes. After all, it was a percentage of the average Jew's hard-earned crops, the Terumah and the Ma'aser, that provided the Kohanim and Levi'im with much of their sustenance. But what, they demanded, were the Kohanim and Levi'im contributing for others in return?

Nowadays, the same questions are raised over the position of the Yeshiva or Kolel student in Jewish society. The Kolel member spends his days learning Torah, and is compensated through the donations of generous Jews. But what do the Kolel members do to deserve this assistance? Are they not avoiding the hard work that others must experience and living the easy life?

What these detractors do not realize is that the Kohanim, the Levi'im, and the Torah scholars are, in fact, benefitting them, too. Through their learning, and through their holy service, they are representing their fellow Jews in the service of Hashem. In this way, they raise the spiritual level of all Klal Yisroel and cause all Jews to be judged in a more favorable light. For one who supports a Torah worker or a Torah scholar secures for himself a share in their holy achievements.

was still entitled to his share of the sacrifices.

Sacrifices, too, had to be free of blemishes. An animal could be offered only after it was eight days old. A mother and its young could not be killed on the same day.

During the year, a number of days were to be proclaimed as holy convocations when the people were to be called together, so that they could worship at the Mishkon. These holy days, on which no work is permitted, were proclaimed in the following order:

a) The Shabbos, the seventh day of the week.

b) The first and last days of Pesach (Passover), the Feast of Unleavened Bread. This festival is to be observed from the 15th through the 21st days of the month of Nissan. Once the Israelites had taken possession of the land of Canaan, they were

(Rambam, Hilchos Shemittah).

This fact was illustrated by the story of a Rosh Yeshiva who was supported by his father-in-law. This arrangement lasted for several years, when the father-in-law became dissatisfied with it. "My son-in-law is fully capable of supporting himself," he announced. "Why should I continue to sustain him?" The father-in-law thus withdrew his support and tragically, within a few days of this act, he died. What he had not realized was that, while his financial help had aided his son-in-law's survival, the son-in-law's learning had guaranteed his survival. Once he withdrew his own support, he undercut his own spiritual salvation (Sefer Ahavas Chesed).

> *Rabbi Yose b. Rabbi Hanina said in the name of Rabbi Eliezer b. Jacob: "If a man entertains a scholar in his house and lets him enjoy his possessions, Scriptures accredit it to him as if he had sacrificed the daily burnt-offering. (Berakhot 10)*
> *He who brings a gift to a learned man is accounted as if he had brought his first fruit offering to the Temple.*
> *Finally, Rava said: "He who loves scholars, will have sons that are scholars; he who respects them, will have scholarly sons-in-law; he who reveres scholars, will become a scholar himself."*

THE SHABBOS FOR HASHEM

"These are the appointed seasons of the L-rd," (Vayikra 23:2) proclaims the Torah when laying down the laws of the Shabbos and Yomim Tovim. "Of the L-rd" are the key words here. They show that these hallowed days are not meant as mere vacations for our own pleasure. No! They must allow us to become more spiritually in-

clined, to move closer to Hashem. G-d designed these days to let His people achieve holiness, and we must observe them according to His wishes. If we do not, we become susceptible to the sickness of secularization and assimilation.

This can be illustrated by the story of a man who had been blessed with several children. One by one the children were stricken with a highly contagious disease. Their father was most concerned and placed an emergency call to the family doctor. The doctor arrived quickly, and after examining each child, prescribed a certain medication and then left.

Some time later, the doctor received another frantic call from the father. "But what is the matter?" asked the doctor. "Didn't you give the medicine I recommended to your children?"

"I certainly did," said the father. "And they recovered beautifully. But now they've suffered a relapse, and I don't know what to do."

"Why don't you give them more medicine?"

"They don't want to take it!"

"In that case," said the doctor, "there isn't anything I can do for you. You have the means to cure them in your hands, and if they do not want to use it, they will remain sick."

We, too, have the means for a spiritual lift from our humdrum daily routine, and its name is Shabbos. It can cure depressions and purify souls. But if it isn't used, if it isn't observed, then nothing can be done. Those who have this medicine in their grasp and do not use it are destined to stay spiritually sick.

> *"Remember the Shabbos day to keep it holy": By what do you keep it holy? By learning Torah and Mishnah, by feasting, by new clothes and by rest.*

to present a sheaf of the first fruits of the barley harvest on the 16th day of the month. This was to be waved on the altar as an expression of gratitude to Hashem, and was referred to as the Omer.

c) Shevuos, the Feast of the Weeks. This is to be observed on the 50th day from the beginning of the Omer, on the sixth of Sivan. Seven weeks were to be counted from the second day of Pesaach, and then a meal offering of two loaves made from the new wheat harvest was to be brought on the altar. The Israelite was reminded of his duties to leave the gleanings of the harvest for the poor.

d) Rosh Hashonoh, Holiday of the New Year, occurs on the first day of the year, Rosh Chodesh Tishrei. This day is special because of the blowing of the shofar.

e) Yom Kippur, the Day of Atonement. This day, which occurs on the tenth day of Tishrei, is a day on which the populace is to fast and pray for the atonement of their sins.

f) Succos, the Feast of Tabernacles. This is to be observed from the 15th

(Tana d'Be Eliyahu 26)

One possible reason for the desecration of Hashem's Shabbos is that observing it is too costly. "If I keep all the laws of Shabbos," some say, "then I will lose money." That this is a short-sighted attitude is demonstrated by the following story:

A certain businessman owned a number of grocery stores. One of his suppliers was a farmer, who helped provide him with eggs.

"I will pay you for every egg you ship to me," said the businessman, "so make sure to keep an exact count of how many eggs you produce."

The farmer looked a bit embarrassed. "You know, I'm not so good at keeping count. I keep on losing the records."

"In that case," the businessman suggested, "why don't you do the following. Every time you send me an egg, put a penny in a bucket. Every now and then I'll come around and count the pennies, and since I trust you, I'll pay you ten cents for every penny in that bucket."

The farmer agreed to this arrangement, and every time his hens produced a usable egg, he put a penny into one of his buckets. After a while, he had quite a sizable number of pennies there. He looked at the bucket longingly, and said to himself, "Isn't it silly to have all these pennies lying there unused? I know the businessman told me to keep them there, but I'll fool him. I'll take some of the pennies out of the bucket and spend them, and he will never know the difference!"

And this is what the farmer did. What he didn't realize, of course, was that he was only fooling himself. For with every penny

he took out of the bucket, he lost the chance to receive ten cents.

Similarly, those who work on Shabbos to earn money are also deluding themselves. True they will be gaining a few pennies for immediate use. But they will be losing out on the chance to secure much greater wealth in spiritual well-being and in the World to Come.

> *R. Tachlifa learned: The entire sustenance of man for the whole year through is fixed for him between the New Year and the Day of Atonement, except for the expenditures for Shabbos, Festivals, and the expenditures for the instruction of his children in the Torah; if he spent less for any of these— he is given less, and if he spent more— he is given more. (Baya 5:16)*

YOMIM TOVIM (HOLIDAYS)

Like Shabbos, the Yomim Tovim serve to commemorate important events in history. They remind us of how the Jewish people were forged into a unified nation and saved from extinction by Hashem. To enhance the Yom Tov, Jews utilize symbolic objects: the Succah, Lulav and Esrog on Succos, the Shofar on Rosh Hashonoh, the Menorah on Chanukah, and the Matzoh on Pesach, and partake in symbolic rituals, again as a reminder of past occurrences. But when observing a Yom Tov, one should not consider it a quaint custom, having no relationship to the present. When we sit in a Succah, when we eat Matzoh, or when we light a Menorah, we should realize that the conditions of the past are still with us today. The Succah and the Matzoh should make us

through the 21st of Tishreï, with great rejoicing. The people are to carry four species (Esrog, Lulav, Hadassim, Arovos) as a symbol of thanksgiving, and live in huts during this period to recall the wanderings in the wilderness. Shemini Atzeres, the 22nd day of Tishrei, is also to be observed as a day of solemn rest.

After this, the people were reminded of their duty to provide pure olive oil for the lamps of the Beis Hamikdosh which were to be kept burning continuously by the Kohanim. The showbread was to be made of twelve loaves of fine flour, arranged in two rows.

A convert that had blasphemed Hashem's name was put to death by the Bes Din (Tribunal).

realize that Jews are still oppressed and wandering in our own times, and the Menorah should bring to mind the many miracles that help preserve the Jewish people today. The Yomim Tovim remind us that the lessons of yesterday can help us cope with the world of today.

Literally, the word "Yom Tov" means "Good Day." A Yom Tov is, usually, a joyous occasion, for it celebrates the survival of the Jews. Therefore, the Torah tells us to mark the Yomim Tovim (with the exception of Yom Kippur) with rejoicing and feasts. We gather with our family and friends, we partake in Seudos (Meals), we sing, and we revel in our Jewishness.

However, these celebrations should not be viewed as an opportunity to lose all self-control and gorge ourselves on pleasure. The pleasures we feel on a Yom Tov, the happy sensations our bodies experience from the feasting and the drinking, are not really ends in themselves. They are the means to better appreciate our Jewish lives and our Creator's benevolence (Rambam, Hilchos Yom Tov; Shulchan Oruch, Orach Chaim 529).

How the Yom Tov festivities can accomplish this is indicated by the tale of a lame man who felt frustrated at having to remain home constantly. The man brooded for a long time, and finally came up with a plan. He would ask his friend to carry him on his shoulders, and together they could go places. The friend readily agreed to this, for he too had a handicap—he was deaf, and he longed for companionship. He hoisted the lame man onto his shoulders and they headed for town. While there, they stepped into a hall. Inside a party was taking place, and sweet, beautiful music was filling the hall. The lame man was entranced by the rhythm, and felt a desire to express his happiness by swaying to the music. Unfortunately, his friend below could not cooperate in this, for he did not hear a note. The lame man thought for a while and arrived at a plan. He guided the deaf man to a table where schnapps was being served, and ordered a drink for his friend. Soon came a second drink, and a third. By this time, the deaf man was in a gay mood and, on his own, began dancing. In this way, the lame man was able to share in the happiness of the moment.

Like the lame man, the Neshomoh (Soul) within us yearns to celebrate the Yom Tov fully. Yet, it cannot do so unless the body joins in this feeling of joyousness. Therefore, we are told to gladden our bodies with good food, drink, and clothing, so that there will be a harmonious enjoyment of the elevating experience known as the Yom Tov.

A man is obliged to rejoice with his children and his household on the Festival, for it is said "and you shall rejoice in your feast, you and your son and daughter, your man-servant and maid-servant, . . . R. Yehuda said: Men with what is suitable for them and women with what is suitable for them. Men with what is suitable for them— with wine; and women—with garments.

After the Jews had taken possession of Canaan, they were to observe every seventh year as a Shemittah (Sabbatical) year for the land. They were not to sow their fields or prune their vineyards, and could not reap the harvest that grew by itself.

Every fiftieth year they were to mark the Yovel (Jubilee), which was to be proclaimed on Yom Kippur. During this year, too, the fields could not be sowed. In addition, Hebrew slaves were to be set free, and all lands were to revert back to their original possessors. Consequently, the price of land that was sold was to be

פרשת
בהר

Parshas Behar

SHEMITTAH AND EMUNAS HASHEM

The decree of the Shemittah year might have appeared to be a harsh restriction when first issued. Here the Jews were being told that they could not work their fields for an entire year. (This was long before farmers learned that leaving their fields fallow for a while would improve them by restoring nutrients and minerals.) The wild grown produce would not belong by right to any individual. The entire land and its products were to be considered "free", under the official ownership of no one but Hashem.

What was the basis for this decree? Why did it apply specifically to every seventh year? And how were the Jews to sustain themselves during this Shemittah year?

The significance of the number seven provides the key to these answers (Eruvin 40b). This number reappears in Jewish life with great frequency. Paroh dreamed of seven fat and seven lean cows. Yehoshua circled the walls of Yericho seven times. Several sacrifices required that the Kohein dip his finger into blood and sprinkle it seven times. Nowadays, the Chosson and Kalloh (Groom and Bride) celebrate their wedding with seven blessings (Sheva Berochos), while the mourner refrains from all public activity for seven days (Sitting Shiva). The prime example of this is the Shabbos, which occurs on the seventh day of the week. This, of course, is based on the fact that Hashem created the world in six days and "rested" on the seventh. In acknowledging His creating the world, and His control over all spheres of human endeavor, we rest on the seventh day. (Rabbeinu Bchaya, Akedas Yitzchok). This reminds us that our souls are of a Divine, spiritual nature, and that our goal is to return to our original state of spiritual rest.

The Shemittah, the seventh year, is of a similar nature. Here the land is allowed to rest and remain fallow. It is an acknowledgment that all earthly possessions, our land, our homes, our money, and even our very personal freedom, all are ultimately under Hashem's dominion. We should never let ourselves be deluded into thinking that we really own and have full control over anything. After all, we can't take anything with us when we depart from this world. Whatever we own is given to us as a temporary possession, to utilize for the utmost good. We are entrusted with money, but it is only a loan really, and we must see that it is used to perform Mitzvos and help the poor. We are allowed title to land, but it is only a transient ownership, and we must give of our produce to the needy. If we forget that we are only temporary guardians of our possessions, we forget Hashem's omnipotence. The Shemittah year, during which we forego actual ownership of the land, makes sure that we remember.

But what is one to do during this Shemittah year? If he lacks possession of his field and its produce, how is he to live? Where will his sustenance come from?

Ultimately, man comes to the realization that his sustenance must arrive from the only source it ever comes from, Hashem. The growth of crops during the previous six years had also been caused by Hashem's good grace. The Jew is promised that if he so deserves, his produce during the sixth year will be sufficiently abundant to supply him for the seventh year as well. It is man's faith in Hashem that will give him the peace of mind to know that help will arrive. One who truly believes in Hashem's control of the world will have no difficulty believing in Hashem's ability to provide him with sustenance.

"The whole world is fed by the

123

based upon the number of years remaining until the Yovel. Land that was sold because of its owner's poverty could be redeemed by a relative of the original owner or by the original owner himself. If someone were to sell a house in a walled city, then he would have a year during which to redeem it. If he did not redeem it within this time, it was too late. However, houses in villages and in cities set aside for Levi'im would revert back to their original owners during the Yovel year.

One should lend money to a poor fellow Jew without charging him interest. If the

benevolence of G-d." *(Berachos 17)*

Unfortunately, not everyone has developed a strong sense of Emunah. Some are like the Jew who asked a certain Rabbi to ascertain that a cow would be slaughtered properly. The Rabbi agreed, and the Jew relied on the Rabbi's authority when eating the meat from it. Some time later, the Rabbi visited the same man to ask him for a contribution. "There is a widow with three children who needs money to continue living," he said. "Won't you help?"

The man, who happened to be quite wealthy, shrugged his shoulders. "Uh . . . I'll have to let you know," he replied.

The Rabbi looked at him sadly and said, "You believed my word when I said that the meat was kosher. Why do you now doubt it when I ask you to aid the poor?"

We, too, cannot be hypocritical. We cannot take the luxury to believe that Hashem created and regulates the world, and then doubt that He will assist us if we deserve it. One who has faith in Hashem must display complete faith, at *all* times.

Avrohom inherited this world, and
the world to come by virtue of the faith
he had in the L-rd. (Bereishis 15:6)
"The steps of man are established by
the L-rd"—no man raises a finger below
without a prior proclamation above.
(Tehillim 27:23)

THE ORAL LAW

The Torah seems to go out of its way to mention that the laws of Shemittah were enunciated at Har Sinai. Why this emphasis? "To inform us," say the Commentators, "that just as all the intricate details of the Shemittah laws were given at Har Sinai, so were the fine points of all laws revealed at Har Sinai" (Toras Kohanim; Rashi, Vayikra 25:1). This point was made in connection with Shemittah, whose laws do not apply outside Eretz Yisroel, to make it clear that even the less obvious laws, and those that do not affect all Jews everywhere, were given in full detail at Har Sinai.

If the minute Jewish laws were given at Har Sinai, where are they written? Not in the Torah, obviously, for many laws there are listed only in general terms. The answer, then, is that these laws were transmitted through a different type of Torah, an Oral one. This is the Torah Shebe'al Peh, which was handed down verbally by the Sages of each generation. When it was in danger of being forgotten, the Torah Shebe'al Peh was compiled in what we know today as the Talmud, the Mishnayos and the Gemorrah.

There have been those throughout history, notably the Karaites, who have denied the authenticity of the Oral Law and have refused to abide by it. Yet, they have always forsaken Judaism in the long run. For how can one who denies the Oral Law follow such laws of the Written Torah as those of Shabbos and Yom Tov? The Written Law is very vague as to what acts are forbidden on Shabbos, and how to celebrate the holidays in detail. How should one build a Succah; how many sounds are blown on the Shofar; how are marriage ceremonies to take place? These matters are not dealt with by the Written Torah, and one must consult the Oral Law for answers. It is only when one studies both the Written and the Oral Laws, when one acknowledges the fact that both were given to the Jews by Hashem at Har Sinai, that he comes to fully appreciate Judaism. This is why the true Torah scholar, the Talmud Chochom, is the one who has mastered not only the Tanach, but the Mishnayos and Gemorah as well.

"Write down the words" refers to the
written scriptures; "for according to the
words have I made with you a
covenant," refers to the Mishnah and
Talmud which separate Israel from the
nations of the world. It has been the
Oral Law that has preserved the Jewish
people and the integrity of its faith.

TAKING INTEREST

The prohibition against charging interest is juxtaposed with the laws of Shemittah.

poor Jew was forced to sell himself into servitude, his Jewish master should treat him as a hired servant with respect; the servant would be set free during the Yovel year. On the other hand, a non-Israelite slave was to remain in servitude after the Yovel year. A rich relative could redeem a Jewish servant by paying his master a sum based on the number of years remaining until the Yovel.

What is the connection between the two? A very clear one. The Shemittah year is designed to remind all Jews that the land they till daily is a gift of Hashem. The prohibition against interest reminds Jews that the money they lend to others is theirs by the grace of G-d, and that it is not proper for them to derive profit from it. All of man's possessions are granted him by Hashem, to be used for the benefit of his fellow man. If he abuses these gifts and uses them selfishly, he does not deserve to keep them.

The Chasam Sofer once lent a neighbor of his a large sum of money for use in a business venture. The man invested it wisely, and was able to repay the loan very quickly. To show his deep appreciation for the Chasam Sofer's favor, he presented him with a beautiful, sparkling diamond.

The Chasam Sofer held the diamond in his hand and expressed amazement at the stone's brilliance. He held it to the light, and examined it carefully. Then he thanked the man profusely, and returned it to him.

"What's wrong?" asked the man. "Does the diamond have a flaw?"

Not at all," said the Chasam Sofer. "It is perfect. But if I would keep it, I would be flawed, for I would then be taking interest for my loan."

"I am sorry, but I do not understand," said the puzzled man. "If you intended to return the diamond, why did you examine it so carefully?"

The Chasam Sofer smiled, and responded, "I looked at the stone to admire its beauty and greatness. But ah! How much greater is the Mitzvah of not taking interest!"

The following are incompetent as witnesses: the gambler and the usurer. (Eruvin 82)

Rabbi Shimon ben Lakish said: "He who loans money is to be preferred to he who donates it." (Shabbat 63)

Sefer Vayikroh concludes with Moshe contrasting the different responses that will follow the Jews' obedience or defiance from Hashem's commandments. Adherence to the laws will result in prosperity and peace for the people. The land will yield abundant produce with the farmers being occupied year-round in planting seeds and reaping the crops. Because of Hashem's protection, no enemies will attack the Jews and they will enjoy peace and contentment.

On the other hand, resistance to Hashem's laws will lead to catastrophe. When the Jews rebel against G-d,

פרשת בחוקותי
Parshas Bechukosai

COMMITMENT TO THE TORAH

As mentioned above, the Torah tells us that the Mitzvos mentioned in this and previous parshios were those that Hashem commanded Moshe at Har Sinai. But was this not obvious? What is the purpose for stressing this?

In reply, Rabbi Eila said, "This underlines the fact that Moshe and Bnei Yisroel performed the Mitzvos *exactly* as Hashem had commanded them, without deviating from them one iota. Only in this way is the Mitz-

vah performed; namely, if the Mitzvah is carried out precisely as was required by the Torah. Otherwise, the act means nothing."

There are those who like to make the Torah more "timely", more "relevant", and more "convenient". They decide on their own that it is perfectly proper to ride to shul on Shabbos, or to install a microphone in the shul to enhance the service, or to eat foods that haven't been certified as Kosher. They try to "bend" the laws of the Torah to suit themselves. But the Torah cannot be

they will be plagued with disease, famine, and the horrors of enemy sieges, to be followed by national exile. But if the people then repent for their wrongdoings, Hashem will once again remember His covenant with the Patriarchs and accept them once more as His people.

Provisions are discussed for those who have made a vow to contribute towards the upkeep of the Sanctuary. If someone dedicates his own worth or the worth of a member of his family to the Sanctuary, the amount of money he is to pay varies,

tampered with. The Torah is timeless, and it will survive the "changes" of the misinformed. It is meant as a blueprint for living for all ages and cultures; if it is made to adapt to certain specific environments, it will become useless as soon as those environments disappear. The Torah does not adapt to the climate; it is the climate that must adapt to the Torah.

Thus, when the leaders of the famed Volozhiner Yeshiva in Eastern Europe were told to alter their curriculum to center it around Czarist propaganda, the leaders made a dramatic decision. They opted to close the Yeshiva rather than have it corrupted into a Czarist propaganda school. They did not want to see the Torah abused and changed beyond recognition, and they were right. The Czarist regime was overthrown shortly thereafter, but the Torah lives on in its original, pristine form.

"G-d will not alter, nor change His law forever, for another." (Siddur, Yigdal)

ACHDUS: UNITED WE STAND, DIVIDED WE FALL

The portion of the Torah called the Tochochoh, admonishment, is very explicit about the punishments that will befall the Jews if they act improperly: "I (Hashem) will set My face against you, and you will be smitten before your enemies. They that hate you will rule over you." (Vayikra 26:17). The text implies that included among the enemies will be those from Yisroel, enemies from within. These enemies, say our Rabbonim, are the most vicious of adversaries. Jews who do not accept their Judaism, and who seek to destroy their fellow Jews, are the most dangerous of all. They are traitors against their own kind and know where their fellow men are the most vulnerable.

It is tragic that often the worst enemy of the Jewish people and those most dangerous to Jews, are Jews themselves. It is most unfortunate that we must be constantly vigilant and on guard against harm from within as well as without.

For example, the first person killed in the Maccabean uprising was the Hellenist Jew killed by Matisyohu when he slaughtered a pig on Hashem's Altar. Another example is the Jew who converted to Christianity and aided the Catholics in debating our Sages during the Middle Ages. Possibly, the most heartbreaking example is that of the kapo in the concentration camps who assisted the Nazis, Yemach Shemam (May their name be erased), in killing his co-religionists.

Thus it has been that when Jews united in fighting for a goal, they have been successful, but when they fought each other selfishly, they invited disaster. When the Jewish kingdom was united behind Dovid and Shlomo, their prosperity was at a peak, and the Beis Hamikdosh was built. However, when the kingdom split in two, the nation became weak and both segments were eventually destroyed. Even after the Beis Hamikdosh was rebuilt, the Jews remained ignorant of this lesson. After the death of Queen Shelomis, her two sons, Hyrcanus and Aristobulos, vied for the throne. Eventually, each side requested the aid of the Roman Emperor. The Emperor readily complied, seeing a way to gain control of Judea (Sotah 49b, Bava Kamma 82b, Menochos 64b). Eventually, neither brother triumphed, for mastery over the nation soon fell to the Roman Empire (Avodah Zara 9a), and this resulted in the destruction of the second Beis Hamikdosh and the Jews' exile from Eretz Yisroel. A petty rivalry had resulted in suffering for all Jews.

Is the situation today any better? Hardly. It is true that when crisis or threats from without appear, Jews unite. Yet once the crisis has passed, Jews turn upon each other, both in politics and personal relationships. The Jewish population becomes fragmented and vulnerable, full of internal disputes and selfish rivalries.

We are all familiar with the story of the father who summoned his sons to his deathbed. He handed each of them an arrow and each of them, at his father's command,

based on the age and sex of the person. If one dedicates a kosher animal, which could be used for a sacrifice to the Sanctuary, he cannot substitute another animal for it. However, he can redeem a blemished animal by paying its monetary value plus an added fifth of the value to the Kohein.

The redemption of a piece of land that was dedicated is to be based on the number of years remaining until the next Yovel year. A firstling (B'chor) cannot be dedicated as a voluntary offering, for it is already the property of Hashem. Ma'aser of agricultural produce can be redeemed by paying its value plus an additional fifth, whereas the tithe of new-born animals (which were set aside for sacrifice) can never be redeemed.

proceeded to break his arrow without much effort. But when he gave each of them a bundle of arrows, they were unable to break them, despite determined efforts. "You can learn from this example, that unity alone creates strength," said the dying father to his children.

Isn't it time for Jews to learn that Achdus, unity, if attained, can be one of their most prized achievements?!

The Midrash (Vayikrah Rabbah) states, "Israel is like a dispersed sheep. Just as all the sheep suffer when one of them is hurt, so it is with Israel, one is hurt and everyone feels the pain."

Samuel stated: A person should never exclude himself from the community. (Berachos 49)

SHIVISEE HASHEM LENEGDEE TOMID

Because the Jews have often strayed from the Torah path, the calamities described in this Parsha have struck. Jews have been abused, oppressed, exiled, and killed, as the Torah here predicts. Often, such calamities cause some Jews to lose all faith in Hashem, and to despair that He has forever abandoned his people. Yet, this is not so. The same Parsha that lists the dreadful punishments assures us that if we repent, Hashem will once again favor us. Therefore, each of us must retain full trust in Hashem, and ask for His gracious assistance at all times. This attitude is expressed by the words "Shivisee Hashem LeNegdee Tomid," (Shulchan Oruch, Orach Chaim 1), meaning that the individual has Hashem in his mind during all actions and at all times. He must constantly see to it that whatever he does is for the sake of Hashem. And he must bear in mind, when something unfortunate occurs,

that Hashem is thereby indicating a need for repentance, which will be followed by renewed acceptance.

Perhaps we can aim for the Bitochon exhibited by Rabbi Yaakov, who found it necessary to travel with a caravan in the desert. Before the trip, Rabbi Yaakov made a special point of giving the Arab caravan leader a large sum of money to make sure he would halt the caravan during Shabbos. As Shabbos approached, the caravan proceeded on its trek, despite Rabbi Yaakov's pleas.

"Are you of sound mind?" asked the leader. "If we stop here for a day, we will certainly die. There is no doubt of that. If you want to stop, you will have to stay alone."

"Then this is what I will do, said Rabbi Yaakov.

The caravan leader shrugged, and ordered the others to move on. Rabbi Yaakov was left entirely alone in the wilderness. There was no one to protect him, except Hashem.

Rabbi Yaakov knew this. Instead of worrying about his situation, he concentrated on thoughts of the Almighty. He began his Shabbos prayers, and recited them so fervently that he lost all conscious contact with the world around him. He did not even notice the desert animals that came seemingly out of nowhere to protect him. They were certainly a Divine response to his prayers for assistance.

Several members of the caravan heard Rabbi Yaakov's prayers, and figured that he and his possessions would be easy prey for them. They attempted to attack Rabbi Yaakov's camp, but turned out to be easy prey for the animals that protected Rabbi Yaakov. Because he had had complete faith in Hashem, and because he kept the image of

The Torah concludes by emphasizing that "these were the commandments given by Hashem to Moshe on Har Sinai."

Hashem's power before him during his time of need, Rabbi Yaakov was rewarded with Hashem's favor, and was saved. (Sefer Agadah).

"The righteous man lives by his faith."

(Chavakuk 2)
"Remember your Creator in tranquility and you will find Him in your hour of trouble." (Peninei ha'Melitzot)

During the second year after the exodus from Egypt, Moshe and Aharon were commanded by Hashem to count all male Israelites aged twenty through sixty. These males automatically became liable for military service. The census revealed that six hundred three thousand, five hundred and fifty men were available for duty in the armed forces. The tribe of Levi was excluded from the general census because of its special duties connected with the Mishkon.

Order and discipline were to be maintained at all times, whether the Israelites were encamped or on the

פרשת במדבר

Parshas Bamidbar

THE HOLY WILDERNESS

The name of this Sefer, Bamidbar, is derived from the fact that Hashem promulgated His laws to the Jews in the Midbar (Desert). Strangely, when a leader wishes to make a momentous announcement to his people, he usually does so from an impressive setting. Yet, Hashem revealed His Torah laws in a barren, desolate desert. Why?

This matter can be clarified by a parable. A very wealthy member of royalty had more money than he could use, but he was not satisfied with being merely rich. He also desired to be a leader of men. Therefore, to achieve his goal, he went to the members of a well-established town and offered to donate a large sum of money to be used for the benefit of the town if they would accept him as their leader.

The members of the town held a private meeting and then returned with their decision. They refused the offer because a new leader would have his own ways of ruling, and the townspeople didn't want to change their established ways.

The man was saddened, but was not left hopeless. He next went to a settlement that had only recently been organized and made them the same offer. They, too, considered it and accepted the offer, for they had not yet become set in their way of life and were still flexible enough to accept the direction of a new leader.

Thus, when Hashem revealed the laws of His Torah, He chose to do so to a newly-formed nation, the Jewish people. And he did so in the desert, a site devoid of established homes and luxuries, a place where the Jews would not want to stay. At this point, the Jews had no permanent home and no set goals. They would be beginning their destiny as a people from this point on, and

would be willing to accept Hashem's guidance, His chosen way and His chosen home. They would be flexible enough to live according to the Torah without having to alter any fixed ways. This is why the desert was such a fitting setting for the presentation of the Torah. It allowed the Jewish people to emerge as a truly unique nation under Hashem's direction, free of the fixed surroundings and influences of the other nations. This was a totally new sort of nation, formed in the barrenness of the desert, breaking with all previous traditions.

This is also why it is said that a person should consider himself as a *Midbar* when learning Torah (Nedarim 55b). Just as a desert exists naturally without being changed by outside influences, so, too, should the Torah scholar retain his natural Torah spirit, without becoming corrupted by alien societal influences (Song of Songs 8).

At the same time, the site of the desert impressed upon the Jewish people the importance of humilty. Just as the desert contains nothing but layers of sand, so too the human body is composed of nothing but dust. But just as the desert was transformed into a holy spot by the appearance of the Divine Presence, so, too, man becomes a source of greatness if he allows his spiritual spark to dominate his actions. It is by following the will of G-d that man reaches his full potential. But man by himself has no supreme power. If he remembers this and remains a humble servant of Hashem, then he has a proper perspective on life.

"Be careful with the sons of the poor, for the Torah shall come from them." (Nedarim 81)

R. Chanina ben Ida said: *"Why are the words of the Torah compared to water? This is to teach you, just as water flows from a higher level to a lower, so, too.*

march. The camp was arranged in the shape of a quadrilateral, with the Mishkon in the center, protected on all four sides by the tents of the Levi'im. The twelve tribes were divided into four groupings, each bearing the name of its leading tribe, all of which formed the outer cordon. Yehudah, together with Yissachar and Zevulun, were stationed on the eastern side of the camp; Reuven, Shimon and Gad were encamped on the south side; Ephraim, Menasheh and Binyomin were on the western side; and Dan, Asher and Naftoli were in the northern area. During the nation's travels, the group led by Yehudah marched first followed by Reuven, Ephraim, and in the rear, Dan. Some commentators maintain that the encampment moved in totality as a quadrilateral, just as it camped.

Originally, the first-borns had been selected by Hashem to perform His holy ser-

the words of the Torah endure only with him who is lowly." (Taanis 7)

YOUR STUDENTS ARE YOUR CHILDREN

"These are the descendants of Aharon and Moshe," (Bamidbar 3:1) begins the Torah in one section, and it then proceeds to enumerate the names of Aharon's children only. The Torah could not have mistakenly attributed Aharon's children to Moshe. Rather, the Torah is in this manner expressing a major concept. When one teaches a child Torah, that child is considered to be the offspring of the teacher. For although Moshe was but the uncle of Aharon's children, the fact that he guided them in the ways of Hashem makes the Torah consider Moshe their father as well. A Torah mentor is in every way a spiritual father of his students (Sanhedrin 19b).

A father brought his only son to the Volozhin Yeshiva. He spoke to Rabbi Naftoli Tzvi Berlin, the Rosh Yeshiva, and asked him to take special care of his son, since he was an only child.

"You have but one 'only' son," said Rabbi Berlin. "I have four hundred 'only' children." (Yechidai Sgulah, pg. 61)

A teacher once came to the Chazon Ish and asked his advice about changing professions. He wanted to become a diamond polisher.

"Aren't you already a diamond polisher?" asked the Chazon Ish of the teacher. (Biog. of Chazon Ish, pg. 229)

It is because of the great influence he has in molding Jewish children, that a Rebbe must be highly conscientious in his work. He should not consider his teaching merely to be a routine job to be forgotten after his school day has ended. (Bava Basra 8b). Rather, he should realize that teaching Jewish children

is a never-ending task, one that encompasses not only classroom lessons, but outside behavior as well. A Rebbe should try to guide his students in the way of the Torah at all times by the way he acts, speaks, prays, and deals with others. He should present an image to be admired and copied by his students. It is by watching the example of others that children learn best. A Rebbe, then, should set an example of the highest moral quality in everything he does. After all, it is his 'own children' that he is teaching.

In some sense, everyone is a teacher, whether he works in a school or not. He does not have to be a professional Rebbe to teach others. If people are impressed with his actions and attitudes and are affected in a positive manner, then he has been an effective instructor.

It is said that a student of a famed Chassidic Rebbe was once asked why he had spent so much time with the Rebbe. Hadn't he learned all he needed to know from the Rebbe's lectures?

"But it is not to hear only his lectures that I want," explained the Chossid. "I go to see how the Rebbe ties his shoes."

It was by watching how the Rebbe performed his daily routine that the Chossid learned how to conduct himself properly. This is why our Talmidei Chachomim who live Torah-true lives are our greatest teachers.

"The one that teaches his neighbor's child the Torah is as if he had himself begotten him." (Sanhedrin 9a)

Rabbi Neharai said: "I put aside all the crafts in the world and I teach my son only Torah." (Kiddushin 82)

YISSACHAR AND ZEVULUN

Parshas Bamidbar lists the various tribes, joining their names with the conjunction

vices. However, after the sin of the Eigel HaZohov, this coveted task was transferred instead to the Levi'im, who had remained faithful to Hashem throughout. Therefore, Moshe was commanded to appoint the Levi'im to Mishkon service under the supervision of Aharon and his sons. A census revealed that there were twenty-two thousand three hundred Levi'im in all.

Each of the three Levitical families, Gershon, Kehoss, and Merari, was assigned separate tasks in the Mishkon service. The Gershonites, on the western side of the Mishkon, were responsible for the transportation of the coverings of the Mishkon. The Kehossites, encamped on the south side, carried the Ark, the Shulchan, the Menorah, and the Mizbochos (Altars). The members of Merari, situated on the north side, were responsible for the transport of the boards, pillars, bolts, and sockets of the Mishkon. The members of Kehoss were warned not to touch or even look upon the sacred objects, which were covered by Aharon and his sons before they were moved. Aharon's son, Elazar, was the general supervisor of the Mishkon,

"and". However, when it comes to enumerating the tribe of Zevulun, this conjunction is missing. Why is Zevulun an exception to the norm?

The Torah has a purpose in doing so. The reason is based on Zevulun's unique relationship with the tribe Yissachar. The men of Yissachar were noted as outstanding Torah scholars. They devoted themselves to the full appreciation of Hashem's law. Consequently, they often did not have sufficient time for working to support themselves and their families.

This is where the men of Zevulun helped. Those of Zevulun were very successful merchants. They, therefore, managed to acquire great wealth. However, they were not selfish. They used their money to help sustain the Torah scholars of Yissachar. Because of this arrangement, the wealth of the tribe of Zevulun provided the basis for the scholarship of the tribe of Yissachar. The efforts of Zevulun in this matter were as essential as those of his brother. It is for this reason that the listing of the tribe of Zevulun is not preceded by the conjunction "and", so as not to accord it a secondary place. The Torah stresses that the contributions of Zevulun are considered every bit as important as those of Yissachar.

It is for this reason that we must give full honors to those wealthy Jews who contribute their money to support Torah institutions and needy persons (Eruvin 86). Hashem has seen fit to grant them riches. But instead of spending everything on themselves, they have used the money for the benefit of others. They have realized that money is valuable only when it is put to good use.

The Chofetz Chaim explains Rabbi Shimon ben Eleazer's quote in Shabbos 151, like this:
Give charity and practice kindness with those versed in Torah by supporting them.

Unfortunately, not all affluent people come to his conclusion. On the Shabbos before Pesach, Shabbos Hagodol, Rebbe Naftali returned to his home after his sermon. He seemed very exhausted and his wife asked him why this was so. "I delivered a very long sermon in the Beis Haknesses today," he responded. "After all, here it is only a few days before Pesach. The expenses for the holiday are very great and many of the poor people cannot afford a decent Seder. I have been trying to convince the wealthy members of the congregation to aid their fellow Jews in preparing for the Yom Tov. After all, if the rich do not use their money to assist others in Mitzvos, what good is all their money?"

"And was your appeal successful?" asked his wife.

"I achieved fifty percent of my goal," said Rabbi Naftali.

"What do you mean?"

"Well," replied Rabbi Naftali, "I convinced all the poor people to accept the money. Now all we need is for the rich people to be willing to give it."

If the richer members of the world would be as ready to contribute some of their wealth as the needy people are to receive it, the amount of happiness in the world would increase infinitely. Fortunately, there are some wealthy Jews who are doing their part to produce this happiness.

The disciples asked Rabbi Nehunia:

watching in particular over the oil for the lamp, the incense, the continual Mincha, and the anointing oil. This is partially discussed in the next sedra.

"What have you done to prolong your life?" He answered: "I have been generous with my money." (Megillah 28)
Rabbi Shimeon ben Yochai taught: If you see towns which have been uprooted, know that it is the result of not encouraging and supporting teachers and scholars. (Yerushalmi Chagiga 1:7)

פרשת נשא

Parshas Nosso

The exact tasks to be performed by the sons of Gershon, Kehoss, and Merari were given, and a census revealed that eight thousand, five hundred eighty such individuals between the ages of thirty and fifty were ready for service.

All impure Israelites were to be sent out from the various Mach'nos. Some were only sent out from Mach'ne Shechina and others from Mach'ne Leviyah. Lepers were to be sent out from all 3 Mach'nos.

Four laws involving the Kohein were then stated:

BIRCHAS KOHANIM AND MATERIAL WEALTH

The blessing recited by the Kohanim on behalf of Klal Yisroel begins with the puzzling expression "Yivorechachoh Hashem Veyishmirecha—May Hashem Bless You and Watch Over You" (Bamidbar 6:24). This seems contradictory. If Hashem blesses us, why does He also have to watch over us? Is not His blessing a sufficient guarantee for our protection?

Part of the answer lies in the differentiation between "Yivorechechoh" and "Veyishmerecha." The former means that Hashem should bless Klal Yisroel's members with material wealth. The latter means that Hashem should also provide the protection that will prevent Klal Yisroel from misusing that wealth. The Jew must at all times remember that it was Hashem's blessing that entitled him to whatever riches he has and that he must use that wealth wisely. He must not let his affluence cause him to be conceited and haughty, but rather he should be humbly grateful for it.

The Rambam writes: "When you give food to a hungry person, give him your best and sweetest food. When you give a needy person clothes, give him your best clothes."

A poor man once came to Rabbi Seligman Baer Bamberger, the Rav of Wuerzburg, while the latter was in the middle of a Talmudic lecture, and told him that he desperately needed a pair of shoes. Rabbi Bamberger interrupted his lecture and brought a pair of his own shoes for the needy person. One of the students asked Rabbi Bamberger why he gave away his best shoes that he had just recently bought. "Why didn't you give him an old pair?"

"The poor man already had torn shoes. I should give him only the best," was the reply.

The Dubno Maggid once expressed the proper attitude of the wealthy individual by means of the following parable:

A rich merchant was traveling home from the great fair in a coach filled with valuable merchandise. He looked up to see a shabbily dressed man walking alongside him, pulling a pushcart filled with cheap material.

The wealthy merchant frowned at the sight and shouted at the man alongside him, "How dare you walk right next to me? People might think you and I are equals, even though I am a member of the upper class and you are obviously just a poor peddler."

"Everyone can see that you are richer than I," replied the peddler. "But let us remember that both of us have bought our wares on credit, not through cash. Then, actually, you who have all that expensive merchandise are more in debt then I am, for you owe your debtors more than I owe mine. If you remember this, then maybe you won't act so abusively towards me."

In the same way, it is the rich man who is more indebted to Hashem for his possessions

1. If a person confessed to wrongfully keeping his neighbor's property, he had to add one-fifth to the original amount and also bring a guilt-offering to Hashem in atonement for his sin. If the rightful owner had died leaving no heirs (this is only true by a convert) the repayment was made to the Kohein.

2. A husband who suspected his wife of being unfaithful to him should present his complaint to the Kohein with the qualifications prescribed in Mesechta Sotah. The Kohein then took holy water from the laver and mixed it with dust from the Mishkon floor. The wife then had to swear to the Kohein that if she was guilty, she would suffer harmful effects after drinking the "waters of bitterness." The words of the oath were written on a scroll, and were blotted out in the water. The woman then drank the water. If she was guilty, the physical deformities that resulted bore witness to her faithlessness, and she was accursed among her people and died. If she was innocent, no injuries resulted and she was promised the blessing of motherhood.

3. The Nazir was one who voluntarily took a vow to become completely consecrated to the service of Hashem for a given length of time. He was obliged to abstain from wine and strong drink which comes from grapes, to let his hair grow and

than the average individual. He should, therefore, behave with greater gratitude towards Hashem than anyone else and should certainly avoid condescension towards others.

"Better off is the poor man who follows the straight path than the depraved man who is rich." (Mishlei 28)

"One man gives freely yet grows all the richer; another withholds what he should give and only suffers want." (Mishlei 11)

BIRCHAS KOHANIM AND PRAYING TO HASHEM

When the Kohanim bless the people, as specified in the Torah, they do something rather unusual. Instead of facing the Aron, as all Chazonim do, they turn around and face the congregation (Sotah 38a, Orach Chaim 128). Why do they shift their attention and their prayers from Hashem and concentrate instead on the assembly? Aren't prayers usually directed towards Hashem?

A parable will help provide the answer. A father, angered by his son's intolerable behavior and unable to reason with him, reluctantly banished him from home. The son left without any support and unable to find a job, walked around town looking hungry and cold. His clothes were nothing but mere shreds. A neighbor of the father saw the sad plight of the son and decided to contact the father.

"I'm glad to see you," he said. "I'd like to speak to you about your son."

Much to the neighbor's surprise, the father nodded and said, "That's just what I want to discuss with you. Did you really think you had to come and ask me to provide for my own son? After all, his happiness is as important to me as my own. It was only to change his ways that I acted as if I no longer cared for him. So if you truly want to help him, don't talk to me but go to him. Tell him that if he only mends his ways, I'll take him back into the house and supply all his needs, as any father would."

The same is true of our own relationship with our own Father, Hashem. Is there really any need for a Kohein to turn to Hashem and ask Him to bless and favor the people of Israel? For Hashem desires that His children, Bnei Yisroel, should at all times be blessed with happiness. It is, therefore, to Bnei Yisroel that the Kohein must direct his words, to urge them to act in accordance with Hashem's Will. If they do so, Hashem will provide for their welfare without the need for any intermediaries (Yerushalmi Berachos, Perek 9 Halachah 1; Rambam, Mishnayos, Sanhedrin, Perek 5).

"Prayer reunites the afflicted with their Father in Heaven."

"G-d wants the heart." (Sanhedrin 106)

"There is no better means of approaching Hashem than prayer, for in the very hour that Israel prays and praises Hashem, lifting their eyes and hearts toward Heaven, the Holy One, Blessed be He looks down upon them, embraces them, and is overjoyed to hear their voices." (Koheles)

to avoid contact with a dead body. If he did accidentally defile himself, he had to shave his head, bring an atoning sacrifice, and begin the counting anew. When the days of Nazirus had expired, he was required to bring a sacrifice, to shave his head, and to have the hair burnt beneath the sacrifice. After the Kohein had performed additional ceremonies, the Nazir was freed from any further restrictions and returned to live a normal life-style.

4. The Kohanim were directed to use a specific series of blessings for the people, as follows: May the L-rd bless you and keep you. May the L-rd make His Face shine upon you and be gracious unto you. May the L-rd lift up His Countenance on you and give you peace.

The Mishkon had been erected and dedicated on the first of Nissan in the second year after the Exodus. The twelve leaders, each representing his own tribe, jointly presented a gift of six wagons and twelve oxen for the transport of the Mishkon and its contents. The members of Gershon, who carried the tapestry, were allotted two wagons and four oxen; the members of Merari, entrusted with the heaviest burdens, received four wagons and eight oxen. On the other hand, the members of Kehoss did not receive any wagons for their duty was to carry the

THE NAZIR

The Nazir is one who voluntarily agrees to refrain from drinking wine, the cutting of his hair, and having contact with the dead. He appears to refrain from certain aspects of living.

Is this an indication that the Jew should withdraw from life and its pleasures?

No, the world and its resources were created for man's benefit. To deny oneself life's pleasures implies that the world is no good and this degrades Hashem's gifts (Nedarim 10a, Taanis 11a, Nazir 3a). True, man must pratice self-restraint in using these pleasures, but Judaism frowns upon asceticism. Thus, whereas the priests of other religions must practice celibacy, the Kohein and the Rabbi are expected to marry.

The Nazir is not one who hides from life. Yet, he feels he needs a strengthening of the will, a renewed dedication to Hashem. Perhaps he senses that he is not as firm in his commitment to Judaism as he should be. He is, therefore, told to develop his willpower and to devote all his actions to Hashem for a given time. He should not drink wine or come in contact with a dead body, for these either confuse his thinking or cause his defilement. His thoughts and body must be pure and his actions must be dedicated entirely to Hashem.

Shimon HaTzaddik disapproved of the Nazirites who vowed to abstain from wine and not to cut their hair for a period of time. He considered it a sin to renounce the pleasures G-d created for the benefit of man.

He made only one exception to this rule of disapproval. A Nazir with beautiful, curly hair came to him one day, stating his desire to cut his hair and thus end his Nazirus period. Shimon HaTzaddik asked him why he wanted to cut off such beautiful hair. The latter replied that he had seen his image in a stream—what a handsome face he had—and feared that he would grow haughty. But he said to himself, "What reason have I to be proud? In the end we all turn to worms." He then swore to cut off his hair in honor of the Almighty.

The Nazirus period is for a limited time only. When he feels that he has overcome any personal weaknesses or doubts, then he is ready to return to his normal life. He is once again a full-fledged member of civilization. Yet, the Torah still refers to him as a Nazir, even after his days of Nazirus are over. Although he no longer has to follow the laws of Nazirus, he is expected to remain at the high spiritual level he achieved as a Nazir. He should continue to direct all his thoughts and actions to the service of Hashem as he did during his Nazirus.

Unfortunately, the influences of society sometimes make us all too much a part of today's world. We sometimes adopt secular ways and overlook the high standards expected of us by Judaism. Then it becomes time to take a lesson from the rite of Nazirus. It is necessary to make an abrupt U-turn and head back in the Torah direction. A major change in lifestyle is helpful in reminding us exactly what our life goals should be. If we break dramatically with alien ways and dedicate ourselves entirely to Hashem, by

holiest of the vessels on their shoulders. Each leader then brought identical gifts of gold and silver vessels, sacrificial animals, and meal offerings, on twelve successive days.

learning in a Beis Hamedrash or coming under the constant guidance of a Rabbi, then we can get ourselves back onto the proper path.

> *Rav said: "Man is destined to give account for all the fruits he saw but abstained from eating." (Yerushalmi,*

Keddushin)
> *Samuel stated: "Whoever spends his days in fasting is dubbed a sinner." (Taanis 11)*
> *Hillel stated: "Separate not yourself from the community." (Avos 2:4)*

Aharon was entrusted with the task of arranging the outer six lamps of the Menorah so that their lights projected towards the seventh and central shaft.

The Levi'im were readied for their service in the Mishkon by purifying themselves through washings and sacrifices. They were told that only Levi'im between the ages of thirty and fifty were to take part in the service, but those between the ages of twenty-five and thirty were to be trained for their future duties.

The first Pesach after the Exodus was observed on the fourteenth day of Nisan. Those who were impure at

פרשת
בהעלותך

Parshas Beha'alos-cha

THE MENORAH

The designers of the Menorah were told to make it "mikshah"—beaten out of a single piece of gold. This meant that the base was the primary feature of the Menorah and that the branches were an outgrowth of the basic shaft. It was built in the manner of a fountain whose sprouts shoot out from a central flow of water.

The design of the Menorah was intended to have an effect on how we design our own lives. Just as the Menorah began with a central base and branched outwards, so, too, should our basic personality stem from within us. Our motives should come from an inner desire to be good and should not be dependent on the other influences of society. No matter what the world at large might consider important, we should remain true to our basic Torah principles.

> *"G-d takes no pleasure even in outwardly attractive deeds unless they are prompted by inward purity." (Abarbanel)*

The Netziv, the head of the illustrious Volozhiner Yeshiva, had great insight into the basic human personality. Once a certain student at the Yeshiva began dressing in an unusual manner. Instead of wearing the normal yeshiva garb, he started wearing clothing favored by the Goyim. His peers

were upset and reported this to the Netziv.

"Look at the clothing he is wearing!" they exclaimed.

"It is not the clothing that worries me," replied the Netziv, "The clothing is not at fault. After all, when a clock stops running, it is not the fault of the hands. Rather there is something wrong with the inner mechanism. Therefore, when a student begins wearing modern clothing, that shows that something is not going well with the basic personality of the student. Let me speak to him and see what is wrong. One must always go to the root of the person's problems and search his inner self before the problems can be solved."

Another lesson provided by the Menorah comes from the term "Beha'aloscha" (Bamidbar 8:2). This comes from the term "to raise". The fire of the Menorah had to be directed in an upward direction. This is to inspire us to strive to reach ever higher goals in our lives until we have dedicated our acts entirely to the service of Hashem Yisborach.

> *"A man should not speak one way with his mouth and another way with his heart." (Bava Metzia 49).*
> *"The heart of the matter is what matters." (Berachos 15).*

that time asked that they also be allowed to partake of the Pesach offerings. A special date, the fourteenth day of Iyar, was set aside for those who were impure or too far away on the regular Pesach day to bring the Korban Pesach.

The cloud of the Lord lifting from the Mishkon was a signal for the members of the camp to continue their journey. Moshe was commanded to make two silver trumpets. They were to be used to announce the commencement of the march forward, to summon the entire assembly to the Mishkon, to sound the alarm before a battle and to proclaim joyous occasions, such as the festivals and the New Moon.

After almost a year in the wilderness of Sinai, the people were told to journey to the wilderness of Paran. Moshe asked his father-in-law, Yisro, to accompany the

CONSISTENT DEVOTION

The Torah tells us that Hashem commanded Moshe to instruct Aharon how to light the Menorah. Then the Torah states, "And Aharon did so ... as Hashem had commanded Moshe" (Bamidbar 8:3). Rashi comments on this last passage that the Torah hereby commends Aharon for not acting differently from Hashem's instructions.

But would one have assumed otherwise? Could one even suspect that Aharon might have altered Hashem's instructions in any way? Of course not!

Therefore, one commentator gives the following psychologically-based explanation of Rashi's statement:

It is human nature for one to begin an assignment with the greatest enthusiasm. Gradually, however, this initial ardor cools. After a while, the person performs his task more out of habit than out of devotion. But this was not the case with Aharon. He began his duties in the Mishkon with the most fervent of devotion and maintained that devotion throughout his years of service. His enthusiasm for serving Hashem never waivered. This, then, is what Rashi is informing us here.

It is sad but true that we have become so used to many of our activities that we perform them mechanically, without any feeling whatsoever. This is why our Tefillos sometimes become exercises in reading Hebrew rather than emotional communications with Hashem. This is why we occasionally treat Shabbos as a day for sleeping rather than as an opportunity to become spiritually enriched. We take these Mitzvos for granted and we do not give them the devotion they deserve.

"Prayer without devotion is like a body without a soul." (Yeshuos Meshilo)
"Zeal for commandments increases the number of good deeds. (Mitzva va'Lev)

Perhaps one way to maintain this consistent devotion is for us to bear in mind that by doing Mitzvos we are performing the will of Hashem. We should not act according to the Torah simply to gain a reward. If the reward does not come immediately we might be disappointed. Rather, we should perform Mitzvos for the reason Aharon and Moshe did, because Hashem wants it (Avos deRabbi Nosson 5; Avodah Zarah 19a).

Antigonos of Socho stated: "Be not like servants who serve Hashem for the sake of reward but like servants who serve Hashem not for the sake of reward." (Avos 1:3)

The Vilna Gaon was another who adopted this attitude. He was known to be especially particular about finding perfect Esrogim and Lulavim for Succos. Messengers were sent to find a perfect pair but they returned empty handed. One messenger, though, came back to report that he had found a most beautiful set. However, it was in the possession of a certain man who refused to sell it. When the man learned that the Lulav and Esrog were to be used by the great Vilna Gaon, he changed his mind. "I will sell it to you on one condition, that when the Vilna Gaon uses this set I get the reward for the Mitzvah."

When the Vilna Gaon heard this, he smiled. "May Hashem be thanked for arranging matters in this way. Now I can finally fulfill one of His commandments without receiving a reward for doing so. Now I can do the Mitzvoh just for the sake of obeying Him."

"Ben Azzai said: The reward of a Mitzvah is another Mitzvah; the reward of transgression is transgression. (Avos 4:2)

PROTECTING OTHER JEWS

When Moshe asked Hashem for aid in leading the destined people of Klal Yisroel,

people but Yisro preferred to return to his native land of Midian.

During the journey, the people began murmuring against Hashem's leadership. Hashem's anger was aroused and He caused a fire to burn in their midst, prompting terror and destruction. The fire abated only after Moshe had prayed to Hashem on the people's behalf.

However, the people had not learned their lesson. Urged by the mixed multitudes that had accompanied them out of Egypt, they complained again, this time about the lack of meat in the desert. Their murmurings led Moshe to feel that the burden of leading the people was too great for him to bear alone. Hashem responded by telling Moshe to assemble seventy Elders who would assist him in leading the people. The Elders were assembled and the spirit of prophecy rested upon them.

In response to the people's complaints about a lack of meat and the boring taste of "Mun," Hashem caused the wind to blow an abundance of quails from across the sea. The people gathered the quails greedily, but when they began to eat, many fell dead.

Miriam, Moshe's sister, was punished with leprosy for defaming Moshe. After one week outside the camp she was completely healed.

Hashem replied by telling Moshe that seventy elders would assist him.

Who were these seventy elders? The Midrash tells us that these men had been appointed by Paroh as overseers for the Jews that were in bondage. They were to make sure that these Jews produced a certain number of bricks every day. If the bricks were not ready in time, someone would suffer.

One day Paroh's aides made a careful count of the bricks. There were less than the required number! The overseers were summoned. "Tell us which Jews did not fill their quota of bricks," they were told, "or else you will be punished."

"We are members of the Jewish people," they replied, "and we are not about to turn against our brothers. We refuse to inform on them and make them suffer. We would rather take the full brunt of the punishment ourselves."

These men were severly punished because they would not incriminate their fellow Jews, but at least their consciences were clear. They knew that they had defended Klal Yisroel. It was these men who were most fit to serve as leaders of the Bnei Yisroel.

From the days of Avrohom Ovinu to our own generation, there have been Jews who have sacrificed their own safety and welfare on behalf of their fellow Jews. They serve as models for us all, and we should devote our efforts to helping Klal Yisroel.

In the year 1895, a great fire destroyed many of the houses in the city of Brisk. Rabbi Chaim Soloveitchik, the beloved Rav of Brisk, worked day and night to help those unfortunate victims who had lost their homes and possessions in the fire. During that period, Rav Chaim did not sleep at home. He slept instead on the floor in a side room of the Shul. He ignored the pleas of his family that he at least rest at night in his own bed. "I am not able to sleep in a bed when so many people do not have even a roof over their heads," was his reply.

"The true friend is he who offers you his money when you are in need and his life when you are in danger."

The Israelites had reached Kadesh in the wilderness of Paran. Twelve representatives, one from each of the tribes, were sent by Moshe to explore the promised land of Canaan and to report back on the condition of its populace, dwelling places, and soil. Yehoshua and Calev were among those in this group of Meraglim (Spies).

The Meraglim secretly crossed the mountain path of the Negev in southern Canaan and traversed the land until the extreme north. They returned to the assembly after an absence of forty days bringing with them huge

פרשת שלח
Parshas Shalach

MOSHE AND YEHOSHUA: QUALITIES OF LEADERSHIP

Among the twelve Meraglim (Spies) was Hoshea ben Nun, of the tribe of Ephraim. Before the Meraglim's departure, Moshe blessed him and changed his name officially from Hoshea to Yehoshua. The meaning of this new name is "Hashem should help". Why this sudden change and what help did Moshe want Hashem to offer Yehoshua?

Moshe knew that the venture of the Meraglim would be a dangerous one and that Bnei Yisroel might react negatively to their report. He also knew Yehoshua to be a quiet, humble individual. Moshe was, therefore, afraid that if the people did rise in rebellion, Yehoshua might say little. He might feel powerless to lead the people away from mistaken opinions. Consequently, Moshe asked that Hashem should help Yehoshua in gaining the strength to be a powerful leader. After all, if Yehoshua was to succeed Moshe in guiding the people he had to exhibit the qualities that make a leader effective. Fortunately, Moshe's prayers were answered and Yehoshua became the forceful leader of Yisroel that Moshe had envisioned.

What qualities are expected of a leader of Klal Yisroel? He must, of course, be a total Ma'amin B'Hashem, (Believer in G-d) and through his personal example, he should inspire others to have the same attitude. He must be one whom others will respect and model themselves after. He should also possess the personal attributes of sincerity, affability, and concern for others that make others admire him. He should feel humble before Hashem and not consider himself superior to his fellow man. Yet, he should also be firm and unwavering in his devotion to Hashem, and if Hashem's supremacy is challenged, he should react with vigor

against those who question His law. In this sense, a Jewish leader should be strong and dynamic rather than meek and vacillating. But at all times, the Jewish leader should not let his position make him haughty. He should remember that he is but dust and ashes and that in the end his bones will rest in the same soil as do those of all other men (Sanhedrin 7b).

"All the prophets as compared with Moses are like the moon as compared with the sun." (Zohar)
"There has never yet arisen in Israel a prophet like Moses." (Siddur, Yigdal)
"A scholar must be as unyielding as iron, or he is no scholar." (Taanis 4)
"The body follows the head." (Eruvin 41)

The Rav of Lublin was a true leader. His followers numbered in the thousands.

He was once asked by a fellow Rav, "Why do you permit so many Chassidim to acclaim you as their Rebbe when you yourself admit that you are not worthy of their honors?"

"What can I do if the Jews flock to me?" the Rebbe asked.

"Why don't you simply ascend the pulpit this Shabbos and announce that you do not really deserve to be their Rebbe?"

The Rav of Lublin decided to follow this advice. He rose and announced that he was just an ordinary Jew and that there was no reason for anyone to seek his blessings.

Those who were present were overwhelmed by his statement. What humility the Rebbe displayed! What humble piety! Word of his greatness spread and an even larger crowd than before came to ask for his blessings.

The Rav's friend saw that the announcement had caused a most unexpected result. He, therefore, suggested that the Rav take opposite approach and announce that he was

clusters of grapes, pomegranates, and figs as evidence of the land's fertility. However, ten of the Meraglim claimed that it would be impossible for the Bnei Yisroel to conquer Canaan. They felt that the cities were too strongly fortified and that the inhabitants were too powerful. Calev and Yehoshua disassociated themselves from this pessimistic report and counseled that the people should march on Canaan. The people, though, sided with the majority report and lost heart. They broke into open rebellion and proposed the election of a leader to lead them back to Egypt. They refused to listen to the renewed pleas of Calev and Yehoshua and threatened to stone them.

Hashem was angered by this lack of faith and He expressed His intention to destroy the people and to form a new nation exclusively from Moshe's descendants. Moshe again interceded successfully on the Israelites' behalf. But while their destruction was avoided, Bnei Yisroel were condemned to wander in the wilderness

in reality a great Tzadik.

"Oh, no!" the Rav of Lublin exclaimed immediately. "When you wanted me to say that I am a simple Jew who does not deserve honor, I more than agreed with you. However, now you want me to lie and say that I am a saint and that I will not do!"

The Rav of Lublin recognized that he held his position only by the grace of Hashem and not because of his own boundless greatness.

"He that pursues greatness, greatness eludes him; he that eludes greatness, greatness pursues him." (Eruvin 13b)

THE SIN OF THE MERAGLIM: A LACK OF BITOCHON

What was the punishment meted out by Hashem for those who sinned because of the Meraglim? Not only were the Meraglim themselves killed by a plague, but the people were condemned to wander in the Midbar for a full forty years. The date of this tragic error was Tisha B'Av which became a day of continued tragedy for Yisroel, including the destruction of both Botei Mikdosh (Temples), the fall of Beitar, and the expulsion from Spain. Seemingly, the sin of the Meraglim paved the way for future sorrows for the Jews. But what was this great crime and why was it so serious?

To comprehend this, one must realize that until this point Bnei Yisroel had adopted the attitude of "Na'aseh V'Nishmah". They had been willing to accept Hashem's leadership without any doubts or questions. When the Meraglim delivered their pessimistic report, though, the people's outlook changed. They became hesitant and fearful. They no longer accepted Hashem's guarantees of protection, but they began to question His strength, and to doubt His promise. They lost their basic

Bitochon (Faith). Their unchallenging belief in Hashem was gone and they no longer accepted His word without proof. It was for this loss of faith that they suffered, and it was this lack of trust that led to the later tragedies.

During times of crisis, and Jews have known many such times throughout their history, it has been Bitochon that has filled Bnei Yisroel with the will and ability to persevere. Without this Bitochon Jews would have succumbed to oppression and despair long ago. Most of those who managed to survive the hellish life of the concentration camps did so only through their Bitochon. If we lose faith in Hashem's ability to aid us then all is indeed lost.

The Ba'al Shem Tov claimed that he learned how to have complete faith in Hashem from a certain innkeeper. Once the Ba'al Shem Tov arrived in a small village and went to the local inn for lodging. The owner was an elderly, pious man who welcomed him most heartily. He prepared an excellent meal for the Ba'al Shem Tov and enjoyed a long conversation with him about the wonders of Hashem. Suddenly, in the midst of their talk, a soldier appeared and knocked on the door three times. The innkeeper ignored the soldier and the Ba'al Shem Tov did likewise. Some time later, the soldier appeared again and went through the same ritual. This time the Ba'al Shem Tov asked what the soldier was doing.

"He is a messenger from the Baron," was the innkeeper's reply. "I owe the Baron some money and the soldier came to warn me that I must pay before the day is up, or lose my inn."

"Can you comply with his wishes?" asked the Ba'al Shem Tov.

for forty years, one year for each day the Meraglim had searched the land, until all over the age of twenty (with the exception of Calev and Yehoshua) had died. Then the new generation would enter the promised land to witness the fulfillment of Hashem's promise.

The ten Meraglim who had delivered the negative report died of a sudden plague. The people belatedly realized their error and attempted to go by themselves to Eretz Yisroel. However, they ignored Moshe's warning that Hashem was not with them and were soundly defeated by the tribes of Amalek and Canaan who lived in that area.

The people were assured that their descendants would possess Eretz Yisroel. Hashem told Moshe to prescribe the following law which would become effective at that time: that meal-offerings and drink-offerings should accompany the offering of animals, that the part of the dough called the Challoh should be set aside for

"No, I have no money. But I have faith in Hashem, and I know that He will help me."

Soon afterwards, the soldier made a third appearance and the innkeeper went to meet him. Just as he stepped outside, a coach drew up, and after a short discussion the coach driver delivered a bundle to the innkeeper. The innkeeper handed over the bundle to the soldier, and returned inside.

"What happened?" the Ba'al Shem Tov wondered.

"The coachman came to repay me an old debt," the innkeeper replied. "It was just enough to pay back my loan to the Baron. I knew I could trust in Hashem's assistance."

When the Ba'al Shem Tov next saw his students, he told them what had occurred and concluded, "Do you see how great is the power of a firm belief in Hashem's aid?"

"He need not tremble, he need not worry, whom G-d aids." (Yomah 22)
"All is preordained by Heaven except the fear of Heaven." (Megillah 25)
"Man fears the king who will be dead tomorrow, lest he punish him; but does not fear the True King who is the eternity of both this world and the world to come." (Eben Ezra, Shemos 20:2)

ACHDUS—BROTHERHOOD

Twelve men were chosen to spy out the land of Canaan and their efforts resulted in tragedy. Yet, when Yehoshua sent two men to spy out the city of Yericho, the outcome was much more successful. Why the difference?

Part of the answer may lie in the different number of men sent out on the two missions. In the first instance, Moshe found it necessary to send twelve men representing the twelve tribes. Why so many? Because

some of the tribes distrusted the others and insisted on having their own leader represent them. This revealed a lack of basic Achdus, unity among Bnei Yisroel at the time, a fact that contributed to their wrongdoing. At the time of Yehoshua, though, the feeling of brotherhood was more firmly established and only two men were needed to represent the people. This new sense of togetherness helped foster the success of this mission.

The Ba'al Shem Tov once emphasized the importance of Achdus by means of the following parable:

A King was riding in a forest with his aides when he sighted an unusually beautiful bird perched on the top of a nearby tree. He ordered that the bird be caught so that he could study it carefully. Unfortunately, no ladder was available so he ordered his aides to form a human ladder to reach the bird. Each man climbed onto the shoulders of the man below him. The uppermost man was about to stretch out his hand to snatch the bird when the man on the bottom became impatient and moved slightly. This caused a chain reaction and men began losing their balance, tumbling down one on top of the other. Meanwhile, the bird, frightened by the sudden noise, flew away.

Just as each man was needed to form the human ladder, so too each Jew's cooperation is needed to form the Jewish nation. The life of each Jew is linked with that of his fellow Jew so that if one part of the link is weak the entire "chain" will suffer, or even collapse. Thus, when one Jew is experiencing misfortune or is in danger of abandoning Yiddishkeit, it is incumbent upon his fellow Jews to come to his aid. If they ignore him and forget the spirit of brotherhood, the entire nation grows weaker.

Hashem, and that if the congregation practiced idolatry by error, it should atone by way of a sacrifice.

While in the wilderness, the people found a man violating the Sabbath. The man was held in custody until Hashem declared to Moshe that the man should be stoned to death by the congregation.

Finally, the law that Tzitzis be worn on the four corners of one's garments was given to remind the people of the need to observe Hashem's commandments at all times.

The Jews today are in exile, or Golus, a word whose base is "Gola". We are scattered throughout the world and look forward to the redemption of the days of Moshiach. In Hebrew, redemption is expressed as "Geulah". The words "Gola" and "Geulah" are basically identical, except for the fact that the latter contains an extra Aleph. A Sage once commented that this Aleph represents the term Achdus (which begins with an Aleph). For it is Achdus, the brotherhood that binds Jews together, that is needed to turn the Gola into a time of Geulah. Hopefully, the day will soom come when Jews will put their petty disputes behind them and live harmoniously with each other. Then, we pray, the day of Moshiach's coming will not be far ahead.

"All Jews are responsible for one another." (Shavuous 39)

Shmuel stated: "A person should never exclude himself from the community." (Berachos 49)

A revolt against Moshe and Aharon was led by a group of Levi'im under Korach and a group of Reuvenites under Dasan, Aviram, and On. Included in this rebellion were two hundred fifty prominent members of the assembly. Korach's rebellion was based on the contention that he should have become Nossi (Leader) of the tribe of Levi. Dasan and his associates claimed the right of leadership based on their descent from Reuven, the oldest of Yaakov's sons.

Moshe challenged Korach and his followers to appear the next day, to meet Moshe's challenge. After

פרשת קרח

Parshas Korach

THE REBELLION OF KORACH

The revolt of Korach against the leadership of Moshe and Aharon was a most tragic episode in Jewish history. What was especially saddening was that Korach attracted such a large and prestigious following.

What was Korach's appeal to the populace? He adopted a deceptively attractive argument. What right did Moshe and Aharon have in acting as the sole leaders of Yisroel? Weren't all the Israelites members of a holy nation? If so, why should not all men be equally fit to rule? Why weren't leaders chosen democratically?

This argument may sound very appealing, but it is highly misleading. For one thing, Korach's motives in leading the rebellion were hardly pure. By disputing the leadership of Moshe and Aharon, he did not wish to strengthen Klal Yisroel. Rather, he wanted to strengthen his own position. As a cousin of Moshe and Aharon (their fathers had been brothers), he felt that he was not being given his due share of leadership for himself. His arguments were, therefore, very hypocritical.

Consequently, Korach's protests were made for personal gain, at the expense of Klal Yisroel's unity. They were destructive rather than constructive and were meant to benefit himself rather than Hashem's law. It is for this reason that our Sages have said, "What type of argument is not meant L'Shem Shomayim? That of Korach and his associates." (Pirkey Avos 5:17). The former took place to help man act in accordance with Hashem's Torah while the latter occurred simply to satisfy one man's jealousy and ego. It was the constructive arguments between Beis Hillel and Beis Shammai, then,

warning the populace to stay clear of Korach and his assembly, Moshe announced the method with which Hashem would indicate His selection of their leaders. If the rebels would die a natural death Moshe would be proved wrong, but if they would be swallowed alive by the earth, then Moshe's leadership would be confirmed.

No sooner had Moshe spoken, than Korach and his fellow rebels, as well as all their possessions, were swallowed alive into the ground. The remainder of the people fled in terror.

Those who had survived began to murmur against Moshe, holding him responsible for the deaths of Korach and his followers. They were in turn punished through a plague, which took the lives of an additional fourteen thousand, seven hundred people. It was only when Aharon walked among the people with a pan of incense, as instructed by Moshe, that the plague subsided.

Hashem then ordered the prince of each tribe to bring a rod with his name on it to

that helped Klal Yisroel to more intensive learning, while the destructive protests of Korach and his associates led to their violent deaths.

"Those who were swallowed up with Korach are forever declaring, 'Moses and his Torah are true and we are liars'." (Bava Basra 74)

"The punishment of the misleader into sin is greater than the sinner." (Toldos Yitzchak)

"Deceiving others is deceiving yourself." (Taharas Hakodesh 4)

But what of the appeal for great democracy within Klal Yisroel? Was Korach not correct in fighting for this?

Democracy is certainly a noble goal for nations establishing governments. However, in the case of the Bnei Yisroel, democracy was superceded by the Will of Hashem Himself. For while the general populace can often make excellent choices of leaders, they can also be wrong. Sometimes they can be swayed by a candidate's attractive appearance, impressive campaign promises, or catchy slogans. But these do not necessarily mean that he will make an effective leader. In fact, he might deliberately avoid making tough decisions so as not to anger those who supported him. He might be willing to bend his principles in order to gain votes. If he were dealing with religious principles, this would be calamitous. A leader who compromises the laws of the Torah to win popularity would, in fact, be undermining those laws.

Hashem, therefore, took it upon himself to appoint leaders for Yisroel who could be trusted not to alter the Torah. These were Moshe and Aharon. Our Rabbis say that Moshe had a speech impediment to show

that he was not chosen because of his glib tongue. They owed their offices to no one but Hashem, and, therefore, paid sole allegiance to Him. This is why Torah leadership is not decided by political means. The members of the Moetzes Gedolei HaTorah, the supreme decision-making body of Agudas Yisroel, are, therefore, not chosen by a national election. Rather, they are selected on the basis of their universally acknowledged mastery of Torah laws and ideals. In this way, their full allegiance to Hashem's Torah can be ascertained.

SEARCHING FOR PEACE BY SWALLOWING PRIDE

The Torah states that after Korach, Dasan and Aviram commenced their rebellion, "Moshe sent to call Dasan and Aviram" (Bamidbar 6:12). Rashi comments that this means that Moshe went himself to search for them and to try to placate them with words of peace. This was the same Moshe who was the great leader of the people and who had spoken with Hashem at Har Sinai. Yet, Moshe did not become aloof because of his high office and wait for the rebels to come meekly to him. Instead, he decided to forego all proprieties and to take the initiative in the search for peace. He did not worry about losing his personal honor at this time. If peace could be achieved by his coming to them, he was more than willing to do so.

It is unfortunate that, for some, quarreling seems to be a pastime. They love a good fight and can't wait to attack their fellow man. Even if they are proven wrong, they do not apologize. Their pride would not permit it. "Let the other person come to me and apologize," they say. And so, the quarrel remains unsettled.

the Ohel Moed. These rods, together with the rod of the tribe of Levi which bore the name of Aharon, were placed before the ark. The following morning, Aharon's rod alone was found to have produced buds, blossoms, and almonds. This was indisputable proof that Hashem had chosen Aharon to be the Kohein Godol. Aharon's rod was preserved in front of the ark as a warning for future generations never to challenge the right of Aharon's lineage to the Kehunah.

Because the Kohanim and Levi'im would have no specific portion of the Promised Land, they would be supported by set contributions from the populace. The Kohein would receive provisions like the Bikurim (First Fruits), the Pidyon Bechorim (First Born), the Terumah (a portion of each person's produce), and various offerings. The Levi would receive Ma'aser Rishon (one-tenth of each person's produce) of which he would have to set aside a portion for the Kohein.

Moshe's attitude in this case shows how foolish this approach is. If the great leader of Bnei Yisroel was willing to relinquish his pride in the search for peace, then how much more so should the average person do this! **Men should not** let their pride stand in the way of progress. If they do, they are like the farmer who went to the barn every day to get milk but returned with an empty pail.

"How come you never bring back any milk?" his wife asked.

"Because the only way to get milk is for me to bend down and milk the cow," explained the farmer. "And I'd rather die than lose my pride and bend down to a cow!"

In Shmoneh Esrai, we take three steps backwards at the words, "Oseh Shalom." This is an indication to us that for the sake of peace one frequently has to go out of his way, even it if means backing off at the cost of his own pride.

> "No good comes of a quarrel." (Shemos Rabbah 30)
> "Even if peace eludes you, go after it and you will catch up with it." (Midrash Shmuel 4:20)

A WIFE'S INFLUENCE

This parsha demonstrates the extent of a wife's beneficial influence on her husband. On the one hand, the wife of Korach helped instigate her husband into leading the rebellion. On the other, the wife of On ben Peles told her husband to disassociate himself from the conspiracy (Sanhedrin 110a.). As a result, he was spared the fate that befell the others.

The role of the wife and mother in influencing world events is often overlooked. Of course, Jewish history has produced such prophetesses as Sorah, Rivkah, Rochel, Leah, Miriam, Devorah, Ruth, and Esther, among others (Megillah 14a). Yet, it is also true that behind almost every great Jewish man was an equally great Jewish woman, giving him support and guidance and maintaining the structure of his home. The Jewish mother has usually been the element that has held her family together and kept it functioning as a pillar of Jewish life.

The Torah calls this helpmate an "Ezer Kenegdo" (Bereishis 2:20). Literally, this means "a helper opposed to him". This seems a most contradictory expression. How can someone who is supposed to support a husband also oppose him at the same time?

Our Rabbonim explain the term in the following manner. A man is often a poor judge of his own character. He cannot see himself objectively and sometimes fails to notice his own faults. His wife, however, can serve as a good reflection of his true features. She knows him well enough to see him as he really is. If he is observant of Hashem's laws and is helpful to his fellow man, then it is her job to aid and encourage him in his beneficial work. On the other hand, if he is abusive towards others and disrespectful to the Torah, then it is her task to oppose him, to show him what he is doing wrong and to help him improve himself. In this sense, she is both a "helper" and one "opposed to him", depending on his tendencies. In both instances, her major role in Jewish life cannot be overstated.

> "It is because of his wife that a man's house is blessed." (Bava Metziah 59)
> "Who is rich?—the one who has a fine wife." (Shabbos 25)
> "A good wife is a handsome gift from G-d." (Ben Sira)
> Rabbi Yose said: "In all my life I never called my wife 'my wife' but 'my home' ". (Gitten 52)

A special purification ceremony was performed for those who had touched or had been under the same roof as a dead body. As part of the rites, a Poroh Adumah (Red Heifer) which was without blemish and which had not been worked was slaughtered outside the camp and burned together with cedar wood, hyssop, and a scarlet thread. Its ashes were gathered, mixed with water from a running stream, and sprinkled upon the unclean person on the third and seventh days of his impurity. At the end of the seventh day, after he had washed his clothes and immersed himself in a mikvah, he could once again partake in Sanctuary worship.

פרשת חקת

Parshas Chukas

"TO SAY . . ."—INFLUENCING OTHERS

"This is the law of the Torah which Hashem commanded, to say" (Bamidbar 19:2). These last two words of the phrase seem unnecessary. Yet, they provide us with a most important principle.

Our Sages comment that the words "to say" are an essential part of the law-giving process. They refer to the fact that the law was not complete until the leaders went about telling others of the Torah's commands. The average Jew had to be informed of how the Torah expects him to behave. Isn't this obvious? After all, how would the law become known if it was not revealed to the populace?

Yes, it seems most apparent. However, perhaps not everyone might feel it incumbent upon himself to transmit Hashem's Torah to others. "Let somebody else worry about the irreligious Jews," some might say. "I don't want to defile myself through them. Let me spend my time perfecting myself." Certainly, self-improvement always deserves a high priority. However, one should not close oneself off in an ivory tower and be unconcerned with the plight of one's fellow Jews. After all, if they sin, all of Klal Yisroel suffers (Introduction to Chasam Sofer on Yorah Deya).

Therefore, it is incumbent upon all Jews to try to bring other Jews closer to Yiddishkeit. This is why we are asked to fulfill two functions: "lilmod u'lelamed"—both to learn Hashem's Torah and to teach it to others.

But how can these tasks be easily fulfilled? Is everyone expected to become a professional teacher and relate Torah laws in a classroom? Teaching Torah is not confined only to the classroom. Rather, conveying Hashem's ideals to others is the full-time occupation of every observant Jew, regardless

of his profession. For it is through his everyday lifestyle and his normal behavior that he can set a good Torah example for others. Most people look to certain models for guidance regarding their own behavior. If a Jew can serve as a Torah-true model for other Jews to follow, then he has served as a most successful teacher, no matter what he does for a living.

Sometimes, though, it is necessary for a Jew to take a more active role in influencing others. This involves admonishing one's fellow Jew who has strayed from Yiddishkeit. Perhaps this Jew has become confused about Judaism's true goals, or perhaps he has been misled by foreign influences. Whatever the case, the process of Kiruv Rechokim, of redirecting an errant Jew to the Torah path, is a most essential one.

At the same time, it is a most difficult one, fraught with frustrations and disappointments. In addition, those involved in Kiruv work must be aware that some methods of admonition are more effective than others. Admonishing others through love and concern usually brings better results than doing so through anger.

Rabbi Elimelech of Lizensk was certainly a most effective Ba'al Mussar. It was once brought to his attention that the Jews of a neighboring city were not observing Shabbos in the proper way. Consequently, he asked for the opportunity to address the city's Jewish inhabitants and was invited to speak in their shul.

He mounted the pulpit, closed his eyes, and seemingly speaking to himself, said, "Elimelech! Beware of the Day of Judgment! Be careful of how you observe the Shabbos day! For when the Almighty will ask you whether you treated His Shabbos with the proper respect, what will you reply? Don't

For thirty-eight years the Israelites roamed throughout the wilderness, during which time all of the older generation between twenty and sixty had died except for Yehoshua and Calev. At the beginning of the fortieth year from the Exodus, the remainder of the populace returned to Kadesh. It was there that Miriam, the sister of Moshe and Aharon, died.

At her passing, the well of water that had miraculously accompanied the Israelites ceased to flow. Once again, the people began to murmur against Moshe for the lack of water. Hashem told Moshe and Aharon to speak to a specific rock and enough water would flow forth from it to satisfy the people. However, Moshe was so angered by the people's constant disrespect that he impatiently struck the rock instead of speaking to it. Because they had not followed Hashem's instructions and thereby dishonored Him before the people, Moshe and Aharon were told that they would not be allowed to enter the Holy Land.

The people were now told to prepare for the final stages of their long journey.

you know how sacred the Shabbos is? Aren't you aware of how to treasure it and treat it properly? If you don't, then it is about time that you learned."

He continued his address listing his own shortcomings and pointing out how he could improve himself. But while he spared the people any embarrassment, his words were not lost on them. Impressed by his own pledges to repent, they decided to do likewise. In this way, by admonishing himself, Rabbi Elimelech most successfully made others see how they could improve themselves.

When Rav Elimelech and his brother Rav Zushe saw someone transgress, they would rebuke him in a way that was guaranteed not to embarrass him. One brother would rebuke the other brother for that same transgression. When the person whom they wished to correct overheard the words of admonition, he would invariably think to himself that he, too, had been guilty of the same transgression, and would repent.

Whenever Rabbi Eliyahu Lopian felt the necessity to rebuke any of his children or students, he would not do so immediately upon finding out about the wrongdoing for fear that he might be rebuking out of anger. He always allowed a sufficient amount of time to elapse to ensure that no trace of anger remained. Once, when one of his children did something that was extremely improper, he waited two full weeks until he censured him.

One who perseveres despite setbacks and helps others appreciate Yiddishkeit has certainly strengthened the entire Jewish nation.

"The virtuous man is a mirror to his fellowmen, for he shows them their good and bad points." (Pninei Melizot 48)

R. Yehudah, in the name of Rav says: *"Whoever withholds a ruling (Halachah) from his disciples is as though he had robbed him of his heritage!"* (Sanhedrin 91)

THE POROH ADUMAH—LAW WITHOUT ANY MEANING

The laws of the Poroh Adumah, the red heifer, are included in the category of Chukim. These are statutes specified by the Torah for which there are no readily apparent reasons. Yet, we must observe these laws for they are the stated will of Hashem.

The Medrash relates that a Roman aristocrat asked Rabbi Yochanan ben Zakkai to explain the strange laws involving the Poroh Adumah to him.

Rabbi Yochanan ben Zakkai replied, "Just as a person afflicted with a certain disease is cured of his illness by taking a certain medicine, so, too, do the ashes of the Poroh Adumah, when prepared in the prescribed way and dissolved in water, disperse the unclean spirit."

The Roman left, apparently satisfied with this answer. Rabbi Yochanan's pupils were not willing to accept this reason. "That answer made the Roman happy but what response do you have to satisfy us?" they asked.

Thereupon, Rabbi Yochanan said, "The dead man does not make a person impure, nor do the ashes make him pure again. My explanation, therefore, is that the law concerning the Poroh Adumah is a Heavenly decree. Consequently, we mere mortals have no right to question it" (Midrash Rabbah on

The only route to the Promised Land that was available to them was through the land of Edom, south of the Dead Sea. Moshe sent messengers to the King of Edom, requesting permission to lead the people through his territory and offering to pay for any water the people and cattle might drink. Not only did the King refuse, but he also barred the Israelites by posing an armed force. The Israelites were, therefore, compelled to take the round-about route by way of the Southern borders of Edom. When the assembly reached a peak in the range of Har Hahor, Aharon died and was buried there. Moshe installed his son Elazar as the next Kohein Godol.

After successfully repulsing an attack by the Canaanite King of Arad, the weary Israelites complained bitterly about their lack of food and water. Consequently, they were punished with a plague caused by the deadly bite of fiery serpents. When the people admitted their error, Moshe set a serpent of brass upon a pole. Whoever looked at this serpent was healed.

Chukas 19:8).

In this response lies the answer to the rationale of the Chukim. We cannot always comprehend the workings of Hashem, for as humans, our understanding is limited. It is sufficient for us to know that by obeying the Chukim we are performing Hashem's Will.

This point was also made by Rav Raphael, who was once stopped by a fellow Jew as he was hurrying through the streets.

"Excuse me, Rabbi," said the other man, "but since you are a learned individual, perhaps you could explain to me why we are prohibited to shave with a blade? There seems to be no reason for this in my eyes."

"Pardon me, my friend," replied Rav Raphael. "I'd like to answer your question but I'm just on my way to the pharmacy to buy some medicine and I must get them right away."

"But why are you making this long trip yourself?" asked the man. "Why didn't you send a messenger to buy the medicine?"

"Because I also want to ask the pharmacist about the effectiveness of the medicine."

"I'm sorry, but I don't understand," said the man. "Why must you ask the pharmacist about the medicine? Isn't the advice of a doctor good enough?"

"Ah!" exclaimed Rav Raphael. "Do you hear what you have just said? You want me to accept the word of the doctor unquestioningly. Then why do you not accept Hashem's laws as they are? If Hashem has ordered us not to use blades for shaving, then He must feel that this is beneficial for us. It is our medicine to take and it works, whether we understand it or not. The duty of a Rabbi is merely to explain how to follow the laws of the Torah correctly, just as it is the job of the pharmacist to explain how to

use the doctor's prescription correctly."

"I have separated you from the people to be mine; if you are separated from the peoples then you belong to me; otherwise, you belong to Nebuchadnezzar, King of Babylon and his associates." (Sifrey Kedoshim)

MIRIAM AND AHARON

This parsha records the passings of Miriam and Aharon. Each aided Klal Yisroel greatly and each was sorely missed.

Miriam was, of course, the sister of Moshe and Aharon but she was a great prophetess and leader in her own right. When the oppression of slavery descended upon the Jews of Egypt and Paroh decreed that all male Jewish children would be thrown into the Nile River, many husbands separated from their wives, and refused to father any additional children. Among these was Amram, the father of Miriam and Aharon. It was Miriam who persuaded her father to change his mind and return to his wife. As a result of her influence, Moshe Rabbeinu was born.

It was also due to Miriam's greatness that the Jews were given a well of water miraculously traveling along with them during their sojourn in the Midbar. When Miriam died, the well disappeared and the Jews began to fully appreciate Miriam's presence (Sotah 12b).

The loss of Aharon was also deeply mourned by the people. The Torah makes a point of stating that when Aharon died, all the congregation—every single man and woman—wept for him for thirty days. This was because Aharon considered it his personal mission to settle all quarrels within the congregation and foster peace among all. He went out of his way to see that husbands and

The journey, which had taken the congregation south, east, and then north, and passed the lands of Edom and Moav, came to a halt when the people reached the river Arnon, the boundary between Moav in the south and Emor in the north.

Sichon, king of the Emorites, refused to allow the Israelites to pass through his land and led his army against them. However, because of Hashem's help the battle ended with the utter defeat of the Emorites. Turning northward towards the fertile lands of Gilad and Bashan, the Israelites overcame the resistance of Og, King of Bashan, and took possession of his country. The land on the east side of the Jordan had now been conquered and the Israelites finally camped on the border of Moav, facing Yericho.

wives who had had a quarrel were reunited. When Aharon died, the entire nation felt that they had lost a great friend (Avos of Rabbi Nosson 12).

Whenever Aharon heard that two people were involved in a quarrel, he would go to one of them and tell him that he had recently met his friend and had heard him say, "The quarrel was my fault, and I bitterly regret it." Aharon would then go to the second person and tell him the same fabricated story. When the two would meet again, they would hug each other and be friends. Thus, the entire nation wept when Aharon died for they remembered his compassion and boundless

love he had for them.

When we are blessed with the presence of a great personality in our midst, we must take advantage of it. We should not take him for granted while he is alive, and only appreciate him after his death. Unfortunately, the latter is all too often the case.

"The righteous are greater at death than in life." (Chulin 7)

"The memory of the righteous is blessed." (Mishley 10)

"Monuments need not be raised for the pious, their deeds are their monuments." (Yerushalmi, Shekalim 2)

Balak, king of Moav, viewed with dismay the victory of the Israelites over Emori. Dreading an invasion of his own country, he formed an alliance with his former enemies, the Midianites. Balak then sent messengers to ask Bilam of Pethor, a noted sorceror, to curse the Israelites. Bilam asked the delegation to stay with him overnight so that he could consult with Hashem as to whether he could comply with their request. During the night, he was warned by Hashem not to go with the men, so he sent them away.

Thinking that a more tempting invitation would

פרשת בלק

Parshas Balak

BILAM'S DUPLICITY AND GREED

Very few Parshios of the Torah bear the names of individuals. It may, therefore, seem surprising that this Parsha is named after Balak, a wicked man who sought to destroy the Israelites. If anything, the Parsha might have borne the name of Bilam, who at least communicated with Hashem and who blessed the Jews. Why did Balak deserve this honor more than Bilam?

Our Sages respond that, for all of Balak's wickedness, he possessed at least one good attribute—honesty. He made no attempt to conceal his hatred of the Israelites. At least everyone knew where he stood.

Bilam, though, did not possess even this good characteristic. He pretended to be a holy man and to aspire to fulfill only Hashem's desires. Yet, his very actions proved how hypocritical he was. When the messengers of Balak came and offered him wealth and honors in exchange for his condemnation of the Israelites, he did not flatly refuse them. No! He told them to lodge with him overnight and await Hashem's verdict, hoping that Hashem would give him permission to comply. The permission was denied. But when the messengers returned with promises of even greater wealth, Bilam again welcomed them to his house. He had not

prove effective, Balak sent a second delegation, a larger and more prestigious one, offering great honors and rewards to Bilam if he would cooperate. Bilam, obviously motivated by personal greed, asked them to remain until he could again receive guidance from Hashem. This time he was given permission to go but to speak only as Hashem directed him. During the journey to Balak, Bilam's donkey saw an angel bearing a sword obstructing the path and so it turned aside. The impatient Bilam struck the animal several times in an attempt to make it proceed. After the donkey protested this undeserved cruelty, Bilam finally saw the angel himself and was told he was at fault by inwardly wanting to accept Balak's offer. Bilam offered to return home but was told to continue on his trip and speak exactly as Hashem ordered him.

Balak met Bilam at the border of the Arnon River and brought him to a nearby city for a feast in his honor. The next day, he took Bilam to a hill sacred to the worshippers of Ba'al, from where he could see part of the Israelite camp. After Bilam and Balak had sacrificed a ram and a bullock on each of seven altars, Bilam told Balak to stay near the burnt-offering while he withdrew to inquire of Hashem.

learned his lesson and remained hopeful that he might fulfill their wishes. How could he turn down all those riches, even if it required cursing Hashem's chosen people? And when Hashem did grant him permission this time, he left to fulfill his mission with astonishing swiftness. Nothing could deprive him of his goal now. When his donkey stopped along the way Bilam beat it mercilessly. His mask of holiness became transparent, and the greed in his character shone through.

Unfortunately, there are many in our modern society who have adopted Bilam's tactics of pretending to have high moral values and then throwing them aside at the first chance to earn money. They mobilize all their efforts in an attempt to become wealthy and forget that money is a means to benefit mankind rather than an end in itself. Their greed becomes an obsession that totally disrupts their lives.

The Chofetz Chaim told of just such a man. He worked feverishly to gather wealth, using his money to buy only the finest delicacies and enjoy only the fanciest luxuries. Unfortunately, this drive for money led him to become a traitor and to sell his country's secrets to the enemy. His treachery was soon discovered and the leader of the country decided upon a unique punishment for him. The man would be allowed to retain all his money and luxuries, but he would be forced to live alone on top of a steep tower which overlooked a deep, deep abyss. The man tried to return to his old fancy-free ways, but every time he looked out of the window and noticed the abyss below him, his happiness evaporated. How could all the

money in the world make him feel secure when the threat of death constantly stared him in the eye?

The same unease can ebe felt by every wealthy person. Money can certainly bring about a great deal of good. But whoever worships money as a god is doomed to live in a high tower of his own, afraid to venture outside lest his money be stolen or lost. For how can a greedy person survive a descent to poverty if he has no other riches to sustain him?

"Money legitimized the mamzar." (Kiddushin 71)
"Money can explain everything." (Koheles 10)

ASCERTAINING HASHEM'S PROTECTION

A nobleman once heard that someone had discovered a magic ointment that, when applied to a person's body, would render him invulnerable. The nobleman eagerly sought the ointment and after procuring it, applied it liberally to every part of his body.

While he was returning home through a thick forest one day, the nobleman was attacked by a band of highwaymen. They tried to beat him, stab him, and shoot him, but all their efforts were unsuccessful. Even their hardest blows seemed to have no effect on the nobleman. Frightened and shaken, the robbers began to run away.

They were stopped by a sudden shout from the nobleman. "Wait! Come back!" The robbers eyed him suspiciously until they noticed that the nobleman was offering them a part of his riches. They couldn't un-

On his return, he delivered his first speech: "How can I curse the ones that Hashem has not cursed?" he asked. ". . . Behold, it is a people that lives apart and not included among other nations."

Angered at Bilam's unexpected praise for the Israelites, Balak took him to the top of Mount Pisgah hoping for different results. However, Bilam once again disappointed Balak by declaring that Hashem would not break His promise of blessing Israel and that no magic could prevail against them. In despair, Balak asked Bilam to desist from either cursing or blessing the Israelites. Before departing, though, Bilam foretold the sovereignty of Israel and the doom of Moav, Edom, Amalek and other enemies of the Israelites.

The Israelites then encamped at Shittim. Here, the heathen women of Moav, advised by Bilam, tempted the Israelites to join in the worship of Ba'al Peor and to participate in an orgy of idolatry and immorality. Moshe sentenced the sinners to death and a plague developed among the assembly. Pinchas, the son of Elazar the Kohen Godol, witnessed a flagrant act of immorality between an Israelite and a Midianite woman. Zealously defending the laws of Hashem, he executed the evil-doers. The plague subsided but only after twenty-four thousand of the congregation had perished.

derstand it. Here, they had been trying to murder him, and now he was giving them gifts! The nobleman noticed their surprise and explained, "I am giving you this money out of gratitude. You see, I just went through great trouble and expense to purchase a miraculous ointment, but I wasn't sure whether it would work. Your attack on me proved that it did and that is why I am grateful to you. You showed that my trust in the ointment had not been misplaced."

"Trust in the Creator is a tranquilizer."
(Mussar Haphilosophim)
"Do not worry for the morrow, for you know not what the morrow may bring."
(Ben Sira)

This was also the benefit of Bilam's actions for the Israelites. Their forefathers had escaped the effects of their enemies' curses in the past. However, the Bnei Yisroel could not be certain that they, too, deserved Hashem's protection against the evil designs of others. It took the episode of Bilam to show them that Hashem's assistance was still present and that the curses of their enemies had no effect.

"Nothing happens to man in life without it being decreed by the Holy One Blessed be He." (Sefer Chassidim)
"Even with a sword at the throat, one should not give up hope for mercy." (Berachos 10)

THE JEWISH FAMILY

"How goodly are your tents, O Yaakov; your dwelling places, O Yisroel (Bamidmar 24:5). This was the blessing that came forth from Bilam's lips when he saw the camp of the Israelites. This same blessing, "Ma Tovu", is recited daily by Jews throughout the world.

Its great importance lies in the fact that it offers appreciation for the foundation of Judaism—the Jewish family. The interaction between the various family members provides the structure that Judaism needs to thrive on. It is the family that provides the individual with love and a sense of worth. It is the family that passes down Hashem's traditions from generation to generation. It is the family that makes the individual feel part of a group, and part of a nation, the Jewish nation. For the Jewish nation is, in reality, one big and cohesive family and its members should emphasize their similarities. This cohesiveness has enabled Judaism to survive during the hardest of times, during anti-Jewish oppressions, within the ghettoes, and throughout days of poverty. And it has been the Jewish family that inspired this cohesiveness and sense of tradition.

"As is the mother, so is her daughter." (Ezekiel 16).
"Like father, like son." (Eruvin 70)
"He who loves his wife like himself, and honors her more than himself, and rears his children in the proper way, will have peace in his home and will be the master of his house." (Derech Eretz 2)

As a reward for his zeal in defending the honor of Hashem, Pinchas was promised that the Kehunah would be retained by his descendants.

The Israelites were ordered to prepare for an offensive war against the Midianites, who had been primarily responsible for their degradation. Before this would take place, though, Moshe and Elazar were told to take a new census of the populace (the previous census had been taken thirty-eight years before). Now that the conquest of Canaan was in sight, it was necessary for Moshe to ascertain not only the number of able-bodied

פרשת
פינחס

Parshas Pinchas

PINCHAS' UNCOMPROMISING ATTITUDE

This parsha begins with Hashem praising Pinchas for his courageous act in killing Zimri and Cozbi, who acted immorally. Normally, one who slays others is condemned. Pinchas, though, is praised for taking the initiative in punishing those who had flagrantly opposed Hashem's laws. The Torah states that he was zealous, not for his own benefit but on Hashem's behalf, and that his extreme action was proper in this instance. He had shown the entire congregation how to act swiftly, decisively, and uncompromisingly to uphold the law.

There might be those who scorn Pinchas' actions as being too "hard-lined" and inflexible. They would rather advocate hesitancy and would have tried to find possible excuses for Zimri and Cozbi. Going further, they might have tried to soften the law itself and advocated compromises and changes. Certainly within the past century a large segment of Jewry has been drifting along this lenient current. They began asking for more flexibility in the Torah laws and ended by first compromising and then totally altering the laws. They looked for 'Heterim' or rationalizations to permit whatever acts their evil inclinations desired, and then finally ignored the restrictions of the law altogether. This Reform and Conservative brand of Judaism is, in reality, a Jewish soup so watered down that the original taste has almost disappeared!

One such Reformer approached a noted Rav and asked, "I know that you Orthodox Jews believe that it is forbidden to smoke on the Shabbos. But I just can't go an entire day without smoking and I don't intend to follow that prohibition. Still, I don't want to be left with any guilt feelings, so can you find a loophole that could make smoking permissible on Shabbos?"

"Certainly," answered the Rav. "Sometimes it is permissible to perform a prohibited act through a 'Shinui'—a change from the normal way of doing the act. Therefore, you can smoke on Shabbos, provided you turn the cigarette around and put that part that is lit into your mouth."

It was Pinchas' great deed to show how firm one must be in following Hashem's law. One cannot compromise statutes that have been designed by the Almighty. That would imply that man is superior to G-d and that is certainly not the case.

The Chofetz Chaim condemned the compromisers through the following parable. A man was once seen taking very expensive goods out of a store. Because he seemed to move in a suspicious manner, a policeman began following him. When the man noticed this, he quickly ran with the goods and dumped them into the river. When the policeman was asked later if he was sure that the objects thrown into the river were stolen goods, he replied, "Well, the way the man was so eager to get rid of them seemed proof enough to me that they weren't his."

So, said the Chofetz Chaim, is the apparent attitude of the Reformers. They seem so eager to compromise Jewish laws and to throw away all the Jewish tradition that they indicate that they never considered these laws to be theirs in the first place. They are denying their Judaism, and that is certainly a great tragedy, both for them and for Klal Yisroel.

"A scholar must be as unyielding as iron, or he is no scholar." (Taanis 4)
"Each generation has its great men, each generations its wise men." (Sanhedrin 39)

men available for war but also the numerical strength of each tribe. This was needed as a basis for dividing the Promised Land fairly among the tribes. The total number of male Israelites over the age of twenty, those liable for military service, came to six hundred seven thousand, seven hundred thirty. The extent of the land area to be allotted to each tribe was to be proportionate to the tribe's size, and its geographical location was to be decided by lot. The Levi'im, who would not share in the division of the land, were counted separately.

Zelophchad, a member of the tribe of Menasheh, had died in the wilderness, leaving five daughters but no sons. The question of whether the five daughters could receive their father's inheritance arose; if not, the portion of land that had been due to Zelophchad would pass into other hands. They brought their case before Moshe who submitted it to Hashem. The final ruling was that if a person left no sons, his daughters had the right to his heritage. It was furthermore declared that if one left neither sons nor daughters, his property would go to his surviving brothers, or if there were none, to his nearest next of kin. The principle that the title to one's land would remain within the family was thus established.

PINCHAS' REWARD

The Parsha places much emphasis upon the fact that Pinchas was rewarded for his meritorious deed. Why was this specific act so highly praised? Again, a parable offers cleearer insight into this episode.

A young man was hired to work as an apprentice to a wealthy merchant. The agreement was that the young man would work diligently in his position, under the merchant's guidance, and in return he would receive free room and board.

One day, the merchant and his family were enjoying a sumptuous meal. The apprentice was also seated at the table. Suddenly, a knock was heard at the door. A stranger entered and asked to speak to the merchant in regard to a business deal he wished to initiate.

"I am in the middle of a feast," replied the merchant, "and I do not wish to be bothered right now."

The stranger was about to leave when the apprentice rose and stopped him. "I'll be able to take care of the matter, if you wish," he said.

All the other parties agreed and the apprentice spent the next several hours working out a most favorable deal, netting the merchant a large profit.

The next day, the merchant asked the apprentice to see him. "I am extremely pleased that you took so much time to work out that business affair," he said. "In what way can I reward you for your zeal?"

"You don't have to give me a special reward," said the apprentice. "After all, our agreement was that I was to receive free room and board for all my services, no matter how helpful they might be."

"I know," replied the merchant. "And until now I had felt that the good job you were doing was because you wanted to earn your keep. Yesterday, though, I saw that you were willing to give up your dinner and your sleep just to help me out. Such selfless devotion deserves a reward beyond the terms of our original agreement. I am, therefore, willing to add a special gift to the free room and board I already give you."

This, in a sense, was the case with Pinchas. Every man who performs the basic mitzvos receives from Hashem the basic "free room and board", the essential means for life such as good health, a home, and a livelihood. However, those like Pinchas who reveal that they are willing to go beyond the call of duty in serving Hashem, by risking their lives to uphold the law, deserve a heavenly reward beyond the normal bounds. It was for this reason that Pinchas' prize was not in the form of merely more earthly possessions, but rather of a permanent heritage for all his descendants, a reward that has lasted to this very day. It is to such rewards that the individual Jew must aspire by exhibiting his faith in Hashem to extraordinary degrees.

"Some achieve immortality in one hour." (Avodah Zarah 6)

Ben Heh Heh stated: "According to the pain is the reward." (Avos 5:23)

THE NEW LEADER

When Moshe was informed that the day of his death was drawing near, he did not

Hashem commanded Moshe to ascend the mountain of Abarim from where he could view the Promised Land. Told that he was nearing the end of his days, Moshe showed immediate concern for the continued welfare of the people and asked that his successor be named. Hashem replied that Yehoshua ben Nun would take over the reigns of leadership and that Moshe should lay his hands upon him to signify the transfer of authority. However, unlike Moshe, who had received guidance directly from the Almighty, Yehoshua would be guided by Elazar the Kohein Godol, who would in turn consult Hashem by means of the Urim and Tumim.

The people were reminded that their sacrificial obligations would continue when they entered Canaan. A detailed description of the public morning and evening sacrifices was therefore given, in addition to the sacrifices for the various Yomim Tovim.

sink into self-pity. Rather, his first thoughts were of his people, Klal Yisroel, and who their new leader would be. His selflessness at this time set the standard for all those throughout Jewish history, the martyrs of Roman persecution, the soldiers of Israel, and the Rabonim who faced Nazi torture rather than leave their followers, who thought only of preserving the Jewish nation in times of crisis.

Moshe knew that the selection of a new leader for Klal Yisroel would be a crucial matter. He was aware of how great the effect of a leader can be on a people. A strong leader can direct even an apathetic nation to great achievements, while a weak or devious leader can cause a nation to disintegrate.

The necessity of choosing a proper leader is illustrated by the following story. A wealthy merchant set out on a journey traveling with many wagons heavily laden with merchandise. Snow had fallen and the caravan lost its way. The wagons made several wrong turns and only after many unsuccessful attempts did they get back on course.

The merchant was very distressed. One of his assistants, noticing his displeasure, tried to cheer him up.

"Why are you so worried?" he asked the merchant. "After all, we finally did find the right road. Besides, it often takes me quite a while and many wrong turns until I find the way on this path, so this is not unusual."

"Perhaps," replied the merchant. "But if you would go on this road, you would be traveling alone. The footprints you would be creating in the snow would quickly become obliterated and no one would notice them a day later. But I am traveling with a lot of loaded-down wagons and they will leave obvious tracks in the snow that will not easily go away. So if I take a wrong turn, others will see the tracks and follow me along an incorrect path. I will be leading all future drivers here astray and that is what I am worried about!"

A leader who himself makes errors cannot easily escape the consequences of his mistakes. For when he sins, others will follow his example, and the blame for the nation's downfall can be laid at his doorstep. That is why he must be exceptionally careful about the actions he takes, and for this reason Moshe was so concerned that his successor be a worthy one.

"As the generation, so is its leader." (Erechin 16)

"The body follows the head." (Eruvin 41)

"When the shepherd becomes angry at his flock, he blinds the leader." (Bava Kama 52)

A vow made to Hashem, whether in a positive form (e.g. vowing a voluntary contribution to the Mishkon) or a negative one (e.g. vowing to abstain from certain activities) was binding. However, this general rule was qualified in cases of a vow made by a woman under the jurisdiction of a father or husband. Thus, a young unmarried woman living in her father's house, or a woman who is on the verge of or who has already entered into a marriage was not bound to fulfill her vow if either her father or her husband (as the case might be) disallowed it. The husband's or father's disapproval

פרשת
מטות

Parshas Matos

KEEPING VOWS

Parshas Matos discusses the laws pertaining to one who has vowed voluntary service for Hashem or his fellow man. The Posuk states that such vows are not recommended: "It is better for one not to vow at all than for him to vow and then not fulfill" (Koheles 5). A person who is lax in observing Torah commandments is not permitted to make any vows at all. After all, if he does not have enough self-control to comply with what has already been commanded, how can he be trusted to fulfill what is not required? If he does not keep his vows, he had accumulated an additional sin. So one should make vows or promises only if he is certain that he can carry them out (Nedarim 9a).

The Dubno Maggid illustrated the Talmud's reasoning in the following manner: Two poor neighbors, each of whom had young daughters, expressed similar fears that they would not be able to afford dowries for their daughters' eventual marriage. When the two met again several years later, one of the men announced proudly that his daughter had become engaged.

"But how did you provide her with a dowry?" asked the other.

"I listened to the advice of a wise man," the man replied. "He told me to place a coin into a locked box every day and to vow that I would not open the box, no matter what. That way, when I opened the box years later, I had more than enough to pay for the dowry."

"That's a good idea," said the other. "But that would never have worked for me. You see, I'm not observant. I break a lot of the commandments, and, confidentially, I sometimes break into people's houses and steal their money. So even if I had kept my

money in a box, it wouldn't have stayed there long. I'm so used to breaking locks that I would have broken the one on the box, too. I would have spent all the money on myself and my daughter's hopes would have been shattered. Better not to raise expectations at all than to raise them and lower them again."

So it it is with one who is considering making a pledge. If he knows that he cannot fulfill it, if he knows that he cannot even keep the basic Mitzvos, then it is better for him not to make the pledge at all. On the other hand, if he does make a promise, then he must do everything within his power to carry it out.

This simple strategy has very practical applications. Naturally, it applies to promises made to others. If you promise to help someone in his work or to aid him in learning, make sure that you don't go back on your word. If you do, you will leave the other individual both disappointed and bitter. But the same is true of pledges you make to yourself. If you tell yourself that you will learn an entire perek of Gemorah a week, even though you know that this will be impossible for you to do, you may become so frustrated that you will wind up learning nothing. Therefore, try to set goals that you can accomplish, goals that will stretch your talents, and goals that will not frustrate you. Avoid inviting deliberate failure and keep your promises within the realm of success.

Seven days after Rabbi Leib Cheifitz died, a large gathering assembled to eulogize him. After the speakers delivered their eulogies, the cantor recited the "Kale Molai Rachamim . . ." the special prayer for the dead. Immediately afterward, Rabbi Yeshoshua Leib Diskin gave the synagogue's charity treasurer a sum of money for charity. He told him that the money was

had to be expressed on the day that he heard of the vow, or else he bore the guilt for the vow's non-fulfillment. The vows of a widow or a divorced woman were binding.

The attack on the Midianites was made by twelve thousand Israelite warriors, one thousand men from each tribe. They were accompanied by Pinchas who took with him the holy vessels, and trumpets for sounding the battle alarm. During the war, every male Midianite was slain, including the five kings of Midian and Bilam ben Beor. The victors took the women, children, cattle, and other possessions of the Midianites with them as spoil. Moshe, though, reprimanded them for keeping alive the women, who had been the cause of the plague on Bnei Yisroel. The soldiers, having become unclean by contact with the dead, were required to stay outside the camp for seven days to undergo the ceremony of purification. All their garments and utensils were cleaned in accordance with the rules laid down by Elazar the

being given on behalf of all those who were present when the cantor recited the prayer.

Having heard the cantor say in the prayer that all the congregation will give charity for the merit of the deceased, Rav Yehoshua Leib wanted to make sure that no one would be guilty of violating the vow to give charity.

> *Rabbi Zera stated: "A man should not promise a child something and then fail to give it to him; for that is the beginning of the perilous path sown with falsehood." (Succah 47)*
> *Better not to vow, than to vow and not pay. (Koheles 5)*
> *What has passed your lips you shall keep. (D'vorim 23)*

TZENIUS AND THE YETZER HORAH (MODESTY AND THE EVIL INCLINATION)

The Israelite warriors returned from the wars with Midian laden with riches and with no casualties. Yet, Moshe reacted angrily to their return, because they had brought with them the Midianite women. These were the women whose allure had caused Bnei Yisroel to sin earlier, leading to the plague that had cost thousands of lives. Their mere presence enraged Moshe, for he knew that even if the men promised not to consort with the women, the temptation to do so would be too great for them to withstand.

Moshe had seen the Yetzer HoRah at work, and he knew the strength of its powers. He knew this Evil Inclination to be rooted within the psyche of every man, giving each one the potential to saisfy his animal instincts at the expense of his spiritual well-being. He had seen men rebel to satisfy their egos, and men commit adultery to satisfy their lust. He knew, therefore, that the best way to fight the urges

of the Yetzer HoRah was to remove the object of the men's passion. In this way, the Yetzer HoRah could hopefully be kept under control.

To dramatize the impact of the Yetzer HoRah, the Chofetz Chaim told the story of the merchant who was returning home in a hired coach.

"Listen carefully," he told the driver. "I have just finished a very heavy meal and I am likely to fall asleep during the drive. However, I want you to keep a careful eye on the horse pulling the coach and to make sure that it keeps going in the right direction."

The driver agreed to do so and the merchant soon fell asleep inside the coach. The driver continued watching the horse but soon the monotony of the trip affected him so that he too slipped into drowsiness. The reins dropped from his hands. The horse, realizing that the driver no longer controlled him, began to trot around at random. It suddenly galloped off to an inviting patch of grass. The resulting jerk in the coach quickly woke up the merchant, who was badly shaken.

"Idiot!" he cried at the driver. "Didn't I tell you to watch exactly where we were going. If I've broken any bones by this sudden rush, I'm going to sue you for everything you've got!"

"Why are you blaming me?" protested the driver. "It wasn't my fault. I trusted the horse to be intelligent enough to travel straight. If you want to blame anybody, blame the horse!"

"You fool!" replied the merchant. "Do you want me to sue your horse? Don't you know that the horse runs wild and doesn't have any sense of its own? That's why it was

Kohein Godol, which he had learned from Moshe. The spoils were then divided equally between all those who had gone to war on the one hand, and the remainder of the congregation on the other. The soldiers contributed one-five hundredth of their spoils to the Kohanim, while the non-combatants gave one-fiftieth of their share to the Levi'im. The returning warriors, thankful that not one of them had perished during the battle, made an additional free-will offering to the Mishkon consisting of the golden ornaments that they had captured.

The tribes of Reuven and Gad possessed large herds of cattle and sought permission to settle in the pasture land of Gilad, on the east of the Jordan. Moshe at first disapproved of this plan. He feared that if these two tribes remained behind during the conquest of Canaan, the other tribes might lose heart. However, when the

your task to control it at all times; and if you didn't, then it's your fault."

In other words, when we are not in full control of our animal instincts, they can easily run wild and lead us astray. It is, therefore, our fault if we do not carefully contain them and stay clear of tempting influences.

It is for this reason that Jews place so much emphasis on Tzenius (Modesty.) We must be careful about the way we dress, the way we talk, and the company we keep. This is why we insist on a separation of the sexes during shul services. It is extremely easy for the Yetzer HoRah to take command of a situation. It is, therefore, up to us to see that the situation remains under our control and that our thoughts and actions remain pure.

"When you fear your G-d and beware of an evil path, you will not be misled into evil."

"Faulty tools produce faulty products."

The following is a most dramatic example of how a certain young woman retained her desire to be modest to the very end. She had been the victim of a notorious Blood Libel by being falsely charged with killing a Christian child to use its blood for the baking of Matzos. The accusers used trumped-up evidence to condemn her and she was sentenced to death by a most horrible means. Her hair was to be tied to the tail of a wild horse and she was to be dragged through the streets until she died.

The woman was asked if she had any last request. To the surprise of her accusers, she asked for some pins. No one could understand why, but they gave them to her. She waited until her hair was tied to the tail of the horse. Then she took pins and, folding her dress tightly around her feet, stuck them through her dress into her skin. That way, she reasoned, her dress would not roll up as

she was being dragged through the streets. She did not want to violate the laws of Tzenius even after her death.

If only everyone would be as modesty conscious as the above-mentioned woman during their lifetimes!

"Purity leads to Holiness, Holiness leads to Humility." (Yerushalmi, Shekalim)

THE REQUEST OF REUVEN AND GAD

The tribes of Reuven and Gad approached Moshe and asked for permission to settle in Gilad, apart from the land to be inhabited by the remaining tribes. Moshe was severely disappointed by this request at first. "Will your brethren go to war across the Jordan while you remain untouched here?" (Bamidbar 32:6).

The tribes quickly reassured him by replying, "We will build sheepfolds for our cattle and cities for our children here, but we ourselves will be armed to go before the Children of Israel until we have brought them to their place." (Bamidbar 32:16).

Moshe was pleased with their declared intention to join the other tribes in battle. However, he noted a few disturbing signs in their priorities and their allegiance. They had mentioned the building of homes for their cattle before that of their children. This implied that they attached more importance to their cattle, their worldly possessions, than they did to their children. Furthermore, they had not recognized Hashem's role in the coming conquest of Canaan, stating only that they themselves would bring their fellow tribes to their place.

To set them straight, Moshe was very meticulous in his reply. "Build your cities for your little ones," (Bamidbar 32:24) he said, giving this task priority, and only then did he add, "and folds for your sheep." In

Reuvenites and Gadites explained that they intended to cross the Jordan and fight alongside their fellow Jews while their families remained in Gilad, Moshe changed his mind. He charged Yehoshua with making sure that this promise be fulfilled. Otherwise these tribes would forfeit any claims they might have had to settling in Gilad.

this way, he was rearranging their values into a proper order. Then he reminded them of Hashem's supreme role in the battle for Canaan by stating, "And arm yourselves to go before the L-rd to the war" (Bamidbar 32:27).

The tribes of Reuven and Gad quickly realized their error and adopted Moshe's changes as their own. Thus, we find them saying, "We will build cities for our little ones and sheepfolds for our cattle"—in that order—and, "As the L-rd has said to your servants, so shall we do; we will pass over armed before the L-rd into the land of Canaan" (Bamidbar 32:32).

Those of us who place greater emphasis on wealth than on human life and who fail to recognize Hashem's hand in all worldly events, should be similarly corrected. (Midrash Rabbah, Matos 22:9).

Rabbi Yisroel Salanter once became angry at the people of a town for not paying the tuition of a young orphan to enable him to learn Torah. He had noticed the child roaming the streets and demanded to know why no one had provided for his tuition. The people excused themselves, explaining that the community funds were all used up. No money was available to help that orphan.

"You must sell the Torah scrolls to pay for his tuition," ordered Rav Yisroel Salanter. So great was his desire to impress upon the people the need for helping the needy and the unfortunate.

"A man trembles for his money."
(Shabbos 117)
"To some, their money is dearer than their bodies." (Berachos 61)
"He who hurries to get rich will not go unpunished." (Mishley 28)

Moshe recorded the itinerary of the Bnei Yisroel through the wilderness from the time they left Egypt to their arrival at the plains of Moav. In all, the Israelites had encamped in forty-two separate places during their forty years of wandering.

After they had driven out the present inhabitants of Canaan, the people were told that they would have to destroy every remnant of idol worship in the country. The land would be distributed by lots in proportion to the size of the tribes. Ten leaders, one from each of the tribes concerned, were appointed. They, together with

פרשת מסעי
Parshas Massei

CITIES OF REFUGE

Bnei Yisroel were commanded to establish six Cities of Refuge, Orei Miklot, when they reached Canaan. These cities were set aside for those who had killed unintentionally, where they could escape the wrath of the victim's closest kin.

Sages tell us that signs announcing the location of these Cities of Refuge appeared on every cross-road in the settled territories. They carefully guided the accidental murderer to the refuge he was seeking. (Makos 10).

The same roads were traversed by countless Olei Regolim, those Jews who came to

Yerusholayim three times a year on the occasions of the Yomim Tovim. Yet, not one sign appeared on the roads directing the travelers to Yerusholayim. If they lost their way, they were forced to ask others how to get there.

This arrangement seems just the opposite what one would expect. Logically, one would think that there would be many signs aiding the many Olei Regolim who came several times a year and no signs for the few occasional accidental murderers. Why was the reverse true?

In fact, there was a carefully-designed plan to this arrangement. If there had been

Yehoshua and Elazar the Kohein Godol, were entrusted with the equitable allotment of the land. The Levi'im were not given separate territory but were instead granted forty-eight cities on both sides of the Jordan.

Six of these Levitical cities, three on each side of the Jordan, were designated as Orei Miklot (Cities of Refuge) besides the other forty-two minor Orei Miklot. They would provide asylum for whoever killed another person accidentally, allowing him to escape any vengeful acts of the dead man's relatives. Following an accidental murder, the perpetrator could flee to one of the Orei Miklot where he would be brought before a judicial tribunal. If the judges decided that this was a case of willful murder, the person would be handed over to the avenger of the victim, (a close relative) and anyone who committed a premeditated murder would be put to death. On the other hand, if the murder was unplanned and without evil intent, the perpetrator would have to stay in the City of Refuge until the death of the Kohein

no signs aiding the accidental murderer, he might have been forced to ask those along the way directions to the Orei Miklot. This might in turn have led those giving directions to spread the word that a murderer was in the area, and this might have caused the accidental murderer to become a marked man. It was to avoid this situation that the Torah ensured the accidental murderer safe and silent passage. He could find the proper directions on his own without having to consult others and thereby give rise to gossip.

On the other hand, the Torah wanted the Olei Regolim to ask the local residents directions to Yerusholayim. That way, the populace would get to discuss the coming Yomim Tovim and perhaps join together in the journey to Yerusholayim. This is why no directions to Yerusholayim were posted. (Rav Aharon Kotler).

The Torah, thereby, encourages public discussion of Mitzvos and good deeds, while trying to limit potentially harmful gossip. In an era when mass media influence so much of our thoughts, we must be especially careful of which topics we choose to discuss. It is easy to make a person's attributes a matter of public discussion, but it is hardly that simple to restore a ruined reputation. If we do talk to others, we should try to concentrate on matters beneficial to all.

The Chofetz Chaim was once traveling in a wagon with horse dealers. During the trip, his traveling companions were discussing topics relating to horses and cattle. In the middle of their conversation, one of the travelers began to speak against another dealer.

The Chofetz Chaim reprimanded them for speaking and listening to "Loshon Hora," and asked them to continue discussing

animals rather than people. When he saw, however, that the dealers refused to pay attention to what he told them, he asked the wagon driver to stop, and got off in the middle of the road.

The Chofetz Chaim was once the guest of a certain Shochet for Shabbos. Before Shalosh Seudos (the third and last meal eaten on Shabbos), the Chofetz Chaim heard the Shochet tell his wife that a certain butcher took one of his regular customers. The Chofetz Chaim left the house and went elsewhere. When the Shochet met the Chofetz Chaim a while later, he inquired why he had left his house so abruptly. The Chofetz Chaim replied that if the Shochet had wanted to rebuke the butcher for dishonesty he should have gone to him directly. No purpose was served in relating "Loshon Hora" about the butcher to the Shochet's wife.

"Life and death are in the power of the tongue." (Mishley 18).

"There is a time to keep silent and a time to speak." (Koheles 3)

—R. Abbahu said: "He who prompts his fellowman to fulfill a mitzvah is regarded by the Scriptures as though he had performed it himself. (Sanhedrin 99)

RELYING ON OTHERS

The Dubno Maggid told the story of an important royal official whose son committed various crimes. The King was very fond of the official and because of his supplications he pardoned the son. The son immediately resumed his dissolute ways. This deeply saddened the father who realized that his son was taking advantage of his high position and relying on that to es-

Godol. Even a willful murderer could not be condemned to death unless there were two witnesses to incriminate him. The willful murderer could not have his death sentence commuted by means of monetary payment, nor could the accidental murderer escape exile in the City of Refuge through the payment of ransom money.

Leaders of the family of Gilad from the tribe of Menasheh raised the problem of land inherited by daughters, such as those of Zelophchad. If these daughters married into another tribe, their property would go with them rather than stay within the rights of their original tribe. This would lead to the reduction of that tribe's holdings. This problem was solved with the decision that, in such cases, an heiress should marry a member of her father's tribe. This is what occurred, in fact, in the case of the daughters of Zelophchad, who married their own cousins, but this law applies only for that generation.

cape punishment. The official, therefore, asked the King to accept his resignation so that his son could no longer rely on the father's protection.

This was the case with the Jewish people's reliance on their leaders. They murmured and rebelled against Hashem's leadership while expecting the merits of Moshe and Aharon to help them escape Hashem's wrath. Moshe came to the point of offering to step down as the people's leader, in the hope that the people would then see the consequences of their errors.

Now Moshe's leadership was coming to a close, and in this Parsha, Moshe reminded the people of all the different stages of travel they had gone through under his command. This was intended as a warning to the Jews that they could no longer rely upon Moshe's merits to carry them through but would have to now accumulate their own merits.

> *"The learned increase the peace and happiness in the world." (Berachos 84)*
> *"The fear of Hashem prolongs your life, but the years of the wicked shall be shortened." (Mishley 10:27)*
> *"As the generation, so is its leader." (Erechin 17)*

ENUMERATING THE STAGES—LEARNING FROM EXPERIENCE

The Torah is usually very careful about each and every phrase it uses. No detail mentioned in it is superfluous. It might, therefore, seem unusual for the Torah to take up so much space by listing all the various stages and stops in the people's wanderings. What is the purpose of this detailed account of the journey?

The Medrash compares this situation to that of a King who took his ailing son to a distant locality for a cure. On their way home, the King lovingly reviewed all the experiences they had gone through at each and every place they had stopped. "This was where we slept, and there was where we found shelter, and there was where you felt ill," he recalled. In this way, he reminded the son of all they had experienced during the successful journey.

This is, in reality, the story of the Jews' trip through the desert. During this time, Hashem guided His children, Bnei Yisroel, through difficult times. Now He was reminding them that each spot along the way held its own unique memories and lessons for them to remember now that they had reached their destination. The people had come a long way, and they should not soon forget the experiences that had helped forge their national development. If they remembered their desert wanderings, then they would remember Hashem's assistance throughout.

> *"None is as wise as the experienced in trials." (Maaseh Ephod)*

As the Jews neared the Promised Land, Moshe reviewed for them the events and experiences they had encountered during their years in the wilderness. He recalled how, at Mount Choreb (Sinai), Hashem had commanded them to break camp and march towards their destination, the land of Canaan. Moshe had claimed that unaided he was unable to bear the burden of leadership, so judges and administrators had been appointed to help him. The people had been on the verge of entering the Promised Land, but they were dismayed by the pessimistic report of the Meraglim (Spies)

פרשת דברים

Parshas Devorim

GREATNESS HAS MANY LEVELS

In his recapitulation of past events, Moshe remembered how he had protested to Hashem, "I am not able to bear the burden of this people alone!" (Devorim 1:12). As a result, Hashem advised Moshe to choose wise men from the assembly to aid him in his duties.

At first glance this episode appears somewhat confusing. Could Moshe have considered himself incapable of judging the people? The very same Moshe who had performed miracles for the people? Why had it suddenly been necessary to give him assistants? Had his own greatness diminished?

Moshe remained as strong and powerful a leader in his last days as he had been when he led the exodus from Egypt. However, Hashem felt that it would not be beneficial for Moshe to monopolize the mantle of leadership. Had Moshe remained the sole judge of Klal Yisroel individual Jews might have felt, "What is the use of trying to reach great heights? After all, who can rise to Moshe Rabbeinu's level?"

That this approach is wrong was demonstrated by the appointment of the 70 Elders. True, they could not hope to equal Moshe's level of eminence, but in their own way, they, too, attained the pinnacle of distinction. This showed all of Klal Yisroel that there are many levels of greatness and that each individual has the opportunity to reach his own degree of prominence. The one who donates to charity, or the visitor of the sick may not receive the respect reserved for a Godol HaDor. Yet on their own level, they have used their given potentials to display greatness. It is the task of every individual to discover how he can best utilize his talents to serve Hashem and the Jewish people. If he fulfills his potential to the fullest by assisting

his shul, for instance, or by teaching Jewish children, then he deserves the honors accorded a Torah leader, and he can never say that greatness is beyond him.

A well-known story is told in the name of many great Chassidic Rebbes, including Reb Zusha. He often said that after a person dies and ascends to the heavens for judgement, he will be required to defend his past actions and behavior. But a person will never be asked why he was not as great as Moshe, or as learned as Rabbi Akiva, or a Torah giant like Rabbi Akiva Eiger. Hashem gave to each individual different capabilities. Not everyone was given the intelligence to be a Rosh Yeshiva, and, therefore, not all can be expected to be a Rosh Yeshiva.

However, each man was given certain abilities. He will be required to explain why he has not used his G-d-given talents to the fullest. He will have to defend his wasting of time and effort. He will be required to show why he did not achieve the highest level of spirituality that his abilities would permit. The only person to whom the individual will be compared is to himself. Was he as great as he could have been?

That is all that Hashem requires.

A poor ignorant Jewish youth spent his days as a simple shepherd. He had not received any schooling and his talents seemed limited to one ability. He could be heard whistling clear across the countryside. This held him in good stead when he was summoning his sheep and his family praised him for it. However, he felt dissatisfied with his lot. He sensed that there was more to life than just herding sheep. Therefore, he let his curiosity roam and began investigating the world around him. One of his expeditions took him to a small hut, whose walls bore a plaque with strange-looking writings. This caught his attention

and complained against Hashem. Consequently, this loss of faith resulted in the extended wandering in the desert, during which time almost all of the older generation had died.

The Israelites had encamped at Mount Seir for a lengthy period. There they had been told to continue their travels by passing through the land of Edom. However, they were not to engage in any hostilities there, for this territory had been promised to the descendants of Esav. Nor were they to attack the residents of Moav, for this land had been reserved for the children of Lot. However, they had defeated Sichon,

and he decided to enter the building. Inside, he found a group of men standing and chanting reverently in the direction of a small ark. The devotion of the men entranced him. He watched as they prayed and wished that he, too, could join in their chanting. But he had never learned the language they were speaking, and he found it impossible to follow them. Finally, his yearnings to participate made him act. He rushed up to the front of the building, faced the ark, and let out an ear-piercing whistle.

The members of the congregation turned to the youth with angry expressions on their faces. Was he trying to mock their worship of the L-rd? But the Rabbi of the shul calmed them by saying, "The boy meant no harm. He simply wanted to join us in prayer, but he didn't know how. The only way he could express his emotions was through whistling, and this is what he did. So please accept this as his form of worship, and realize that he was using his greatest talent in the service of Hashem."

The congregation greeted the youth as one of their own and they came to admire him greatly. He was determined to serve Hashem as best he could, and he had successfully achieved his own level of greatness.

The heart of the matter is what matters. (Berachos 15)

The Holy One, blessed be He, seeks the heart. (Sanhedrin 106)

It doesn't matter how much or how little, so long as he directs his heart to Heaven. (Berachos 5)

SPEAKING THE TRUTH

"Eileh Ha'Devorim Asher Diber Moshe El Kol Bnei Yisroel . . . These were the words spoken by Moshe to the entire people of Israel . . ." (Devorim 1:1). Moshe began a lengthy address to the Jewish nation. Apparently, the lecture he presented was well-delivered, for it had a dramatic impact on the populace. This seems quite a feat for

someone who had once felt too tongue-tied to speak in Paroh's court. Moshe had called himself "Kvad Peh"—slow of speech. If so, how had he been able to address the Jewish nation so successfully throughout their stay in the desert?

The answer lies in the different situations during which Moshe spoke. Moshe could indeed feel tongue-tied, but only in the court of Paroh where intrigue and duplicity were the rule. Moshe felt ill at ease among such rampant liars and could not join in their double-talk. It was only within the holiness of Hashem's camp that Moshe felt secure in his speech. He knew that here he could speak only Emes (Truth) and this allowed him to speak to the people with ease.

The word "Emes" is composed of three letters: Alef, Mem, and Tof. Each of these has two "legs" on which to rest, as if the word can stand securely on its own. The word "Sheker" ("Falsehood"), though, is composed of three letters (Shin, Kuff, and Reish) which have only one "leg". This implies that falsehood places one in a very unstable situation, whereas truth gives him a firm footing. (Shabbos 104a).

A man of truth stands on solid ground. His word is accepted by all, and his reputation for integrity will hold him in good stead. On the other hand, the liar can never be relied upon. His friends will not remain friends for long, because they never know whether they can trust him. He is indeed leading a very shaky existence. His lies will entrap him in the end.

How important a trustworthy reputation can be is demonstrated by the story of Rav Yisroel of Ruzin and Rav Tzvi Hakohen of Riminov. When they were about to arrange the marriage of their children, the Ruziner Rav turned to the Riminover Rav and said, "Before I enter into such an agreement, it is my custom to list my Yichus (Heritage). Therefore, I want you to know that my grandfather was Rabbi Berish, my great uncle was the famous Rabbi Nachum of Tser-

the King of Cheshbon, who had refused to allow them to pass through his domain. A similar fate befell Og, King of Bashan. Fear of the Israelites began to spread among the neighboring nations.

The Land of Gilad had been given to the tribes of Reuven, Gad, and part of Menasheh, with the provision that they would join their fellow Israelites in the conquest of Canaan. Moshe encouraged Yehoshua not to fear the nations living in Eretz Yisroel.

nobel, and my uncle was the noted Rav Motel. Now, please tell me of your heritage."

Rav Tzvi replied, "I regret that my parents died when I was very young. As an orphan, I was apprenticed to a master tailor, who raised me. All I can say is that whatever work I performed for him was done honestly."

The Ruziner Rav smiled heartily. "Then that completes the arrangements," he said. "If a man is honest, that is his greatest heritage."

> Who shall dwell upon Your Holy mountain? He that . . . speaks truth in his heart.
> There are six things which Hashem hates: . . . a false witness that breathes out lies . . . (Mishley 6:16)
> Know the truth—and you'll know its bearers. (Moznei Zedek)
> Truth proves itself. (Adnei Kessef, 1)

THE RIGHT ASSOCIATION
In describing the travels of the Jews, Moshe refers to the Euphrates as "The Great River". What attribute merited it the adjective "great"? Rashi comments that because it is mentioned together with the land of Israel it merits that description.

This rule is not limited to rivers. The same process can be applied to men. If they associate with great leaders and scholars, they can be called great, too. For they are like satellites coming into contact with the sun. Some of the sun's illumination will be reflected upon them, so that they, too, can dazzle. The Medrash compares these followers to servants of a king. When the king and his entourage pass by, the king's subjects bow down not only to the king, but, automatically to his servants as well. (Rashi, Shavous 47b).

This is why the company one chooses is so important. If he selects the companionship of undersirable characters, their corrupt ways are bound to rub off on him. If, on the other hand, he seeks the company of Talmidei Chachomim and Ba'alei Midos, then he will gain for himself not only a good name, but also a model on which to base his own behavior. If he is truly successful, then he can eventually become the guiding sun, the beneficial magnet, for others. (Rambam, Perek 6 Hilchos Daios, Halachah 1 & 2).

> He that associates with the unclean becomes unclean. (Bava Kama 92)
> We say to the bee: I want neither your honey nor your sting. (Bamidbar Rabbah 20)
> Woe to the wicked and woe to his neighbor. (Succah 56)
> Environment influences action. (Avodah Zorah 8)

Continuing his criticism of the people, Moshe recalled how he had entreated Hashem for permission to cross the Jordan River. However, his request had been denied. Instead, he was told to view the Promised Land from the peak of Mount Pisgah, and Yehoshua had been appointed to assume the role of leadership in Eretz Yisroel.

Moshe appealed to the people to adhere meticulously to Hashem's statutes and edicts. In this way, they would be recognized by other peoples as a great nation. They would prevail despite their small numbers. They

פרשת
ואתחנן
Parshas Vo'escha-nan

"ALL THE DAYS OF YOUR LIFE"
"That you might fear Hashem your G-d to keep His statutes and His commandments which I commanded you; you, and

would be aided by the memory of their experience at the foot of Mount Chorev, where they had heard the Voice of Hashem proclaim the Ten Commandments. Hashem had not appeared in any form or shape, and this should remind the people of the prohibition against forming graven images of any kind. Should the Children of Israel disobey this injunction in the future, they would be exiled and scattered among the nations. However, even if this occurs, their sincere repentance will lead to Divine mercy and forgiveness.

Moshe then designated the three cities of Bezer, Ramos, and Golan, in the east of Jordan, as Orei Miklot (Cities of Refuge) for whoever kills someone else accidentally.

Moshe followed by repeating the Ten Commandments, the foundation of

your son, and your son's son, *all the days of your life . . .''* (Devorim 6:2) The final words seem slightly misplaced. Wouldn't the verse be clearer if it said, "All the days of your life, and that of your son and your son's son"? Why did the Torah return to a discussion of the person's own life after having mentioned his grandchild?

This was done deliberately to impress upon us an important concept. Never, even after your grandchildren have been born and you are nearing the end of your days, take your adherence to Judaism for granted. As our Sages said, "Do not be sure of yourself until the day of your death." (Pirkey Avos, 2:4). If you are not constantly vigilant about your religious observance, you may stray from the Torah's path. You may innocently experiment with lifestyles alien to Yiddishkeit, "just to sample the opposition," and you may then come to abandon Judaism. You may experience the fate of Yochanan Kohein Godol who remained devout for most of his very long life, and then, towards his death, joined the camp of the irreligious Saducees (Berachos 29a, Yoma 9a). To avoid this, never assume that you can withstand any tests of your faith. Never say that you are not afraid to associate with outsiders. If such activities are necessary, remain constantly on guard to make sure that outside influences do not leave their mark on you. Be careful to remain true to Hashem *all* the days of your life.

Rav Yisroel of Rizhin was traveling in his carriage when he encountered Rav Meir, who was riding in a simple cart pulled by one undernourished foal. Rav Yisroel took pity on his friend and said, "Can I assist you in any way? After all, my carriage is being pulled by four magnificent horses. That way, if my carriage gets stuck in a ditch, the four of them will have no difficulty pulling

me out. You have only one horse leading you. What will happen if you get stuck?"

Rav Meir thanked him for the offer, but declined it. "On the contrary," he said, "It is I who should be offering you aid. I am acutely aware that I have only one horse. Therefore, I am particularly careful not to come near any ditches. You, on the other hand, might feel very secure with your four horses, and may not take the necessary precautions to drive carefully."

Rav Meir's observation can help us as we travel down the path of life. We should never become so confident about our way of living that we do not watch out for any pitfalls that may appear.

The greater the person, the greater his evil impluse. (Succah 52)

Hillel said "Don't have overconfidence in yourself until the day of your death." (Avos 2:5)

LIFNIM MI'SHURAS HA'DIN

In this parsha, we are confronted by an apparent redundancy. We find several admonitions throughout the parsha commanding us to observe the laws taught by Moshe. Then, towards the end of the Parsha, we are told, "And you shall do that which is right and good in the eyes of the L-rd." (Devorim 6:18). What new instruction does this verse add? Why would the Torah, which does not contain any unnecessary material, repeat a warning that has apparently appeared earlier?

Two famed commentators, Rashi and Ramban, explain that this verse contains a new, additional command. In their view, doing "right and good" means going above and beyond the letter of the law in serving Hashem and in aiding one's fellow man. This willingness to go beyond the strict requirements of propriety is termed *"Lifnim*

Hashem's covenant with Israel. The people assembled at Mount Sinai had been terrified by the wonders they witnessed, and had pleaded with Moshe to speak to them in place of Hashem.

Moshe then expounded the Shema, affirming the unity of Hashem, Whom all should love, and Whose commandments should be transmitted to the next generation. His laws are to be remembered by the appearance of a "sign" upon one's hand and forehead, (the Tefillin) and inscribed on the doorposts of one's house (Mezuzah).

Moshe cautioned the people not to forget Hashem even after they had settled in

Mi' shuras Ha'Din''.

Lifnim Mi'shuras Ha'Din implies a great inner devotion to do what is right and good. The person who does this shows that he acts not only out of a sense of duty, or to gain rewards, but also out of a sincere desire to do Hashem's bidding for its own sake. Rabbi Yochanan maintained that the city of Yerusholayim was destroyed centuries ago because its populace at that time was not sufficiently willing to act *Lifnim Mi'shuras Ha'Din.* (Bava Metziah 30b).

One who insists on contributing only the minimum amount possible for charity, or who gives his parents and teachers only the barest respect, or who spends only a miniscule portion of the day learning Torah may be adhering to the letter of the law, but he could certainly do better. (Ran, Nedorim 8a). On the other hand, those who go out of their way to care for the poor and give of their free time to help a needy friend, are certainly of a very high caliber.

Our sages have provided stirring examples of how one can act *Lifnim Mi'shuras Ha'Din.*

The story is told of a man wno came to the Brisker Rav before Pesach. "Can I use milk instead of wine for the Arba Kosos?" he asked.

The Brisker Rav did not reply. Instead, he removed five rubles from his own pocket and gave the money to the man

The Rav's wife, puzzled but not begrudgingly, asked him, "Would not one ruble have been more than enough money for him to buy wine?"

"Perhaps," said the Rav. "But from his question, I understood that he had no money for meat either, for one cannot eat meat and use milk for the Arba Kosos at the same time. I, therefore, gave him enough money to buy both wine and meat for his Pesach meal."

In this act the Brisker Rav displayed both great perception and great righteousness towards his fellow man.

Rav Yisroel Meir Hacohen, better known as the Chofetz Chaim, was a great Sage who authored the Mishna Berurah and many great ethical works. He chose for himself the life of a poor teacher rather than that of a highly respected member of the Rabbinate. This decision led to many difficult moments for his family who struggled to survive.

Their plight was alleviated by a legacy left by one of the Chofetz Chaim's aunts. With the 150 rubles left to him in her will, the Chofetz Chaim was able to open a small grocery store which he hoped would provide a sufficient income for his family. The day-to-day management of the store was assumed by his wife, while the Chofetz Chaim himself pored over his Torah volumes in a side room. From time to time, he would emerge to assist his wife. Word soon spread that the great Torah leader occasionally made an appearance, and this guaranteed an unusually large number of customers in the store. Business was booming, but the Chofetz Chaim looked distressed.

"What is wrong?" asked his wife. "Haven't we earned more than enough to provide for our Shabbos needs?"

"That is just what concerns me," he replied. "We have more than we need, but how are the other stores in the area faring? Aren't we taking away business from them? That is hardly fair!"

And so, to ensure that his fellow storeowners would not suffer because of his fame, the Chofetz Chaim insisted that his store close early. That way, the other storeowners would recapture a portion of their lost business. The Chofetz Chaim did not have to do this under the strict guidelines of the law, but he felt that it was proper for him to do so even though it meant a loss of money to himself.

It was this same rightousness that made him feel distressed when a customer paid

the Promised Land and enjoyed prosperity. They should, therefore, avoid all forms of idol worship, for this would lead to their destruction. Future generations of Jews should be trained in Hashem's commandments, and should be told of His wonderful acts in delivering their ancestors from Egypt. Moshe warned them against intermarrying with the heathens, for this would lead to the abandonment of Hashem. Israel is a holy people for whom Hashem showed His love by redeeming them from bondage, and it is their duty to reciprocate by observing His commandments.

him for a herring and then walked out without the fish. The Chofetz Chaim could not recall who this customer was, and he could not locate him. A lesser individual might have let the matter rest there, but not the Chofetz Chaim. The next day, he decided to give, at his own expense, a free herring to every customer who entered the store. That way, he reasoned, the customer who had walked out might indeed receive his herring after all. This, truly, was acting *Lifnim Mi'shuras Ha'Din.*

> The righteous say little and do much. (Bava Metzia 87)
>
> Happy are those that observe justice, that execute righteousness at all times. (Tehillim 106:3)
>
> The righteous are greater in death than in life. (Chullin 7)

MEZUZAH AND TEFILLIN

The words of Hashem are our holiest possession. In the Shema, part of which is contained in this Parsha, we are told to bind them as a sign on the hand, between our eyes, and to write them on the doorposts of our homes. These instructions refer to the Tefillin of the Hand, the Tefillin of the Head, and the Mezuzah on our doorpost. Each of these contains a portion of Hashem's teachings to Yisroel. As a result, they serve as a link to Hashem, a constant reminder that we are guarded by His presence and that it is our task to perform His mitzvos. (Rambam, Perek 6, Hilchos Mezuzah, Halachah 13).

Onkelos ben Kalonymos was a close relative of the Roman Emperor and was not Jewish. He was attracted by the beauty of Judaism, and having sampled its teachings, decided to convert. The Emperor did not look upon this development kindly, considering it a threat to his own paganism. Consequently, he sent several groups of soldiers to Onkelos, demanding his return to Rome.

One group of soldiers was particularly determined to carry out the Emperor's

charge. They came to Onkelos' house and insisted that he accompany them. His words of praise for Judaism and his new life had no effect upon them at all. They almost dragged him out of the door.

Suddenly, though, Onkelos insisted that they stop. He went over to the doorpost of his house, raised his hand, and placed it on a small box attached there. He then removed his hand and kissed it.

The soldiers gazed at him in astonishment. Onkelos smiled. "Do you see the difference between your human ruler and my G-d?" he said. "A human emperor stays inside his house and his guards stand outside to watch over him. But my G-d stays at the door of the house and guards all the common people inside. For this little box is a Mezuzah, and G-d's holy words are inside it, protecting those Jews who live in the house."

These words had a dramatic impact upon the soldiers. They had never before heard of such a leader, such a Supreme Power, and they, too, converted. The Emperor's command went unfulfilled. (Avodah Zarah 11a). And Onkelos the convert became one of the great names in Jewish history known to this very day as the author of the Targum Onkelos (Megillah 3a).

> Rabbi Yehudah HaNossi told the king in response to a Mezuzah he gave as a gift:
>
> "The gift you sent me is so valuable that it will have to be guarded, while the gift I gave you will guard you, even when you are asleep!"
>
> He who wears Tefillin . . . is like one who has built an altar and has offered a sacrifice. (Berachos 15)
>
> The tefillin are called Pe-eir—"Glory", as it is written, per-eirkha havosh alekah—"thy glory (Tefillin bind around thy head). (Moed Katan 15)
>
> I have heard many righteous sages say that "when they tied the knot of the tefillin, on their left hand, they were teying multitudes of Jews to Hashem." (author of Siddur Lev Semeach)

Continuing his address to Klal Yisroel, Moshe assured the people that prosperity and good health would follow their observance of the Mitzvos. They had no need to fear the numerous Canaanites, for Hashem would be their protector. However, the conquest of the land of Canaan was to be followed by the destruction of all forms of idolatry.

Moshe commented that the forty years of wandering in the desert served to test the people's loyalty to Hashem's commandments. The hardships there had disciplined them to learn that "man does not live by

פרשת עקב
Parshas Eikev

LOVE OF HASHEM

When comparing the first and second sections of the Shema, we notice a major distinction between them. Whereas the first portion is addressed to the individual person "Ve'ohavtoh", meaning "And you (singular) should love" (Devorim 6:5), the second portion refers to the group "Ve'haya im Shoma Tishmeu el Mitzvosai," meaning "And it will be if you (plural) will listen to My commandments." (Devorim 11:13). Why the shift in emphasis?

Our Sages explain that the second section of Shema refers to the observance of Hashem's Mitzvos which are accomplished most effectively when performed by the group. Examples include Tefillah (Prayer) and Limud (Learning). While they can certainly be performed by an individual, they take on added importance if performed by Jews serving Hashem together en masse. On the other hand, the first part of Shema deals with the love of Hashem. This emotional attachment to G-d is to be achieved by every individual Jew on his own level, and the Torah, therefore, uses the singular in this portion.

It is for this same reason that mention of reward and punishment is made in the second section only. The performance of Mitzvos can be increased through the incentive of reward, just as sinful conduct can be deterred through the threat of punishment. Loving Hashem, though, is not an act that can be affected by incentives or deterrents. It is an emotional response that comes naturally, and is the result of one's ultimate realization of Hashem's importance in his life.

There are numerous stories of the love of Hashem displayed by great Jews throughout the ages. In some cases, the feeling of oneness with Hashem, entered the very subconscious of our pious sages. Once Rabbi Pinchas of Koritz came to Rabbi Baruch's

home and found him asleep in the bedroom. Rabbi Pinchas turned to his companion and said, "Watch Rabbi Baruch carefully and you will see something most unusual." The man did so, and Rabbi Pinchas walked to the doorpost of the room. He placed his hand over the Mezuzah which contains the holy words of Hashem. Rabbi Baruch immediately became restless and started tossing and turning in his sleep. When Rabbi Pinchas removed his hand, Rabbi Baruch lapsed into peaceful slumber once again. Rabbi Pinchas turned to his amazed companion and said, "Do you see how saintly Rabbi Baruch is? Even in his sleep he feels an attachment to Hashem and when his direct connection with Hashem is disturbed, he feels ill at ease."

The ultimate test of one's love for Hashem comes when one is forced to die for his loyalty to the Almighty. One of the many Jews who passed this test one generation ago was the Radiziner Rav.

This Tzaddik was a Jewish leader when the Nazis began their murderous rampage throughout Europe. As the butchers approached, the Radiziner Rebbe began planning an escape for fellow townfolk. Word of the plan leaked out, though, and the Rebbe was forced to flee. The Gestapo arrived in the town and demanded his return. They laid down an ultimatum: either the Radiziner came forward, or the entire town population would be killed instead.

When the town's Gabbai heard of this, he donned his white Kittel and his Tallis, and presented himself to the Germans. The Gestapo seized him and killed him instantly, believing him to be the Rebbe. He had sacrificed his own life to save his leader.

However, the Germans were soon informed of the trick. Their anger grew, and they delivered their final set of conditions: either the Rebbe emerged from hiding within two hours, or the people of the town would

bread alone, but by everything that proceeds from the mouth of the L-rd." Moshe described the bountiful Eretz Yisroel including the seven Minim (seven varieties of fruit). Moshe warned that the prosperity the Jews would enjoy in the Promised Land might lead them to disregard Hashem's role in their welfare. Such ingratitude would be severely punished, and the disloyal Jews would share the fate of the heathen nations who perished.

Moshe reminded the people of their earlier acts of rebellion. After he had spent forty days on the mountaintop receiving the Luchos (Tablets of Stone), he had returned to find the people worshipping the Eigel HaZohov (Golden Calf). Hashem had declared His intention to destroy the people, but Moshe interceded on their behalf. He had broken the Luchos, destroyed the Eigel HaZohov, and punished those who had honored it. He also recalled four other instances of the people's disobedience, at Taberah, Massah, Kibros HaTa'avah and Kadesh Barnea.

After Moshe had championed the Bnei Yisroel's cause by asking Hashem to recall the merits of the Patriarchs, Hashem had told him to return to the mountain

be taken out one by one and shot.

The moment the Rebbe heard of this, he knew what he had to do. He left his refuge and declared, "I am the Radiziner. I am more than prepared to die in place of my fellow Jews, and to die in the service of Hashem." The remorseless Nazis dragged him in front of the town and murdered him on the spot. Before the final shots rang out, though, the Rebbe managed to cry out to his fellow townfolk, "Do not surrender to these murderers! Resist! Remain loyal to Hashem! Shema Yisroel, Hashem Elokeinu Hashem Echad! (Hear O Israel! Hashem is our L-rd, Hashem is One!)"

A similar story is told about Rebbe Akiva (Berachos 61b). Even at his dying moment, this sage expressed his kinship with the Almighty. This is the closeness to Hashem that we should strive to attain.

> *Rabbi Akiva who in sacrifice of his life in the service of Hashem explained*
> *"With all your soul"—even if He takes your soul.*
> *He who worships out of love, all his worship is love.*

FEAR OF HASHEM

Our love for Hashem should be mingled with a sense of awe and fear towards the Creator. The Torah comments, "And now, Israel, what does Hashem request of you? Only to fear Him." (Devorim 10:12). A feeling of respect is only natural towards the Divine Regulator of the Universe. If one possesses fear of Hashem, then it will supersede all fear of his enemies and he will perform His Mitzvos despite all opposition and enmity.

A pious person was traveling on a long, dusty road, when dusk fell. The man paused on his journey to pray. As he was in the midst of reciting the Shemoneh Esrai, an officer of the king approached him and asked for directions. The man did not respond immediately, only after he had finished his prayers.

The officer was livid with anger. "You fool! Why didn't you return my greeting? Don't you know that this might have cost you your life?"

The man replied, "Please allow me to explain my actions. If you were standing before a king, and your friend came by and greeted you, would you have returned his greeting?"

"No," said the officer.

"And if you had responded to his greeting, what would have happened to you?"

"I would have lost my life."

"Therefore, you can now appreciate why I did not answer you. If you would be afraid to speak to others while standing before a mere mortal king, then how could you expect me to respond when I was standing before the King of the Universe?"

The officer was most pleased with this reply. "I see now why you Jews are so loyal to your religion," he commented. "Your fear of your G-d is greater that your fear of the most powerful of men." (Berachos 32b).

> *The beginning of wisdom is the fear of Hashem (Mishley 9:10)*
> *The fear of Hashem prolongs days but the years of the wicked shall be shortened. (Mishley 10:27)*
> *A good deed and fear extinguish the fire*

to receive a second set of Luchos. These were placed in the Holy Ark, the Aron HaKodesh. The Kohanim and Levi'im had been appointed to perform the services of the Mishkon, and permission had been given for the people to continue the journey from Sinai towards Canaan.

All that Hashem requests from the Jews, Moshe said, is for them to love, fear, and serve Him by keeping the Mitzvos. Their personal knowledge of His greatness, manifested by such incidents as the deliverance from Egypt, the miracle of the Red Sea, the experiences in the desert, and the miraculous punishment given to Korach, Dasan and Aviram, should be sufficient to assure their observance and fulfillment of the Mitzvohs. The commitment to Hashem's laws would ensure a successful harvest through the regularity of the autumn and spring rains; but these would be withheld if the people became disobedient. Moshe assured the people that their adherence to the Torah would result in their victory over the Canaanites and the acquisition of extensive territory in the Promised Land.

of lust.
The fear of Hashem is strength and glory.

THE JEWISH HOMELAND

"For the land that you are going to possess is not like the land of Egypt from where you came."

Eretz Yisroel is a land that has been claimed and coveted by many nations and religions. It is the focal point of world history. Why, indeed, has Hashem granted this holy land to the Jews and placed the other nations elsewhere? A parable offers an explanation.

There once lived a man who was blessed with a son of fine character and exceptional piety. The young man married, and in time he, too, became a father. As he was preparing for his new-born son's Bris Milah party, he came to his father for advice.

"Could you counsel me," he asked, "on how I should seat the guests? If I am forced to seat the rich guests in places of honor and leave the poor in positions at the end of the banquet table, I will feel upset because I don't want to embarrass the poor. Wouldn't it be better if I make the rich sit at the far end of the table, and enable the poor to sit at the head for once?"

"Your intentions are most noble, my son," replied the father. "However, if you carry out your plan, none of your guests will be very happy. You see, the custom of placing the rich at the head and the poor at the end of the table is based on common sense. After all, the poor are hungry, and they care more for the food at the end of the table than for the honor at the head. The rich, on the other hand, have their own sumptuous food at home. When they come to a banquet, they are not seeking nourishment, but honor. This is why it is best to seat them at the head of the table, where they can receive the recognition they crave. So, my son, let the poor sit at the foot of the table, where they can eat undisturbed and out of the limelight. Let the rich sit at the head of the table, where they can receive honor."

This same differentiation can be made between Israel and the other nations. The heathens of the world, like the poor at the banquet, seek only to satisfy their bodily needs. They could accomplish this in any part of the world, not in the holy land of Eretz Yisroel. The nation of Israel, though, does not place its emphasis upon materialistic satisfaction. The Jews have always sought the higher, spiritual aspects of life. They are to be recognized and honored by the other nations of the world. Therefore, they have been placed in Eretz Yisroel, where the eyes of the world are fixed upon them. (Tehillim 104). In this way, their good deeds can be observed by all. At the same time, however they must be especially careful not to desecrate Hashem's laws. If they unfortunately do so, they will be degrading the Torah in full view of all other nations, thereby causing the unspeakable tragedy of "Chillul Hashem."

"If I forget you, O Jerusalem, let my right hand forget her cunning."
(Tehillim 137:5)
The exile is harder than anything else. (Sifrey, Ekev)
R. Yochnan said: Great is the day of ingathering of the exiles as the day of the Creations of Heaven and Earth. (Pesachim, 88)

Moshe informed the Children of Israel that they may choose between receiving Hashem's blessings for observing His commandments or suffering His curse for rejecting His laws. A ceremony would be held on the mountains of Gerizim and Eival, immediately after entering Eretz Yisroel, during which the consequences of the blessing and the curse would be pronounced.

Moshe then turned to the exposition of a number of religious, civil, and social laws which were to regulate the life of the nation in the Promised Land. He dealt first with the principle of centralized worship, which

פרשת
ראה

Parshas
R'ei

THE BLESSING OR THE CURSE

"Behold, I set before you this day a blessing and a curse; the blessing, if you heed the commandments of the L-rd, and the curse, if you will not observe His commandments."

Bnei Yisorel are offered a clear-cut choice, either the blessing or the curse. There are no compromise alternatives; it is either one or the other. One cannot opt for a half-filled cup of religion. Either one commits himself fully, or his commitment is lacking. Based on his decision, one receives either the blessing or the curse.

The blessing need not be in the form of gold dropping from heaven, nor need the curse be manifested through a supernatural calamity. The happiness that is derived from a good deed, or the satisfaction that comes from being unblemished by sin, are blessings in themselves. Likewise, the feeling of guilt, the pangs of loneliness, the sense of being hated are all the effects of a curse. They are all the result of Divine remuneration, based on a person's deeds. And they are well-deserved, in one sense or the other.

The mechanisms of reward and punishment, of blessings and curses, are often difficult to comprehend. On the surface, it may seem as if many people who do the will of Hashem live their lives in poverty and discomfort, while the reverse seems true of many evildoers. The naked eye, however, generally fails to perceive the truth that lies beyond the surface. This point is illustrated by a parable related by the Chofetz Chaim.

There was once a well known man who served as the king's personal adviser on important matters of the kingdom. To the great shock and dismay of the king, this adviser was discovered to be a traitor to the kingdom. Determined to punish this man's treachery in a way that would serve as a lesson to all, the king erected a large glass structure in the center of the capital city to serve as a prison. The traitor would be locked in this structure and would receive no food or drink. Notices were posted throughout the kingdom proclaiming the sentence imposed upon the traitor and inviting all to observe the man's punishment through the glass walls.

A large crowd formed on the day the traitor was placed in his jail. He had eaten a hearty meal prior to being imprisoned, and all observers were surprised to see him in good spirits. As the days wore on, however, the lack of nourishment took its toll on the prisoner. By the end of the sixth day, he could not move at all. The observers realized that the man could not survive another day without food and drink. On the seventh day, the crowd watched in horror as the prisoner, in desperation, bit into his arm until he was able to tear off a mouthful of his own flesh. The prisoner chewed on this meat with great enthusiasm.

Just then, a countryman arrived at the glass prison. He had not seen the proclamation until the seventh day and was curious to observe the king's former adviser in his miserable condition. To his great bewilderment, he saw the prisoner chewing on some meat, and he wondered aloud, "Is this the man who was sentenced to starve to death as a traitor to the king?"

"That's the one," replied a number of people in the crowd.

"But how could that be? He is eating a piece of meat! Is this the way the king punishes traitors?"

The moral of the story is that reward and punishment are not always apparent to the casual observer. We on this world are often able to perceive only that which is readily visible, but the truth will be revealed to all in the World to Come, when the entire pan-

was directed against the idolatrous practice of individual worship at any site. All sacrifices were to be brought only to the place chosen by Hashem. Those portions of offerings permitted to the lay worshipper were to be eaten there. However, an animal intended for ordinary consumption rather than for a sacrifice could be slaughtered and eaten anywhere, provided its blood was not consumed.

The Bnei Yisroel were warned not to imitate the hideous rites of the Canaanites, such as sacrificing living children to their gods. The false prophet who attempted to entice them to worship idols was to be put to death. All the inhabitants of a city who, after having been investigated, were convicted of idol worship, were also to be put to death, and the city (called an Ir Hanidachas) was to be totally destroyed by fire. Self infliction of wounds on the body or head as a sign of mourning is prohibited.

As a holy people, Israelites are to refrain from eating anything abominable.

orama of blessings and curses will be made clear to everyone.

> Say of the righteous that it shall be well with him; for they shall eat the fruit of their deeds. Woe to the wicked! It shall go ill with him; for the work of his hands shall be done to him. (Isaiah 3:10) Know that for all these things Hashem will bring you to judgement. (Koheles 11:9)

INTENTIONS

The Torah states that the curse will befall those who "do not listen to the commandments of Hashem your G-d, but turn aside from the way which I have commanded you, to go after other gods . . ."

Once again, the Torah appears to contain a redundancy. If one does not listen to Hashem's Mitzvos, does he not automatically turn aside from Hashem's chosen way? Why was the Torah so explicit about the unfortunate actions of the miscreants?

Again, the extra wording provides a moral lesson. For one to be considered a wrongdoer, he must have actually taken action in a negative sense. He must have made the most to "turn aside from" Hashem's way and to actively "go after" forbidden fruits. Merely having sinister intentions is not considered a serious crime, as long as the intentions are not acted upon. There is a wide gulf between the intention and its execution. If the individual shows enough self-control to refrain from carrying out his sinful designs, he avoids punishment.

On the other hand, if one intends to perform a Mitzvah, he receives credit for this even if he is not able to fulfill his desires. Thus, if someone sincerely plans to give Tzedokoh but is unable to do so because of

an unexpected loss of money, he is credited with the good deed nevertheless.

> R. Assi said: Even if one merely thinks of performing a precept but is forcibly prevented, Holy Writ ascribes it to him, regarding it as though he has actually performed it. But on the other hand there is no punishment for a mere intention to do wrong, so long as it has not been implemented.

GENEROSITY AT ALL TIMES

Charity is an important Jewish trait to be encouraged at all times.

A person might claim, though, "here is the Shemitta year, I will not be allowed to work my fields or harvest the produce for an entire year. How, then, can anyone expect me to contribute any of my precious money to charity during this time?"

To the Torah this is not at all acceptable. Charity is one of the mainstays of the Jewish religion. As the Talmud states, "Israel is known by three characteristics: mercy, chastity, and charity." If the Jew tries to garner wealth at the expense of the needy," says the Torah, "it will be considered a sin."

It is especially incumbent upon the Jew to give charity during a difficult financial period such as during the Shemitta year. Hard times should not induce him to turn entirely inward and become oblivious to the concerns of his fellow man. This is dramatized by the following parable:

A great ship was sailing proudly on the high seas. She carried many important merchants, bringing huge quantities of merchandise to markets abroad. One day, a violent storm arose, and it became evident that the ship was in danger of sinking. The captain assembled his passengers and told

Moshe, therefore, reviewed the dietary laws already revealed at Sinai. He said that a second Ma'aser (Mas'aser Sheini), consisting of a tenth of one's annual produce of the soil including grain, wine, and oil, was to be brought by every Jewish man to the Sanctuary and consumed by him there. Any Israelite who lived too far away from the Sanctuary to bring the Ma'aser Sheini there, could bring its monetary value instead, purchase food there with the money, and enjoy a festive meal with his family and the Levi'im. At the end of every 3rd and 6th year of the Shemitta cycle, this tenth was to be given to the poor (Ma'aser Oni) at home rather than brought to the Sanctuary.

At the end of every seventh (Shemitta) year, during which the land is to remain fallow, a creditor is to release his fellow Jews from any loans which may be due. Yet, this should not discourage anyone from lending money to the needy, for such acts of kindness will be repaid by Hashem.

them to throw overboard whatever heavy merchandise they carried with them, lest they all be drowned. However, he permitted them to keep with them whatever they found absolutely essential.

This created a great uproar on the ship. Every man raced to his cabin, and proceeded to save his most valuable possessions, packets of jewels, bags of gold, cases of coins. Then they reluctantly threw overboard the rest of their possessions.

One of those aboard observed what was happening, and shook his head sadly. He went to his cabin and saved only two small items, his Tallis and his Teffilin. Everything else, including his money and jewels, he agreed to have thrown overboard.

"But why are you doing this?" asked someone who noticed this. "Why don't you save your money instead?"

"How could I?!" reported the man. "Even if I throw away my money, I could always earn more later. But how can I throw out the holy symbols of my religion? Those are my life. If I abandon those, I might just as well have absolutely nothing; all the money in the world won't help me."

When people experience hard times, they often decide to throw overboard not their luxuries, but, rather, their religious scruples, their tendency to be charitable and merciful. But if they do this, then they are abandoning their very lifeline, the very basis of their humanity. This is why the Torah advises us to retain our generosity even during difficult times. This is the period when charity is all the more needed, and one who remains generous even at times of personal duress will be all the more rewarded.

The consequences of being uncharitable are often unforeseeable. A story was once told of a man who enjoyed all the good graces of life, a successful business, a devoted wife, and a spacious, comfortable home. He was very content to continue this life of pleasure indefinitely.

One day, as he was sitting down to a sumptuous meal, he heard a knock at the door. He opened it and found a wretched-looking beggar facing him. "Sir, I have not eaten for two days," the beggar pleaded. "Would you have a few morsels of food that you could spare?" He looked at the man hopefully.

The man responded only with scorn. "Why don't you go out and earn a living instead of depending upon others to support you?!" he said, and angrily shut the door in the beggar's face.

It was not long afterwards that the man noticed his business beginning to decline. Sales were not what they had once been and the man was forced to cut back on his lifestyle. First he shed his frills—his art collection and his extra wardrobes. But the business' downward turn continued unabated. Was it simply luck, or a matter of fate? Whatever the case, the man eventually found himself pawning what he had once taken for granted. Out went his furniture, his clothing, and, finally, the house itself. His wife volunteered to find work to pay for food, but the man refused. He felt so ashamed at not being able to support her, that he gave her a divorce, and she sadly agreed to it.

After several months, the wife found a new suitor. He was a newly wealthy man, and they married and set up house. One day, as they were preparing for dinner, they heard the doorbell ring. Once again, a beggar appeared at the door and asked meekly for

In addition, a Hebrew slave who had been sold into bondage was to be freed at the beginning of the seventh year, and liberally assisted with material means to enable him to make a fresh start on life. If the slave should choose to remain in his master's service, his ear was to be pierced, as a sign that he selected slavery rather than freedom, contrary to G-d's wishes.

In amplifying the laws of the Feasts of Pesach, Shevuous, and Succos, Moshe emphasized that every male Israelite was to make a pilgrimage three times a year to the Sanctuary, bringing with him sacrifices, each person according to his means.

food. But this new husband was of a more charitable bent than the previous one. He invited the emaciated beggar inside and provided him with enough food and money to satisfy him for weeks. The beggar kept his eyes downcast, but he accepted the charity gratefully.

After the beggar had departed, the husband noticed that his wife had a strange expression on her face. He asked her if anything was wrong.

"I knew that beggar," she said in a tone of wonder. "He was my first husband. He looked so thin and pale that I hardly recognized him. How sad to see a man sink so low."

The husband thought for a moment and said, "If that was your first husband, then I

just realized something. Do you remember that a beggar once came to your previous home asking for bread and was turned away? Well, that beggar was me. Somehow, good fortune seemed to come my way after that, and I became quite wealthy. "Do you suppose there was any reason why our fortunes became reversed?" The wife nodded solemnly. "I most certainly think there was. For we are told, *'He who closes his ears to the cry of the poor will himself cry out and not be heard.'* " (Mishley 21.13)

The world is like the wheel at the well; the full bucket is enptied and the empty one filled. (Vayikra Rabbah 34)
Love the poor, so that your children should not be reduced to poverty. (Derech Eretz Zutta 2:4)

Moshe proceeded to review the regulations needed to insure the conditions necessary for a civilized society. Local judges and officers were to be appointed in every city, and justice was to be administered righteously and impartially. A judge was, therefore, strictly forbidden to display bias or accept a bribe. If a local judge were to find a case too difficult to decide, he should refer it to a higher authority, namely, the Kohanim and the Supreme Court sitting at the Court of the Sanctuary. Their decision would be final, and refusal to abide by their verdict may be punishable by death.

פרשת
שופטים
*Parshas
Shoftim*

"JUSTICE, JUSTICE YOU SHALL PURSUE"

In guiding the Jews towards achieving justice, the Torah is quite explicit in its instructions for judges. It commands the deciders of law to be completely impartial, to remain unswayed by the identities of those involved in the case, and to steer clear of all bribes. In this way, justice will emerge unblemished, and those innocent and guilty will be clearly identified.

The true Jewish judges have taken great pains to comply with these requirements.

One Sage who served as head of the Beis Din (Rabbinical Court) used to cover his face with a Tallis whenever two individuals came for a decision. He did this to ensure that he would not be influenced by the identities of the plaintiff and defendant. If he could not see them, he would not be tempted to weigh his decision in either one's favor. The sage knew that justice can easily be perverted, so he went out of his way to pursue it.

Rabbi Joseph Schor, who was appointed by the Austrian government as the Chief Justice of the civil court of Tarnopol, was

The crime of idolatry, determined after a thorough inquiry, was to be punished by death by stoning. The accused was not to be condemned through the testimony of a single witness alone. Instead, the testimony of at least two witnesses was required, and these witnesses were to be the first to carry out the execution.

Moshe noted that the time would come when the people might desire a king to rule over them, as was the case with other nations. When this occurred, the appointed ruler was to be a native Israelite chosen by Hashem. He was not to misuse his power to amass many horses, or maintain a harem, or accumulate greath wealth. He was to write a copy of the Torah Law, so that he would be G-d-fearing and Torah-observant.

After enumerating the gifts that the Kohanim were to receive for their

also extremely careful about rendering decisions. He was asked to preside over a case where five men claimed that a certain Jew had set fire to a house. The five men testified under oath that they had observed the Jew go into the house and ignite the flames. Had they not discovered the conflagration in time, they said, it would have destroyed the entire city.

Throughout the testimony of the five men, Rabbi Schor sat quitely, not even joining the other five judges in their discussions of the case. Finally, the trial evidence had been entirely presented, and the judges retired to consider the verdict. Each of the other judges immediately offered his opinion: "Guilty". But when it came Rabbi Schor's turn to speak, he said, "It is my position that the accused is completely innocent of the crime, and I accuse each of the five witnesses of having given false testimony."

The other judges were amazed. How could Rabbi Schor, the chief Justice, make such an unfounded statement? On what did he base his opinion?

"I will explain it to you," replied Rabbi Schor. "Here are five strong, healthy young men, all of whom claim to have been present when a thin aged Jew started a fire. Yet, they admit that they simply watched the Jew set the fire and did nothing to prevent him or to put out the flames. Does this make sense? Not to me. Rather, I feel that their story is merely a figment of their anti-Semitic imagination. Do not be so hasty to condemn the defendant in this case. I would suggest that you investigate the matter further, and perhaps you will change your mind."

The other judges did just that, and indeed found that the Jew had been nowhere near the site of the fire, and that the accusers had fabricated the story to serve as a cover up of their own part in the fire. The five were

sentenced to stiff jail terms, and the Jew was set free. He owed his liberty to Rabbi Schor's stubborn insistence that justice be pursued to the fullest.

This same meticulousness was displayed by Rabbi Shmuel Salant when he was head of a Rabbinical Court. One morning, several men entered the court, assisting an obviously injured man. The victim had scars all over his face and body, and he limped noticeably. His companions said that he had been beaten by a certain individual, whom they named. They demanded that the other party be brought to justice.

"I will certainly bring the assailant to justice," replied Rav Salant. "But first, I would like to ask my assistant to visit the other party and see if he is in good condition."

"Why is that necessary?" the men demanded. "He should immediately be brought to trial for assault!"

But Rav Salant was not to be rushed. "Until I see the other man, how do I really know which of the two is really the victim? Perhaps the other party isn't here now because he has been too seriously injured to walk?"

Some investigation revealed that the other man had indeed been the real victim of the fight, and that it was he who deserved to receive payment. Once again, careful consideration and examination proved superior to undue haste and enabled justice to triumph.

A warning to the courts—not to be lenient with one and harsh with another. (Kesubos 46)

The Judge who accepts a bribe will not leave this world with a sane mind. (Kesubos 105)

The Judge must consider a matter just as his eyes see it. (Niddah 20)

sustenance, Moshe ruled that if a Kohein from another city would come to the Sanctuary, he would be allowed to minister together with the Kohanim already there and to share in the dues they received.

The Torah forbids all forms of superstition and "magic" practiced by the soothsayer. Israel had no need to resort to such tricks, for Hashem would provide inspired prophets from among the Israelites themselves. These would communicate Hashem's will to them. False prophets who spoke in the name of idols were to be punished with death. The false seer could be distinguished from the true one by the non-fulfillment of his predictions.

The removal of a landmark to enlarge one's own estate constitutes theft. Before

THE LEVI'IM'S SHARE

One who considers the Torah's instructions regarding the Levi'im might be puzzled. The Levi'im were, after all, the jewel in the crown of Yisroel. They were the group whose loyalty prompted Hashem to appoint them as guardians of His Sanctuary. They were considered princes of the people, models of holiness. And yet, for all their high position, they were not granted their own territory in the Promised Land. Instead, they had to be sustained through the donations and offerings of the rest of the populace. Why was this so?

The matter can be clarified through the following parable. A wealthy merchant set out on a lengthy journey and he asked his sons to accompany him. To avoid unnecessary expenses along the way, he told his servants to remain at his home, and he expected his sons to compensate for their absence by performing all the necessary chores. However, soon after the trip began, it became evident that most of the sons were not able to prepare food properly. Only one of the sons had received training in the art of cooking, and the others looked to him to feed them. However, this son tended to be both lazy and selfish. He rarely considered the needs of his father and brothers, and he devoted most of his attention to satisfying his own wants. The father was afraid that this son would prepare enough food for only himself. To forestall this, the father made sure to acquire only the largest cooking utensils, a very big pot and very large pans and ladles. In this way, the son would be forced to prepare very large portions, so that if he cooked for his own benefit, he would be cooking for the others at the same time. If the son filled up the pot with food sufficient for only himself, it would quickly burn. Therefore, he had no choice but to cook enough food for everyone, and did not have

a chance to indulge in selfishness.

A similar situation was prepared for the Levi'im. Hashem knew that they were worthy of special duties and tasks. Yet, he was concerned that if they were allowed to cultivate their own land and to raise their own crops, they would let human nature take over and would become increasingly self-centered. If they prayed for assistance, they might have their own needs in mind, and might forget to intercede on behalf of the rest of Klal Yisroel as well. They might also devote most of their efforts towards improving their own lot, and perform their services for Hashem only half-heartedly. To make sure that they continued to pray for the welfare of the entire Jewish nation, Hashem made their sustenance dependent on the well-being of the rest of the Jews instead of allowing them to own their own lands. Even princes must be aware of the fact that they cannot separate their fate from that of the rest of the people.

He that prays for his friend, while being himself in the same need, will be answered first. (Bava Kama 92) Turnusrufus asked Rabbi Akiva: "If your G-d loves the poor, why does He not feed them? Answered Rabbi Akiva: "That we may, through our supporting them, save ourselves from Gehennum. (Bava Basra 10)

A "COMPLETE" NATION

"Tomim Ti'hiyeh im Hashem Elockecha:" "You shall be Tomim (Complete) with Hashem your G-d." This same word Tomim is used to describe Hashem's Torah: "Toras Hashem Temimah—The Torah of Hashem is complete." Thus, we find that both the nation of Israel and the Holy Torah have been, and must remain a complete, unified whole.

This description is, of course, appropriate with regard to the Torah. The Torah is the

anyone could be convicted of a crime, his criminality had to be confirmed by at least two witnesses. If a witness was shown to have given false evidence, he was to receive the punishment intended for his innocent victim.

The Israelites should not display any fear before engaging in battle against a powerful enemy, for Hashem would protect them. Three categories of men were to be exempt from military service: the man who had just built a new house but who had not yet dedicated it; one who had planted a vineyard and had not yet enjoyed its fruits; and one who had just become betrothed.

Before Israel attacked a hostile city, she should try to negotiate a peaceful entry, in which case the city's inhabitants would become subservient to Israel. Only if these peace overtures failed could war be waged. If Israel were victorious, all men of the enemy were to be put to death, but their women and children were to be spared.

complete blueprint of life as transmitted to man by Hashem. Its laws contain the definitive plan for the Jew's lifestyle, and they cannot be altered or "modernized".

In addition, the Sefer Torah, the Scroll on which the Torah is written, must be perfect. That is, it must not contain any mistakes. If it does, it is called a Sefer Torah Posul, a scroll that is still a Torah, but which cannot be used for Torah readings. It makes no difference which letter is missing or incorrect. Any significant error is sufficient to render a Sefer Torah unusable.

But how does the term Tomim apply to the Jewish nation? Of course, each individual Jew must strive to be perfect in his own way. His actions and personality should not be blemished by any errors, any missing Midos Tovos or incorrectly performed acts. However, the same is true of the entire Jewish nation. The nation itself is meant to be complete, with all its members faithful to the way of Hashem. If there are Jews who abandon this way, then Klal Yisroel is considered an incomplete entity. It is then the duty of each Jew to try to persuade his straying brother to return to the fold. As in the case of the Torah's missing letter, it does not matter if the alienated Jew is rich or poor, seemingly important or apparently insignificant. The fact is, when a Jew abandons Yiddishkeit the nation as a whole loses. It is for this reason that Jews must never consider one of their number to be permanently "lost", and must do all they can to embrace all Jews within the family of Judaism. We must never consider any fellow Jew inferior. If Jews do not care for one another's welfare, who else will?

This concern for one's fellow Jew is a basic element of Judaism. We have been blessed by a host of miraculous sights, Jews

being salvaged from seemingly hopeless situations, third generation American Jews being welcomed back into the fold, and even Jews from atheistic countries rediscovering their ancestral traditions. We are confident that these miracles will continue to occur if we continue to display Ahavas Yisroel to all our brethren.

Israel is like a dispersed sheep. Just as all sheep suffer when a limb of one of them is smitten, so it is with Israel, one sins and everyone is punished.
(Vayikrah Rabbah)
All Jews are Princes (that is, all Jews have an equally noble ancestry—the poor like the rich). (Shabbos 67)
Jews are responsible for one another. (Shavuos 39)
When one Jew is being beaten all Jews feel it. (Midrash on Shir Hashirim 6)

A Rebbe once spoke to a group of yeshiva high school students about the merits of continuing their Torah education in an institution of higher learning after their graduation. He then asked each one individually what their future plans were. Each in his own way explained why he could not devote the coming year to intensive Torah learning, one had to learn a trade, others had made plans for college. Finally, somewhat discouraged, the Rebbe was left with a student who had shown little proficiency in learning throughout the years. "Surely he wouldn't be interested in continuing in yeshiva," the Rebbe said to himself. Nevertheless, with a "Why not?" attitude, the Rebbe proceeded to ask this student, too.

To his amazement, the student expressed a desire to continue his study of Torah in a post high school yeshiva.

"But why didn't you ever say you were in-

Fruit trees were not to be destroyed during a siege, where there were other things available, so that they could continue to benefit the new inhabitants of the conquered city.

If the body of a murdered person were found in the field, and the murderer could not be discovered, responsibility for the murder rested with the city nearest the scene of the murder. In atonement, the judges and Elders of the city, acting on behalf of the other inhabitants, were to slaughter a young heifer in an uncultivated valley containing a stream. They then were to wash their hands in the presence of Kohanim, testify that they were in no way responsible for the murder, and pray for forgiveness.

terested before this?'' asked the Rebbe.

"Because no one ever asked me before," was the reply.

The student was true to his word. He went to the post high school yeshiva, gained a true love of learning, and eventually became a Rebbe himself. Had he been given up for lost, the nation of Israel would have emerged poorer.

Every person in Klal Yisroel has "Chashivus" (special worth) and great potential. No matter how low a person may seem, one should make the effort to help a person develop his traits in a positive manner.

Rabbi Shimon ben Lakish, also known as Resh Lakish, started out his adult life in the company of robbers and ended up as one of the greatest of the Amoraim, thanks to Rabbi Yochanan who first befriended him. Rabbi Yochanan saw a man of great strength, but he had the depth of perception to see beyond the physical. He saw strength that could be utilized for Torah learning and to achieve greatness. As an added inducement, he offered his beautiful sister as a wife to

Resh Lakish if in turn he would devote his life to Torah. Rabbi Yochanan's trust was not in vain. Resh Lakish attained prominence, in fact so much so that some say he was even greater than his teacher and mentor, Rabbi Yochanan.

Rabbi Yisroel Yaakov Lubchanski once tried to influence a certain student for many months. Although he spent much time with the boy, his efforts were to no avail. The boy simply would not yield. Rav Yisroel Yaakov admitted that it came to the point where he sensed an indifference within himself toward the lad.

One day, it dawned on him. "G-d did not bless me with any children. Suppose the boy were mine. I would not ignore him. Then why do I reject him now? Because he belongs to someone else?"

Rabbi Lubchanski became overwhelmed with a feeling of love for the boy. His previous indifference turned to a deep concern. He began to work with him anew, and eventually the boy grew up to be an outstanding leader.

If an Israelite were to capture a female prisoner of war in a battle outside Canaan, he could not take her into marriage immediately. Instead, she must first shave her head, cut her nails, remove her garments of captivity, and mourn her parents for a full month, so that she would become unattractive to the Israelite. If he would then still wish to marry her, he could; but if not, he could not treat her as a slave.

A first-born son is to inherit a double portion, even if his mother is not beloved by his father. A rebellious son (i.e., one who has stolen and eaten and drunk a certain

פרשת
כי תצא
Parshas
Ki Seitsei

THE RIGHT MARRIAGE PARTNER

The Torah tells us that if an Israelite captured a woman in the process of war, he could not marry her immediately. Rather, she had to first make herself unattractive, thereby providing an opportunity for the man's passionate lust to dissipate.

In this way the Torah warns us not to act in the heat of passion. One should not become a captive of his desires and lose all self-control in the process. Instead, he should try to wait until his strong yearnings for physical pleasure have died down. Only then can be act with caution and common sense.

This is particularly true of the process of choosing an appropriate marriage partner. If one marries solely on the basis of physical attraction, the marriage rests on a very shaky foundation. If the partners' outward attractiveness fades, so, too, does the marriage. The resulting offspring will grow up as witnesses to a stormy union, and may themselves emerge scarred. It is for this reason that the Torah juxtaposes the passages of marrying a captive woman and raising a rebellious son (Ben Sorer U'Moreh). The act of marrying simply for beauty rather than true love can result in the development of a disrespectful son. On the other hand, one who is careful in choosing a marriage partner of fine character can be blessed with righteous children. Thus, we find Aharon the Kohein Godol marrying Elisheva, the daughter of the Tzaddik Aminodov (whose son Nachshon was also a great leader and was the first to cross the Yam Suf). Among their descendants were Eliezer, the next Kohein Godol, and Pinchas, whose great merits were discussed earlier. Pinchas' sterling character was no doubt molded by parents and grandparents, whose own personal qualities set a fine example for the growing boy.

A good wife is a handsome gift from Hashem. (Ben Sira)

A woman is beautiful when she is virtuous. (Shabbos 25)

It is only because of his wife that a man's house is blessed. (Bava Metzia 59)

RETURNING LOST PROPERTY

This Parsha discusses the importance of Hashovas Aveidah, returning a lost object to its rightful owner. The laws regarding lost property are discussed very extensively in the Talmud. One who finds an article must go to great lengths in locating the owner. Only if he is absolutely certain that the owner cannot be located may the finder keep it himself. This is another reminder to man not to appropriate property that is not his. It would be very easy for the finder to simply keep the object without telling anyone about it. Yet, the Torah tells him to go out of his way to return it. Possessions in this world are only temporary, and one cannot afford to have his earthly record besmirched with sin just for the sake of such possessions.

Rabbi Zundel of Salant was in the middle of davening on Yom Kippur when he noticed through a window that someone's goat had wandered into the garden of a non-Jew. In order to save the owner of the goat from loss (the owner of the garden was likely to kill it), Rabbi Zundel ran out of the Shul, cloaked in his talis, and chased the goat out of the garden.

A guest once forgot his umbrella in Rabbi Ziv's Yeshiva in Kelm. Thirteen years later, he returned to the yeshiva and found his umbrella in the exact spot where he had left it.

Rabbi Naftoli Riff, an associate of Rabbi Eliyahu Henkin of Ezras Torah, recalled that

amount of meat and wine, and who had been warned not to do so) is to be stoned. The body of a man who has been hanged should not remain on the hanging tree overnight, but he should be buried that same day.

One should return all lost articles to their rightful owners. To promote safety, one should build a railing around his roof. One should not wear Sha'atnes (wool and linen together). One should wear Tzitzis on his garments.

A husband who falsely accuses his bride of having been unfaithful to him before their marriage but after betrothel, is to receive lashes and a fine. If the charges prove to be true, the wife is to be stoned. If a woman commits adultery, both she and the man involved are to be killed. One should not marry his father's wife, or a member of Ammon or Moav.

One should not charge interest of a fellow Jew. Whoever utters a vow must fulfill it.

When a husband has grounds for divorce, the marriage is to be dissolved in a for-

Rav Henkin frequently referred to a small notebook. The notebook contained a record of those minutes during the day that he did not utilize for Ezras Torah. He was not involved with personal business during those minutes. But when someone came to his office at Ezras Torah to discuss Torah thoughts, or if he received a telephone call, as he frequently did, asking his opinion on a particular halachic problem, he immediately looked at the time and noted in his record how many minutes he had borrowed from Ezras Torah. He would then know how many minutes to 'make up' on behalf of Ezras Torah related work.

When the Chazon Ish settled in Stoibz, his wife opened a textile shop enabling him to devote his entire time to Torah study. On market day, however, the Chazon Ish would come to help out in the store. Since the store would be more crowded on those days, the Chazon Ish feared that in the hustle and bustle, mistakes might be made and customers might be cheated. Therefore, the Chazon Ish himself would carefully measure each piece of cloth that was sold.

Rabbi Eliezer Gorden, founder of Telshe Yeshiva, personally checked the weights and measures of the storekeepers in the city of Telshe to ensure that they were exact. Even the non-Jews in the neighboring areas knew about this and insisted on buying only from the stores whose weights were checked by the Rabbi.

It is for this same reason that the Parsha warns businessmen to be extremely ethical in their dealings. Too many Jews have succumbed to the lure of a few extra dollars and have given their approval to shady business deals. The fact that this wrong could lead to

great Chilulei Hashem does not seem to concern them. Yet, this, too, is considered stealing, and these misguided individuals all too often soil their characters for the sake of temporary profits.

The end of a lie is shame. (Adnei Kessef, 1)

A lie has no legs to stand on. (Tikkune Zohar 422)

The wicked say much and do little. (Bava Metzia 87)

We fix the evil on the evil-doer. (Bava Basra 110)

Even when the circumstances are not so clear-cut, one must take the safer path to ensure the honesty and propriety of his behavior.

A Jewish employer was seeking a reliable worker in his firm. Several applicants expressed interest in the job, and the employer interviewed each one separately. Part of the interview consisted of this question: "Suppose that you ordered a pen from a company, and they accidentally sent back not one, but two pens. What would you do?"

Almost all the applicants found different reasons for keeping the extra pen. After all, they reasoned, would a big company miss a single pen? And hadn't it been the company which had made the mistake, anyway? What would be so terrible about keeping a little pen?

Only one applicant replied, "I would send back the extra pen since it wouldn't be mine." This was the person who got the job. The employer knew that here was one individual who was totally reliable and trustworthy. He would not let his own desire for material possessions supersede his ethical training. Here, again, honesty was the best

mal legal proceeding, involving a Get (Bill of Divorce). If the woman marries again and becomes a divorcee or a widow, she cannot remarry her first husband.

If one lends money to a fellow Jew, he should not take as a security something that provides the borrower with a livelihood. If the borrower is poor, the lender should return the security at night if it is needed then. One should pay a hired worker at the completion of the work.

If a married man dies childless, his surviving brother is to marry the widow and inherit the estate. In this way, the deceased brother's line will not die out. If the surviving brother refuses to marry the widow, he would be subjected to the degrading ceremony of Chalitzah, because he did not perpetuate his brother's name.

A warning is given to merchants and businessmen to be extremely scrupulous in their trading. They must not have faulty scales and weights or try to cheat the customer.

policy.

The following story illustrates how careful one must be in not taking even the slightest thing that belongs to another:

A student of Rabbi Eliyahu Dushnitzer relates that once while walking with his teacher, the two became involved in a deep discussion. At one point they stopped walking and stood in the same spot for a long time. Without realizing what he had done, the student tore off a leaf from a nearby tree.

Rabbi Dushnitzer grabbed his hand and censured him, "What did you do? Even if the value of what you took is less than a "prutah" it is still considered stealing."

> Who shall dwell upon Your holy mountain? He that walks uprightly and performs righteousness, and speaks truth in his heart. (Tehillim 15:1)
> "He that engages in deceit shall not dwell within My house." (Tehillim 101:7)
> Truth is a heavy burden, therefore, its bearers are few. (Meiri, Mishley 3:18)
> The seal of Hashem is "TRUTH". (Sanhedrin 64)

THE CRIME OF AMMON AND MOAV AGAINST BNEI YISROEL

"An Amonite or Moavite shall not enter into the assembly of the L-rd," says the Torah, (Devorim 23:4) "because their countrymen met you not with bread and water on the way when you came forth from Egypt, and because they hired Bilom the son of Beor from Pesor to curse you" (Devorim 23:5).

The Torah's priorities in this passage seem to be reversed. Wasn't the hiring of Bilom, an act directed against the spiritual well-being of the people, of a more serious nature than the withholding of bread and water,

which affected only the Jew's physical condition? Why, then, did the Torah mention the matter of Bilom only after mentioning the bread and water?

The following is a parable that helps explain the order of the passages. The father of a beautiful young girl was hopeful that his daughter would find a distinguished and wealthy member of society for a husband. He was, therefore, shocked to learn that she had fallen in love with a poor yeshiva bochur who spent his days learning. "But if you marry him, who will support you?" asked her father.

"I will try to find work," she replied, "And if you could occasionally help us, we would be extremely grateful."

But the father would have none of this. As soon as the couple married, the father considered them outcasts. He vowed not to give a penny for their support, and he kept his promise even when he heard that they were living in poverty. He hoped that the difficult life his daughter was now experiencing would induce her to return to him.

However, when it became clear that she would not leave her husband, the father resorted to more desperate methods. He went to a soothsayer and, for an enormous sum of money, asked that an evil spell be cast over his son-in-law. In this way, he thought, their marriage would surely fall apart.

The Rabbi in the father's community heard what was occurring, and went to visit the father. "How can you let your daughter and her husband live in such abject poverty?" he demanded. "Isn't it your paternal duty to support them?"

"But I can't possibly pay for all their needs," replied the father. "I don't have enough money."

Finally, the Jews are told to remember for all time the perfidious actions of Amalek, who attacked the Bnei Yisroel when they were weak. They must blot out the remembrance of Amalek from the earth.

"I am afraid that your excuse is hardly a good one," retorted the Rabbi. "After all, didn't you have enough money to pay the soothsayer for casting a curse on your son-in-law? Why, then, couldn't you put that money to better use by supporting him?"

The same accusation was made against Ammon and Moav. Their initial error was in not having the human decency to provide Bnei Yisroel with basic sustenance. And if Ammon and Moav were to claim that they did not have the means to supply this food, the Torah reminded them that they had paid sufficient funds to gain Bilom's services to curse the Jews. It is to point out the invalidity of this excuse that the Torah mentioned Bilom's deed last. The hiring of Bilom pointed out the hypocrisy of Ammon and Moav, and it is because of this that no members of these nations could enter the nation of Israel.

Moshe concluded the legal section of his discourse with an account of the ceremonies to be performed in the Promised Land involving the Bekurim, *the* first fruits of *the* seven Minim (Species). These were to be brought to the Kohein in the central Sanctuary. The donor was then to recite a prayer of thanksgiving, recalling how Hashem had delivered his ancestors from Egypt and brought the new generation into a land flowing with milk and honey.

The Ma'aser (Tenth of the Crop) of each third year of the Shemittah cycle was to be given to the poor.

פרשת כי תבא

Parshas Ki Sovo

DOING MITZVOS QUICKLY AND EAGERLY

"Vi'ata Hinei Heiveisi," says the bringer of the first fruits: "And now, behold, I have brought." Our Sages tell us that the word "Vi'ata", means right away, the word "Hinei" signifies happiness, and "Heiveisi" indicates that one gives of himself. Therefore, the performer of this Mitzvah, like the doer of any Mitzvah, is indicating his willingness to perform Hashem's law quickly, eagerly, and selflessly. This is the proper approach to all of Hashem's commandments.

The importance of not letting the opportunity for a Mitzvah pass by is demonstrated by the story told of Nachum Ish Gamzo. He suffered greatly from pains that wracked his entire body. Yet, in other ways he was most fortunate. His house started to deteriorate and his students came to his aid. They removed all his possessions from the house and moved them to a new location. Then, just as Nachum Ish Gamzo had left the house for the last time, it collapsed. As long as the Tzaddik was in the house, his merit delayed its collapse.

His students turned to him and asked, "That you have many merits can be seen from what just occurred. Only a man worthy of Hashem's favor could have escaped injury like that. Tell us, then, why you should be made to suffer so."

Nachum Ish Gamzo replied, "I was once traveling on my donkey in the wilderness when a poor man stopped me and asked for food. He looked extremely faint and I took great pity on him. Yet, I told him to wait until I had unsaddled my donkey. I thought that he could surely wait until then. However, after I did this, I looked and saw that the man had fallen to the ground. I tried to revive him, but it was no use, he had already died of hunger. Had I rushed to do the Mitzvah of providing him with food, he might have survived. I have never forgiven myself for not performing the Mitzvah with more haste, and that is, no doubt, why I deserve these pains."

If we do not take quick advantage of a chance for good deeds, we may never again get the chance. Haste in performing Mitzvos is better than losing a precious opportunity. Furthermore, one should perform Mitzvos

After this, the donor was to offer a prayer in which he declared that he had obeyed the commandment to set aside Ma'aser for the Levi, orphan, and widow.

Moshe and the Elders instructed the people to observe several solemn ceremonies once they had crossed the Jordan River. Firstly, they were to erect large stones on Mount Eival, and clearly inscribe on them all the words of the Law. Secondly, they were to build an altar of stones and sacrifice burnt-offerings and peace-offerings on it. The sacrificial meal which followed the latter was to be eaten in an atmosphere of rejoicing. Thirdly, the acceptance of the Law was to be ratified by the twelve tribes in the following manner. Six tribes were to stand upon Mount Gerizim, representing the blessings, while the remaining six tribes were to stand upon Mount Eival, signifying the curses. The Levi'im were to stand in the valley midway between the mountains and were to pronounce curses upon those who committed the following

not only without delay, but also with great enthusiasm. **This enthusiasm was** evident in the manner in which Rabbi Levi Yitzchok of Berdichev fulfilled the Mitzvos of Succos. When he removed the Esrog from its container, he would handle it with the same care that one would ordinarily reserve for a precious jewel. He would hold the Esrog and Lulav lovingly and then recite the blessings on them with great concentration. He would then proceed into a joyous dance with the Lulav and Esrog, all the while glowing with sublime happiness at being able to carry out the Will of Hashem.

Once a Torah scholar who was not a follower of Rabbi Levi Yitzchok, observed this dance and frowned disapprovingly at it. He felt that this was below the dignity of a religious Jew, and so he remained aloof from the festivities. Rabbi Levi Yitzchok noticed this, and came over to the scholar. "Does the Torah not tell us to rejoice in our festival?" he asked. "This is why I feel so ecstatic. If it were not commanded for us to enjoy the holiday, I would not behave in this manner. My happiness comes because I am observing the commands of Hashem in the way He wants them performed with great zeal and spirit!"

The righteous say little and do much.
(Bava Metzia 87)
The zealous do their religious duties as early as possible. (Pesachim 4)
Be as fierce as a tiger, swift as an eagle, fleet as a deer and brave as a lion, to do the will of Hashem. (Avos 5:23)
There is no joy like that of fulfilling a precept.

THE "CHOSEN NATION"

The Jews are referred to as the "Am Segulah", the "Chosen Nation" of Hashem.

We are compared to a precious stone which is carefully watched and proudly displayed. The Jews are unique in world history. No other nation has survived as long under such adverse conditions. And no other nation has been so prominent in world history contributing to the welfare of such countries as Greece, Rome, Spain, England, Germany, France, Russia, and the United States. Such great Torah scholars as the Rambam, the Abarbanel, and Rabbi Samson R. Hirsch offered great services to the countries in which they lived. Jews have stimulated the business of many countries and have shown mankind the way to monotheism and greater morality. Proportionally, the Jewish people have contributed more inventions, discoveries, and works of art than any other. They have always been in the forefront of academic achievement. And yet, Jews have long found themselves persecuted. Perhaps the world is jealous of this "Chosen Nation". If so, it is acting against its own best interests; for every country that has discriminated against Jews has gone into decline. Rome, Spain, and Czarist Russia, are several examples. Still, the Jews have persevered as the Chosen People of Hashem.

A gentile once turned to a man sitting next to him and said scornfully, "You're a Jew, aren't you?"

"Yes," the other replied.

"Well, I'm glad I'm not," continued the gentile, "And I'm proud to say that the little village where I come from contains not a single Jew."

"I see," said the Jew. "Maybe that's why it's still only a little village."

Even the most sinful Jew is as full of virtue as the seeds of the pomegranate. (Eruvin 19)
Israel is the light of the world. (Shir

sins, and blessings upon those who avoided them:

a) Idolatry

b) Dishonoring one's parents

c) Removing a neighbor's boundary line

d) Misleading the blind

e) Acting unjustly towards the stranger, orphan, and widow

f) Behaving in an immoral fashion

g) Murdering someone in secret

h) Taking a bribe to give false testimony in a case involving capital punishment

i) Failing to observe the commandments in general.

All members of the twelve tribes were to respond to each curse and blessing with the refrain of "Amen" (Truth).

The people had frequently been warned of the consequences of disobeying

HaShirim)
Leave it to Israel—if they are not prophets, they are the children of prophets. (Pesachim 66)

MA'ASER FOR THE POOR

In this Parsha, the Torah reminds us that a tenth of one's crop should be reserved every third year for the poor and needy. Once again, the Torah calls to our attention the plight of the destitute, and tells us that it is our obligation, we who have benefited from Hashem's graces, to help them.

Sometimes we may feel that the task of supporting the poor is too burdensome. Why must we be "pestered" so much by paupers? Can't we enjoy our own money without having to give it away?

Those who follow this line of thinking should consider the attitude of Rabbi Akiva Eiger. When a Jew asked him for a loan of fifty rubles, Rabbi Eiger promised to assist him, but found that he had no cash on hand. Rather than let the man leave empty-handed, he gave the man a lamp, and told him to pawn it for fifty rubles.

Some weeks later, someone told Rabbi Eiger that the man had pawned the lamp for not fifty but one hundred rubles, and had then failed to redeem the lamp. That meant that the man had not only neglected to repay the loan, but had also received twice as much for the lamp as he had been told to.

But Rabbi Eiger was not upset at the man's actions. Rather, he chastised himself. "If the man did this," he said, "then he must have needed the hundred rubles badly, but was ashamed to ask for so much. I should have been more sensitive in asking him what his total needs were, and he would not have

been forced to lie about them. The next time, I must remember to tell someone like that that I can give him more money if he needs it." To Rabbi Akiva Eiger, the major concern was not his own wealth, but the welfare of the poor person.

One who contributes to charity should not think that he is losing through his donations, for he will actually gain in the long run. The rewards for giving Tzedokoh are great. It is said that "Tzedokoh Tatzil Mi'movess—Giving Charity Spares One From Death." Sometimes, the reward comes in unexpected ways, such as described in the following story.

A certain man was so dedicated to the good deed of distributing alms that he sold his own house to be able to continue doing so. Once, on Hoshana Rabboh, the man's wife gave him a few pennies and told him to buy something for their children in the marketplace. While on his way there, the man met someone who was collecting money to clothe an orphan. The man readily gave away all the money his wife had given him. But then, ashamed to return to the children empty-handed, he searched for something he could take from shul, where he found some abandoned Esrogim used by children for play. He collected a sackful of them and brought them home.

It so happened that the man had to go overseas, and while packing his belongings, he accidentally included the sack of Esrogim. When he arrived at his destination, he heard that the country's king was suffering from a severe stomach ailment. The king's physicians decided that only the fruit of citron could provide relief, but no one could secure such a fruit on short notice. It was then that

Hashem's laws. Now that they were about to enter the Promised Land, Moshe felt it his duty to place even greater emphasis upon the results their future behavior would bring. If the Bnei Yisroel observed Hashem's commandments, they would receive numerous blessings. These would include prosperity from the fields and within their cities, abundant livestock, the subjugation of enemies, and supremacy over other nations. The alternative would lead to disaster; disease, famine, and death would result. The land of the Israelites would be overrun by a cruel nation. The Jews would be scattered throughout the world and they would once again become slaves.

Moshe then began his third and final discourse to the people. He appealed to them to remember Hashem their G-d, who watched over them in Egypt, during their wanderings in the wilderness, and who would continue to protect them in the future.

the Jew looked in his bag and discovered the Esrogim, just the cure for the ailing king. He brought them to the palace, and upon the king's recovery, was handsomely rewarded for his contribution. The money he had spent to aid the poor had been returned to him many times over. He indicated his gratitude by making a very large donation to those in need.

Sometimes the reward for the charity-giver consists of the expressions of thanks offered by the recipients. But the donor should not demand this of the poor before contributing. He should be willing to give Tzedokoh simply because it is a Mitzvah to do so. In fact, say our Sages, the greatest form of Tzedokoh is achieved when the recipient does not know who donated the charity. In this way, he will not feel embarrassed at accepting it.

Rabbi Eliyahu Chaim, the Rav of Lodz, opened his home to visitors from all over. One evening, a tired traveler came to call on him. Rav Eliyahu Chaim went to the guest bedroom to check on the guest's welfare, and noticed that his shoes were tattered and torn. He waited until the man was asleep. Then he tiptoed into the room, took away the torn shoes, and substituted his own.

The next morning, the guest arose and dressed hurriedly, not realizing what Rav Eliyahu Chaim had done. He departed early to resume his journey, and, as the streets were not well-paved, his shoes soon became muddy. As a result, he was not able to identify them as having belonged to someone else. When Rav Eliyahu Chaim realized that his guest had left without noticing the switch, he was pleased. "Wouldn't it be wonderful if he never finds out," he pondered. "Then not only won't he have to suffer from the effects of torn shoes, but he will also never know that he has accepted charity."

This, indeed, is Tzedokoh of the highest order.

If you are a generous giver, you will never come to harm. (Derech Eretz Zotta 2)

What kind of almsgiving delivers the giver from an unnatural death? That which is given without knowing to whom, and is received-without knowing from whom.(Bava Basra 10)

Each day Hashem lauds the rich man who distributes charity in private. (Pesachim 112)

Rabbi Yanai saw a man giving a coin publicly to a poor man. He told him: "It would have been better not to give in such a manner, rather than shame him!" (Chagiga 5)

On the day he was to die, Moshe assembled every man, woman, and child of Israel, to bring them into a Covenant with Hashem. The Covenant confirmed the Bnei Yisroel as Hashem's Chosen People, and applied not only to those present on that day, but to all future Jewish generations.

A warning was issued to anyone who contemplated rejecting Hashem in the belief that the curses mentioned earlier would not apply to him. Such behavior would arouse Hashem's anger, and the individual involved would be blotted out from the earth. If the

פרשת
נצבים

Parshas
Netzavim

ALL STAND AS EQUALS BEFORE HASHEM

You are standing this day, all of you, before Hashem your G-d, your leaders, your tribes, your elders, and your officers, all the men of Israel. Your little ones, your wives, your stranger that is in your camp, from the cutter of your wood to the drawer of your water. (Devorim, 29:9-10)

So begins Parshas Nitzavim. This passage notes that all members of Klal Yisroel, from the greatest leader to the simplest woodcutter, stood together as equals before Hashem. This was dramatic proof that to Hashem each individual, no matter what his station in life, has the same potential for spiritual greatness. Every person can, in his own way, rise to the summit of holiness. Thus, the poor woodchopper who is devout in his ways and who raises his children as true Jews is elevated to the same level as the wealthy supporter of Jewish causes. No man should consider himself too insignificant to be a partner in the Covenant between the Jews and Hashem.

On Rosh Hashana, Rabbi Levi Yitzchok of Berditchev rose to blow the Shofar. He ascended the Bimah, led the congregation in the prayers of Lamnatzeiach and Min Hameitzar, and then waited until the congregation stood silently and expectantly. All waited without a sound for the blowing of the Shofar to commence.

Then, to their consternation, Rabbi Levi Yitzchok stopped, removed the Shofar from his lips, and put it down. He seemed to be pausing, waiting for something to happen.

The people grew restless. Had the great Rabbi forgotten what to do? Finally, he smiled, and began to offer an explanation.

"My friends," he said, "in the rear of the shul today sits a Jew who spent his early years among the gentiles. He had been kidnapped as a child, brought up by a gentile family, and placed into the king's army. When he was 40 years old, he was finally freed and allowed to return to his people.

"This man had not been inside a shul since he was a youngster, until he joined us today. He could not possibly remember the prayers that he heard so long ago. And yet, he was overcome with emotion at his return to the House of G-d. He yearned to join in the expressions of devotion to the Holy One, Blessed be He. And so, I saw him speaking the only remnants of Hebrew that he recalled from his youth, the letters of the Alef Beis. But he said these with such feeling that they have risen straight to the heavens. I therefore paused before blowing the Shofar so that his letters would have time to reach Hashem Yisborach, Who will Himself form them into the words of our prayers. Now we can begin the blowing of the Shofar."

To Rabbi Levi Yitzchok of Berditchev, the ignorance of the man mattered not at all. It was his devotion that mattered.

All Jews are princes (that is, all Jews have an equally noble ancestry—the poor like the rich). (Shabbos 67) Whether you be good or bad, you are the children of Hashem. (Kiddushin 36) A Jew, even if he has sinned, is still a Jew. (Sanhedrin 44)

SEARCHING FOR THE TREASURE WITHIN YOURSELF

For this commandment which I command you today is not hidden from you, nor is it far off. It is not in heaven that you could say, 'Who will go up to heaven for us and bring it to us and make us hear it that we can do it?' Nor is it beyond the sea that you could say

public sinned, then the land would be destroyed. When later generations would wonder about the cause of this destruction, they would be told that it had come about because of the abandonment of Hashem and His ways.

After the Jews have experienced Hashem's blessing and curse and they have returned to His fold, Hashem will gather them from dispersion and return them to the Promised Land. Then the curse will be transferred to the enemies who had persecuted and oppressed the Jews. The Jews, on the other hand, would experience the blessings of prosperity and happiness, provided that they would accept Hashem's commandments fully.

'Who will go over to the other side of the sea for us and bring it to us and make us hear it that we can do it?' But the matter is very near to you: in your mouth and in your heart, that you can do it. (Devorim, 30:11-14)

With this passage, the Torah reminds the Jewish nation that the secret of life lies not in a hidden, unreachable treasure, but directly in the Torah, accessible to all.

Rabbi Yitzchok of Cracow was a poor man who had experienced many years of struggling for survival. One night, he had a dream that if he would go to the city of Prague and look under the main bridge there, he would find a great treasure. He thought nothing of this at first, but when he had this dream for several days in succession, he grew very curious. Finally, he decided to make the trip to Prague and see if there was any truth to the matter.

When he arrived at the main bridge there, he discovered that this task would be much harder than he had imagined. Stationed at the bridge was a large contingent of the king's soldiers, who were guarding the area very carefully. Rabbi Yitzchok returned day after day, hoping to find an opportunity when the soldiers were away so that he could begin his search, but no such opportunity occurred. Finally, one day as he paid his daily visit, he was approached by a high-ranking army officer. "I see you coming here every day," the officer said to Rabbi Yitzchok. "What are you looking for?"

Startled, Rabbi Yitzcok decided to tell the truth, and related his dream in its entirety.

After he had finished, the army officer laughed. "Why waste your time believing in dreams? Why, if I believed in dreams, I would not be here right now. I would be in Cracow instead, for I have dreamt that if I went to the home of a certain Rabbi Yitzchok there, I would find a treasure hidden in the yard. I, therefore, suggest that you forget this foolishness and return

home."

Return home is just what Rabbi Yitzchok did. As soon as he arrived, he searched in his own yard and, as the officer's dream had predicted, he found a treasure buried there. Rabbi Yitzchok became the richest man in the city, and was known far and wide as a most generous donor to charity.

Rabbi Yitchok had to travel miles to learn that the riches he was seeking were in his own back yard. We can spare ourselves the trouble of such a treasure hunt by realizing that the treasures of life are revealed in the Torah that is in our very midst.

Knowledge is not in heaven, nor is it beyond the sea. (Devarim 30)

The Torah speaks in the language of human beings. (Berachos 31)

"The law of your mouth is better unto me than thousands of gold and silver." (Tehillim 119:72)

RETURNING WHILE THERE'S STILL TIME

Moshe informed the Bnei Yisroel that even if they abandon the laws of the Torah and are plagued by calamities, they can still regain Hashem's favor, but only if they repent. They must declare that their sinful ways are wrong, and then they must actively change them.

Teshuva, the returning to Hashem's fold, is not a simple matter. It often requires a lengthy, difficult process, complete with frustrations and backslidings. It sometimes takes place in stages; first the person works at improving one aspect of his behavior, and his success then gives him the impetus to proceed further. One should never become so frustrated by lack of progress that he gives up the battle for Teshuva entirely. As long as one is still alive, there is still time for repentance.

Rabbi Yisroel Salanter once went to a shoemaker to have his shoes repaired. The hour was late and darkness had already

Therefore, the people should realize that the choice between life and death—between good and evil—is placed before them. The heaven and earth are eternal witnesses to this offer. If the Bnei Yisroel choose to cling to Hashem, then they will thrive; but if they do not, then they will perish.

descended. Rabbi Yisroel noticed that the shoemaker might have trouble repairing the shoes in the dim light, and so he suggested that perhaps the job could wait until the next day.

"Do not despair," the shoemaker replied. "I can work very well by candlelight. So as long as the candle burns it is still possible to fix the shoes."

Rabbi Yisroel immediately realized the significance of the shoemaker's words. As long as the candle burned, he could still repair what was broken. And as long as the spark of life still flickers in a person, that person could still repair his sinful ways. One can never resign himself to spiritual doom.

"**Repent one day** before your death," say the Sages.

A man once quoted this to a Rabbi, and then asked, "But how can I do this? How do I know when I will die?"

"That is exactly the point," replied the Rabbi. "No one knows when he will die. Perhaps it will be this very day! That is why everyone should start doing Teshuva immediately!"

> Man sacrifices all his tomorrows for one today so that he should not have to give up all his todays on account of one tomorrow. (Yoseph Horowitz)
> The knowledge that a thing is evil is halfway to repentance. (Meiri)
> R. Chama ben Chanina said: "Great is penitence, for it brings healing to the world." (Yoma 86)
> R. Yochanan said: Great is penitence, for it averts the evil decree. (Rosh Hashana 17)

Moshe was 120 years old, and he announced that his leadership was drawing to its close. He revealed that Yehoshua had been chosen by Hashem as his successor who would take command and lead Israel successfully to the Promised Land. In the presence of the entire assembly, Moshe urged Yehoshua to be strong and courageous, and to place his full trust in Hashem.

Moshe then committed the Law to writing and delivered it to the Kohanim and the Elders. When there would be a king over Yisroel he would be charged with reading it publicly on Succos during the year after the

פרשת וילך
Parshas Vayeilech

A TRUE LEADER OF THE PEOPLE

This was the last day of Moshe's life. He was 120 years old and would die without seeing the beloved Promised Land. Yet, he was filled not with self-pity, but with concern for his people. "And Moshe went out and spoke . . ." begins the Parsha. He did not wait for the people to come to him. Rather, he actively went out and gathered the people to him. A true leader must give of himself to his followers, and to take the initiative in speaking to them. This was Moshe, a true leader to the very end.

Rav Eliyahu of Vilna was another such leader. He was called the Vilna Gaon, and no term described him better. So great was his brilliance and leadership that he dwarfed all other great men of his era. Yet he never considered himself aloof from the common folk, and went out of his way to display concern for them.

Once, while engrossed in a difficult passage of the Talmud, he did not notice that one of his young students had entered the room to greet him. The student extended a friendly hand, but the Gaon did not acknowledge it. Thinking he had been rebuffed, the student left hurt and depressed. While exiting, he met Rav Chaim Volozhiner, one of the Gaon's foremost students, and complained of how the Gaon had snubbed him.

Rav Chaim tried to console the young student, but to no avail. "The master must have

Shemitta year to the Israelites assembled at the Sanctuary. In this way, every man, woman, and child of Israel would be constantly reminded of their obligation to obey Hashem.

The Book of the Law, written by Moshe, was to be placed by the Levi'im at the

found something wrong with me," he said sadly.

Rav Chaim left the student and entered the Gaon's chambers. Seeing his favorite disciple, the Gaon greeted him happily. "But why do you look so downcast?" he asked.

"Master," said Rav Chaim, "one of your pupils feels insulted because you ignored him when he greeted you in this room a few minutes ago."

"Chas v'sholom!" exclaimed the Gaon. "I never realized that he was here because I was so involved in my thoughts. Where is this young man now? I must go to see him."

The Vilna Gaon rushed out of his room and through the study hall, until he caught sight of the student walking through the streets. The student heard someone calling his name, and turned around to see the greatest Sage of his time hurrying to reach him. The student watched in amazement as the Gaon came up to him, embraced him, and said, "My dear son, forgive me if I unintentionally caused you any anguish. I love you as dearly as I do all my other students. If I did not notice you, it was solely because my thoughts were elsewhere. Will you forgive me?"

The young man was overwhelmed by this display of affection, and his eyes welled up with tears. He became one of the Gaon's most devoted followers, a true tribute to the leadership qualities of this great man who put concern for others before self-pride.

The Chazon Ish was once walking home on Simchas Torah, when he met a "Ger" (Convert to Judaism). The latter complained to him that people were not befriending him, even though the Torah obliges them to love a convert. Thereby, the Chazon Ish, one of our great Sages, told the "Ger" that he would honor him with a song. The Chazon Ish burst into song and danced before him in the street, not stopping until he saw that the convert had been appeased.

People constantly came to the Chazon Ish for advice on all types of problems. Two days before he died, his relatives wanted to stop people from disturbing him because he was extremely weak. The Chazon Ish, however, refused, saying, "How is it possible not to allow them to come in? They come with broken hearts."

Abba Shaul said: "You have to emulate Hashem's attributes—Just as He is compassionate, so must you be.

The whole message of the Torah spells mercy from the All-Merciful. (Bechaya, Re'eh 29)

INCLUDING THE CHILDREN

The Torah seems to make a special point of mentioning the fact that the children were assembled with their fathers and mothers during Moshe's discourse. This might seem unnecessary, for one would automatically assume that when the parents were summoned, they would bring along their children. However, the Torah wants to emphasize the need for parents to maintain close watch on their children's development. It is their task to set the proper example for their children, especially during the early years when they are the children's primary role models. The so-called "permissive parents", who allow their children to run rampant, are in reality abandoning their parental responsibility. They do not care enough for the children's welfare to guide them properly, and the children consequently feel neglected. This often leads to a marked increase in childhood problems.

The spiritual leader of a certain small town noticed that parents were allowing their children to roam the streets late at night without any supervision whatsoever.

The next day, he delivered the following sermon to his congregation: "One night, I saw a woman wandering in the streets searching for her missing goat. I asked her, 'What is so terrible about letting the goat spend the night in the fields.'

" 'But the fields are full of wolves and other wild animals! If I leave the goat there, it will be in great danger.'

" 'Don't you have any children to send to search for the goat so that you don't have to be out so late?' I asked her.

" 'Yes,' she replied, 'but they're out with their friends in the streets!' "

" 'Woe to you, foolish mother,' I responded. 'You are concerned enough about

side of the Aron HaKodesh, to bear witness against Israel if they were ever to deviate from its teachings.

Then Moshe was told to assemble the people to teach them the passages of

your goat to go out and search for it. Yet, you let your children roam the streets at will, even though they are in great danger of being corrupted there. No wonder our youth are in such unfortunate straits!' "

It is one thing for parents to avoid being overly strict towards these children, but for parents to provide no moral leadership whatsoever is most regrettable, and the results may be tragically disheartening.

> The world is preserved only by the innocence of the school children. (Shabbos 119)
> The one that teaches his neighbor's child the Torah, is as if he had himself begotten him. (Sanhedrin 99)
> Instruct the child in that which he is inclined to; even in his old age will he not part from it. (Mishley 22)
> Withhold not from chastising a child: if you will apply the rod, he will not die therefrom. (Mishley 23)

THE HIDDEN FACE OF HASHEM

In one of his final messages to the people, Moshe prophesized that after his passing, the people of Israel would turn away from Hashem. They will suffer greatly, go into exile, and feel that Hashem has forsaken them; for "in that day. . . . I will hide My face from them, and they will be devoured."

There have been times throughout history when this "Hastoras Ponim," hiding of Hashem's face, appears to have occurred. Many tragic expulsions and massacres have cost the lives of many Jews, often in societies where Jews at one point felt secure. Certainly the Jews of Spain and Germany had every reason to believe that they had contributed greatly to the welfare of those countries. Perhaps some of them felt too secure in these foreign lands, too willing to adopt the gentile way of life.

Assimilation has always been a greater threat to the Jewish nation than oppression. Many Jews have retained their identities throughout the worst ghetto conditions, but have succumbed to the blandishments of the "good life" by abandoning their religion. Persecutions have always served as tragic reminders that the Jew is, in fact, still considered a Jew wherever he is, even if he no longer considers himself one.

Yet, Hashem's face has never been completely hidden. If it had been, the Jews would have long ago ceased to exist as a viable nation. This has not happened. Hashem must, therefore, still be their guardian, even though His presence may sometimes not be obvious.

An example of this hidden protection is the miracle of Purim. Although no supernatural events occurred to save the Jews, the series of coincidences that took place could have been engineered only by Hashem.

A further example of this is the story of how Dovid was able to escape from King Shaul who sought to kill him. Dovid hid in a cave with King Shaul's men drawing near. When Dovid's enemies came to the cave, they stopped short. "Look," one said, "the spider's web is still whole. If Dovid had entered this cave, he would have caused the web to tear. That proves that he is not inside, so let us look elsewhere." Hashem, working through the veil of nature, had provided Dovid with protection.

We devoutly hope for the day when Hashem's Face will once again be turned directly and openly to the Children of Israel, and when we will once more enjoy His full favor. But for this to happen, we cannot rely solely upon the merits of our ancestors. To do so would be like the man who went into a department store and asked to be given some merchandise on the credit of his father and grandfather.

"But that is impossible!" replied the salesman. "Your father and grandfather were excellent customers and I suppose you may become one also. But their credit is insufficient. You must establish your own trustworthiness to prove to me that you, too, are deserving of such credit."

Our ancestors had excellent credit ratings with Hashem and they received their rewards for their service to Him. It is time to establish our own credit rating by practicing good deeds, and, hopefully, in this way we can earn the eventual coming of the Moshiach.

> Nothing happens to man in life without it being decreed by the Holy One blessed be He. (Sefer Chassidim)

187

"Ha'azinu," which would again remind them of the consequences of turning against Hashem.

> It is Hashem who ultimately contrives that the sinner goes forward to meet his own punishment. (Meleches Machshevet)
> Hashem performs His designs through everything, even a serpent, insect, or a frog. (Bereishis Rabbah 10)
> The physician's error is the Creator's design. (Hagiz)

פרשת האזינו
Parshas Ha'azinu

Moshe commenced this poetic discourse to the people by invoking the heavens and the earth as eternal witnesses of his warnings. He contrasted Hashem's faithfulness and justice with the corrupt ways of His chosen nation. If the Bnei Yisroel would but inquire of the older generation, they would be told how Hashem had selected Israel from among the other nations and had cared for them in the wilderness, as an eagle guards its young. However, in later generations, they may turn to other objects of worship.

Consequently, Hashem promises to repay their lack left alone.

FORGETFULNESS

Hashem in His great mercy, gave mankind the ability to forget past events. When someone uses this ability properly, he will forget about past indignities caused him by others, and will forgive them for whatever wrongs they have done him.

However, Bnei Yisroel have often misused this power of forgetting. Instead of allowing themselves to become more merciful towards others, they have allowed themselves to become forgetful of past favors. This is especially true of favors shown them by Hashem. They have forgotten that He defended them in battles and redeemed them from Egypt and have instead turned to other sources of power, i.e., human armies, science, and money, thereby turning their backs on the Ultimate Power. In doing so, they have taken a heavenly gift and misused it.

The insolence of such action is demonstrated by the following story. A man was so heavily in debt that he could find no possible way to repay all those to whom he owed money. He asked a friend for advice, and the friend suggested that whenever someone asked him for repayment, he should act insane. That way, the people would no longer bother him.

The man took his friend's advice, and to his delight, the plan worked perfectly. Whenever someone came to claim his loan, the man acted as if he were crazy, and he was

One day, the man who had given the advice came to ask for repayment of his loan. Again, the other one put on his act of insanity and hoped that he could get away with it.

But his companion was not amused. "You fool!" he shouted. "I was the one who advised you to act insane in the first place. Now you're using the trick I taught you against me!"

The Dubno Magid used this parable to translate this posok: "Tzur yelodchah teshi vatishkach Kail mechollelechah" as follows: Hashem created you with the power of forgetfullness but you have used that power to forget Him.

If we owe the gift of forgetting to Hashem, then we most certainly should not be so two-faced as to use it against Him!

> Let everything that draws breath praise Hashem. (Tehillim 150:5)
> Know your soul and you will know Hashem. (Nishmas Chaim, Introduction)
> He who studies the Torah and then forgets it is like the woman who gives birth and then buries her offspring. (Sanhedrin 99)

PROSPERITY AND REBELLION

When Bnei Yisroel were enslaved in Egypt, they accepted Hashem's leadership most willingly. When they were attacked by their enemies, they pleaded for His protec-

of appreciation with the denial of His favor. Both young and old will be ravaged by disease and the cruelty of the enemy. It will be only His concern that the enemy should not gloat that will prevent Israel's complete destruction.

Israel should, therefore, realize that it is only through Hashem's providence that

tion. Yet, when they became established in their homeland, and when they later gained some prosperity in Golus, they turned to other gods. They had "grown fat", tasted a bit of affluence and esteem, and then they rebelled. They no longer acknowledged the original source of their success, and they experimented with other deities. They joined other religions, worshipped materialism and nationalism, placed their faith in human leaders, and looked to scientists for the answers to the universe's puzzles. Yet in the long run, the result was always identical. The attraction of other gods proved to be a mirage and the Jews were faced with disaster.

There once lived a famous lion tamer whose skill in controlling the wild beasts of the jungle was legendary. Working with him was a youngster, who assisted him in his feats. They toured the country and their fame and wealth grew.

However, the youthful assistant let this success go to his head. After the performance one day, he flippantly informed the lion tamer that this had been their final appearance together. After all, the youth had been with the act long enough to know all the tricks of the trade, and he was now just as rich and famous as the lion tamer himself. He had, therefore, decided he no longer needed the guidance of his mentor, and had persuaded another circus owner to provide him with an act of his own. With that he arrogantly left, without even thanking the lion tamer for all his help throughout the years.

Soon, the time came for the youth to give his debut performance. His billing made no mention of his teacher's name, for he confidently assumed that he would do better on his own. In addition, he would no longer have to perform the act the way his teacher had wanted. He was now free to run the show his own way, and to garner all the acclaim for himself. And so, he entered the ring with all the assurance in the world.

What he did not realize was that his teacher had a natural knack for controlling the lions. They were instinctively afraid of him. But this fear did not carry over to the youthful assistant. When the lions looked at this young man cracking a whip at them, they charged at him en masse, and severely mauled him. It was only when the lion tamer himself, who had been watching from the sidelines, appeared to take control, that the animals beat a hasty retreat, and the youth's life was barely saved.

When Jews became materially successful, they sometimes feel that they no longer have to rely on Hashem's mercy and kindness. But they are soon brought back to reality, as they find that all their wealth does not protect them from their enemies. It is only when Hashem is there to guard them that they survive.

> *He who appreciates his soul, depreciates the materialistic world. (Mivhar 42)*
> *Better off is the poor man who follows the straight path than the depraved man who is rich. (Mishley 28)*
> *Envy, cupidity and ambition drive a man out of the world. (Messilas Yesharim 11)*
> *Man's vision is far-sighted; but every little coin blocks the line of his vision.*

THE FEW CHASING THE MANY

In Parshas Ha'azinu, Moshe reminds the Bnei Yisroel that when they find themselves capable of defeating a vastly superior army, it is Hashem Who is responsible for their victory.

There have been many occasions when vastly outnumbered Jews have amazed the world by overcoming a powerful enemy, most recently during the Israeli-Arab wars. Many instances of miraculous occurrences during these wars have been recounted, all of which serve to show that Hashem's mighty hand was the decisive factor in these victories.

During the 1973 "Yom Kippur War," an Israeli tank was advancing towards the Suez Canal, when the men inside suddenly noticed three Egyptian tanks approaching. Though outnumbered three to one, the men geared up for battle. First, though, they thought it wise to ask for Hashem's assistance in their struggle, and so they recited several verses of Tehillim. The officer

they are able to fight off vastly superior armies. They should acknowledge that there is only one G-d whose might and power are complete.

After completing this address, Moshe was told to ascend Mount Nevo so that he would be able to see the Promised Land before he dies.

inside then pressed the firing mechanism. But there was no response, the mechanism was jammed! The others inside made desperate attempts to fix it but to no avail, and the enemy tanks were advancing rapidly! All the men joined in resorting to the only protection they had left—prayer.

Suddenly, one of the men noticed that all three enemy tanks had hoisted white flags of surrender. And to their amazement, men soon emerged from the enemy tanks with arms raised. "They're our men!" one of them finally shouted. "They're Jews!"

"That's right," one of the approaching men confirmed. "We blew up one of the enemy's tanks, and they escaped from these three, leaving them entirely to us. We were bringing the tanks back to our home base, and we were hoping that none of our own men would assume that we were Egyptians. We saw you aiming your gun at us. Why didn't you shoot?"

"That," replied one of the men in the Israeli tank, "was the result of Hashem answering our prayers."

In the same war, an Israeli paratrooper was about to parachute into the city of Yerusholayim. Snipers were shooting at the soldiers as they descended, so the paratroopers had to travel very lightly. The

paratrooper assembled his backpack with great care. Then he came to his bag of Tefillin. He was about to leave it behind on the plane, but then reconsidered. "These Tefillin have been with me wherever I've gone," he thought to himself. "Perhaps having the words of Hashem with me when I jump will bring me good fortune." Consequently, he put the bag into the backpack as well and then jumped.

The snipers' fire was there to greet him as he landed. He managed to scurry to safety, and later, examined himself and his belongings. The first thing he removed from his pack was the bag of Teffilin. Immediately, he noticed a hole in it. He opened it, and found a bullet lodged inside the Siddur that had been inside the bag.

"It's a good thing I decided to take my Tefillin along," said the soldier. "If I hadn't, that bullet would have gone straight through my sack and into my body."

The soldier, and the entire army, had much to be thankful to Hashem for that day.

The whole world is fed by the benevolence of Hashem. (Berachos 17) Every year designs are made to exterminate the Jews but Hashem brings them to nought. (Yalkut Shimoni, Malachai 1)

Before his death, Moshe issued a blessing to Israel. In very stylistic and formal language, he described the good fortunes that would be granted to each of the tribes. He concluded with praise of Hashem whose protection of and love for the people are everlasting, provided the people reciprocate with recognition and acceptance of Hashem's Lordship.

The life of the great leader was nearing its end. Moshe ascended from the plains of Moav to reach the heights of Mount Nevo, the summit of Pisgah. There, alone with G-d, he was shown all the land of Gilad, un-

פרשת וזאת הברכה

Parshas V'zos Ha'brochoh

TORAH TZIVA LONU MOSHE, MORASHA KEHILLAS YAAKOV

This verse, which means, "Moshe commanded us the law, the inheritance of the congregation of Yaakov," is a most important one in the framework of the Jewish religion. The Talmud states that it is this

verse which every father must teach his young child. A child who appreciated this will develop into a loyal Jew.

Note the inclusion of the word "congregation" in this passage. The Jewish people can thrive only if it remains a congregation, a unified whole. Certainly, the entire law

til Dan, all of Naftoli, Ephraim, Menassheh, and Yehudah, until the sea, the Negev in the·South, and the Valley of Jericho, as far as Zoar. This, Hashem promised him, was the land that would be given to the Children of Israel, as their forefathers had been told.

Then Moshe, in the land of Moav, went to his everlasting peace. He was buried in the valley, but, to this day, no one knows the exact site of his burial. Although Moshe had been one hundred twenty years old when he died, he had remained

cannot be fully observed unless the entire congregation of Jews accepts it. Certain laws pertain to holy Kohanim; some apply only to property owners; still others apply only in Eretz Yisroel, but not in the Diaspora. All of Jewry must worship G-d before all of the commandments can be fulfilled, since some are applicable to only specific segments of the people. Only if the entire congregation performs what Hashem has demanded of them, is the full body of Torah law fulfilled.

It is also important to note that the Torah laws encourage the maintenance of a congregation, an association of people serving Hashem together. Thus, we are told to daven together in a Minyon (quorum of at least 10 males), to eat together in groups (allowing a group recitation of the Birchas HaMozon, the Grace After Meals), and to celebrate joyous occasions like births and weddings together. When an unfortunate occurrence such as death takes place, we are told to visit the mourners, and to remind them that they are an integral part of the group. It is as a congregation that we can best survive and that we can best fulfill Hashem's laws.

The only child of a friend of Rabbi Yitzchok Greenberg, Menahel Ruchani of the Lomzhe Yeshiva, contracted polio and died. The father of the child was deeply depressed. Friends and relatives who would have comforted him in his sorrow, refrained from coming because they feared the communicability of polio.

The bereaved father asked Rabbi Greenberg to request the Chazon Ish to pray for him. When Rabbi Greenberg related the message to the Chazon Ish, the latter asked, "Do you think if I go to comfort him, it would prove beneficial?"

"I'm certain it would," replied Rabbi Greenberg.

The Chazon Ish immediately ordered a taxi and even refused Rabbi Greenberg's offer to pay the fare. At the house of mourning, the Chazon Ish spent twenty minutes speaking words of comfort to the bereaved parent, who was greatly consoled by the visit

of this great man.

> Knowledge of the Torah cannot be thoroughly acquired unless studied in a group. (Berachos 63)
> Samuel stated: "A person should never exclude himself from the community. (Berachos 49)

THE PUBLIC WEDDING

Why is the completion of the Torah celebrated on Simchas Torah which occurs several months after Shevuos, when the Torah was actually given to Yisroel? The Dubnow Maggid responded to this question with the following parable:

A king was blessed with great power and wealth. Yet, one huge void saddened him greatly—he had no children. However, his spirits were raised when he was told that a certain resident of a nearby village, a very saintly man, seemed to have the power to guarantee the wishes of those he considered worthy.

The king promptly visited this man, and poured out his heart to him. The man replied that the king would indeed be blessed with a daughter, but that he had to first promise that he would let no member of his kingdom rest eyes upon her until after she was married. The king reluctantly agreed to this condition.

When a daughter was born to him, the king was overjoyed. Nevertheless, he raised his daughter in absolute privacy, in accordance with the man's demands. The king waited patiently until his daughter was of marriageable age, and then invited all the eligible young men in his kingdom to his palace. They were all told that the king's daughter was interested in marrying one of them, but that there was one condition. She could not be seen until after the marriage. The young men present felt very uneasy. After all, they murmured, who knew what type of monster this girl must be if the king was forced to keep her in hiding? Slowly, one by one, all the young men slipped out of the palace, leaving behind only one man who

physically, spiritually, and intellectually vital until the very end.

The Bnei Yisroel mourned the great loss of their leader for thirty full days. Then they turned towards Yehoshua, their new leader, who would guide them towards the conquest of the Land of Canaan under Hashem's supervision. The Torah concludes with the statement that "There has not arisen a prophet since, in Israel, like Moshe, whom the Lord knew face to face. . . .''

was willing to go through with the marriage. The king joyously agreed to the match. The young couple were married and only then was the man allowed to see his new bride. To his surprise and delight, instead of looking like a witch, she was the most lovely young woman he had ever seen.

But doubts still troubled him. If she was so beautiful, why had the king kept her locked up for so long? Was there something else, something not readily noticeable, that was wrong with her? The young man took his bride to their new home, determined to learn what her true character was.

Several months later, the couple returned to the palace. Everyone surrounded the young man and asked for his reaction. He smiled and announced, "Now that I have lived with her for several months, I can say without a doubt that there is nothing wrong with her and that she is the most wonderful bride possible in the entire world!" And he immediately arranged for a lavish party, to celebrate his bliss.

When Bnei Yisroel accepted the Torah on Shavuos, after it had been rejected by the other nations, they were not familiar with its contents. It took them some time to fully appreciate its greatness. By Simchas Torah, though, they had become totally convinced of the Torah's beauty and goodness. This is why, even though the Torah was given at Shevuos, we publicly celebrate on Simchas Torah the confirmation of Yisroel's blissful union with Hashem's Torah.

> On the verse: "And I praised joy"
> (Koheles 8:15) uttered by King
> Solomon, our Sages commented:
> This refers to the joy of doing a commandment. (Shabbos 30)
> There is no real joy in life except in that involving the service of Hashem.
> (HaKemach)

THE TORAH IS ETERNAL

The Torah teaches us: "Torah Tzivah Lanu Moshe Morasha Kehilos Yaakov. Vayehi Beshurun Melech Behesaseif Roshei am Yachad Shivtei Yisroel.''

The Rogotchover Gaon, offered the following beautiful interpretation. These two verses are connected for a special reason. The Torah is an eternal inheritance of the Jewish people. It is ours to treasure, protect, love and obey. It will remain ours no matter what circumstances we live in. Whether Jews are in a country that has a monarchy such as Medieval France or Germany (Vayehi Beshurun Melech), an oligarchy of sorts like Athens or Rome (Behesaseif Roshei Am)or a democracy, as in the United States, where the individual has a say in government (Yachad Shivtei Yisroel), The Torah will remain the same and the Jews must remain true to it.

V'zos Ha'brochoh is the last Parsha in what we call the Chumash. However, it is not the end of the Torah. The fact is that there is no end to the Torah. Like the water to which it is compared, it flows forever, sustaining each new generation with its spiritual nourishment.

This is symbolized by the fact that we always conclude every cycle of Torah readings by beginning anew. On the very same day that we finish V'zos Ha'brochoh, we commence the reading of Parshas Bereishis. There is never a moment when we can exist without the Torah being a part of our lives. It remains an ever-fresh spring from which every new generation of Jews can draw.

The Torah is nothing less than the Book of Life. With its teachings to guide them, the Jews can persevere and triumph. Without it, they are lost.

> If your head aches, study the Torah; if your throat aches, study the Torah; if your stomach aches, study the Torah; if your bones ache, study the Torah; the Torah is a cure for all ailments. (Eruvin 53)
> The splendor of men-is their Torah (D'be Eliyahu Uta 15)
> Ben Bog-Bog said: Turn it over (the Torah) and turn it over, for everything is there. And look into it, and become grey and old therein; do not budge from it do not budge from it, for you have no better standard of conduct. (Avos 5:25)